Name, Shame and Blame

Criminalising Consensual Sex in Papua New Guinea

Name, Shame and Blame

Criminalising Consensual Sex in Papua New Guinea

Christine Stewart

PRESS

Published by ANU Press
The Australian National University
Canberra ACT 0200, Australia
Email: anupress@anu.edu.au
This title is also available online at http://press.anu.edu.au

---

National Library of Australia Cataloguing-in-Publication entry

Author: Stewart, Christine, author.

Title: Name, shame and blame : criminalising consensual sex in Papua New Guinea / Christine Stewart.

ISBN: 9781925021219 (paperback) 9781925021226 (ebook)

Subjects: Sexual consent--Social aspects--Papua New Guinea.
Prostitution--Social aspects--Papua New Guinea.
Prostitution--Law and legislation--Papua New Guinea.
Homosexuality--Law and legislation--Papua New Guinea.
Homosexuality--Social aspects--Papua New Guinea.
Papua New Guinea--Social conditions.

Dewey Number: 306.7409953

All rights reserved. No part of this publication may be reproduced, stored in a retrieval system or transmitted in any form or by any means, electronic, mechanical, photocopying or otherwise, without the prior permission of the publisher.

Cover design and layout by ANU Press

Cover photo: The *bilum*, the string bag made originally from bush twine, is the symbol of womanhood and femaleness throughout Papua New Guinea. The rainbow colours denote the global LGBT movement. The frangipanis represent the PNG Friends Frangipani sex workers network. Photo by Christine Stewart.

This edition © 2014 ANU Press

Contents

List of Illustrations	vii
Dedication	ix
Acknowledgements	xi
Glossary	xv
Maps	xxiii
Prologue. The Perfect Storm	xxv
1. Through the Window	1
2. From the Bush	39
3. In the Courtroom	81
4. On the Streets	137
5. In Trouble	191
6. At the Intersection	225
7. Where to Now?	267
Appendix 1. Respondents	305
Appendix 2. Sample Antecedent Report	309
Appendix 3. Review of Homosexuality Cases	313
Appendix 4. Summary of Sentences	319
Bibliography	321

List of Illustrations

Figures

1.1.	A main street in Boroko today—all the trees planted in the colonial era have grown and gardens flourish.	16
1.2.	A 'tuckerbox' store constructed in a fence beside a suburban road in Tokarara, heavily screened for security. The graffiti are unsurprising.	17
1.3.	High-covenant houses and apartments built to take maximum advantage of the spectacular ocean views. The houses are owned by politicians and other *elites*, and the apartments are mainly rented to expatriates.	18
1.4.	'Sodomy Shock.' Front-page headline from the *Post-Courier*, 21 January 2006.	36
2.1.	*Kiap* presiding at a Native Affairs Court hearing, 1950s.	49
2.2.	Thomas Vinit, 'S̲EX IS S̲ACRED AND S̲PECIAL.'	63
4.1.	Poro Sapot outreach workers leave the Project yard to conduct site visits.	139
4.2.	MSM drop-in centre in Poro Sapot's front yard.	139
4.3.	FSW drop-in centre at the rear of the building. A literacy class, conducted by a teacher funded by Dame Carol Kidu, is in progress.	140
4.4.	Many women sleep, dress and prepare themselves for work at the FSW drop-in centre. Their only possessions are stored in bags in the rafters.	141
4.5.	Laundry at the tubs.	142
4.6.	Project workers in their condom costumes, ready for the motorcade around town, World AIDS Day Port Moresby.	144
4.7.	Here the police are shown placing posters on their escort vehicles.	145
4.8.	Market—selling soft drinks, boiled eggs, ice blocks and vegetables—and in the background, sex, 2006.	153
4.9.	Up-market—free-lance workers wait outside one of Port Moresby's classier hotels for security guards to summon them to work, 2006.	155

4.10.	Harbourside sales. This landfill site has now been built over and no longer exists.	158
4.11.	Typical club, with bar and snooker table.	159
4.12.	Drag show contestant.	181
4.13.	Notice of MSW meeting posted on the 'notice-board' at Poro Sapot.	182
4.14.	The Ela Beach beat downtown.	184
5.1.	'Males "freed"…but 31 suspected female prostitutes charged!'	197
5.2.	Front-page, 'Forty held in capital city brothel raid,' *Post-Courier*.	200
5.3.	*Post-Courier* report of 1998 raid, referring to a 'forced march.'	201
5.4.	*Aito Paka Paka*, flowers, brightly coloured sarongs, outrageous hats … and fruit.	215
6.1.	Poster (carried by a man) from the 'Stop Violence Against Women' march of 2006, displaying some of the prevalent arguments against nightclubs.	236
6.2.	Good or Bad? – A cartoon from 1981.	258

Maps

0.1.	Map of Papua New Guinea.	xxi
0.2.	Map of Port Moresby.	xxii
1.1.	Port Moresby today, showing the harbour at upper left, the original town site on the peninsula, the steep slopes of the coastal hills, the urban and suburban development inland to the east and the airport to the far right on the eastern edge of the city.	11
4.1.	Aerial view of Hanuabada (HB), beside and in the harbour, with the Yacht Club to the upper right. Each row of houses is arranged by family and clan relationships.	178
7.1.	Prostitution laws of the world.	280
7.2.	LGBT rights by country or territory.	283

Table

3.1.	Formal court system in PNG before and after Independence.	86

*For Anna, Clemence, Christopher, Johnny, Kuragi, Mama, Margaret, Monika, Peter, Piku and all their sisters and brothers who have suffered the full force of the law's justice
and to the memory of Carol Jenkins, Jason Lavare and John Ballard.*

Acknowledgements

Without the encouragement and support of several wonderful people, this book would never have been written. Two amazing women have long provided inspiration for my work in HIV and gender. The late Dr Carol Jenkins was a wonderful colleague and co-conspirator since we first met twenty years ago in Port Moresby at a Health Department National AIDS Committee meeting. Together (she the biologist and medical anthropologist, I the lawyer) we wrangled, tested ideas, hatched the original plan for the PNG National AIDS Council, played devil's advocate to each other. PNG lost a wonderful asset when she was forced to leave in the late 1990s. Dame Carol Kidu, three times elected Member of Parliament in PNG and Minister for Community Development from 2002 until the political turmoil of 2011, inspired me to carry on. Her efforts to assist the 'meek of the earth'—battered wives, evicted squatters, illiterate street-dwellers, the sick and needy, and the stigmatised, harassed and bullied sex sellers and gays of the city—have marked her as extraordinary. She has achieved far more than I could ever hope to do. PNG has been lucky to have her, and I have been lucky to know her.

Professor Margaret Jolly of The Australian National University blessed me with her mentoring at all stages of this process, through some very trying times. Her encouragement, guidance, wisdom and faith in me and my project, despite all reservations, have been the foundation upon which this book has been constructed. It has been an immense privilege to have been associated with her, first as a doctoral student in the Gender Relations Centre of the former Research School of Pacific and Asian studies, and then as a Visiting Fellow with her Australian Research Council Laureate Project.

The late Dr John Ballard, a friend from UPNG days of long ago, supported my first faltering steps back into academia after an absence of several decades. He provided an excellent supply of background information and later, a meticulous reading of my drafts, as well as being a comprehensive source of information about life in Canberra. I was immensely flattered when, at the conclusion of my project, he retired from academic life with a satisfied sigh, declaring: my job is done.

Professor Jean Zorn, law teacher in New York and Florida, has been a firm friend since UPNG days, where she started teaching my UPNG law class about Torrens title and livery of seisin by introducing us to the notion of customary law. We have shared much together, and her thoughtful insights on many things, particularly feminist law, customary legal systems and scholarship on intersectionality, have been most welcome.

Dr Katherine (Kathy) Lepani has also been a good friend from PNG, and is now a colleague at The Australian National University. She helped immeasurably by sharing many useful insights and hints into the research process, as well as much information from her work with HIV in PNG. From the outset, she has provided sage advice and reading suggestions, and has always been ready to act as a sounding board for many of my ideas and theories.

I owe much to many other teachers, near and far (both in space and time), and particularly (in chronological order): Professor Peter Lawrence, who nearly made a full-time anthropologist of me; C.J. (Joe) Lynch, who first introduced me to law by showing me how legislative drafting can be a truly exciting, creative, significant process; Professor Peter Fitzpatrick, who, Buddha-like, taught jurisprudence under a tree behind the UPNG Forum, and recently, with Ben Golder, imparted much new insight about Michel Foucault.

The staff and students of the former Gender Relations Centre at The Australian National University, and of the current School of Culture, History and Language, and many other academics and staff of the former Research School of Pacific and Asian Studies, gave willingly of their friendship, support and camaraderie. Particular thanks go to Aileen Pangutalan-Mijares, Dr Frances Steel, Dr Greg Dvorak, Dr Cathy Hine and Dr Ruth Saovana-Spriggs, for sharing office spaces, lunches, discussion, tips and workload generally. Wherever you all are now (some near, some far), I thank you. I also thank principals and staff, past and present, of Burgmann College for providing a wonderful base from which to operate for so many years. Dr Carolyn Brewer has proved to be a wonderful editor, as well as a good friend. Thanks go also to Professor Gil Herdt, Dr Vicki Luker, Professor Sally Engle Merry, Wayne Morgan and Dr Laura Zimmer Tamakoshi, for critical reading and inspiring comment on the manuscript through its various metamorphoses.

Most of all though, my thanks go to the many in PNG who have helped in some way. I thank Josepha Namsu Kiris and Keith Stebbins for their treasured friendship over the years, for shelter and cheer, for being always there for me when I needed them. I owe much to all those who assisted in my field research, but I wish particularly to acknowledge the Port Moresby branch of the Poro Sapot Project, a project of the international NGO Save the Children, and all its staff and volunteers past and present, particularly Topa Hershey, Paula Neville, Janet Kilai and the late Jason Lavare, who gave unstintingly of their time and friendship. I thank Dr Fiona Hukula-Kenema, Jim Robins and the library staff of the National Research Institute, the staff of the National Court library and archives, and of the National Archives in Port Moresby, who in various ways helped my research. A special thanks to Moses Tau and CHM Recording Studios for making his wonderful music available for my use; and to my many friends at the bar and on the Bench, particularly Sir Robert Woods, Justice Sao Gabi and Justice David Cannings, for much useful legal information and mentoring.

Finally, I wish to express my deep regret that I am not able to name and thereby honour those to whom I owe the greatest thanks, whose contribution to this book was a *sine qua non*. They tolerated my intrusions into their personal lives, opened their hearts and gave freely of their thoughts, their fears and their stories, and I am still at a loss as to how I might reciprocate. I can only hope that this work of mine will somehow, sometime, help to repay the debt and ease the burden.

Glossary

Key terms

Languages

There are well over 800 distinct languages in Papua New Guinea (PNG), with significant variations in the number of speakers of each. Several *linguae francae* have developed, or been developed. Foremost today is English, the 'official' language used for business and governmental purposes, as well as being spoken in a myriad other situations. But as it has done in so many English-speaking ex-colonies, English itself has now taken on a PNG national form, with its own accent and some of its own unique vocabulary.[1]

A multiplicity of statutes is frequently termed 'legislations,' nouns become verbs (I heard a teenage boy once declare that he was expelled from school 'because I homosex with another boy,' and so on. I have retained these features in my reproduction of interviews.

Each of the two Territories developed its own *lingua franca*. In New Guinea in the north, this was 'neo-Melanesian,' 'Melanesian Pidgin' or most recently, 'Tok Pisin,' derived from the original Chinese trade Pidgin, with an admixture of terms from Malay, German, and Kuanua (the language of the Tolai people, of East New Britain, where the Germans established their principal plantations). In Papua to the South, a 'pidgin' version of Motu, the language of one of the peoples dwelling around Port Moresby, was adopted by the administration and known first as Police Motu, now as Hiri Motu.[2] Tok Pisin had not been adopted by Papuan people even by the time of Independence, although that has changed, with it now being spoken nation-wide, while Hiri Motu is now spoken by many non-Papuan residents of Port Moresby and environs.

'Custom' and 'customary law'

In an endnote to her chapter on custom in a recent volume *Passage of Change: Law, Society and Governance in the Pacific*, Jean Zorn discusses the various ways in which scholars and writers have used and distinguished the terms 'custom'

---

[1] For example 'tuckerbox' in Chapter 2, which refers specifically to a small locally-run store carrying a limited range of foodstuffs and other household items.
[2] 'Pure' *Motu* is distinguished, among other things, by a far more complex grammar, notably a detailed set of noun and pronoun inflections and verb-tenses. These were stripped from Hiri Motu.

and 'customary law.'[3] The most significant of these is the approach which treats 'custom' as referring to the norms and usages of indigenous peoples, which become 'customary law' when they are recognised and applied by the formal courts of law. This however is resented by others who consider that this demeans 'custom' if it is not 'law' with the same force as the system which was introduced by colonisers. More recently, however, Miranda Forsyth in her analysis of *kastom* and state justice systems in Vanuatu has preferred the term 'non-state justice systems' as more accurately describing the collectivity of substantive norms, non-formal judicial processes and non-state institutions.[4] She then adopts the terms 'state justice system' and 'state law' to refer to the corollary of the introduced legal system. I have taken a hybridised approach, and use the terms 'state law/legal system,' 'custom' when referring to situations of everyday usage in PNG, and 'customary law' where describing that which is defined and used in the state legal system.

Legal forms and terms

Act, Bill, Ordinance, Regulation, Statute

These terms all refer to various types of written laws, referred to generically as 'statutes.' In PNG, an Act is a law made by the National Parliament. Before enactment by Parliament, it is a Bill. During the colonial period, laws made by the local legislature (first the Legislative Council, then the House of Assembly) were termed Ordinances. At Independence, all Ordinances were repealed and re-enacted as Acts.[5] Regulations are laws made under and in accordance with Acts or Ordinances: they amplify and provide detail to the governing statute.

PNG Acts and Regulations are cited in italics with the year of passage un-italicised. Where the statute appears in the *Revised Laws of Papua New Guinea* with a Chapter number, that is usually given instead of the year, although with the updating of Chapter numbering having ceased, the year of passage is often cited, even for statutes with Chapter numbers. Divisions of statutes (sections, Parts etc.) are usually named in full for ease of understanding by non-lawyers, using PNG style regarding capitalisation. Where abbreviations are used (as for example in footnote references) the abbreviations follow PNG citation style.

---

3   Jean G. Zorn, 2003, 'Custom then and now: the changing Melanesian family,' in *Passage of Change: Law, Society and Governance in the Pacific,* ed. Anita Jowitt and Tess Newton Cain, Canberra: Pandanus Press, 95–124, 113n3.
4   Miranda Forsyth, 2009, *A Bird That Flies With Two Wings: Kastom and State Justice Systems in Vanuatu,* Canberra: ANU E Press, 29, online: http://press.anu.edu.au?p=49351, accessed 28 July 2014.
5   *Constitution* Schedule 2.4.6.

Repealed Acts and Ordinances are usually not italicised. However, where it is more appropriate in the context (for example, in narrating the history of legislation) I have italicised repealed laws.

Case referencing

Not all court decisions are written down. A decision may be so straightforward as to require no more than the judge's oral delivery and the court clerk's record. Or a judge may decide to write down his decision (and his reasoning). This written decision may go no further than distribution to the Court Registry, judges and other interested parties. It will bear identifying details such as the place, the date, the judge, etc. In PNG this is known as an Unnumbered, Unreported decision.

A decision may be considered important enough that it should reach a wider audience. If so, it is given a number in the Court Registry. In PNG, that number will be preceded by letters indicating the court: N for National Court, SC for Supreme Court, DC for District Court, FC for pre-Independence Full Court. In PNG, this is an 'Unreported' case decision, and is cited by the court letter and the number. Citation of Unreported cases follows PNG citation, as (Unreported)/Judgement Number/date of judgement.

Each year, the most significant cases are gathered together in a law report for the year, as 'Reported' decisions. The PNG reports are referred to as PNGLR and the year is indicated in square brackets [ ] which identifies the volume. I have used the referencing styles appropriate to PNG legal materials, with cases being cited by their Reported reference (*case name* [year of reporting] PNGLR first-page), or Unreported numbered reference (*case name* (Unreported) court initial number place date). Where a case is Unnumbered, judge's name, place and date are added. Judges themselves are referred to as [surname] J or CJ (Chief Justice), DCJ (Deputy Chief Justice) or AJ (Acting Justice) as appropriate, and JJ in the plural.

Otherwise, case and statute citation styles follow those given in the *Australian Guide to Legal Citation* (AGLC).[6] All references to statutes and cases are to those of Papua New Guinea unless otherwise indicated, and in that case they are cited according to the style of their jurisdiction.

---

6   Melbourne University Law Review Association Inc 2010, *Australian Guide to Legal Citation* [3rd ed.], Melbourne: Melbourne University Law Review Association Inc.

Other referencing

I have not however followed the legal style of citation of law journal articles, which relies on a somewhat obscure (especially to the non-lawyer) system of abbreviated journal names. All journal articles, whether appearing in law journals or otherwise, are cited using the full journal name. Pinpoint page numbers normally appear, both in legal journals and in cases, without a preceding 'p,' so I have followed this practice throughout for the sake of consistency, and have made other minor variations in punctuation.

I have made extensive use of the online postings of PNG newspapers. In this case, I have omitted the full URL, as it often tells little more about the article than I have noted for myself. For some years, these online versions of the newspapers gave no indication of date, either in the text or the URL.

International treaties and the like are cited according to the format used by the University of Minnesota Human Rights Library at www.umn.edu/humanrts.

Presentation and format

Gendering language

The language of PNG law is not gender-neutral, and 'words importing the masculine gender include females.'[7] No implications of gender bias should be read into any quotation in which such a word appears, unless there is a clear intention indicated in the text.

Italicisation

Italicisation has generally followed the principles of the AGLC. As well as italicising foreign terms, I have italicised the terms *grassroots* and *elites*, and dropped the 'é' from the latter, to indicate that I am using these terms in a non-English sense to refer to a perceived dichotomy in social class in modern PNG. Italicisation in quotations has been retained.[8]

---

7 *Interpretation Act* 1975 Section 6(*a*).
8 In this I follow Tom Boellstorff in his italicisation of *gay*, *lesbi* and *normal*, to indicate that they are Indonesian terms, not English: Tom Boellstorff, 2005, *The Gay Archipelago: Sexuality and Nation in Indonesia*, Princeton and Oxford: Princeton University Press, xv.

Glossary

'Tales'

A brief note on my use of the word 'Tale' to introduce many of the case and interview summaries. I have been urged to substitute 'story,' but to me the term *stori* in Tok Pisin (and hence in PNG English) is used to indicate a leisure-time chat with friends, as opposed to a purposeful narrative. In this I am supported by Dr Ruth Saovana-Spriggs, teacher of PNG Tok Pisin in the Pacific Studies course at ANU. So I have retained 'Tale,' and cite in support Geoffrey Chaucer and Charles Dickens.

Acronyms and abbreviations

AFAO	Australian Federation of AIDS Organisations
AGLC	*Australian Guide to Legal Citation*
AIDS	acquired immune deficiency syndrome
ak	Askan
ANU	The Australian National University, Canberra, Australia
askan	lit. arse-cunt, a highly derogatory term for the recipient partner in anal sex, or gays in general
AusAID	the former name for the Australian Government's overseas aid program, absorbed in 2013 into the Department of Foreign Affairs and Trade and renamed 'Australian Aid'
bilum	net carry-bag, traditionally slung behind from the head, and thereby capable of carrying loads of considerable weight. The *bilum* is a standard accessory (and gender signifier) for rural women in most of PNG, and particularly in the Highlands region
boihaus	domestic quarters built in the colonial era, usually in the back yards of high-covenant houses allocated to expatriates at the time
Boroko	suburb of Port Moresby, originally developed for expatriate residence
boss-boi	foreman or similar
buai	betelnut, chewed with lime and mustard of various kinds, very popular, sold in markets and from small stands on the streets of Port Moresby, and responsible for the red stains of expectorant which colour streets, walls, buildings and roads
CEDAW	*Convention on the Elimination of All Forms of Discrimination Against Women*[9]
CJ	Chief Justice (and see J)
CLRC	Constitutional and Law Reform Commission
CPC	Constitutional Planning Committee, the pre-Independence body responsible for preparing directions for the *Constitution*
CRC	*Convention on the Rights of the Child*[10]
DCJ	Deputy Chief Justice (and see J)
Derham Report	Report made in 1960 to the Australian government on the administration

---

9 *Convention on the Elimination of All Forms of Discrimination against Women*, GA res 34/180, 34 UN GAOR Supp (No. 46) at 193, UN Doc A/34/46, entered into force 3 September, 1981 (CEDAW).
10 *Convention on the Rights of the Child*, GA res 44/25, annex, 44 UN GAOR Supp (No 49) at 167, UN Doc A/44/49 (1989), entered into force 2 September, 1990 (CRC).

	of justice in the Territories of Papua and New Guinea, which gave rise to widespread reforms to courts, applicable laws, etc.[11]
discourse	historically produced, loosely structured combination of concerns, concepts, themes, and types of statement which establish systems of knowledge
distinguish	in relation to a legal decision: to identify a point or points by which two cases differ
elite(s)	term used to describe the emerging middle class, juxtaposed with *grassroots*
European	term used mainly in colonial times to denote white expatriates, who at the time were mostly of Australian origin
expatriate, expat	non-indigenous, foreigner—used to denote both Europeans and foreigners from other regions, such as Asia
flower	term used in the gay community for a non-heteronormative man—divided into 'closed flower' (closeted) and 'open flower' (out)
FSVAC	Family and Sexual Violence Action Committee
FSW	internationally accepted acronym for 'female sex worker'
GBH	grievous bodily harm
grassroots	term used in contrast to elites, variously describing rural village-dwellers, urban settlers, unemployed, operators in the informal sector, the 'man/woman in the street,' etc.
HALC	HIV/AIDS Legal Centre, Sydney, Australia
hauswin	lit. air-house—an open, roofed raised sitting platform in a house yard, used for daytime living
HB	slang for Hanuabada, the 'Great Village,' located next to the original township of Port Moresby
HRW	Human Rights Watch, an international NGO 'dedicated to protecting the human rights of people around the world'
HIV	human immunodeficiency virus
HIV/AIDS	term used globally when PNG management legislation was introduced. Despite subsequent changes at international level, this term is still used widely in PNG
ICCPR	*International Covenant on Civil and Political Rights*
ICESCR	*International Covenant on Economic, Social and Cultural Rights*
ICRAF	Individual and Community Rights Advocacy Forum, a PNG human rights NGO specialising in upholding women's rights, providing legal advice and assistance
IDLO	International Development Law Organization
IMR	Institute of Medical Research, PNG
J	Judge (of the National and Supreme Courts). It is PNG citation practice to place this abbreviation (or CJ, DCJ, as appropriate) after the name of the judge
kaikai, kai	food; to eat
kiap	patrol officer (by various names); the means by which the colonial Administration maintained a presence and extended the 'rule of law' throughout the colony
kina	basic unit of PNG currency, currently worth approximately 40 cents Australian; symbol K, as in K2.00, K50.00

---

[11] David Plumley Derham 1960, *Report on the System for the Administration of Justice in the Territory of Papua and New Guinea*, Melbourne: Report to the Minister for Territories (*Derham Report*).

Koitabu	ethnic group dispersed throughout villages around Port Moresby, intermarried for generations with Motuans
Lae	PNG's second-largest city, a port town on the north-east coast of the mainland, the coastal endpoint of the Highlands Highway which runs west through the Highlands Range of the mainland
landowner	term for village-dweller (supposedly) who is receiving royalty payments for a resource extraction project on his customary land
laplap	sarong, cloth worn around the waist, usually of a brightly coloured tropical-theme print
LMS	London Missionary Society
luluai	administration-appointed village leader in the territory of New Guinea
MDGs	Millennium Development Goals
meri	woman, wife
meri-blouse	a loose-fitting short-sleeved top worn throughout PNG, related to the 'mother hubbards' worn by women throughout the Pacific. The fabric (usually colourful cotton print) is gathered to a yoke and the blouse is capable of concealing breasts, pregnancies and other female bodily identifiers
Motu	ethnic group in villages around Port Moresby, intermarried for generations with Koitabuans; also, the name for their language, used in simplified form as Hiri Motu, a *lingua franca* in Papua
MP	Member of the National Parliament
MSM	internationally accepted acronym for 'men who have sex with men'
MSW	internationally accepted acronym for 'male sex worker'
NAC	National AIDS Council
NACS	National AIDS Council Secretariat
national	Papua New Guinean citizen
NCD	National Capital District, located in but not of Central Province, where Port Moresby the capital is situated
NCDC	National Capital District Commission
NGO	non-government organisation (including here international organisations)
NHASP	AusAID's National HIV/AIDS Support Project 2000–2005
nolle prosequi	a legal term used in criminal proceedings when a prosecution is suspended. It is not the same as an acquittal, it is merely an acknowledgement that no further action will be taken for the time being, thereby permitting the prosecution to be resumed at a later date
NRI	PNG National Research Institute
OV	PSP outreach volunteer
PAC	Provincial AIDS Committee. These committees have been established by the National AIDS Council for each province and the NCD, in line with the government policy of the decentralisation of powers
palopa	gay or transsexual, particularly one who exhibits effeminate behaviour
pamuk	slut, prostitute (derogatory)
Papua	although this is the term currently used for the Indonesian territory known at various times in the past as West Papua, Irian Jaya etc., it is used herein to refer to the former Australian colony constituted by the southern part of the eastern half of the island of New Guinea

pasinja	lit. passenger; person in transit or visiting who relies on others for shelter and sustenance[12]
pasinja-meri	lit. passenger-woman, one who has left home and (usually) engages in transactional sex or casual relationships for survival
PLHIV	People living with HIV
PMV	lit. passenger motor vehicle; bus
PNG	Papua New Guinea
PNGLR	Papua New Guinea Law Reports
poro	friend
PSP	Poro Sapot Project
raskol	criminal, member of a criminal gang
Simbu	or Chimbu, a Highlands province
STD	sexually transmitted disease (now replaced by STI)
STI	sexually transmitted infection
stori	chat, hang out, tell stories
Tok Pisin	a *lingua franca* originating in New Guinea and now used throughout the country. Its use, together with that of English and Hiri Motu, another *lingua franca* used in Papua, is encouraged in the Preamble to the Constitution
Tolai	ethnic group in East New Britain
TP	abbreviation used for Tok Pisin
tukina, (K2.00)	lit. two kina, slang for prostitute. Two kina (originally £1) was the standard price charged in and even after colonial times
UDHR	*Universal Declaration of Human Rights*
UNAIDS	Joint United Nations Programme on HIV/AIDS
UNGASS	United Nations General Assembly Special Session on HIV/AIDS
UNICEF	United Nations Children's Fund, active in PNG
UNSW	University of New South Wales, Sydney, Australia
UPNG	University of Papua New Guinea, Port Moresby, PNG
VD	venereal disease (former term for STI)
wantok	literally 'one language.' Refers to a friend, relative, or simply someone from the same culture group or area
WWII	Second World War

---

12   Alan Rew, 1974, *Social Images and Process in Urban New Guinea: A Study of Port Moresby*, St Paul: West Publishing Co.: 43; Joan Drikoré Johnston, 1993, 'The Gumini *Bisnis-Meri*: a study of the development of an innovative indigenous entrepreneurial activity in Port Moresby in the early 1970s', Ph.D. thesis, Brisbane: University of Queensland, 66n27.

Maps

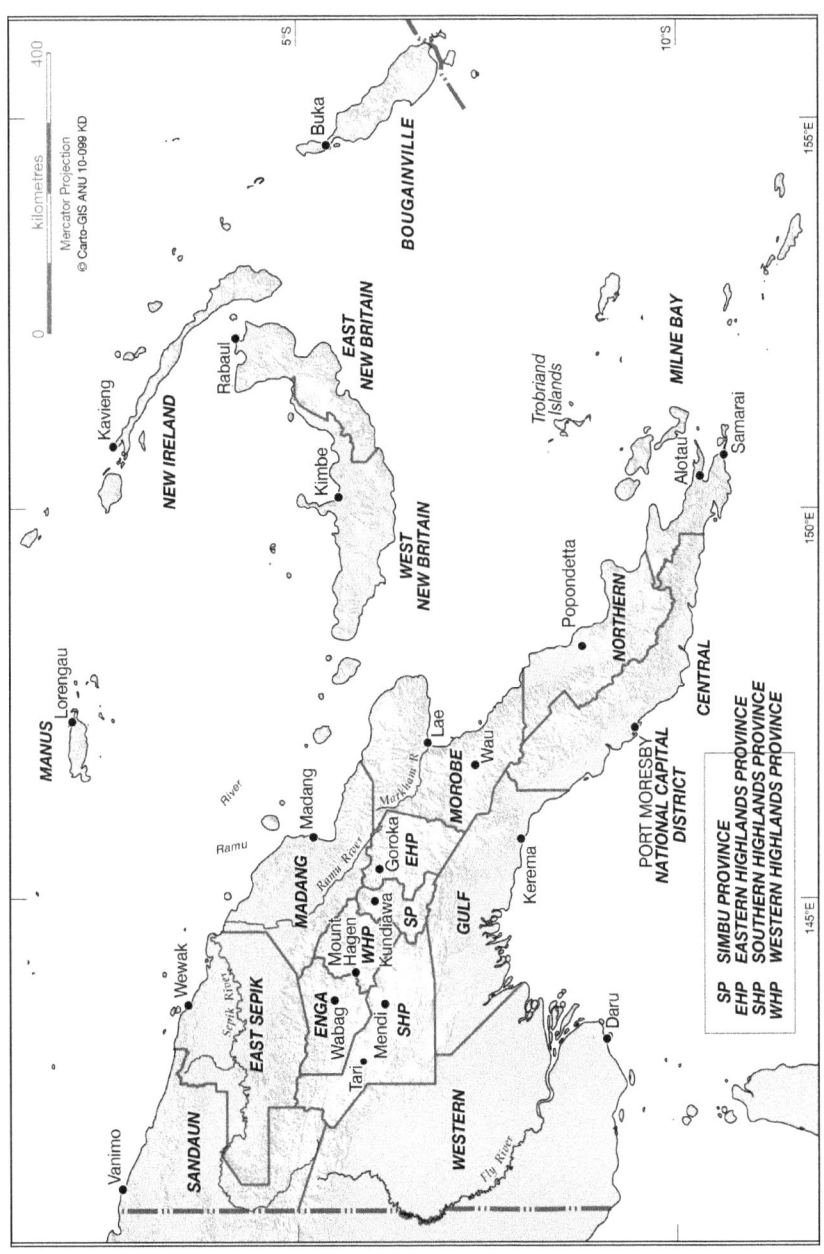

Map 0.1. Map of Papua New Guinea.

Source: Kay Dancey, CartoGIS, The Australian National University, Canberra, 13 January 2014.

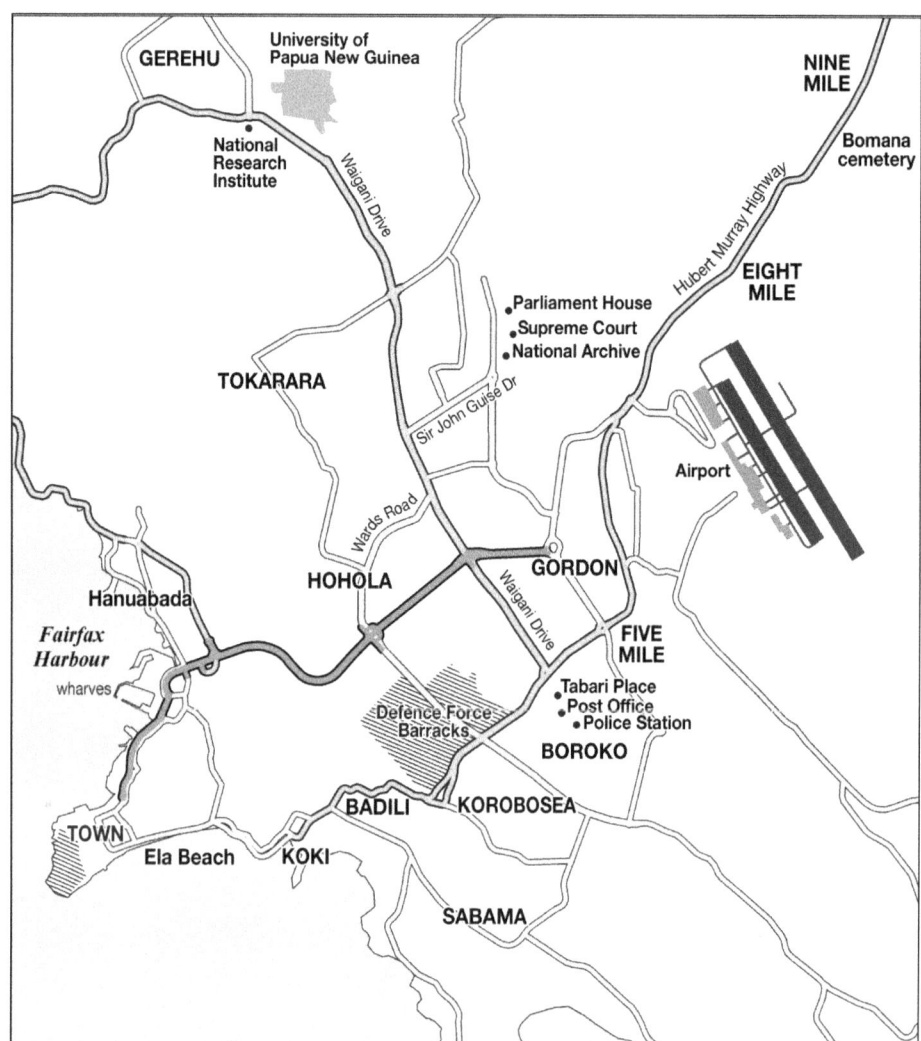

Map 0.2. Map of Port Moresby.

Source: Kay Dancey, CartoGIS, The Australian National University, Canberra, 10 January 2012.

Prologue. The Perfect Storm

Late in 2010, the Minister for Community Development Dame Carol Kidu convened a meeting of the Decriminalisation Reference Group in her Ministry Office conference room.[1] It was a formidable gathering: the then Minister for Justice and Attorney General, the Secretary for Justice, the National AIDS Council Secretariat Director, United Nations and AusAID HIV project personnel, NGO representatives … and yes, quite a few representatives of the criminal classes, in the form of gays, *Palopas* and sex sellers. The monsoon was approaching, the air-conditioning was painfully absent, but nobody cared. Everybody was listening to Dame Carol's great news.

It was the third and last term in Parliament for 'Dame,' as she is fondly and respectfully known. She did not intend to stand again, and had saved the most contentious issues on her reform agenda for this final term. During her previous terms, she had already established a semi-formal Decriminalisation Task Force to start looking into the decriminalisation of sex work and sodomy. When she was re-elected in 2007 and the National Alliance Party to which she belonged became the principal member of the governing coalition, she moved quickly to formalise the Task Force and reconstitute it as the Reference Group.

Now she told the Group how she had been trying for three years to take submissions to Cabinet, only to be rejected by the all-male pre-screening committees. Eventually though, she succeeded in an alternative strategy: Cabinet had endorsed her proposal to refer a review of the laws in question to the Constitutional and Law Reform Commission (CLRC), with instructions to undertake widespread and lengthy community consultation, and to work in conjunction with the Reference Group.

Meanwhile, she had persuaded the then Attorney-General Ano Pala MP to take an interest in another strategy: a Supreme Court case to challenge the constitutional validity of laws which criminalised consensual sex between adults in private, the sodomy laws. The Attorney-General instructed the Secretary for Justice to start immediately on preparing the case. Everyone was urged to assist by providing as much background data as possible, as soon as possible.

Outside, the atmosphere was sultry, but inside the crowded room, it was euphoric. 'Let us create a perfect storm,' said the Minister.

---

1 Sole female member of PNG's National Parliament since 1997 and widow of the late Sir Buri Kidu, the first and arguably the greatest national Chief Justice.

1. Through the Window

The question

> In more than 40 of the 54 nations of the Commonwealth, homosexual activity is illegal, even when conducted in private between consenting adults. The 'white' dominions and a few others have got rid of these laws, and many of the attitudes they reinforce. But in the 'new' Commonwealth, they remain resolutely in place. Likewise, laws and policies on prostitution. Getting fresh thinking on these topics is very hard.
>
> Michael Kirby, former judge of the High Court of Australia, 2011.[1]

Papua New Guinea (PNG) is one of those 'new' Commonwealth nations referred to in the epigraph above which 'resolutely' retain the criminalisation of homosexual activity and prostitution. In this book, I explore the effect of this criminalisation, in an attempt to provoke and support some of the 'fresh thinking' which is desperately needed. Like Justice Kirby, I also make a connection between the two 'topics' of homosexuality and prostitution. This is not new. The 'proscribed forms of "deviant" sexuality—homosexuality and prostitution' have lent themselves to many studies of state regulation and control of sexualities.[2] In nineteenth-century England, the linkage of the two was the result of the construction of the wanton prostitute as the 'other' to the virtuous woman, and the homosexual as the 'other' to the heteronormative man.[3]

As one schooled and experienced in the legal system of Papua New Guinea, where I lived and worked for many years in government advising, law reform and legislative drafting, I was already familiar with the plight of such people. Although they were consenting adults involved in sex in private, they were adjudged criminals under PNG law. In 2001–2002, I worked for the Australian government-funded PNG National HIV/AIDS Support Project (NHASP), preparing legislation for the management of HIV. This drew my attention to the

---

[1] 'Speaking in tongues on AIDS,' 2011, *Sydney Morning Herald Online*, 21 February, online: http://www.smh.com.au/opinion/society-and-culture/speaking-in-tongues-on-aids-20110220-1b0y8.html, accessed 23 February 2011.
[2] John Ballard, 1992, 'Sexuality and the state in time of epidemic,' in *Rethinking Sex: Social Theory and Sexuality Research*, ed. R.W. Connell and G.W. Dowsett, Carleton, Vic: Melbourne University Press, 102–16, 104 and the several references there and at 107.
[3] Ibid., 108–09.

role of poverty, discrimination and human rights abuses in spreading the HIV epidemic, and much of the focus of my work was on the incorporation of human rights and anti-discrimination principles into the draft.

Two factors impelled me to undertake this study. The first was news of an incident which took place in the PNG capital Port Moresby in March 2004. The police raided a guesthouse which operated a bar and served as a venue for sexual networking, on the grounds that it was a brothel and prostitutes there were spreading HIV. The raid was accompanied by violent abuse inflicted on those present by the police. The incident, I have termed the Three-Mile Guesthouse Raid, was notified internationally on several email discussion-group lists. Locally, it featured over many days in the PNG daily newspapers. I was greatly shaken by the news, and resolved to study the challenges and issues it presented.

The second factor, consequent on the first, was my recollection of a friend, a long-time Australian resident in PNG, requesting me many years ago while I was working in the PNG Law Reform Commission, to 'do something' about the 'sodomy law,' adding that expatriates can leave, but the nationals have nowhere to go. They must endure discrimination and abuse everywhere, he told me—bullied and even raped by police, open to blackmail, thrown out of home, sacked from work, forced by custom into marriage.

In my HIV work, I had relied on the existing work of international bodies to support my view that management of the HIV epidemic would only succeed if an enabling legal environment was provided. But I needed hard evidence on the ground in PNG. I determined to research the effect of PNG's state legal system on social perceptions of and attitudes to sex-selling and sodomy. I would study the reasons for the retention of these state laws controlling sexuality, and then examine current moves towards decriminalisation and resistance to the moves. Although at first glance it may seem strange to combine 'prostitution' and 'sodomy' in one study,[4] they do have one outstanding feature in common—both involve sex between consenting adults in private; they are both 'victimless' crimes.[5]

---

4   There is however a long tradition for this combination: for example the 1957 *Report of the Committee on Homosexual Offences and Prostitution*, London: HMSO, Cmnd. 247 (*Wolfenden Report*).
5   This is not to say that sex-selling and sodomy may not involve the participation of minors, forced sex, or other forms of violence, but that is not my focus. Sex with minors, forced sex and physical abuse are another matter, and the law is capable of dealing with them in other ways.

PNG as home and workplace

I have spent more of my adult life in PNG than anywhere else. I come to this research from a BA (Hons) degree from Sydney University in the 1960s, which included a major in Anthropology, although my Honours field was Indonesian and Malayan Studies. This was followed by some nine years of living, working and studying in PNG before and during Independence in 1975.[6] During this period, I obtained a law degree from the recently established University of Papua New Guinea (UPNG). Nearly all the academic staff was expatriate. Only a very few students were not Papua New Guinean, and I was one of those. This era, from the early- to mid-1970s, was one of major experimentation and enquiry in the field of law reform, and although relations between lawyers and anthropologists were not generally good,[7] some attempts were made to enlist anthropologists in the reform project.[8] A Law Reform Commission was established at Independence and given the statutory mandate to review the law with a view to modernisation, simplification and 'the development of new approaches to and new concepts of the law in keeping with and responsive to the changing needs of Papua New Guinea society and of individual members of that society.'[9]

Later, I spent most of the 1990s working first in this Law Reform Commission and then in the Attorney-General's Department. In 2001–2002, as Policy and Legal Adviser to NHASP, I was largely responsible for drafting the *HIV/AIDS Management and Prevention Act* of 2003 (HAMP Act). In 2006, I worked for three months with the United Nations Development Programme Pacific Sub-Regional Centre in Fiji, reviewing the HIV-related laws of fifteen Pacific countries and preparing instructions for rights-based law reform. In all, I have spent over twenty years living in the Pacific, working mainly in the field of law reform.

My early associations with PNG differed somewhat from those of most other pre-Independence expatriates. I fell into none of the three usual categories of government, mission or private sector. My first years were spent working with and for the fledgling *Pangu Pati*, PNG's first political party, which gave me an insight into Westminster-style parliamentary processes, a deep aversion to racism, a readiness to spring to the defence of the underdog and considerable

---

6   See Patricia Mary Reid, 2005, 'Whiteness as goodness: white women in PNG and Australia, 1960's to the present,' Ph.D. thesis, Brisbane: Griffith University, 78–84, for an analysis of the changes already taking place in this 'de-colonisation era.'
7   Peter Lawrence, 1970, 'Law and anthropology: the need for collaboration,' *Melanesian Law Journal* 1(1): 40–57; Bernard Narokobi, 1989, Lo Bilong Yumi Yet: *Law and Custom in Melanesia*, Suva: Institute of Pacific Studies of the University of the South Pacific and The Melanesian Institute for Pastoral and Socio-Economic Service.
8   For example, in the project to reform the criminal law: see Marilyn Strathern, 1975, 'Report on questionnaire relating to sexual offences as defined in the Criminal Code,' Boroko, PNG: New Guinea Research Unit.
9   Law Reform Commission Act 1975, Section 9.

fluency in Tok Pisin. At the same time it earned me the distrust of many in the colonial establishment, to the point where (as I was to learn years later) my application to study law at UPNG in 1972 was very nearly rejected for political reasons.

This was a time of great change, as the colony moved rapidly towards self-government and Independence. V. Lynn Meek describes how the establishment of UPNG helped spark dramatic changes in the relationship between 'white' colonial expatriates and 'black' indigenous students, who in those early days constituted the privileged few, and were regarded with extreme distrust by the colonial establishment.[10] So also were many of the academic staff, who were recruited internationally from a wide range of countries and strove to develop high standards for the university. Most of them were far more closely associated with students and emerging indigenous politicians than with the administrative and commercial colonial establishment. At the same time, however, many were also involved in assisting the moves towards self-government and independence in various fields: politics, law reform, structural rearrangements, education curricula and so forth. These were heady days in the colony, a time of equal rights, anti-racism, freedom and feminism. As one academic described this milieu:

> We were, in the early '70s, a happy, busy, enthralled with PNG, devoted to the shining ideas of a better non-colonial life for its peoples, and therefore an independence-fomenting group—we'd come from everywhere—PNG, Kenya, Tanzania, Northern Ireland, England, the U.S., even a few from Oz—we included just about every Papua New Guinean with a university degree—a rare thing in those days, when the Australians had kept education from so many—though, given they were the leaders of Our Gang, I guess the colonizers had made a wise self-interested choice.... Meetings all the time—so much work to do—so much conversation about principles and policies and philosophy and goals and history and even a little anthropology.[11]

The site of struggle

Like many of those expatriate UPNG teachers, I have been and continue to be involved, sympathetic and ready to offer my services and assistance to causes I consider to be just. During fieldwork, I was several times asked to assist with the preparation of background papers and awareness materials on legal matters

---

10   V. Lynn Meek, 1982, *The University of Papua New Guinea: A Case Study in the Sociology of Higher Education*, Brisbane: University of Queensland Press, 75.
11   Pers. comm., Jean Zorn, former UPNG law lecturer, on the occasion of Bernard Narokobi's death in 2010.

affecting my 'subjects.' I let those interviewed know my views on the human rights abuses I had noted in my studies and research. I make no apology for this personal bias. In so doing, I am reminded of Ruth Behar's exposition of the objective/subjective dilemma confronted by anthropologists,[12] and Nancy Scheper-Hughes's declaration that 'anthropology must exist on two fronts: as a traditional, disciplinary field *and* as a force field, a more immediate and reactive site of struggle and resistance [emphasis in original].'[13]

My 'site of struggle and resistance' is that of working towards bringing to public attention the situation of sex sellers and gays in PNG. Recently, the HIV epidemic has thrown a fierce spotlight on sexualities in the country. We hear calls to 'ban prostitution' as a means of prevention; explanations which blame it all on 'those *pamuks* or *gelis*,'[14] or which say that homosexuality is a foreign import; we know that gays face continual harassment in public and sometimes from their own families; we realise that the economic situation forces more and more people, male and female, young and old, into selling sex for survival.

Many international aid organisations and United Nations bodies consider that an approach to the HIV epidemic based in human rights is essential. Failure to protect human rights fuels the epidemic by driving people underground through fear of detection and punitive measures, thereby inhibiting care and support and blocking achievement of the desired goals of preventing new infections. The impact of the epidemic on those infected or presumed to be infected is increased, by depriving them of economic and social support. Even the ability of civil society to respond to the epidemic is hindered by criminalising or otherwise curtailing their outreach activities.[15]

Hence the Joint United Nations Programme on HIV/AIDS (UNAIDS) and the Office of the United Nations High Commissioner for Human Rights have resolved that, globally

> criminal law prohibiting sexual acts (including adultery, sodomy, fornication and commercial sexual encounters) between consenting adults in private should be reviewed, with the aim of repeal….
>
> With regard to adult sex work that involves no victimization, criminal law should be reviewed with the aim of decriminalizing, then legally

---

12 Ruth Behar, 1996, *The Vulnerable Observer: Anthropology that Breaks your Heart*, Boston: Beacon Press: especially 1–33.
13 Nancy Scheper-Hughes, 1996, 'Small wars and invisible genocides,' *Social Science and Medicine* 43(5): 889–900, 892.
14 Derogatory terms for 'prostitute' and 'effeminate gay' respectively (see Glossary).
15 Joint United Nations Programme on HIV/AIDS (UNAIDS), 1999, *Handbook for Legislators on HIV/AIDS, Law and Human Rights: Action to Combat HIV/AIDS in View of its Devastating Human, Economic and Social Impact*, UNAIDS/99.48E, Geneva, UNAIDS, 24–25.

regulating occupational health and safety conditions to protect sex workers and their clients, including support for safe sex during sex work.[16]

Despite these exhortations, it is proving exceedingly difficult to implement these reforms in PNG. Regardless of private sentiments, public opinion is outraged by reports of sex between males, and many are opposed to any moves towards decriminalising sex-selling. However, upon her appointment as Minister for Community Development in 2002, Dame Carol Kidu launched a multi-sectoral effort to seek a review of the criminal laws on sex-selling and sodomy. In 2009 this effort was re-cast as a Reference Group, comprising civil society organisations and public and private sector representatives, working to seek decriminalisation.[17] This was the group that assembled in the Ministerial office, that sultry day in 2010, to create a 'perfect storm.'

But is decriminalisation the answer? Why not just attempt to influence the discourse,[18] train and sensitise the public, the law-enforcers and the media, change the thinking, overcome the stigma? If the laws are not enforced, or in any way relied upon, won't they simply cease to matter?

This way of thinking has been called the 'enforcement principle': the belief that if proscriptive laws are not enforced, they are harmless. Both commentators and courts have long relied upon it to dismiss arguments for decriminalisation. One example is the US Supreme Court in *Bowers v Hardwick*, a case which upheld the constitutionality of the sodomy law of the State of Georgia.[19]

The enforcement principle has been challenged by several writers. In 2001, American lawyer Ryan Goodman contended that as long as such laws remain on the statute books, they operate to form and inform social norms. He believed that to understand the effects of law in general, and laws which criminalise sexual conduct in particular, one must take into account the law's role in a wider social context. He used empirical data from fieldwork to support his challenge, comparing information gathered from South African gays and lesbians before and after sodomy was decriminalised there in 1998. He learned that various social institutions operate in life, working both for and against the law, to shape identity, regulate social relations, and influence personal behaviour.

---

16 Office of the United Nations High Commissioner for Human Rights and Joint United Nations Programme on HIV/AIDS, 1998, *HIV/AIDS and Human Rights: International Guidelines*, HR/PUB/98/1, United Nations.

17 Carol Kidu, 2011, 'A national response to the HIV epidemic in Papua New Guinea,' *UN Chronicle* 1, online: http://www.un.org:80/wcm/content/site/chronicle/home/archive/issues2011/hivaidsthefourthdecade/nationalresponsetohivpapuanewguinea, accessed 20 August 2011.

18 I use this term in the Foucauldian sense, to refer to historically produced, loosely structured combinations of concerns, concepts, themes and types of statement which establish systems of knowledge.

19 478 U.S. 186 (1986); overturned in 2003 by *Lawrence v Texas* 539 U.S. 558, 578, 123 S.Ct. 2472, 156 L.Ed.2d 508 (2003).

Criminalisation reinforced antagonism in other institutions of cultural ideology, such as medical and religious discourse, and decriminalisation effected clear changes. Individuals felt a heightened sense of placement and acceptance in the community, a sense of relief that their primary legal burden had been removed, and new feelings of freedom in public spaces and in interactions with police.[20]

Although Goodman was primarily concerned with the criminalisation of same-sex conduct, much of what he has had to say is applicable also to the criminalisation of the selling of sex. I was delighted to discover Goodman's work, and situated my own in relation to his critique of the enforcement principle, a critique which I consider reinforces the case for decriminalisation in PNG.

Goodman based his approach on the theories of twentieth-century French philosopher Michel Foucault, who studied the organisation of knowledge and power in the modern world through case studies of the history of medicine, psychiatry, penal systems and sexuality.[21] Although Foucault's theories have spoken directly to a multitude of scholars of colonialism, he himself rarely directed his gaze beyond Europe.[22] Others however have applied his work to colonial situations, tracing the multiple ways in which colonists exerted power through control of sexuality. But to what extent can Foucault's analysis of Europe be extended beyond the European colonists to the colonised and the formerly colonised, and to their own post-Independence laws governing sexuality? This is crucial to the question I set out to explore.

My goal, then, is to research the criminalisation of the selling of sex and sex between males under PNG's state legal system, and the effects of that criminalisation on perceptions of and attitudes to these two sexual behaviours. If I agree with Goodman's opposition to the enforcement principle and accept that proscriptive laws, even if they are not enforced, nevertheless continue to have an effect on the lives of those whose behaviour is proscribed and the attitudes of others to them, then I must also accept that the law is not operating in isolation from other normative discourses, but in interaction with them. Thus, I aim in the first place to study the operation of these discourses upon the colonised in pre-Independence PNG, and then ask whether this process has persisted into the era of Independence. I then ask what are the effects on those still criminalised, and on the moves towards decriminalisation prompted by the spread of HIV.

---

20   Ryan Goodman, 2001, 'Beyond the enforcement principle: sodomy laws, social norms, and social panoptics,' *California Law Review* 89: 643–740, and 648nn19–20 for details and references regarding the process of gathering data.
21   Michel Foucault, 1978 [1976], *The Will to Knowledge: The History of Sexuality: Volume 1*, London: Penguin Books.
22   Ann Laura Stoler, 1995, *Race and the Education of Desire: Foucault's History of Sexuality and the Colonial Order of Things*, Durham and London: Duke University Press, vii, 1, 19.

PNG as field

> It seems most useful to us to attempt to redefine the fieldwork 'trademark' not with a time-honored commitment to the *local* but with an attentiveness to social, cultural and political *location* and a willingness to work self-consciously at shifting or aligning our own location while building epistemological and political links with other locations [emphasis in original].
>
> Akhil Gupta and James Ferguson, 1997.[23]

The nature of the field

This book is not the result of a classic live-in study of a static, spatially fixed group of people. My fieldwork, like much other anthropological work conducted today, subverts many of the conventional anthropological concepts of 'field.' Rather, it is concerned with a set of behaviours, practised nation-wide, by people with little in common other than their sexual practices, their self-images, and the insistence of PNG society on viewing them as discrete and coherent groups, both *de jure* and in practice. As Akhil Gupta and James Ferguson point out, the classic assumption of the 'spatialisation of difference' which relies on constructs of 'home' and 'abroad' can easily be upset by gender and sexuality studies, which start from the opposite premise: that 'home' may be a place of difference.[24] A fieldwork site need not be geographically bounded: rather, it can be constructed upon a point of unequal power relations, a 'political' location.[25] The entire nation of PNG bounds my 'field.'

In this, I adopt the reasoning of Tom Boellstorff who, in his study of *gay* and *lesbi* culture in Indonesia, points out that the dominance of anthropological studies grounded in 'ethnolocality' means that there is virtually no ethnography of Indonesia as a whole, but only that confined to individual ethnicities. He suggests that this 'mode of representation' shares a genealogy with the colonial project which tried to block the emergence of 'translocal spatial scales' inherent in nationalism and anti-colonial religious movements. His own study defies such traditional boundedness. His respondents are scattered throughout the nation, their sites embedded in a national 'Indonesian' culture.[26]

---

23   Akhil Gupta and James Ferguson, 1997, 'Discipline and practice: "the field" as site, method and location in anthropology,' in *Anthropological Locations: Boundaries and Grounds of a Field Science*, ed. Akhil Gupta and James Ferguson, Berkeley: California University Press, 1–29, 3, 5.
24   Ibid., 32–33.
25   Ibid., 35.
26   Tom Boellstorff, 2005, *The Gay Archipelago: Sexuality and Nation in Indonesia*, Princeton and Oxford: Princeton University Press, 18–20.

PNG can be viewed in much the same way. Most ethnographies focus on one particular ethnic group of the many hundreds in the country. But the post-Independence era has seen a melding of local ethnicities to the point where Tok Pisin has become creolised,[27] many city dwellers of all classes claim 'mixed' parentage and do not speak the language of one or both parents,[28] and despite a multitude of ethnically based activities (traditional dance performances, weddings and funerals, church activities and so on) many of them locate themselves in day-to-day socialising through common interests and lifestyles, rather than through kinship. Sex-sellers and gays are no exception. Many of the women involved in the Three-Mile Guesthouse Raid were of mixed parentage, and many local sex-worker groups around the country see each other as united in their efforts to survive, as evidenced by their careful choice of names for themselves. Many of my gay respondents claimed both the same mixed parentage and 'sister' friendships with those of different ethnic origin—in fact my first group interview was conducted with three 'sisters' each from a different part of the country.

Nowhere is this melding more prominent than in the major coastal towns, Lae and the capital Port Moresby. Freedom of movement throughout the country is a right guaranteed to all citizens under Section 52 of the *Constitution*, as a reaction to colonial laws which from time to time restricted movement, particularly into towns,[29] and PNG's independent citizens have taken full advantage of this right.

If my field does have a spatial location, it has been the capital city of Port Moresby. The reason for this limit was purely pragmatic. Whereas Boellstorff moved around Indonesia with comparative ease, and was therefore able to select various sites for his study, I was less advantaged. Finances prohibited much inter-province travel, which in PNG must be undertaken by air, boat or foot, and I was told that research conducted outside Port Moresby required additional clearances from the relevant Provincial Governments. I also needed to carry out archival research in the National Archives and the National Court Archives. So I submitted to the need for some boundedness to my site and confined myself to the spatial field of Port Moresby where I had lived and worked for many

---

27 I use the term to refer to 'a form of language, originally a pidgin, that has become the mother tongue of a speech community through a process of linguistic development whereby an increasing proportion of a community uses the pidgin as their primary mode of communication and children begin to adopt it as their mother tongue.' Andrew M. Colman, 2006, *A Dictionary of Psychology*, Oxford: Oxford University Press, s.v. creole; *Oxford Reference Online*. Oxford University Press: The Australian National University, online: http://www.oxfordreference.com/views/ENTRY.html?subview=Main&entry=t87.e1975, accessed 16 April 2007; and see Don Kulick, 1992, *Language Shift and Cultural Reproduction: Socialization, Self, and Syncretism in a Papua New Guinean Village*, Cambridge and New York: Cambridge University Press, 83–84; Darrell T. Tryon and Jean-Michel Charpentier, 2004, *Pacific Pidgins and Creoles: Origins, Growth and Development*, Berlin and New York: Mouton de Gruyter, 5–6.
28 In the sense that their parents came from differently identified places or ethnic groups in PNG.
29 Edward P. Wolfers, 1975, *Race Relations and Colonial Rule in Papua New Guinea*, Sydney: Australia and New Zealand Book Company, 95–96.

years. Within it I studied a specific habitus, 'a cluster of *embodied* dispositions and practices.'[30] Research in Port Moresby was made easy for me by the many friendships and associations I have established over the years. Doors were open to me which might have remained closed to other outsiders. Rather than needing to spend time tracking down contacts, I found that many were already waiting for me.

My experiences in PNG have served to minimise the distinction between 'field' and 'home' which persists as the traditional criterion for good fieldwork.[31] Anthropologist friends have gone into the field to meet subjects, and emerged having made friends: I was obliged to restructure many friends as subjects, at least temporarily. This positioning has also coloured my perceptions and understanding to the point where I am often unable to distinguish what I have learned from research and reading from what I have absorbed over the years. I can 'know' something to be true, without being able to locate an academic reference to support it. I can recall many conversations and events which have subsequently become relevant to my research. Where I refer to such matters in my work, I can only propose them as 'personal knowledge.'

Mosbi, an urban site

> Port Moresby is girt with mountains and is beautiful with its lake-like harbour.
>
> Captain John Moresby, 1873.[32]

> Here in the dusty streets is the most polyglot town population.... Here the new order is being born; and this is the germ of the new nation. The melting in this pot ... is limited to the indigenous groups for the most part; and the Australian sauce on top does not melt officially.
>
> Charles Rowley, 1966.[33]

Port Moresby's 'discoverer' was right about the beauty afforded by the great sweep of Fairfax Harbour. Unfortunately, however, he arrived in the middle of the wet monsoon season, when the hills were lush with long green grass, and it never occurred to him that the reason for the absence of tall trees and jungle

---

30 James Clifford, 1997, *Routes: Travel and Translation in the Late Twentieth Century*, Cambridge, MA: Harvard University Press, 69.
31 Gupta and Ferguson, 'Discipline and practice,' 12–13.
32 Captain John Moresby, quoted in Ian Stuart, 1970, *Port Moresby Yesterday and Today*, Sydney: Pacific Publications, 13.
33 Charles Rowley, 1966, *The New Guinea Villager: The Impact of Colonial Rule on Primitive Society and Economy*, New York: Praeger, 201.

1. Through the Window

was the local rainfall pattern.³⁴ An exceptional rainshadow along this part of the coast means that only scrawny sclerophyll eucalypts dot the harbour slopes and the plains beyond, and by the end of the dry season even the grass is dead.

The town grew on a peninsula separating harbour from ocean, flanked on both sides by a line of Motu-Koitabu villages strung along the coast from west to east. The Koita were originally an agricultural people who moved towards the coast from the foothills of the ranges to the east, while the Motu were fishing and trading immigrants. Intermarriage and mutual gain saw former enmities transformed as their villages joined forces in symbiotic relationship.³⁵

Map 1.1. Port Moresby today, showing the harbour at upper left, the original town site on the peninsula, the steep slopes of the coastal hills, the urban and suburban development inland to the east and the airport to the far right on the eastern edge of the city.

Source: Google Earth V7.1.2.2041. (16 October 2013). Port Moresby, Papua New Guinea. 9° 28′ 39.62″S, 147° 09′ 01.61″E, Eye alt 8.85 kilometres. DigitalGlobe 2014. http://www.earth.google.com [20 June 2014].

Nigel Oram describes how topography, land tenure systems and legislation, the self-serving wishes of the colonial administration and subsequent piecemeal

---

34 Stuart, *Port Moresby Yesterday and Today*, 18.
35 Cyril Shirley Belshaw, 1957, *The Great Village: The Economic and Social Welfare of Hanuabada, an Urban Community in Papuai*, London: Routledge & K. Paul; Nigel Oram, 1968, 'The Hula in Port Moresby,' *Oceania*, 39(1): 1–35, 2; interview with 'Robin,' 9 September 2007.

planning have combined to produce a scattered and formless city, with residential and commercial areas interspersed with undeveloped land, much of it too steep to build on,[36] and too high for the water supply to reach.[37] To this list, Alan Rew has added the colonial policies of racial segregation which divided even the indigenous immigrants into ethnic groupings.[38]

The harbour is bounded on its southern side by a long peninsula on which the original township was built. The Motu and Koita villages dotting the harbour's edges hindered expansion along the shoreline to the north and west, so the town spread eastwards along the ocean shore past the canoe anchorage at Koki Point to Badili where, during much of the colonial era, most indigenous town workers were confined in barracks after the 9:00pm curfew excluded them from the town and confined them indoors.[39] Curfew regulations and other laws restricting the movement of Papua New Guineans to and in towns, probably the most stringent in the world outside South Africa at the time, were gradually relaxed through the 1950s and finally repealed in 1959 following criticism from the United Nations.[40]

Despite its poor climate and limited local agricultural resources, Port Moresby went from southern administrative headquarters to base for the Allied Forces in the southwest Pacific during World War II, to capital of the joint territory of Papua and New Guinea.[41] After World War II, the town spread over the steep coastal hills and inland to the east. Extensive residential suburbs sprang up, including that of Hohola, the first experiment in indigenous housing. Urban development in colonial times followed a western pattern, predominantly by and for non-indigenous people, and the implementation of municipal management processes lagged well behind town growth. The repeal of laws restricting movement around the country and into towns led to a vast increase in urban migration during the 1960s, with permanent residence starting to replace temporary urban migration and the sex-ratio imbalance starting to even out, so that by the mid-1960s, according to Oram, migrant workers and their families had increased to an estimated 80 per cent of the population. The rate of urban population growth has continued to be high.[42] Charles Rowley, however, pointed out that the sex ratio was by no means equal. In 1956, there

---

36 Nigel Oram, 1976, *Colonial Town to Melanesian city: Port Moresby 1884–1974*, Canberra: Australian National University Press, 100–01.
37 Rowley, *The New Guinea Villager*, 207.
38 Alan Rew, 1974, *Social Images and Process in Urban New Guinea: A Study of Port Moresby*. St. Paul: West Publishing Co, 13.
39 Wolfer, *Race Relations and Colonial Rule*, 50–54.
40 Ibid., 45, 127–32.
41 Rew, *Social Images and Process in Urban New Guinea*, 5.
42 Oram, *Colonial Town to Melanesian City*, 96–97; G. Koczberski, G.N. Curry and J. Connell, 2001, 'Full circle or spiralling out of control? State violence and the control of urbanisation in Papua New Guinea,' *Urban Studies* 38(11): 2017–36, 2020.

were four thousand single men living in labour compounds, and he assumed that this number must have increased in the following ten years, influenced by the wage structure which was incapable of supporting a family in town. In his view, this situation provoked an increase in sexual offences, prostitution and homosexuality.[43]

When I first arrived in PNG in the late 1960s, expatriates shopped in 'Town' on the peninsula, where the Pacific-wide trading companies Burns-Philp and Steamships operated department stores close by the main wharf, and the Hotel Papua and its adjacent movie theatre were the principal focuses of colonial social activity. Another retail centre complete with Burns-Philp supermarket at Boroko, one of the inland suburbs, competed with 'Town,' while the former site of the native-worker barracks, the Koki-Badili area with its market, tradestores and industrial area, had become the indigenous commercial centre.[44] Increasing numbers of Highlanders were joining the ranks of urban migrants,[45] and village ties were gradually being loosened by many urban settlers,[46] although this process has not progressed to the extent anticipated by writers of that period.[47] At that time, the unskilled migrant majority of the population was largely invisible to expatriate officials and academics, their settlements hidden in the hills, their comings and goings barely noticed.[48]

The Motu-Koitabuan resentment of these immigrants grew as the newcomers began appropriating the informal sector economy. Percy Chatterton attributes the origins of the Papuan separatist movement of the early 1970s to the smaller size and compact character of this former British territory compared to that of New Guinea, and the impact of Sir Hubert Murray's long rule as a paternalistic and protectionist Lieutenant-Governor. These facilitated the growth of a concept of Papuan unity in a way which did not happen in New Guinea, a growth which was then reinforced, as immigration increased, by the economic neglect of Papua brought about by the adoption of World Bank policies of the 1960s.[49]

Port Moresby of the decolonisation era has been described as

---

43 Rowley, *The New Guinea Villager*, 199–200, 207.
44 Oram, 'The Hula in Port Moresby,' 4.
45 Oram, *Colonial Town to Melanesian City*, 105.
46 Ibid., 111.
47 Anou Borrey claims that economic and land pressures have led to the multi-ethnic nature of settlements, as people live where they can. Borrey, 2003, 'Understanding sexual violence: the case of Papua New Guinea,' Ph.D. thesis, Sydney: University of Sydney, 82, 88.
48 Joan Drikoré Johnstone, 1993, 'The Gumini *Bisnis-Meri*: a study of the development of an innovative indigenous entrepreneurial activity in Port Moresby in the early 1970s,' Ph.D. thesis, Brisbane: University of Queensland, 71.
49 Percy Chatterton, 1974, *Day That I Have Loved: Percy Chatterton's Papua*, Sydney: Pacific Publications, 114.

hung in a state of endless becoming, caught midway between its earlier role as a small, European center with a surrounding galaxy of native villages and labor compounds, and the more integrated role its apologists would wish for it in the future … no longer, as it was between the wars, a small European town with a fringe of native villages and compounds. It is now a complex network of functional and spatial positions creating distinctive settings for social life while it gathers a culturally highly diverse population to fill them.[50]

Everyone lived in the town, or wanted to—but no-one owned it.

Gina Koczberski and others consider that the colonial control of the urban population has been replicated in contemporary times, often in more draconian form such as police raids and the bulldozing of informal housing.[51] Attempts to provide low-cost housing failed to satisfy the accommodation needs of the influx of migrants, even before Independence. A substantial proportion of the population, which, in 2014, has been estimated as anywhere between 300,000 and 800,000,[52] now lives in comparatively unplanned, unstructured locations known as 'settlements.' John Connell estimated that there were over eighty informal settlements around Port Moresby in 2003.[53] Keith Barber describes one such settlement, composed mainly of related families from an area in the north of the country, who deliberately moved from formal housing dispersed around town to a reproduced 'village' in a settlement area, which enabled them to be together, carry out a little gardening, intermarry and provide their own internal security.[54] Anou Borrey describes another, with a multiplicity of ethnic groups and less internal cohesion—inhabitants from one section of the settlement do not move freely through another part, especially at night.[55] But these settlements are not segregated from the rest of the town. Outsiders may see a city divided in simple spatial and socio-economic terms, with a working

---

50   Rew, *Social Images and Process in Urban New Guinea*, 229, vii.
51   Koczberski, Curry and Connell, 'Full circle or spiralling out of control?' 2032.
52   'The largest cities in Papua New Guinea, ranked by population,' in Mongabay.com, online: http://population.mongabay.com/population/papua-new-guinea/, accessed 28 March 2014; 'Port Moresby,' in Wikipedia, 2014, online: http://en.wikipedia.org/wiki/Port_Moresby, accessed 28 March 2014; 'Swelling Port Moresby population taxing city infrastructure,' *PNG Engineering*, online: http://www.pngengineering.com/2011/swelling-port-moresby-population-taxing-city-infrastructure/, accessed 29 October 2011 (no longer available). The figures depend a lot on whether or not settlements and peri-urban villages are included in the count, and how accurate the count is.
53   John Connell, 2003,' Regulation of space in the contemporary postcolonial Pacific city: Port Moresby and Suva,' *Asia Pacific Viewpoint* 44(3): 243–57, 245.
54   K. Barber, 2003, 'The Bugiau community at Eight-mile: an urban settlement in Port Moresby, Papua New Guinea,' *Oceania* 73(4): 287–97.
55   Borrey, *Understanding Sexual Violence*, 74–78, 88. Anou Borrey, despite many years of living in Port Moresby and her close associations with many *grassroots*, was nevertheless unable to stay overnight in her field site, the settlement of Morata, because of her hosts' disquiet regarding her safety. This was confirmed in conversation in May 2006 with a PNG friend of mine who lived in the same settlement. She told me how she must insist that a taxi taking her home at night drops her right at her door, rather than leaving her at the end of the street.

population living in 'legitimate' housing contrasting to an underclass of the uneducated, the unemployed and the criminal; but closer investigation reveals a city of complex social organisation, with regional enclaves established in many areas, and complex degrees and forms of socialities pervading the entire town—Michael Goddard's 'unseen city.'[56]

My impression of Port Moresby over the years since the 1960s has been one of space both resisting and adapting to attempts from on high to manage and control it. These adaptations can sometimes happen with remarkable speed. A retail centre is developed, or grows around a major retail enterprise (usually a supermarket/variety store). Gradually it becomes a hunting ground for pickpockets, bag-snatchers and carjackers; its storefronts provide an outlet for the venting of frustrations in demonstrations and riots, requiring extensive boarding-up and security grilles. The colourful thronging crowds through whom I once threaded my way thin and disappear; eventually, the centre becomes a 'no-go zone' for most shoppers; commercial enterprises relocate elsewhere; the crowds migrate there and the cycle repeats itself.

Unofficial roadside markets selling *buai* (betelnut), fresh produce and second-hand clothes spring up and many are eventually 'legitimised,' achieving official recognition from the city's governing body, the National Capital District Commission (NCDC). Residential suburbs, originally planned as spacious single-family accommodation, are transformed into multi-residential compounds with houses and their colonial domestic quarters converted to communal hamlet-style residences, offices, professional suites or 'guesthouses'; at the same time, industrial and commercial yards in other suburbs include small living quarters originally intended for single security staff but today occupied by extended families. Roads, even the main highways, are prone to develop alarming potholes in the tropical climate; mounds of refuse compost quietly along their verges; flamboyant gardens flourish everywhere; and the most noticeable change I observed when returning in 1988 after an absence of twelve years was that all the tree saplings planted and nurtured in the dustbowl of the pre-Independence town had grown strong and tall, greening the ever-growing city.

---

56 Michael Goddard, 2005, *The Unseen City: Anthropological Perspectives on Port Moresby, Papua New Guinea*, Canberra: Pandanus Press, 3–8. In a twist of supreme irony, recent times have seen a reversal of the concept of settlement as the 'breeding ground' of criminals: a 2008 newspaper report told of the concerns of Lae police that gangs were now active in settlements 'prey[ing] on innocent people because of regular police presence in the main city centres.' 'Gangs turn to settlements for crime,' *Post-Courier*, 3 September 2008.

Figure 1.1. A main street in Boroko—all the trees planted in the colonial era have grown, and gardens flourish.

Source: Photo by Christine Stewart, 4 September 2007.

The informal sector is everywhere evident, constantly defying efforts to manage and curtail its activities. Itinerant vendors roam the streets offering cold drinks and tourist artefacts. Increasingly these days, goods offered for sale include Asian imports of pencils, bootlaces, razors and so on. In the morning, these pedlars are joined by men (and recently, the occasional woman) selling the daily newspapers. Stationary vendors of food, iceblocks, cigarettes and most ubiquitously, *buai*, are to be found everywhere. Security issues have seen many vendors shift from the pavements outside their houses back into their front yards where they continue their business through wire-mesh fences. Inside many yards too are makeshift shelters for pool tables, dart boards and 'black-market' beer supplies. Or a tiny store constructed against the front fence sells basic tinned and packaged foodstuffs through a weldmesh security screen.

Figure 1.2. A 'tuckerbox' store constructed in a fence beside a suburban road in Tokarara, heavily screened for security. The graffiti are unsurprising.

Source: Photo by Christine Stewart, 4 September 2007.

Most of the steep hillsides are still under direct government control. They are ribbed by garden plots built in the Highlands style, with downhill drainage which suits a high rainfall climate and contributes to soil erosion in Port Moresby's rain-shadow climate. Once considered impossible to build on, the slopes are increasingly leased to land developers, particularly where water views are involved. This often involves 'eviction' of settler housing and destruction of food gardens.

An important feature of the city is its remarkably effective public transport system. A bus service was already operating vehicles of doubtful quality in the 1950s.[57] In the late 1960s, the Port Moresby bus service, which provided huge vehicles on limited routes, was largely superseded by a local company, Buang Taxi Trucks, which operated a fleet of flat-top trucks with canopies and bench seats. Similar vehicles still operate rural services out to those Central Province villages which are served by road. In town today, however, the twelve- to twenty-seater passenger motor vehicles (PMVs) swarm everywhere. Most of

---

57 Gloria Chalmers, 2006, *Kundus, Cannibals and Cargo Cults: Papua New Guinea in the 1950's*, Watsons Bay, NSW: Books & Writers Network Pty Ltd., 14.

these are operated as part of large fleets belonging to prominent businessmen; registration, routes and fares are controlled by a statutory body, the Land Transport Board. Taxis are more often individually owned and operated, and most are of dubious trustworthiness. Attempts to regulate their presentation, roadworthiness and fare charges are consistently foiled or ignored. Regardless of appearance and even safety, though, the PMVs and taxis of Port Moresby enable even the poorest of the population to move readily around the city. Meanwhile, the *elites* drive in air-conditioned four-wheel-drives, with windows rolled up and all doors locked, along 'safe' routes between destinations which are modelled on modern global lifestyles—supermarkets with fenced car parks patrolled by security guards with their leashed guard-dogs, five-star hotels, air-conditioned restaurants with elaborate security measures, apartments in walled guarded compounds.

Figure 1.3. High-covenant houses and apartments built to take maximum advantage of the spectacular ocean views. The houses are owned by politicians and other *elites*, and the apartments are mainly rented to expatriates.

Source: Photo by Christine Stewart, 27 January 2006.

The *elites* are not, however, completely insulated from their surroundings. Complex kin and ethnic networks continue to bind them into ongoing relationships which cross spatial and class boundaries. For example, a prominent lawyer friend once told me that she numbered many *raskols* among her relatives.

Another friend of mixed ethnicity often found herself hosting visiting relatives from the home villages of both her parents, along with those of her husband who came from a different province again. Port Moresby has flung itself together, it belongs to everybody and nobody, and the process of its self-determination and self-definition is ongoing. This then is the site and setting for my study.

Methodology

I have employed a range of methods in my project: fieldwork interviews and group discussions; and textual historical, legal and archival research.

Fieldwork

Several factors inhibited my field research in PNG. Within the city, movement and personal security were issues. I was doubly disadvantaged as a white woman. From the outset, this limited my accommodation options—rental properties and hotel/motel accommodation of a sufficiently secure standard are priced for the business and international aid market, and were far beyond my finances, while cheaper accommodation presented real dangers. I was lucky to be able to stay with friends, but I had to purchase my own car, as nowadays it is not safe for white women to use public transport—in fact, any women travelling alone in buses or taxis are liable to be robbed and even raped, and white women are an even more conspicuous target. I was limited too in the locations I could visit for talk and 'hanging-out.'[58] I should have liked to spend more time for example in the urban-fringe village of Hanuabada observing the day-to-day life of the gay households there, and at nightclubs while the sexual networking process was operating, but personal security was always at issue, and I could go there only in the company of friends or outreach workers. I was able to persuade friends to drive me around some settlement areas in the daytime, for purposes of viewing and photography, but they were not entirely comfortable with this. On the other hand, my large range of friends and acquaintances, and familiarity with the city itself, enabled me to pinpoint destinations and get myself there safely, and to network swiftly and effectively.

---

58   I am not alone in this. Even PNG women researchers experience such inhibiting measures. Fiona Hukula, a PNG researcher with the National Research Institute, was advised by her peers to recruit a male research assistant when interviewing convicted rapists at Bomana Prison outside Port Moresby. Fiona Hukula, 2012, 'Conversations with convicted rapists,' in *Engendering Violence in Papua New Guinea*, ed. Margaret Jolly and Christine Stewart with Carolyn Brewer, Canberra: ANU E Press, online: http://press.anu.edu.au?p=182671, accessed 28 March 2014.

Interviews

I conducted interviews with 'background respondents' and 'subject respondents.' Although I contacted many respondents through an NGO, Save the Children's *Poro Sapot Project* (PSP or Poro Sapot), this project was not my only source of interviews. Moresby is not so large that people can disappear completely, and it is easy to locate and connect with those from all walks of life. What helps most are the kinship and pseudo-kinship networks which operate throughout the city and beyond. Some of those I interviewed were friends of long standing, others were contacted through a snowballing process. Limitations of time and finance precluded any form of exhaustive, quantitative surveying of sex sellers and gays, even in the circumscribed locale of Port Moresby, and besides, I was more interested to hear my respondents speak for themselves. My interviews were thus largely unstructured.

Despite my long acquaintance with PNG, or perhaps because of it, I was acutely sensitive to the possibilities of my status as the 'other,' on several counts—as an expatriate, as an older woman who had never sold sex, as a woman interviewing gays, as a comparatively well-off, highly educated researcher from overseas. I realised that this would probably affect my interviews in various ways.

I was aware that women who sell sex had been intensively surveyed for at least a decade in PNG, principally for the purposes of behavioural research related to HIV. I felt uneasiness at the prospect of approaching these women to 'study' them yet again, so I held off seeking interviews until I had established some measure of friendship. My contacts were limited mainly to those I contacted and learned about through Poro Sapot. They were representative of the freelance women of the streets and guesthouses. Although I was able to observe women and girls at various nightclubs on site visits, these visits were conducted for outreach workers to establish and confirm early contact, conduct awareness discussions and encourage them to visit the Poro Sapot clinic. I did not want to disturb this valuable work by trying to arrange or take interviews.

By contrast though, while I had thought that I would encounter serious difficulties and embarrassments interviewing gays and transgenders,[59] I was quite wrong. The fact that I was a woman and an expatriate seemed to make it easier, not harder. The floodgates opened, and I was treated to detailed descriptions of the first love affair, the greatest love affair, 'the worst event in my life,' 'how I came out to my family' and so on; not to mention several requests to me to source an expatriate partner. I think I became viewed as a kind of *mama* and my subjects were more than comfortable to treat me to their

---

[59] Contrast the difficulties encountered by Fiona Hukula in interviewing male prisoners convicted of sexual offences. Hukula, 'Conversations with convicted rapists.'

confidences. This in itself said a lot about their place in society, how outcast and rejected they often felt, how much they needed someone, anyone, and especially surrogate 'family,' to confide in, even to use as a mouthpiece:

> When people doing a research, what are you coming out with? what's the whole idea of the research? you trying to let people ... you trying to let the government, even let the leaders know that we exist?... I don't mind about people doing research, when people doing research, we are happy, because at that time that we be coming out. When people make a research on MSM ... let's go there, give information ... they can work for us, because we can't work and talk for ourselves (Timothy).

Another difference is that between identity and behaviour. Same-sex attraction, often though not always acknowledged as an identity, is what one can or may feel, whereas selling sex is something one does. The gay community of Port Moresby has learnt how to conceal identity in public spaces, so there is less to lose in coming out in a safe space to a sympathetic companion. By contrast, women selling sex in PNG may be 'clerks, betel-nut sellers, housewives, collectors of firewood, struggling widows, girls doing Grade 8, job applicants, and women seeking to marry expatriate boyfriends,'[60] and it is these identities, not that of 'sex worker,' which predominate. Selling sex is what many women do, whether short- or long-term—and they must advertise themselves, however subtly. In situations where women are identified as 'sex workers' or 'prostitutes' and are being questioned as such, the stigma and discrimination that they anticipate can cause discomfort and embarrassment.[61]

By contrast, while there is a wealth of information, study and public debate on sex-selling, there is little on issues of homosexuality. These differences are part of the reason why I ended up with numerous interviews with gays and far fewer interviews but more other data on selling sex.

In order to discover what adverse consequences gays in Port Moresby faced due to the criminalisation of anal sex and 'indecent dealings' between males, I interviewed and talked with gays of various ages, from various social and class backgrounds, both within PNG and from overseas. I cannot state definitely that my sample of gays was representative of all gays in Port Moresby, much less throughout the country. Sexuality must be concealed in public, and there is a large measure of denial. For example, of the grand finalists in a drag competition in late 2006, all of whom came out openly about their sexuality during the

---

60 Lawrence Hammar, n.d., 'The 'S' words: 'sex', 'sex worker', and 'stigma' in Papua New Guinea,' paper for Papua New Guinea Institute of Medical Research, 4.
61 I was interested to observe at a sex workers' forum organised in Port Moresby by the Australian Sex Workers Association Scarlet Alliance in 2006 that the predominantly street-work women attending were largely reticent and very casually dressed, while the *Palopas* present were gorgeously attired, carefully made-up, and cheerfully forthcoming about selling sex.

event, five were married men who had male partners for casual sex, but kept a low profile so as to hide their sexuality from their wives.[62] *Elites* had more to lose and proved harder to contact than, for example, impecunious *grassroots*. Nevertheless, as many of my interviews were arranged via networks of friends from many walks of life, I was able to obtain a reasonably wide sample. I have seen a study conducted under the auspices of the PNG Institute of Medical Research (IMR),[63] purportedly using a sampling method (respondent-driven sampling, RDS) which if properly used should result in a sample which is representative of the target population with respect to key indicators.[64] I consider that the sample derived for that study is more limited than mine, but I still cannot claim that my sample is truly 'representative' of all groups in Port Moresby. However, I do know that the gay community of this city, which is in reality a small post-colonial town, is close-knit, with long-standing interwoven relationships, and I can guess that I have covered a reasonable range.

My gay respondents fell into three broad categories: the self-identified transgenders who corresponded to those in the IMR study, many of whom were unemployed; gays, usually employed, who may or may not be open about their sexuality, although all have identified to some degree and formed or joined networks of both nationals and expatriates; and expatriate gays who have lived for a considerable length of time in PNG and have long-standing associations (not only sexual) with PNG men. As my research is not behavioural or related to HIV, I was not concerned with enquiring about sexual behaviour or HIV status, and I made a point of explaining this from the outset. Nevertheless, occasionally these matters would come up spontaneously.

Sex sellers, however, were less accessible—those working in clubs were subject to continual scrutiny by the management, and I was only able to talk with the street workers who came to the safety of the PSP drop-in centre. But still, informal meetings in safe spaces were one thing—finding a private space and going through the formalities of obtaining consent for a recorded interview were another. Even where this process had been completed, I still learned as much if not more during casual conversation with those interviewed, while driving, sharing a meal or meeting in other such informal circumstances. I was however able to observe other forms of sexual networking, for example in nightclubs, but deliberately kept a low profile there so as not to jeopardise the HIV awareness work of the outreach workers who took me to these sites, or the operations of the clubs themselves, which have come under repeated attack

---

62 *Poro Sapot Project* database 4 October 2006 (from fieldnotes). These events are held in 'safe' clubs with heavy security.
63 Geraldine Maibani-Michie and William Yeka, 2005, *Baseline Research for Poro Sapot Project: A Program for Prevention of HIV/AIDS among MSM in Port Moresby and FSW in Goroka and Port Moresby Papua New Guinea (PNG)*, Goroka: Papua New Guinea Institute of Medical Research.
64 Ibid., 8.

from politicians and other leaders in recent years.[65] By contrast, however, there was a wealth of documentary material relating to selling sex. In addition to the Three-Mile Guesthouse Raid interviews, I found debates of decriminalisation and legalisation spanning decades in the daily newspapers, reports and publications stemming from behavioural surveys in connection with HIV, and so on. While the sale of sex was over-studied and commented upon, gays were largely invisible. This contrast moulded my own methods.

I was also aware that much of my sampling, both of gays and sex sellers, was skewed towards the least educated and most socially disadvantaged, those with the least to lose by agreeing to exposure to the extent of being interviewed by me.[66] This was truer in the case of the women I interviewed who sold sex, as many of the gay respondents contacted through my own networks were of significantly higher social status: employed, sometimes in very good positions. The more socially disadvantaged, however, were more forthcoming and more relaxed in large groups.

The subject positions I detected or assumed in my respondents may also have placed some constraints on what they told me. I was aware that much of the information I received was given for a reason. Whites in PNG are highly visible and assumed to be very rich. Indeed, despite my financial constraints, I was well-off in comparison with most of the people I mixed with. This perception introduced a 'victim' discourse into many interviews. Gay interviews for example often elicited declarations such as 'it's hard being a gay man in PNG,' etc. I was sometimes expected to provide a high level of financial and other support (for example, money for the purchase of costumes for the drag shows which I was invited by participants to attend). My interviews with women who sold sex all elicited the reason for their situation as being that of abused or rejected wife, eventually obliged to take to the streets to support herself and possibly her children—the narrative of the events leading to their current situation was told in great detail, but little was said about their daily lives selling sex. However, the abused-wife narrative may not be the only one available to them: rather, the 'victim' narrative is usually the first and easiest to reproduce; the expectation of stigma following an admission of selling sex provokes the wish to avoid it.[67] This contrasted with the group of male sex sellers I interviewed who were quite happy to describe where, how and to whom they and their friends sold sex.

---

65   One site visit in 2006 involved our group (some eight people, including two field staff from USAID) waiting for at least half an hour outside the door while the PSP outreach workers talked us in—the management was very nervous after a recent public attack on nightclubs by politicians, reported widely in the press.
66   Christopher Hershey, 2008, 'Reflections on Poro Sapot: one model of care for men's sexual & reproductive health,' paper presented at the Men's Sexual and Reproductive Health in PNG Conference, Port Moresby, PNG, 12 June, 4.
67   Pers. comm., Friends Frangipani outreach worker, Port Moresby, 23 August 2008. Friends Frangipani is a sex worker network for PNG established by Scarlet Alliance, the Australian Sex Worker Association.

I was also aware that the statements made by the women involved in the Three-Mile Guesthouse Raid, being made for a specific purpose (a possible court case for damages), were for the most part deliberately lacking any outright admission of selling sex, while at the same time dwelling at length on the injuries they sustained. Only one or two of those making statements admitted to selling sex, and then felt obliged to proceed to explain the domestic circumstances which compelled them to follow this course. This stand reflects not only the fact that they were advised to conceal their allegedly criminal activities, but also illustrates my point that they were simply ordinary women and girls engaged in earning some form of living from PNG's extensive informal sector.

Interviews—language and translation, names and textual references

Most interviews were conducted in English, sometimes mixed with Tok Pisin. Many of the negotiations and informal conversations were conducted in a mixture of English and Tok Pisin. I am comfortable using Tok Pisin or a mixture of Tok Pisin and English in written and verbal contexts, and all translations are my own, unless otherwise specified. As English was usually not a first language for most respondents, many of the interviews were disjointed, with words or phrases repeated or altered. I have omitted these repetitions and hesitancies, indicating them only with ellipses. Spelling and grammatical errors in interview statements and original texts, particularly those in English, have been reproduced uncorrected, as have disjointed statements in interviews. Where I offer a translation or an alternative for a term, or an explanation of a matter in a quote, it appears in square brackets.

Names of 'subject respondents' have been changed where appropriate or requested. All respondents were given this option, and many chose their own pseudonyms. However, many of my respondents did not fully understand the implications of confidentiality. Some gays chose obvious nicknames, 'stage names' from drag shows, or the fairly identifiable 'girl' names they used amongst themselves. In these cases, I have altered and re-coded their names. A list of respondents with their names (or pseudonyms), date of interview or document receipt and other relevant matters is given at Appendix 1.

I have used the generic term 'outreach worker' to refer to the various officers, workers and volunteers involved with organisations and bodies in PNG which are involved in some capacity with sex-sellers or gays. Unless permission to use a name was specifically given and its use is appropriate, 'outreach worker' is used for purposes of confidentiality. Third persons named in interviews have all been referred to as X, unless the person referred to is a public figure and/or has given permission to be referred to by real name. All places are referred to as Z, where it was thought necessary to conceal a place-name for the protection of respondents.

Regarding names appearing in cases and case files, etc., I have proceeded on the following basis: written case judgements, whether Reported, Unreported or Unreported and Unnumbered, are in the public record (the first two categories may be found on the shelves of The Australian National University Law Library, and more recently, online at www.paclii.org). Records pertaining to cases for which no written judgement was made or is extant are nevertheless (in principle, at least) accessible to the public at the PNG National and Supreme Court registries. It would be absurd to change names and then be obliged to cite the real name in a case or file reference. I have not therefore altered or concealed any names in case materials except for names of witnesses where they do not appear in judgements.

Textual materials

Legal materials

Case decisions are in the public domain and comparatively easy to access, being the foundation upon which the law of the courts is constructed.[68] PNG case decisions may be located in hard copy in various libraries, and in digital form online at the *Pacific Islands Legal Information Institute*[69] or via the digital database *pngInLaw*.[70] Statistics on trials and convictions may be compiled from Annual Reports.[71] But the case files themselves, which often tell a far more intriguing story than the bare bones of the law reports and statistics, can be much harder to discover. The court files were undergoing restoration at the time of fieldwork and very little could be located there.[72] I relied principally on legal files held in the PNG National Archive. In the main, these were Crown Prosecution files dating from before Independence, preserved in Australia and subsequently returned to PNG in the 1980s.

One of the principal constraints that I encountered was in locating information on prostitution cases in the courts. While charges relating to sex between males

---

68 But see Jean G. Zorn, 2010, 'The paradoxes of sexism: proving rape in the Papua New Guinea courts,' *LAWASIA Journal*, 17–58, 44n70, where she explains why 'one can never be quite sure that one has found every Papua New Guinea court decision.'
69 *Pacific Islands Legal Information Institute*, n.d., online: http:www.paclii.org, accessed 28 March 2014.
70 'pngInLaw,' *NiuMedia Pacific: The Legal Information Network*, n.d., online: http://www.niumedia.com/pnginlaw/, accessed 28 March 2014.
71 For a relevant example of this process see Robert Aldrich, 2003, *Colonialism and Homosexuality*, London & New York: Routledge, 251.
72 I am deeply grateful to the National Court library and archivist staff who did their best to assist me.

are brought in the superior courts,[73] charges for prostitution are brought in the lower District Courts. Although some magistrates have recently begun reporting their decisions, I was advised that general District Court records are most unlikely to have survived. Apart from two significant appeal cases in the National Court, I have had therefore to rely on random accounts of prosecutions, such as newspaper reports.

Research in the National Archive proved difficult. Archives are in a sorry state in PNG, either uncatalogued, poorly indexed or vanished forever. Unfortunately the National Archive proved the least cooperative and most inaccessible of repositories. In 2006 when I conducted most of my fieldwork, it opened only three days a week for limited hours. Justice files were all stored in a separate and run-down building to which I was denied access, and items I wanted had to be ordered at least half a day in advance, a fairly standard practice, but in this case the requirement sometimes led to mix-ups in requests, and some files when finally delivered proved to be empty. I was not allowed to photograph documents, as I was told that the Archive relies on making money through the sale of photocopies.[74] Here again, mix-ups occurred: many files had to be sent back for re-copying several times before the correct versions were obtained. All this was time-consuming. And last but not least, the Archive building itself is in a dangerous location, and friends constantly warned me to take particular care there. The town-planners of the more easy-going 1970s had decided to conceal such buildings as the Archives, the National Library and the Arts Theatre in hollows between artificial hillocks, which these days provide perfect cover for Port Moresby's notorious *raskol* gangs bent on armed robbery. I would arrive in the morning, scuttle from my car into the safety of the heavily fortified building, out again when it closed for the lunch hour, back again afterwards for two more precious hours of work, and then out again. These anxieties about my personal security provided an ironic backdrop to my scholarly search for records of old crimes.

Other documents

As well as reviewing the historical and anthropological literature on sexuality, colonialism and the Independence era in PNG, I combed newspaper and magazine records held in the Australian National Library, Canberra, and the PNG National

---

73 Termed the Supreme Court before Independence and the National Court after Independence: see Table 3.1.
74 The same income-generating principle applies in other places, for example the National Research Institute library, but I was always allowed to photograph documents there and in other library and archive collections in PNG. The National Archive was an unfortunate exception.

Research Institute (NRI). The two current PNG dailies, the *Post-Courier* and the *National*, have become available online in recent years. The Pacific Manuscripts Bureau has been particularly helpful in tracking down documents and images.[75]

I obtained further assorted materials from various sources. These have included a detailed personal account of the circumstances surrounding *Mala's Case*; a compilation of accounts of blackmail and accompanying violence provided by a gay friend; a broken series of an annual compilation 'Summary of Sentencing' for most of the 1990s, provided to me by the National Court judge who compiled them, and which show the number and type of 'unlawful carnal knowledge' cases coming before the National Court; the *Poro Sapot Database* for the years 2005–2007, which records the activities of outreach volunteers (OVs) in distributing condoms and promoting HIV awareness among sex sellers, their clients, gatekeepers and receptionists at clubs, guesthouses etc., and includes background comments by workers on issues raised; various reports and publications prepared in connection with the management of the HIV epidemic in PNG; items posted to electronic mailing lists, chiefly concerned with anthropology or HIV; and other documents in my personal possession, collected over time. Much of this material was only accessible through the contacts I have referred to above.

The Three-Mile Guesthouse Raid materials include accounts in the PNG daily newspapers of the time; statements made by those caught up in the raid for the purposes of mounting a claim for damages for infringement of human rights;[76] accounts from interviews with social workers involved in assisting those arrested; and background information from others involved. Materials on selling sex in general in Port Moresby consisted of interviews with past and present street workers; observations at brothels, nightclubs and known sex-selling venues in Port Moresby; notes which I took upon attending a forum organised under the auspices of Scarlet Alliance, the Australian Sex Workers Association, in 2006; and further material obtained from officers of the international organisation Human Rights Watch, who visited PNG in 2004 after calling in at The Australian National University.[77]

---

75 The Pacific Manuscripts Bureau is based in the College of Asia and the Pacific at The Australian National University, Canberra. It is a non-profit organisation sponsored by an international consortium of libraries specialising in Pacific research, online: http://asiapacific.anu.edu.au/pambu/about.php.
76 These statements were later verified by the makers who gave permission for their use in my research.
77 See Human Rights Watch, 2005, *'Making Their Own Rules': Police Beatings, Rape, and Torture of Children in Papua New Guinea* 17(8(C)), New York: Human Rights Watch; Human Rights Watch, 2006, *'Still Making Their Own Rules': Ongoing Impunity for Police Beatings, Rape, and Torture in Papua New Guinea* 18(13(C)), New York: Human Rights Watch.

Key concepts

Papua New Guinea

Throughout its colonial history, the now Independent State of Papua New Guinea underwent several name changes, effected by the legislatures of the metropole: from British New Guinea to the Territory of Papua, and from New Guinea to the Territory of New Guinea; the two amalgamated first as the Territory of Papua and New Guinea, and then as the Territory of Papua New Guinea. Ultimately the name Papua New Guinea was adopted upon Independence. For simplicity's sake I use the term Papua New Guinea (commonly abbreviated as PNG) throughout, regardless of the precise name pertaining to the period under discussion (except where the context requires otherwise). I also follow Edward P. Wolfers in using the term 'Papua New Guineans' to refer throughout to the indigenous inhabitants of the two territories and the subsequent nation, whether before or after the Independence era of the 1970s when the term came into general use.[78]

The term 'Papua' has undergone some dramatic changes. Until Independence, it was used to describe the southern part of the country, and the boundary between it and 'New Guinea' was that drawn up in 1899 between Britain and Germany to demarcate their respective spheres of influence.[79] At Independence, this division was abolished, but de facto differences of cultural tradition, languages etc. have remained. Recently, the name has been applied to the Indonesian province of the western half of the island. Where I use the term however, I intend it to apply to the region formerly constituting the Territory of Papua to the south, and particularly those coastal areas bordering the Gulf of Papua.[80]

Prior to Independence, the divisions of the country were termed 'district'; this was changed to 'province' at Independence. I have used 'district' when talking about pre-Independence times, and 'province' thereafter. Some names and spellings were subsequently altered too, so that 'West Sepik' became 'Sandaun,' and 'Chimbu' became 'Simbu.' The legality of the name changes has been questioned, so I have used the name most commonly in use today, except where directly quoting text.

---

78 Wolfers, *Race Relations and Colonial Rule*, 10n1.
79 Herman Hiery and John MacKenzie (eds), 1997, *European Impact and Pacific Influence: British and German Colonial Policy in the Pacific Islands and the Indigenous Response*, London: Tauris Academic Studies, 4.
80 The situation is further complicated by the use of 'Papuan' to denote language family, ethnicity and political division.

Selling sex

The terminology used for transactional sex is highly problematic. Terms have been imported from overseas, derived from various PNG languages, and invented (both as applied by others and for self-application). Many terms in common use are rejected by those to whom they are applied. Localised groups may invent their own terminology.

The familiar English terms 'sex work' and 'prostitution' and their variants are not universally accepted in PNG. 'Prostitute' and its variants are the language of the law, and still used frequently in the media. Similarly, the term 'brothel' is used in the law but rarely appears elsewhere, except in newspaper reports intended to excite and scandalise. Only very recently have establishments appeared which may truly be termed brothels.

In many countries including Australia, the term 'prostitute' has fallen into disrepute due to its connotations of immorality and unworthiness.[81] To represent the discursive shift from moral to economic terms, 'sex worker' is preferred instead.[82] For example, in 2004 the then Coordinator of the Global Network of Sex Work Projects, an informal alliance of sex worker rights' activists working within sex work projects around the world, posted a defence to the network's eForum of the term 'sex worker' in preference to the stigmatising 'prostitute.'[83] The term 'sex work' implies a modern form of freely-chosen employment whereby money is exchanged for a sexual service of some kind, thereby focusing attention on the economic rather than the moral aspect of the activity, and assuming individuated agency on the part of its practitioners.

But there are those who do not agree. The term 'sex worker' is shaped by specific (and for PNG, foreign) cultural assumptions regarding the purpose of selling sex and the agency or lack of it involved. In third-world situations, there are many other forms of sex-for-money and the sale of sex is not necessarily seen as a profession, but as a means of survival.[84] Terms such as 'survival sex' or 'transactional sex' seem more appropriate in the PNG setting.

---

81 Gail Phetersen, 1993, 'The whore stigma: female dishonor and male unworthiness,' *Social Text* 37 (Winter): 39–64, 39.
82 Holly Wardlow, 2004, 'Anger, economy and female agency: problematizing "prostitution" and "sex work" among the Huli of Papua New Guinea,' *Signs* 29(4): 1017–39, 1017; 'Terminology,' *Scarlet Alliance*, 2007, online: http://www.scarletalliance.org.au/issues/terminology/, accessed 21 March 2009.
83 P. Longho, 2004, 'Defending the term sex-work,' *SEX-WORK eForum*, online: sex-work@eforums. healthdev.org 17/9/2004, accessed 17 September 2004.
84 Janet Maia Wojcicki, 2002, '"She drank his money": survival sex and the problem of violence in taverns in Gauteng Province, South Africa,' *Medical Anthropology Quarterly* 16(3): 267–93, 268; Janet Maia Wojcicki, 2002, 'Commercial sexwork or *ukuphanda*? sex-for-money exchange in Soweto and Hammanskraal area, South Africa,' *Culture, Medicine and Psychiatry* 26: 339–70, 340.

Holly Wardlow challenges all of these, however, pointing out that although the Huli passenger women of the Southern Highlands whom she has studied exchange sex for money, their 'initial motives have little to do with material necessity and everything to do with anger and resistance.'[85] And Martha Macintyre challenges the whole culture of devising 'harmless' terminology:

> Calling them 'sex workers' seems to me to be a bit ludicrous in all societies—changing the name is an especially middle-class liberal response that confuses the subject of the hostility—which is selling sex—with a word. If the sex worker is still selling her body, she's still stigmatised.[86]

The HELP Resources report on the commercial exploitation of children in PNG also queried the term and its implications of agency when it is applied to children and young people. In this situation, it fails to take into account the reality of their experiences in selling, or being sold for, sex. The report preferred to use the term 'child prostitution.'[87] In 2008, UNAIDS supported this limited use of the term 'prostitution,' and proposed the terms 'commercial sex,' 'sex work' or 'the sale of sexual services.'[88] In 2010, stakeholders in the *Askim na Save* survey of sex-selling and associated violence in Port Moresby agreed on the term 'people who sell and exchange sex.'[89]

A variety of terms from Tok Pisin is used in PNG to describe commoditised sexual conduct, depending on the person talking, the nature of the conduct and the locality in which it is carried out. For example, *pamuk* [slut],[90] *raunraun meri* [lit. mobile woman], and *tukina* [two kina, a reference to the long-standing price standard] are common; *pasinja meri* [passenger-woman] has displaced the

---

85 Holly Wardlow, 2001, '"Prostitution", "sexwork", and "passenger women": when sexualities don't correspond to stereotypes,' paper presented at the 3rd IASSCS Conference, Melbourne, 1–3 October: 1018; Wardlow, 'Anger, economy and female agency,' 1037; and see also the testimony of Kuragi Ku in *Monika Jon and Others v Dominik Kuman and Others* (unreported), N253, 8 August 1980 (*Monika Jon's Case*).
86 Pers. comm. with Martha Macintyre per email, 25 January 2009.
87 HELP Resources Inc., 2005, 'A situational analysis of child sexual abuse & the commercial sexual exploitation of children in Papua New Guinea' (draft), report prepared for UNICEF, Port Moresby, PNG, 5.
88 Joint United Nations Programme on HIV/AIDS (UNAIDS), 2008, *UNAIDS Terminology Guidelines (2008)* UNAIDS: Geneva, 14.
89 Angela Kelly et al., 2011, Askim na Save *(Ask and Understand): People who Sell and/or Exchange Sex in Port Moresby*, Sydney: Papua New Guinea Institute of Medical Research and the University of New South Wales, 6. This survey sampled people nine years of age and older, and at a community feedback pre-publication session in Port Moresby to which I was invited, we were told that ethics approval for sampling minors without parental consent took a year to obtain, and required the construction of a category of 'liberated minors' (field notes, 4 Nov 2010).
90 *Pamuk* comes originally from the Samoan *pa'umutu* (slang pronunciation *pa'umuku*) where it referred to a girl who lost her virginity without the appropriate ceremony in pre-Christian times, but has come to mean a prostitute or slut in modern Samoan parlance. It was probably introduced into PNG either by labourers returning home from work on German plantations in Samoa between 1880s and 1914, or by Samoan LMS missionaries—pers. comms, Penelope Schoeffel, 27 February 2005 and 2 March 2005; and the Reverend Latu Latai, Canberra, December 2011.

former *haiwei meri* [highway-woman]; and in the Highlands, *fo'kopi* [4-coffee, a reference to the fourth or lowest grade of coffee] has recently come into use.[91] All are highly derogatory. Variants on the term 'sister' (*asidua, sista-sista*) are used by sex-seller women themselves;[92] and another term currently in use in several places is 'problem mother,'[93] referring to the fact that most women on the streets are there because they have fled, or been cast out from, abusive marriages, and consequently live with problems.

I decided wherever possible to refer to the process rather than the practitioner and have used variants on the terminology of the *Askim Na Save* report, which uses 'selling or exchanging sex.' I use 'sex worker' in the context of international movements, and 'prostitute' where appropriate, particularly when discussing the law. On occasion, I also refer to 'the sex trade.'[94]

Homosexuality

The terminology in respect of male-male sex is similarly problematic. The connections between the social constructs of 'sex' (a person's biological sex determined from genital attributes), 'gender' (the social dimension of personhood) and 'sexual orientation' (the direction of sexual or affectional desire) have long been the subject of intense scrutiny and debate in the West,[95] where this categorisation is constantly changing and evolving.[96] The distinction between identity and action, so crucial in the law, is blurred. Moreover, the standard accepted categories and the terminology applied to them are not

---

91 Holly Buchanan et al., 2010, *Behavioural Surveillance Research in Rural Development Enclaves in Papua New Guinea: A Study with the WR Carpenters Workforce*, Port Moresby: National Research Institute, 39.
92 The provincial groupings of the Friends Frangipani network have chosen names involving 'sisters': 'Sky Sisters' for Port Moresby, 'Paradise Sisters' for Goroka, and so on.
93 I have heard 'problem mother' in Port Moresby, and was informed by a friend that it is also used in Wewak, on the northern coast of mainland PNG. See also Elizabeth Reid, 2010, 'Putting values into practice in PNG: the Poro Sapot project and aid effectiveness,' *Pacificurrents* 1.2 and 2.1, (April), online http://intersections.anu.edu.au/pacificurrents/reid.htm/, accessed 9 August 2010.
94 While it may be argued that this refers to the entire scope of commercial sexual activity (see for example Anne McClintock, 1993, 'Sex workers and sex work: introduction,' *Social Text* 11 (Winter): 1–10, 2), I use it here in its PNG context.
95 Definitions taken from Martha Chamallas, 2003, *Introduction to Feminist Legal Theory* [2nd edn] New York: Aspen Publishers, 161–69. I acknowledge that they are open to debate and challenge.
96 Judith Butler, 1993, *Bodies that Matter: On the Discursive limits of 'Sex,'* New York: Routledge; Moira Gatens, 1991, 'A critique of the sex/gender distinction,' in *A Reader in Feminist Knowledge*, ed. Sneja Gunew, London & New York: Routledge, 139–57; Henrietta L. Moore, 1999, *Anthropological Theory Today*, Cambridge; Malden, MA: Polity Press; Jeffrey Weeks, 1989, *Sex, Politics, and Society: The Regulation of Sexuality Since 1800* [2nd edn], London and New York: Longman, 6.

necessarily applicable in non-western countries such as PNG.[97] Nor is the presumed direct and immutable connection between behaviour and identity.[98] Much is borrowed, but much also is adapted.

I will deal first with the localised terminology of homosexual identity. As with sellers of sex, a range of names and terms is applied to non-heteronormative men in PNG: *manmeri* [manwoman]; *geligeli* [girlie-girlie]; *askan* [arse-cunt], also abbreviated to *AK*; *suckers*; *vavine* or *kekeni* (Central Province language terms for woman, girl). Some of these appellations are derogatory.

The internationally recognised terminology 'men who have sex with men' or 'males who have sex with males' and its acronym MSM describe behaviour, not identity, but is becoming accepted in many countries and cultures, as an identity appellation.[99] The term 'encompasses a range of identities, networks, behaviours and collectivities, and includes sexual behaviours of those who do not self-identify as practicing sex between males at all.'[100] It has been imported into PNG as part of the HIV discourse, and is most commonly used in NGO settings.[101] But it has encountered a measure of disfavour:

> Even when used as a description of persons with a particular behaviour, rather than an ascription of identity, it is obfuscating in a culture where the sexual practices of the men may include regular and transient sex with women as well as men, the sale and purchase of sex with both women and men, and non-commercial sex.[102]

I found that in Port Moresby, MSM is rarely used outside the NGO working environment—the only occurrence in interview that I came across was a tentative,

> I got into high school and then I was introduced to—what do you call it? MSM? Then I didn't know what it was, and why I was getting involved' (Fred).

---

97 Dennis Altman, 2001, *Global Sex*, Sydney: Allen & Unwin; Chris Berry, Fran Martin and Audrey Yue (eds), 2003, *Mobile Cultures: New Media in Queer Asia*, Durham NC: Duke University Press; Boellstorff, *The Gay Archipelago*; Gilbert Herdt (ed.), 1994, *Third Sex, Third Gender: Beyond Sexual Dimorphism in Culture and History*, New York: Zone Books; Peter Jackson, 1997, '*Kathoey*><gay><man: the historical emergence of gay male identity in Thailand,' in *Sites of Desire Economies of Pleasure: Sexualities in Asia and the Pacific*, ed. Lenore Manderson and Margaret Jolly, Chicago and London: University of Chicago Press, 166–90; Peter Jackson, 2000, 'An explosion of Thai identities: global queering and re-imagining queer theory,' *Culture, Health & Sexuality* 2(4): 405–24.
98 Sonia Katyal, 2002, 'Exporting identity,' *Yale Journal of Law and Feminism* 14(1): 98–176, 99–100.
99 UNAIDS, *UNAIDS Terminology Guidelines* (2008).
100 Definition used at the 'Risks and responsibilities male sexual health and HIV in Asia and the Pacific' International Consultation, New Delhi, India, 23–26 September 2006, and set out in *Pukaar* 56, January 2007, 15.
101 Hershey, 'Reflections on Poro Sapot,' 6; Elizabeth Reid, 'Putting values into practice.'
102 Elizabeth Reid, 'Putting values into practice'; and see Maibani-Michie and Yeka, *Baseline Research for Poro Sapot Project*, 20.

The term *geligeli* is sometimes used but usually carries similar negative connotations to those attaching to *pamuk*; *geli* as an adjective however is often used by gays for 'effeminate.' Many respondents prefer the term *gay*:

> When people say 'gay,' then I put myself into that category (Len).

> I don't like being called homosexual or *geligeli*. The word I like is 'gay' (Douglas).

The gay and transgender people of Port Moresby have formed strong bonds. In the absence of any established categories or indigenous names such as can be found in Polynesian countries to the east,[103] they are constantly inventing their own terminology. While I was doing fieldwork, they were using one such invented term, *Palopa,* which I was told was derived from 'Jennifer Lopez.' They developed a complex system of ascriptive and descriptive terms for themselves:

> *Palopa* is the general term, but 'sister-girl' refers to the ones that are so obvious, any time you see them you know that sister-girls are transgendered, 'open flowers.' 'Closed flowers' are the ones at the moment you cannot tell.… 'Sister-girls' refers to … all the pretty ones. *Palopa* is just a big term for all of us (MSW).[104]

'She,' 'girl' and 'sister' are often used by gays to refer to each other. 'Sister-girl' has replaced *Palopa* for some. Other terms have come and gone.

Categorisation in itself is problematic. As Carol Jenkins points out, 'Sexual identity has little meaning in PNG,'[105] although some have tried. As Len explained,

> I never got myself involved with the gay people from the village [Hanuabada]. And when I say a gay person from the village, I would normally refer to those who are feminine. And so those are the people that you would call *geligeli* in the village. Some people would see me as I'm not gay, because I don't get myself involved with…. I'm not feminine, I'm not dainty-dainty, so they wouldn't put me in the same category as the ones that they call *geligeli* in the village.

Timothy had been to international meetings and conferences, and was grappling with all he had learned there:

---

103 Stephen O. Murray, 1992, *Oceanic Homosexualities*, New York: Garland Gay and Lesbian Studies; Niko Besnier, 1994, 'Polynesian gender liminality through time and space,' in *Third Sex, Third Gender: Beyond Sexual Dimorphism in Culture and History*, ed. Gilbert Herdt, New York: Zone Books, 285–328.
104 Despite my avoidance of acronyms, I have used 'MSW' (male sex worker) to denote an unidentified participant in one group discussion where no names, real or pseudonym, were used, see Appendix 1.
105 Carol Jenkins, 2006, 'Male sexuality and HIV: the case of male-to-male sex,' paper presented at the Risks and Responsibilities: Male Sexual Health and HIV in Asia and the Pacific International Consultation, New Delhi, India, 23–26 September, 57.

Sometimes we have tags on.... I have a special kind of a tag, it's a permanent tag on me, meaning that I'm a gay ... gay meaning that I have sex with men, some gays may be a bisexual, they are playing both ways, or some sex can be insertive-receptive, they can give and they can take, but they come under one tag ... when you open it, there are lots of colours coming up. Sometimes it's very hard to identify a straight man but he's a gay ... it's a gender problem!... We know where we are going to, we know how we are playing.... But sometimes I confuse myself, I sometimes sit down and think, what am I?... I'd like to know why people don't understand people—because of inability in gender, or otherwise ... people put people into boxes ... that's my identity, anyway ... I cannot change overnight to become a 'real man,' it takes time to ... you know, to come to a stage where we think we need to be stable.... I will never become a real man.

Or categorisation may be rejected altogether:

To be honest, I don't like labels, like 'you are gay.' I'll categorise myself as a man who likes other men. Even though I'm straight-acting, most girls they like going out with me, but I don't prefer them, I prefer going out with guys. I don't like to call myself like, I'm gay. I just like going out. If when someone finds me attractive, that's it. I don't like to identify myself (Colin).

Many gays, both expatriate and Papua New Guinean, borrowing from practice overseas, have assumed female nicknames which they use amongst themselves:

We do have *geli* names, 'she' names, just for fun, when we're sending emails or sms, calling up, then we use these names (Barry).

I have used 'gay/gays,' '*Palopa*,' or 'sister-girl' as appropriate to the context throughout. I prefer not to use the term 'gay men' as many gays do not always identify as 'men.'

The labelling of behaviour is similarly fraught with confusion. Until 2003, when significant amendments were made, the *Criminal Code* as adopted from Queensland used the arcane term 'carnal knowledge against the order of nature' for anal sex, whether involving a male or female person or an animal. 'Carnal knowledge' is used in reference to other sexual acts in this version of the Code (incest, sex with a child, defilement and so on) and has been understood to refer to sexual penetration,[106] though it is nowhere defined as such—the only explanatory provision states:

---

106 'Carnal knowledge' has been replaced by 'sexual penetration' by the 2002 *Criminal Code* amendments.

When the expression 'carnal knowledge' or 'carnal connection' is used in the definition of an offence, the offence, so far as regards that element of it, is complete on penetration (Section 6).

The consequence of the ubiquitous use of this term has been that the usual court and legal office classification system of criminal cases categorises all such cases under 'carnal knowledge,' making it difficult to separate out cases of sex between males, as I found when consulting the indexes in the PNG National Archives.

'Carnal knowledge,' however, is a term confined to legal circles. Common parlance in PNG (and elsewhere) has resorted to the Biblical 'sodomy,' although exceptionally, in a 1972 Full Court judgement, one of the judges, an Australian, made repeated reference to 'buggery.'[107]

The term 'sodomy' has had an interesting journey through PNG English. It was used from earliest times when homosexual behaviour and practices were suspected or discovered by early administrators,[108] unless coy circumlocutions were employed.[109] Gradually, 'sodomy' in media and urban middle-class discourse has acquired new meanings. A long string of cases dealing with male rapes and sex with boys has dominated the legal discourse, to the point where factors of age and consent are no longer taken into consideration. In addition to its broad meaning of anal sex irrespective of the gender of the recipient,[110] it has come to be applied to any form of sex between males, irrespective of age and questions of consent or force. The *Post-Courier* front-page headline of 21 January 2006 heads a story of forced sex with and between juveniles in prison (Figure 1.4):

---

107 Prentice J, in *R v M.K.* [1973] PNGLR 204: 210. At 211, he applied the same term to a United Kingdom case of bestiality involving a dog.
108 E.g., Edward Beardmore, 1890, 'The natives of Mowat, Daudai, New Guinea,' *The Journal of the Anthropological Institute of Great Britain and Ireland* 19: 459–66, 464; Francis Edgar Williams, 1969 [1936], *Papuans of the Trans-Fly*, Oxford: Clarendon Press, 158; and see various *Annual Reports for British New Guinea*.
109 E.g., 'unnatural vice,' 'immoral purposes,' 'filthy customs' in Sir Hubert Murray, 1925, *Papua of Today: or an Australian Colony in the Making*, London: P.S. King & Son, Ltd., 94, 259.
110 E.g., Clifford Faiparik, 2004, 'Wife accuses man of sodomy,' *National*, 21 July 2004.

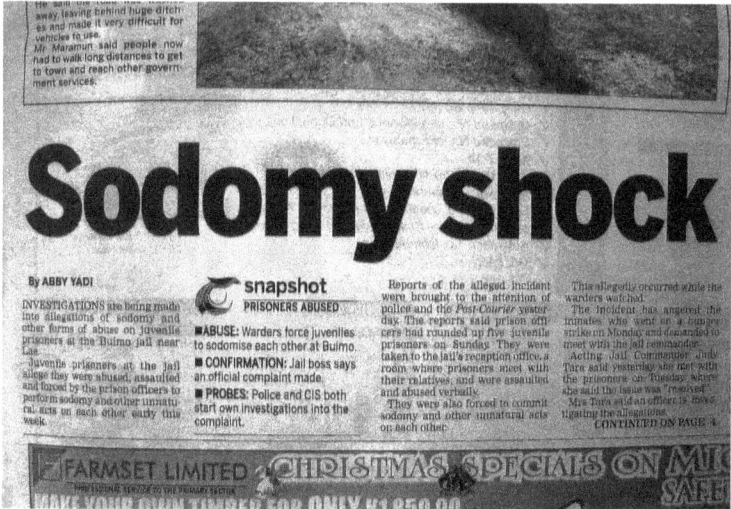

Figure 1.4. 'Sodomy Shock.' Front-page headline from the *Post-Courier*, 21 January 2006.

Source: Author's collection.

For non-anal sex between males, the *Criminal Code* at Sections 211 and 212 uses the terms 'indecent treatment,' 'indecently deal with' and 'act of gross indecency.' Although the 2002 amendments to the Code replaced 'carnal knowledge against the order of nature' with the term 'sexually penetrates' (and its variants) and repealed Section 211, the language of Section 212 remained undisturbed.

My use of terminology throughout this work is similarly confused, and strongly reliant on context and associated quotations. I have in the main used 'gay' when referring to identities, 'homosexual' when discussing theory, the relevant specific terms when discussing case law, 'male-male sex' or 'sex between men' as generic terms for activity, 'MSM' in the context of modern international activism, and so on. In this confusion, at least, I am on a par with my respondents.

The goal

I ask whether the law has had an effect on PNG society's perceptions of and attitudes to these two forms of criminalised sex between consenting adults in private. Do those who sell sex and males who have sex with other males suffer adverse consequences due to this criminalisation, as Goodman found in South Africa, and if so, what are the consequences? What other influences affect them? Should these acts be decriminalised, and relegated to the sphere of private and personal morality? If so, how and to what extent should the law's control be relaxed? These and related questions form the major concerns of this book. Sex worker Elena Jeffreys asks, why should a researcher research sex workers?[111] My own answer in relation to my research on both sex sellers and gays in PNG is this: I want their stories told. I want to expose the effects of criminalisation, I want people to know how the laws and the rhetoric which keep these activities criminalised is dramatically influencing the collective future of PNG.

This chapter has provided an introduction to the theme and approach of this book. It describes the setting of Port Moresby the capital, my long association with PNG, and the personal knowledge and experience which I bring to my work. I outline my reasons for the goal I have set myself, and summarise my terminology, methodology and materials.

Chapter 2 sets out the theoretical framework to my research, based in Foucault's theories of societal sexual self-regulation and the deployment of discourse, and then presents the PNG background as it relates to my question: colonial regulation of sexuality, the development of the PNG police culture and human rights; the religious and medical discourses of sexuality in PNG; the development of a middle class and some effects of modernity.

In Chapter 3, I introduce some recent commentary on Foucault's theories, and arguments which uphold a view that in Foucault's modernity, law has not disappeared, rather it has retreated to police the boundaries of the societal norms. Through its fixed nature, law maintains the boundaries and works to constitute the norm. But its responsive aspect enables it to be re-constituted by changing societal norms, which compel it to alter the form and limit of those boundaries in the law-reform process. The chapter looks at the ways in which sex sellers and gays have been and continue to be disadvantaged by the law. It describes the PNG system of state law, its relationship to customary legal systems, its development and its composite nature, and special features of the criminal law. Laws criminalising sexual minorities are still on the statute books. Through the lens of specific court cases, this chapter studies how their parameters have been developed through case decisions and legislative intervention over the years: how they have been altered and adapted but not repealed.

I extend the discussion of Foucault's law in Chapter 4 by considering the operation of law at the boundary of the norm. I give a brief historical outline of selling sex and homosexual relations in PNG. Then I summarise my fieldwork findings on the ways in which the lives of sex sellers and gays are constructed, played out and viewed in modern-day PNG.

---

111   Elena Jeffreys, 2010, 'Sex work, migration and trafficking identity matters: non-sex workers writing about sex work,' in *Intersections: Gender and Sexuality in Asia and the Pacific* 23 (January), online: http://intersections.anu.edu.au/issue23/jeffreys_review-essay.htm, accessed 11 March 2010.

The operation of the laws which criminalise sexualities is focused on in Chapter 5. By recounting tales told to me by various individuals, I expose some of the effects of criminalisation which they have experienced. Today's police culture, and the positioning of the police as the lead enforcement agency of the state, has led to abuse and violence far in excess of their legal powers, but which can be exercised unchecked by law.

Chapter 6 sets out the results of textual investigations—surveys, studies and media reports—which demonstrate the ways in which the *elites* of PNG society today have formed their opinions and attitudes to criminalised sexual minorities. It poses some puzzling questions emerging from the data, and then deploys some concepts from intersectionality theory, as developed in feminist legal studies, in an attempt to explain them.

In Chapter 7, I return to my original goal: to discover, present and attain an understanding of evidence which might further the arguments for decriminalisation. It canvasses successful law reforms overseas, by legislative intervention and through landmark case decisions, and traces the history of activism in PNG to date. The fundamental issue, it appears to me, is that of the relationship of law to morality, the understanding of morality, and how Christianity in PNG today is often deployed to justify the law's intrusion into the realm of the private. This enables me to ask, and present some answers to, the main question: what are the chances for decriminalisation of consensual sex in PNG?

2. From the Bush

> The political autonomy, economic habits, religious practices, and sexual customs of organized native groups, in so far as they threaten European control or offend Western notions of morality, must be abandoned.
>
> Stephen Winsor Reed, 1943.[1]

Introduction: The background

In Chapter One, I described how Ryan Goodman challenged the 'enforcement principle' (the belief that proscriptive laws which are not enforced have no social effect), arguing that laws which criminalise certain sexualities operate far more broadly, to form and inform social norms. The laws which I examine were introduced into Papua New Guinea (PNG) by the Anglo-Australian colonial enterprise, so in this chapter I describe how the colonisation process took the many peoples of PNG from their villages in the bush to the management of their own affairs as citizens of an independent nation. I pay particular attention to the colonial regulatory management of indigenous sexuality, some of the processes and discourses which aided this management, and the enduring effects of colonisation, even after Independence, on the many peoples of PNG.

I start by outlining the work of the philosopher Michel Foucault which is the basis for Goodman's critique of the enforcement principle. Foucault argues that the legal processes by which the modern state is regulated are supported by other normative discourses, mainly those of religion and medicine. To these, in the context of the colonial enterprise, should be added the languages of race and class. Writers on colonialism both in and beyond PNG have analysed specific examples of the operation of the regulation of colonial sexuality and, whether or not they acknowledge the influence of Foucault, his insights can be discerned in much of what they describe.

---

1 Stephen Winsor Reed, 1943, *The Making of Modern New Guinea with Special Reference to Culture Contact in the Mandated Territory*, Philadelphia: The American Philosophical Society, xvii. Reed, an American anthropologist working under the auspices of the US Institute of Pacific Relations, conducted a 'sociological' study of government, missions, planters, traders and labour recruiters in the Mandated Territory of New Guinea just before World War II. His writing reflects little of British anthropological traditions: a contemporaneous review of his book, Lennox A. Mills, 1943, 'Reed, Stephen Winsor: The Making of Modern New Guinea,' *The ANNALS of the American Academy of Political and Social Science*, 229, 202, refers to terms and phrases such as 'neolithic natives of New Guinea,' 'head-hunting, cannibalism, and a small amount of trade,' and 'a lively fear of malevolent spirits who could be recognized by their possession of fiery red buttocks.' For these details see Reed, *The Making of Modern New Guinea*, 1–71, especially 53–55 and 67. Nevertheless, Reed's work appears to reflect generally accepted views of white inhabitants of the Territory during the inter-war period.

First, though, I provide a background to those aspects of the history, cultures and development of PNG during and following colonisation which are germane to the book and preface the case studies I present in later chapters. As Martha Macintyre puts it:

> Colonialism and the forces of Australian neo- and postcolonial dominance have shaped the world that urban and industrialised Papua New Guineans inhabit. The economy, the institutions of government, the legal system and the prevailing religious beliefs have developed within Australian hegemony.[2]

The rural and subsistence population was also affected in many ways, although the present decline in government services (such as infrastructure, health and education) may lead a casual observer to think otherwise.[3] The effects of this newly shaped world have been felt everywhere. So I describe the institutions (patrol officers, native regulations, police) through which the colonists imposed an administrative, regulatory and political system on the colonised. These processes established colonial rule and bequeathed to the independent nation a western-style, centralised legal system, a policing culture which is semi-military in nature, and frequent public claims that all society's ills can be solved by making more state laws. The post-colonial legal discourse has been tempered to an extent by the constitutional entrenchment of an elaborate system of human rights.

I then review other discursive systems which arguably support that of legal regulation. The Christian message brought by the early missionaries has been absorbed into traditional belief systems and practices, both changing and being changed by them. The spread of exotic diseases was accompanied by the intrusions of western medical practices and the deployment of medical discourse to assist legal control of indigenous sexualities and sexual practices, now heightened by the recent emergence of a serious HIV epidemic. These discourses on sexuality are simultaneously created by and used to support the unequal power relations in society, so I also describe how the discourses of race, ethnicity and class which divided coloniser from colonised in PNG have been reconfigured in the post-colonial era around a new binary of *elites* and *grassroots*. Changes have taken place in the configuration of PNG communities. I discuss whether and how far identity has shifted from the collective to the individual in a vertically divided modern society, increasingly affected by cultural globalisation.

---

2 Martha Macintyre, 2011, 'Money changes everything: Papua New Guinean women in the modern economy,' in *Managing Modernity in the Western Pacific*, ed. Mary Patterson and Martha Macintyre, Brisbane: University of Queensland Press, 90–120, 91.
3 For an illustration see Nicole Haley, 2009, 'HIV/AIDS and witchcraft at Lake Kopiago,' *Catalyst* 39(1): 115–34.

The power of sexuality

> The primary concern was not repression of the sex of the classes to be exploited, but rather the body, vigor, longevity, progeniture, and descent of the classes that 'ruled.'
>
> We must say that there is a bourgeois sexuality, and that there are class sexualities.
>
> Sexuality is not the most intractable element in power relations, but rather one of those endowed with the greatest instrumentality.
>
> Michel Foucault, 1976.[4]

Foucault has been widely analysed and criticised,[5] but his work is helpful for the many ways in which it provides us with reference points from which to develop an understanding of the role of sexuality in the social construction of power and knowledge. Three main themes can be found in his work: systems of knowledge, modalities of power, and the self's relationship to itself.[6] He suggests that power has come to be exercised not through the repressive mechanisms of the sovereign's law over entire populations but through disciplines of the body which demand of each individual the effort to develop and maintain a moral stance. It is this shift in modern times which underpins his theories of the relationship of sexuality to the operation of systems of knowledge and power.[7] In his work *The Will to Knowledge: The History of Sexuality Volume 1*,[8] he reasoned that modern society is shaped by normative processes that operate largely by exclusion—of the criminal, the insane, the sexually deviant and so on. The management of sexuality plays a highly significant role in this process, governing populations and creating and buttressing class divisions. Laws which criminalise sexual conduct and the individual internalisation of the project of self-discipline represent an exercise of social power via the control of human bodies.

But although law has a significant place in the regulation of society, it is not supreme. Laws cannot operate in isolation from other influences.[9] For Foucault,

---

4   Michel Foucault, 1978 [1976], *The Will to Knowledge: The History of Sexuality: Volume 1*, London: Penguin Books, 123, 127, 103.
5   For example David Couzens Hoy (ed,), 1986, *Foucault: A Critical Reader*, Oxford and New York: B. Blackwell, 1; and see Ben Golder and Peter Fitzpatrick, 2009, *Foucault's Law*, Abingdon, UK: Routledge, discussed in Chapter Three and thereafter.
6   Arnold I. Davidson, 1986, 'Archaeology, genealogy, ethics,' in *Foucault: A Critical Reader*, ed. Hoy, Oxford and New York: B. Blackwell, 221–46, 221.
7   Ibid., 228–29.
8   Foucault, *The Will to Knowledge: The History of Sexuality Vol. 1*.
9   Goodman, 2001, 'Beyond the enforcement principle: sodomy laws, social norms, and social panoptics,' *California Law Review* 89: 643–740, 719–21.

'bourgeois sexuality' was an outcome of the displacement of church power by the state, and the triumph of a capitalist class structure over a feudal order. Since the Middle Ages in Europe, the church had managed social relations through canon law. But in the eighteenth and nineteenth centuries, the state came to assume this role, developing disciplines and laws to produce a sense of sexuality which was an aspect of bourgeois self-regulation, self-discipline and self-definition, set in opposition to working-class immorality on the one hand and aristocratic decadence on the other.[10] 'The old power of death that symbolized sovereign power was now carefully supplanted by the administration of bodies and the calculated management of life,' a process which Foucault termed 'biopower.'[11] Matters of sex and sexuality, far from being 'repressed,' were animated as an ever-present danger, through a multiplicity of discourses.[12] The three realms of sin (religion), sickness (medicine), and crime (law) worked to reinforce one another, giving rise to the four sexual objects of power and knowledge: the hysterical woman, the masturbatory child, the psychotic pervert and the properly socialised and state-controlled procreative couple.[13] Laws became self-regulating by operating as internalised norms rather than as overt exercises of power.[14]

Bourgeois sexuality is male-dominated, defined and policed by the bourgeoisie themselves, and demands adherence to the only lawful sexuality, that of the monogamous heterosexual married couple. Procreative behaviour is approved—all other sexual conduct is illicit and those who engage in it, such as prostitutes and homosexuals, are relegated to the realm of the outclasses. The prostitute acts out the unrestrained sexuality of women, and is constructed as the 'other' to the chaste and virtuous woman; the homosexual represents an extreme in perversion, remote from the disciplined heterosexual married couple and the 'other' to the gentleman, father and patriarch.[15] Sexual order is generated and social barriers demarcated by the exercise of power through the legislative

---

10   And from the exotic others of Africa, Asia and the Pacific see, Margaret Jolly and Lenore Manderson, 1997, 'Sites of desire and economies of pleasure in Asia and the Pacific,' in *Sites of Desire, Economies of Pleasure: Sexualities in Asia and the Pacific*, ed. Manderson and Jolly, Chicago: University of Chicago Press, 1–26, 7.
11   Foucault, *The Will to Knowledge: The History of Sexuality Vol. 1*, 139–40.
12   Ibid., 103–05.
13   To these four, Stoler added a fifth, the erotic savage of the colonial experience. See Ann Laura Stoler, 1995, *Race and the Education of Desire: Foucault's History of Sexuality and the Colonial Order of Things*, Durham and London: Duke University Press.
14   Foucault, *The Will to Knowledge: The History of Sexuality Vol. 1*, 144.
15   Ballard, 'Sexuality and the state in time of epidemic,' 109.

production of these categories of deviance,[16] and through the processes of self-definition and self-regulation produced by the disciplining processes of the law.[17]

Foucault in the colonies

Foucault wrote exclusively for and about the European metropole, and although he did not concern himself with colonial laws governing the sexuality of the colonised, others have applied his analyses.[18] 'Colonialism,' Sally Engle Merry reminds us bluntly, 'is an instance of a more general phenomenon of domination.'[19] This process of domination involved the wholesale transfer of laws from the core to the periphery, whereby one society strove to rule and transform another. This process of imposing the coercive control of coloniser over the colonised through the local imposition of imported legislation, has been termed *lawfare*: 'the effort to conquer and control indigenous peoples by the coercive use of legal means.'[20] As Merry demonstrates, through the power it wields colonial law can play a critical role in defining identity and ethnicity and thus citizenship, nationality, political participation, and access to land and other resources.[21] US lawyer Katherine Franke points out, in writing about the creation of post-colonial homophobia in Zimbabwe and Egypt, that where there is sex, there is likely to be power; but the reverse may also be true: where there is power, there is likely to be sex. The state's management of sexuality becomes a tool of governance 'that produces individual unfreedom in the name of expanding national freedom or independence.' And where power is transferred from colonial to post-colonial control, sex can be an 'especially

---

16 Foucault, *The Will to Knowledge: The History of Sexuality Vol. 1*, 87; Ballard 'Sexuality and the state in time of epidemic,' 104–05.
17 Margaret A. McLaren, 2002, *Feminism, Foucault, and Embodied Subjectivity*, Albany, NY: State University of New York Press, 87–90.
18 Stoler, *Race and the Education of Desire*, viii, 9; Peter Fitzpatrick, 1982, 'The political economy of law in the post-colonial period,' in *Law and Social Change in Papua New Guinea*, ed. David Weisbrot, Abdul Paliwala and Akilagpa Sawyerr, Sydney, Melbourne, Brisbane, Adelaide, Perth: Butterworths, 25–55; Peter Fitzpatrick, 1984, 'Traditionalism and traditional law,' *Journal of African Law* 28: 20–27; Peter Sack, 1997, 'Colonial government, "justice" and "the rule of law": the case of German New Guinea,' in *European Impact and Pacific Influence: British and German Colonial Policy in the Pacific Islands and the Indigenous Response*, ed. Hermann J. Hiery and John M. MacKenzie, London: Tauris Academic Studies, 189–213; John L. Comaroff, 2001, 'Colonialism, culture, and the law: a foreword,' *Law & Social Inquiry* 26(2): 305–14; and for a view from the other side of the fence, Bernard Narokobi, 1977, 'Adaptation of western law in Papua New Guinea,' *Melanesian Law Journal* 5(1): 52–69.
19 Sally Engle Merry, 1991, 'Law and colonialism,' *Law and Society Review* 25(4): 889–922, 890.
20 Comaroff, 'Colonialism, culture, and the law,' 306; and see also Sally Engle Merry and Donald Brenneis, 2004, 'Introduction,' in *Law & Empire in the Pacific: Fiji and Hawai'i*, ed. Merry and Brenneis, Santa Fe: School of American Research Press, 3–34, 6.
21 Sally Engle Merry, 2004, 'Law and identity in an American colony,' in *Law & Empire in the Pacific Fiji and Hawai'i*, ed. Merry and Brenneis, Santa Fe: School of American Research Press, 123–52.

dense transfer point.'[22] So it is not surprising that control of sexuality features prominently in many colonial regulatory schemes, to be carried forward into the post-Independence era.[23]

The law's focus on the sexuality of the colonised is apparent in PNG. Because of the diversity of cultures encountered by the newly arrived colonists, and because contact by private entrepreneurs and missions usually preceded the arrival of any form of governmental apparatus, few societies were studied and objectively described early enough to provide details of pre-colonial systems—this is particularly true for pre-colonial sexuality, much of which was quickly concealed in the face of mission and administration disapproval.[24]

The colonists were quick to make their mark. Sinclair Dinnen notes how the early colonial administration displayed a 'persistent concern with indigenous criminality.'[25] Racial and sexual anxieties gave rise to draconian and discriminatory legislation in an atmosphere of paternalism and authoritarianism. A surprisingly large number of matters which concerned the formal courts of the colony were sexual in nature. Alongside murder and sorcery, cases of rape, incest and sodomy featured frequently. Adultery was punished by the criminal law too, because it seemed so often to lead to breaches of the peace.[26]

Colonial discourses of sexuality in PNG were largely qualified and directed by principles of social organisation upon which the introduced state legal system was based. Whereas the sexuality of the colonisers was idealised in this system as controlled and restrained,[27] the colonised were viewed as 'licentious savages': to be reformed by missionaries; to be studied by early anthropologists intent on understanding 'the sexual life of savages';[28] and to have their (introduced)

---

22 Foucault, *The Will to Knowledge: The History of Sexuality Vol. 1*, 103; Katherine M. Franke, 2004, 'Sexual tensions of post-empire,' *Columbia Law School Pub. Law Research Paper No.04–62*, 2, online: http://ssrn.com/abstract=491205, accessed 12 November 2006.
23 And see Ann Laura Stoler, 2003, *Carnal Knowledge and Imperial Power: Race and the Intimate in Colonial Rule*, Berkeley: University of California Press, 43–45.
24 Bernard Narokobi, 1989, 'Law and custom in Melanesia,' *Pacific Perspectives* 14(1): 17–26; Carol Jenkins, 1996, 'The homosexual context of heterosexual practice in Papua New Guinea,' in *Bisexualities and AIDS*, ed. Peter Aggleton, London: Taylor and Francis, 191–206, 193. Nevertheless, many early missionaries were also enthusiastic students of culture and language, even if their reports and views were tempered by their own moral stance and their projects of conversion.
25 Sinclair Dinnen, 1989, 'Crime, law and order in Papua New Guinea,' *Melanesian Law Journal* 17: 10–25, 10–11.
26 David Plumley Derham, 1960, *Report on the System for the Administration of Justice in the Territory of Papua and New Guinea*, Melbourne: report to the Minister for Territories (*Derham Report*), Appendix H.
27 In reality, the opposite was true as regards relations between white men and indigenous women. For accounts of the uneasy attitudes of the Administration to such liaisons, see Wolfers, *Race Relations and Colonial Rule*, 127; and Amirah Inglis, 1974, *Not a White Woman Safe: Sexual Anxiety and Politics in Port Moresby, 1920–1934*, Canberra: Australian National University Press, 13–19.
28 Bronislaw Malinowski, 1948, *The Sexual Life of Savages in North-Western Melanesia: An Ethnographic Account of Courtship, Marriage, and Family Life among the Natives of the Trobriand Islands, British New Guinea*, [third ed], London: Routledge & K. Paul.

venereal diseases and dwindling populations controlled by the medical branch of the colonial administration.[29] However, the colonial management of 'savage' sexuality was concerned not with the development and regulation of an indigenous bourgeoisie but rather with securing the dominance of (male) colonisers over colonised and the protection of chaste white womenfolk from the depredations of this 'lascivious savage.' Although colonised later than many other parts of the non-western world, these processes were pervasive in the territories of PNG as well.

Objects of public surveillance

> New Guinea … was originally divided into hundreds of small groups speaking different languages and living in a state of fear and enmity towards one another…. There was no single religious belief and nothing in the nature of a priesthood but only the fear of the dead and the power of the sorcerer. The existence of most of the people was hand-to-mouth from the garden and the jungle straight to the cooking pot…. In their primitive condition the expectation of life was short because of disease, violence and the absence of medical knowledge or hygienic practice. The country itself is made difficult by jungle, precipitous mountains, torrents and vast swamps…. To this country of close upon 2,000,000 people, who lived originally in a condition of the most primitive savagery, separated from each other into hundreds of hostile groups, we have brought law and order without bloodshed.
>
> Paul Hasluck, Minister for Territories, to the Australian Commonwealth Parliament, 1960.[30]

The European colonists brought with them to PNG not only their administrative practices, their laws and their cash economy, but their social norms as well. Whether or not they adhered to them in practice (a far-flung outpost of empire is always a good place to flout the social strictures of home), lip-service at least was paid to the conventions.[31] Writers such as Ann Laura Stoler and Anne McClintock have argued that beliefs in the patriarchal family and evolutionary theory provided the colonial setting for disapproval of non-(re)productive women (including prostitutes) and men (including homosexuals); concubinage produced problematic mixed-race offspring, while the importation into and

---

29 Jolly and Manderson, 'Sites of desire, economies of pleasure in Asia and the Pacific,' 8; Adam Reed, 1997, 'Contested images and common strategies: early colonial sexual politics in the Massim,' in, *Sites of Desire, Economies of Pleasure*, ed. Manderson and Jolly, Chicago: University of Chicago Press, 48–71.
30 Commonwealth of Australia, *Parliamentary Debates*, House of Representatives, 23 August 1960, 259 (Paul Hasluck, Minister for Territories).
31 Robert Aldrich, 2003, *Colonialism and Homosexuality*, London and New York: Routledge.

maintenance in tropical colonies of white wives was expensive and fraught with the danger of the (presumably unstable) women themselves transgressing the boundaries of white supremacy.[32] And so it was in PNG.

The early administrations of both territories tried to protect villagers from the 'sexual depredations' of single white males, who sought both casual sex and concubines—the latter arrangements were regarded as liaisons 'unworthy of white men.'[33] The infamous *White Women's Protection Ordinance* of 1929 was drawn up in Papua to protect white women from the fantasised savage 'other,'[34] and also partly to protect them from themselves, women being then considered weak and prone to lapse into 'savagery.' Years later, on the insistence of male villagers, laws were passed for the 'protection' of native women. In Papua, this was effected by the *Native Women's Protection Ordinance* in force from 1951 to 1962, which forbade any indigenous woman to be on expatriate premises at night without her husband, or any expatriate to be in a village at night, effectively confining those women to their villages—a measure designed ostensibly to protect them from the depredations of white men, but probably also to assist in preserving white prestige.[35]

The late-nineteenth and early-twentieth centuries were times when selling sex and sexual relations between men were high on the social regulation agenda. In many colonies, state laws criminalised sexualities with little regard for the realities of the cultures they encountered. The laws were enforced wherever some feature of local social practice was identified which might fall within their ambit. In both PNG territories, 'prostitution' and 'homosexual dealings' were thus criminalised. And the rationale for this drew upon Foucault's familiar discourses of crime, sin and sickness.

Imposing peace, bringing law, creating disorder

'Enlightened colonial methods'

> We went to New Guinea solely and simply to serve our own ends, and this fact should never be forgotten in dealing with the natives of that country.
>
> Sir William MacGregor, first Administrator of Papua, 1912.[36]

---

32 Anne McClintock, 1995, *Imperial Leather: Race, Gender and Sexuality in the Colonial Conquest*, New York and London: Routledge; Stoler, *Carnal Knowledge and Imperial Power*.
33 McClintock, *Imperial Leather*, 55, 81.
34 Inglis, *Not a White Woman Safe*; Wolfers, *Race Relations and Colonial Rule*, 58.
35 Wolfers, *Race Relations and Colonial Rule*, 128.
36 Sir Hubert Murray, 1912, 'Introduction,' *Papua or British New Guinea*, London: T. Fisher Unwin, quoted in B. Jinks, P. Biskup and H. Nelson, 1973, *Readings in New Guinea History*, Sydney: Angus and Robertson, 67.

The eastern half of the island of New Guinea was progressively colonised from Europe from the mid-nineteenth century, by Germany in the north and Britain in the south. While the German colony was established primarily for economic exploitation, the southern half (originally named British New Guinea and later Papua) was possessed at the insistence of Queensland, mainly for purposes of defence.[37] When World War I broke out, German New Guinea was occupied by the Australian Naval and Military Expeditionary Force. Laws promulgated by the Germans remained in force 'so far as is consistent with the military situation,' until Australia assumed post-war administration in May 1921 under the Commonwealth *New Guinea Act*, first as a Class C mandated territory and then after World War II as a United Nations Trust Territory.[38] In the inter-war period, the two territories were administered separately, but following World War II they were amalgamated under a single administrative and judicial system.[39]

Following the assumption of the administration of both territories, Australia's main concern was with their commercial prospects, agriculture and mining. Pacification was the first task, to enable these enterprises to take hold. Administrative policy was based on concepts of social evolution and the goal of ultimate assimilation. The colonised were to remain villagers, protected in the first instance from the worst effects of social and economic change, until through the application of western and Christian principles and the introduction of colonial law, they would eventually be civilised.[40] As the Administrator of Papua, Sir Hubert Murray, put it:

> So, as the Papuan has no Courts of Justice of his own, we must establish Courts for him. This is direct rule of the most bare faced kind, but the Court is after all only the machinery, and in the actual administration of justice we come back to our principle of indirect government. From here we give due weight to native custom, especially in the sentences that we pass…. But the main thing to remember … is that it is our criminal code and not that of the Papuans that is going to survive.[41]

---

37   John Goldring, 1978, *The Constitution of Papua New Guinea*, Sydney Melbourne Brisbane Perth: The Law Book Company, 6; Jinks, Biskup and Nelson, *Readings in New Guinea History*, 60, 154; Allen M. Healy, 1987, 'Monocultural administration in a multicultural environment: the Australians in Papua New Guinea,' in *Colony to Coloniser: Studies in Australian Administrative History*, ed. J.J. Eddy and J.R. Nethercote, Sydney: Hale & Iremonger, 207–24, 210, 216; D.C. Lewis, 1996, *The Plantation Dream: Developing British New Guinea and Papua, 1884–1942*, Canberra: The Journal of Pacific History, 16; Hank Nelson, 1982, Taim Bilong Masta: *The Australian Involvement with Papua New Guinea*, Sydney: Australian Broadcasting Commission, 23, 67.
38   Jinks, Biskup and Nelson, *Readings in New Guinea History*, 202–06, 227, 230; Wolfers, *Race Relations and Colonial Rule*, 74–79.
39   J.R. Mattes, 1969, 'The courts system,' in *Fashion of Law*, ed. B.J. Brown, Sydney: Butterworths, 71–82, 71.
40   Healy, 'Monocultural administration in a multicultural environment,' 215; Murray, *Papua or British New Guinea*, 360; Wolfers, *Race Relations and Colonial Rule*, 66–70, 92.
41   J.H.P. Murray, 1929, *Indirect Rule in Papua*, Port Moresby, quoted in Jinks, Biskup and Nelson *Readings in New Guinea History*, 128.

Alan M. Healy claims that Australia lacked the basic interest in its colony which was necessary for developing a modern colonial administrative practice designed to manage acculturation.[42] Its involvement in the colonial enterprise was confined to a very limited and poorly implemented set of self-interested objectives. No properly professional public service was ever developed, administrative interaction with the colonised was limited in the main to police action, very little political attention was ever paid to the colony and the approach was one of white paternalism, which nevertheless was considered to be the epitome of enlightened colonial methods—a 'benevolent type of police rule.'[43]

The colonial enterprise in PNG involved the bringing of peace and order into what was perceived to be a disordered situation (the reality that this 'order' was often brought by non-peaceful means was ignored).[44] So laws of general application in each territory, based on or even copied directly from those of the metropole, were applied both to colonisers and colonised. But there was a further step. Part of the *lawfare* process of colonial control included the creation of 'customary law,' so that local norms and dispute settlement processes were restricted and incorporated into the lowest level of the state legal system. As Peter Fitzpatrick puts it, 'The European created the native and the native law and custom.'[45] Customary norms and principles were explicated, codified and, where deemed by the colonists to be overly primitive or dangerous, criminalised.[46]

So a host of 'native regulations,' applying only to 'natives' carefully defined, was promulgated: the *Native Regulations* in Papua commencing in 1888, and the *Native Administration Regulations* in New Guinea from May 1921 (collectively the Native Regulations).[47] In the absence of clearly visible chiefs, kings or other forms of hierarchical ruler with whom to react directly, the colonists brought governance to the people by appointing faux-chiefs, the *luluais* and *tultuls*, and administered it by means of a travelling administrative officer (the patrol officer or *kiap*) who walked (or in coastal or islands areas, sailed) around his designated area of command. Among his many other duties the *kiap* adjudicated the Native Regulations in specially established Courts of Native Affairs (Figure 2.1).

---

42   Healy 'Monocultural administration in a multicultural environment,' 208–10.
43   Ibid., 210–21.
44   Peter Fitzpatrick, 1980, 'Really rather like slavery: law and labour in the colonial economy in Papua New Guinea,' *Contemporary Crises* 4(1): 77–95, 82; Peter Fitzpatrick, 1992, *The Mythology of Modern Law*, London and New York: Routledge, 107–14; Peter Fitzpatrick, 2000, 'Magnified features: the underdevelopment of law and legitimation,' *Journal of South Pacific Law* 13(1), online: http://www.paclii.org/journals/fJSPL/vol04/5.shtml, accessed 28 March 2014; see also Sinclair Dinnen, Tess Newton and Anita Jowitt (eds), 2003, *A Kind of Mending: Restorative Justice in the Pacific Islands*, Canberra: Pandanus Books, 5.
45   Fitzpatrick, *The Mythology of Modern Law*, 110.
46   Comaroff, 'Colonialism, culture, and the law,' 306; Peter Bayne, 1975, 'Legal development in Papua New Guinea: the place of the common law,' *Melanesian Law Journal* 3(1): 9–39, 13, 20.
47   See also David Weisbrot, 1982, 'Integration of laws in Papua New Guinea: custom and the criminal law in conflict,' in *Law and Social Change in Papua New Guinea*, ed. Weisbrot, Paliwala and Sawyerr, Sydney: Butterworths, 59–103, 65–67.

Figure 2.1. *Kiap* presiding at a Native Affairs Court hearing, 1950s.

Source: PMB Photo 6_12, District Officer holding court, from PMB Photo 6. Sir Paul HASLUCK, New Guinea Administration Series of Photographic Slides, 1956, Nos. 00121–00188.

These regulations were borrowed in the first instance from those of the British colony of Fiji,[48] and remained in force, albeit with frequent revisions, insertions, deletions and alterations, until a complete repeal process commenced in the 1960s.[49] The regulations were based on the assumption that the colonists had the right to unilateral intervention in almost every aspect of village life; and that the form and principles of the legal system they knew were applicable to everyone everywhere. Sprinkled through the Papuan regulations (the New Guinea version is mercifully free of them) are brief homilies on the reason for these massive intrusions into private village life, penned under the administration of the first Administrator Sir William MacGregor and retained in subsequent revisions,[50] such as:

> Clothes are good to wear if they are kept clean, and if they are taken off when they are wet and dried before they are put on again. Otherwise they are bad, for they cause sickness and death. Some natives know how to keep their clothes clean and do not wear them when they are wet, but

---

48 Wilfred Norman Beaver, 1920, *Unexplored New Guinea: A Record of the Travels, Adventures, and Experiences of a Resident Magistrate*, London: Seeley, Service & Co, 292.
49 This process was consequent on the *Derham Report*.
50 Wolfers, *Race Relations and Colonial Rule*, 21–24.

many others are foolish and wear them when they are very dirty, and keep them on, and even sleep in them, when they are wet. To protect these foolish men and women it is necessary to make a law about the wearing of clothes.[51]

Sorcery is only deceit, but the lies of the Sorcerer frighten many people and cause great trouble, therefore the Sorcerer must be punished.[52]

The practice of people abandoning their old homes in settled villages and scattering themselves in small groups over the face of the country is growing in the land. Experience proves that this isolated way of living tends to breed animosities, to increase superstitious fears and to debase those that follow it. On the other hand people persist in living in villages that are built on unhealthy sites even when it is easy for them to remove the village to a healthy site.[53]

The first aim of the Native Regulations in both Territories was to establish law and order by stopping warfare and murder.[54] Practices 'repugnant to humanity' (according to the definitions of the colonisers) were proscribed, and then the perceived needs of the villagers themselves were addressed. Populations and their whereabouts were controlled through regular census-taking and strict control of movement in both territories. Health and well-being were promoted through a wealth of regulations governing (among other matters) dress, housing, sanitation, disease—and not surprisingly, sexuality.[55] Native marriage was recognised as being governed solely by custom—the regulations in both jurisdictions are at pains to ensure that this is acknowledged. Consensual sex outside marriage, and indeed outside heteronormativity, was made illegal: adultery, prostitution and 'indecent practices' between males were all offences under the regulations, as well as appearing in criminal laws of national application.

This was the situation until well into the post-World War II era. One consequence of the trusteeship of New Guinea was regular inspection of Australia's administration by international missions. In 1962, one mission considered Australia's administrative approach to its colony to be outdated and unworkable, and felt it should be changed.[56] But it was too late. The Australian

---

51   *Native Regulations* 1922 (Papua), Regulation 87. The regulation does not apply to 'village' clothing, which is not clothing at all for the purposes of the law.
52   Ibid., Regulation 80.
53   Ibid., Regulation 90.
54   Rowley, *The New Guinea Villager*, 67–68.
55   This very brief overview of the development of the native regulations of both territories elides much of the historical processes that underpinned their making. For this see for example, Healy, 'Monocultural administration in a multicultural environment'; Wolfers, *Race Relations and Colonial Rule*; Nelson, *Taim Bilong Masta*, 185–191, for greater detail.
56   *Report of the 1962 United Nations Visiting Mission to the Trust Territory of New Guinea*, Chairman Sir H. Foot, New York, 1962 (*Foot Report*), referred to in Healy, 'Monocultural administration in a multicultural

colonial administration had already imposed an administrative, legal and political system on PNG which has persisted to this day.[57] The adoption of a *Constitution* at Independence in 1975, the many repeals, consolidations and amendments of the laws described in more detail in Chapter Three, have not altered the basic systems of governance introduced by the colonial regime.

'Benevolent police rule': Creating dis-order

> The two finest and best institutions I left in New Guinea were the constabulary and village police, and the missions.
>
> Sir William MacGregor, first Administrator of Papua, 1912.[58]

MacGregor established the Armed Native Constabulary for British New Guinea in 1890, and was proud to report that the process of pacification had never required military assistance.[59] The same was not true of German New Guinea, although the *Neu-Guinea-Kompagnie* had already established a small armed native police force there, as Germany's naval presence was only intermittent.[60]

The foundations for today's police culture in PNG were laid in these origins. In Europe, the role of policing had shifted from the maintenance of an orderly environment in which trade and commerce could flourish to one of focus on criminal activity and the maintenance of social order through increased surveillance and restrictions on the use of violence.[61] In the Territories, however, community pacification and regulation was carried out by the peripatetic *kiaps*, accompanied, assisted and protected by an armed native constabulary. The demarcation of functions between police and army was blurred and the 'pacification' was sometimes anything but peaceful.[62] Particularly in New Guinea, police were selected for the warrior-like traditions of their societies. Police on patrol, and even on the government stations, were required to repel attacks and enforce the colonial presence, and to do this they were entitled to

---

environment,' 207, n1.
57 Healy, 'Monocultural administration in a multicultural environment,' 224.
58 Sir William MacGregor, in Murray, 1912, 'Introduction,' *Papua or British New Guinea* (1912), quoted in Jinks, Biskup and Nelson, *Readings in New Guinea History*, 69.
59 Ibid., 60–61. MacGregor did not proceed to the obvious inference, that an army was not needed because the police fulfilled this role already. Minister's Hasluck's reference to the lack of bloodshed in the epigraph which commences this section is wishful thinking.
60 Peter Sack, 2001, *Phantom History, the Rule of Law and the Colonial State: The Case of German New Guinea*, Canberra: Division of Pacific and Asian History, The Australian National University, 72.
61 John Braithwaite, 2009, 'Foreword,' in Miranda Forsyth, *A Bird That Flies With Two Wings: Kastom and State, Justice Systems In Vanuatu*, Canberra: ANU E Press, xi–xiv, xi, online: http://press.anu.edu.au?p=49351, accessed 10 April 2014; Sinclair Dinnen and John Braithwaite, 2009, 'Reinventing policing through the prism of the colonial kiap,' *Policing and Society* 19(2): 161–73; Alan Hunt and Gary Wickham, 1994, *Foucault and the Law: Towards a Sociology of Law as Governance*, London; Boulder, Colorado: Pluto Press, 99.
62 Sinclair Dinnen, 1998, 'Criminal justice reform in Papua New Guinea,' in *Governance and Reform in the South Pacific*, ed. Peter Larmour, Canberra: National Centre for Development Studies, The Australian National University, 253–72, 260.

use armed force, often against people with whom they had no prior relationship (although they were both 'Melanesian') and whom they regarded as alien. They also acquired power over all native servants and employees of the colonists, including the power of physical punishment.[63] During the 1960s, though, *kiap* control of the constabulary was removed, it became more of an unarmed professional police force,[64] and its rural regulatory role was eclipsed by a new emphasis on urban paramilitary crime control.[65] This quasi-militaristic tradition has left its legacy in the retributive and violent nature of policing today. Even before Independence, a private lawyer practising in Port Moresby felt obliged to declare that

> authorities directly involved in the administration of law generally give order and punishment more weight than they give to law … this policy will slowly, but nonetheless surely, lead to a crisis between the community on the one hand and the law-enforcement agencies, especially the police, on the other.[66]

Dinnen argues that the cause is to be found in those early pacification strategies—'many features of state strategies of control in the post-independence period represent a return to the pacifying strategies of early colonial rule'—and points to such present-day actions as punitive raids, orders to 'shoot to kill,' and violence against the civilian population.[67] A second facet of policing is derived from a congruence of traditional cultural constructs and 'modern' views of the function of a police force. The police in PNG constitute themselves as guardians of the community, not of individuals, in much the same way as the warriors of traditional times did.[68] A further feature of modern-day police culture in PNG was recently described by Macintyre.[69] She examined representations of masculinity by today's youth, not only in towns but rural settings as well. Traditions which stress male physical strength and the propensity for violence

---

63 Jinks, Biskup and Nelson, *Readings in New Guinea History*, 61–64; Nelson, Taim Bilong Masta, 52–56; Bill Gammage, 1996, 'Police and power in the pre-war Papua New Guinea Highlands,' *Journal of Pacific History* 31(2): 162–77, 162, 168–69; August Ibrum K. Kituai, 1998, *My Gun, My Brother: The World of the Papua New Guinea Colonial Police, 1920–1960*, Honolulu: University of Hawai'i Press.
64 Donald Denoon, 2005, *A Trial Separation: Australia and the Decolonisation of Papua New Guinea*, Canberra, Pandanus Books, 35, 150–51.
65 Dinnen and Braithwaite, 'Reinventing policing through the prism of the colonial kiap,' 163.
66 Michael F. Adams, 1975, 'Law versus order,' in *Lo Bilong Ol Manmeri: Crime, Compensation and Village Courts*, ed. Jean Zorn and Peter Bayne, Port Moresby: University of Papua New Guinea, 97–103, 97.
67 Dinnen, 'Criminal justice reform in Papua New Guinea,' 260.
68 A present-day analogy to this may be seen in the current accounts of witch-killing, where it is often the community at large, or in some places its young men, who carry out the inquisition, torture and killing of a suspected witch. See for example 'Suspects appear in court,' *National*, online, 17 March 2009; Philip Gibbs, 2012, 'Engendered violence and witch-killing in Simbu,' in *Engendering Violence in Papua New Guinea*, ed. Margaret Jolly, Christine Stewart with Carolyn Brewer, Canberra: ANU E Press, http://press.anu.edu.au?p=182671, accessed 31 March 2014.
69 Martha Macintyre, 2008, 'Police and thieves, gunmen and drunks: problems with men and problems with society in Papua New Guinea,' *The Australian Journal of Anthropology* 19(2): 179–93.

translate into the wearing of modern military-style clothing, possession of firearms and the consumption of drugs and alcohol, all signalling socially approved manifestations of masculinity.[70] These presentations by rebel *raskols* overlap with those of the police, supposedly their opponents. But it is less of an oppositional relationship than a continuum. Both groups share class origins and ideals of masculine comportment and consumption, and both groups feel betrayed by a state which fails to provide employment for the unemployed (the *raskols*) or decent living and working conditions for those it does employ (the police). Meanwhile, the community is ambivalent about the police. While people want a greater police presence in the community as a deterrent to crime, police are considered to be inefficient, corrupt, given to improper conduct, violent and even involved in crime themselves.[71]

The fundamental rights and freedoms of the individual

> We Papua New Guineans are all too familiar with authoritarian governments, having been ruled by them for almost ninety years. The last years of colonial rule have, of course, been enlightened by world standards, but in earlier times the basic rights and dignity of our people were frequently suppressed or ignored.
>
> Constitutional Planning Committee, 1974.[72]

Independence in 1975 was achieved with a minimum of fuss and a maximum of flurried preparation. Experts from all around the world assisted in the preparation of a national constitution. The House of Assembly established a Constitutional Planning Committee (CPC), and the *Constitution*, hailed as one of the most detailed and lengthy of its time, was based on the Committee's Report.

The Preamble to the *Constitution* declares that 'all persons in our country are entitled to the fundamental rights and freedoms of the individual … subject to respect for the rights and freedoms of others and for the legitimate public interest.' The *Constitution* then includes a lengthy set of human rights provisions, and the means of enforcing them.[73] The need for the colonial administration to control the native population, effected through the Native Regulations and other colonial legislation, had meant that all the best aspects of the common

---

70   Ibid., 180–83.
71   National Research Institute 2005, *Port Moresby Community Crime Survey, 2005: A Report Prepared for the Government of Papua New Guinea's Law and Justice Sector's National Coordinating Mechanism*, Port Moresby: National Research Institute, 48, 51; and see Human Rights Watch, '*Making Their Own Rules*'; Human Rights Watch, '*Still Making Their Own Rules.*' Negative attitudes to the police on all these grounds are regularly voiced in the newspapers, producing a reference body too large for detailed citation.
72   Constitutional Planning Committee, 1974, 'Final Report of the Constitutional Planning Committee,' Port Moresby: Papua New Guinea House of Assembly: 5/1/4.
73   *Constitution* Part III Division 3. Enforcement mechanisms appear at Sections 57 and 58. Section 57 had its origins in the *Human Rights Ordinance*, 1972.

law system—the jury system, the separation of powers, the independence of the judiciary, the prohibitions against unreasonable search and seizure, the role of the independent defence lawyer, the presumption of innocence and the guarantee of equal protection before the law (to name some)—were either not available in practice to most of PNG society or not imported into the colony's legal system at all.[74] Small wonder then that the CPC regarded the incorporation of human rights into the *Constitution* as a matter of high priority, as witnessed by the rhetoric in the epigraph above.

The model for these rights was already at hand, in the *Human Rights Ordinance* 1972. The Ordinance had been moved by Private Member Percy Chatterton in response to the Administration's *Public Order Ordinance* 1971, which he considered 'made substantial inroads into the right of freedom of assembly, and it still gave very great powers to the police without providing ... adequate legal checks on the exercise of these powers.'[75]

Human rights in the *Constitution* are of two kinds. The civil and political rights of the *Universal Declaration of Human Rights* (UDHR)[76] and the *International Covenant on Civil and Political Rights* (ICCPR)[77] are termed Basic Rights, and may be enforced by the courts.[78] Other rights of a more socio-economic nature, some contained in the UDHR and some in the later International Covenant on Economic, Social and Cultural Rights (ICESCR),[79] were considered at the time of framing the *Constitution* not to be capable of judicial enforcement.[80] But the nation's founders wanted to see many of these principles embedded in the *Constitution*, along with others more removed from the traditionally western concepts of state and nation,[81] so they were incorporated into the Preamble and a provision inserted that courts and government bodies should apply and give effect to them as far as possible.[82]

Since Independence, the Supreme and National Courts have often been called upon to adjudicate and pronounce on constitutional rights.[83] Many cases involve conflicts between custom and the rights of the individual. For example, in 1991,

---

74 Bayne, 'Legal development in Papua New Guinea,' 12; Weisbrot, 'Custom and the criminal law in conflict,' 66–67.
75 Chatterton, *Day That I Have Loved*, 108–11.
76 GA Res 217A (III), UN Doc A/810 (1948) ('UDHR').
77 G.A. res. 2200A (XXI), 21 U.N. GAOR Supp. (No. 16) at 52, U.N. Doc. A/6316 (1966), 999 U.N.T.S. 171, entered into force 23 March 1976 ('ICCPR').
78 *Constitution* Div III.3, ss 35-57.
79 GA Res 2200A (XXI), 21 UN GAOR Supp (No. 16) at 49, UN Doc A/6316 (1966), 993 UNTS. 3 ('ICESCR').
80 Frans Viljoen, 2009, 'International Human Rights Law: a short history,' *UN Chronicle: The Magazine of the United Nations*, online: http://www.un.org:80/wcm/content/site/chronicle/home/archive/Issues2009/internationalhumanrightslawashorthistory, accessed 6 August 2011.
81 Constitutional Planning Committee, *Final Report of the Constitutional Planning Committee*, 2/1-2/2.
82 *Constitution* Section 25.
83 Even though, as I recall, the first Rules of Court for the appropriate procedures were not drawn up until around 1990.

a woman gaoled by a Village Court for adultery was released on the grounds that the detention was unlawful and unreasonable and that 'customs which denigrate women should be denied a place in the underlying law because they conflict with the National Goals of equality and participation laid down in the *Constitution*.'[84] Another the same year decided that a customary requirement which obliged a murderer to hand over one of his daughters to the family of his victim was akin to slavery, proscribed under *Constitution* Section 253.[85] A third case held that the giving away of a young woman as part of a compensation payment for wrongful death contravened her right to freedom and equality.[86]

But this approach of the formal courts is not reflected in the views and actions of the general public. Constitutional rights are a prime example of the kind of alien imported concepts discussed by Michael Jacobsen below. They are based in liberalism, the dominant western ideology of the twentieth century,[87] with its emphasis on the concept of civil liberty and the fundamental value of political organisation; on the individual, whose liberties lie at the heart of society; and on John Stuart Mill's 'harm principle': that harm to others in the form of interfering with their rights is the only legitimate ground for interfering with liberty through legal sanctions.[88]

Today, this ideology has been criticised in the West by a more radical jurisprudential school of thought which holds that these rights in fact belong only to the privileged groups of society, are a screen to hide the nature of oppression in society, and do not necessarily produce substantive justice or equality.[89] In the Pacific, where the discourse of nationalism includes antagonism to European and colonial traditions, these formal constitutional protections become a source of tension.[90] The chief conflicts are claimed to arise between the communal rights upheld by custom and the rights of the individual espoused by state law;[91] and

---

84 *Re Wagi Non and Section 42(5) of the Constitution* [1991] PNGLR 84. Village Courts were established in 1974 independently of the formal court system, to dispense justice at the local level according to custom and subject only to the limitations of the *Constitution*.
85 *The State v Kule* [1991] PNGLR 404.
86 *In the Matter of an Application under Section 57 of the Constitution; Application by Individual and Community Rights Advocacy Forum Inc (ICRAF); In re Miriam Willingal* [1997] PNGLR 119 (*Willingal's Case*).
87 Maila Stivens, 2000, 'Gender politics and the reimagining of human rights in the Asia-Pacific,' in *Human Rights and Gender Politics: Asia-Pacific Perspectives*, ed. Anne-Marie Hilsdon et al., London and New York: Routledge, 1–36, 5.
88 Margaret Davies, 2008, *Asking the Law Question*, Sydney: Law Book Co., 203–08.
89 Ibid.
90 Martha Macintyre, 2000. '"Hear us, women of Papua New Guinea!": Melanesian women and human rights,' in *Human Rights and Gender Politics: Asia-Pacific Perspectives*, ed. Hilsdon et al., London and New York: Routledge, 147–71, 152; Pacific Regional Rights Resource Team, 2005, *Pacific Human Rights Law Digest: Volume 1*, *PHRLD*, Suva: Pacific Regional Rights Resource Team, xv.
91 This promotion of individualism by the formal law is supported by the missionising process, which aimed from the outset to promote the individual as a discrete entity. See Anne Dickson-Waiko, 2003, 'The missing rib: mobilizing church women for change in Papua New Guinea,' *Oceania* 74(1/2): 98–119, 104.

between male precedence and domination and gender equality.[92] Protecting the rights of the individual at the expense of collective rights of groups ignores the reality of collective group rights that characterise Pacific communities, and may well contribute to their disintegration.[93]

But this distinction between collectivism and individualism may not be as clear-cut as received wisdom would have us believe. The Enlightenment tradition in the West was equally concerned with collective rights in such matters as the democratic process and citizenship, while the emphasis on collectivity in Melanesia overlooks individual agency and action even in the remotest of villages.[94] Recent discussions of the effects of modernity, consumerism and of 'individualistic' Christian conversion on Marilyn Strathern's Melanesian 'dividual,' a person embedded in social relations and manifesting self through the reciprocity of exchange,[95] have simultaneously dismantled and supported the concepts of relationality, gift-exchange, agency and individualism in PNG.[96]

It is not just this perceived tension between collectivity and individuality which prompts the reluctance of Papua New Guineans to espouse the principles of equality. Various other reasons have been advanced for the eschewing of human rights and the principles of individualism that underpin them. The 'collision' between introduced and traditional political practices has produced a hybridised 'non-liberal democratic political culture,' involving cronyism, bribery, coercion, and a marked absence of morality and ethical standing on the part of leaders.[97] PNG is extremely vulnerable to the international economy.[98] Women

---

92   Laitia Tamata, 2000, 'Application of human rights conventions in the Pacific Islands courts, *Journal of South Pacific Law* 4 (Working Paper 4), online: http://www.paclii.org/journals/fJSPL/vol04/12.shtml, accessed 30 April 2010; Macintyre '"Hear us, women of Papua New Guinea!"' 150–51.
93   Bernard Narokobi, 1980, *The Melanesian Way: Total Cosmic Vision of Life*, Boroko: Institute of Papua New Guinea Studies.
94   Margaret Jolly, 1996, '*Woman ikat raet long human raet o no*?: Women's rights, human rights and domestic violence in Vanuatu,' *Feminist Review* 52 (Spring): 169–90; Macintyre, '"Hear us, women of Papua New Guinea!"' 162–64; Margaret Jolly, 2012, 'Introduction—engendering violence in Papua New Guinea: persons, power and perilous transformations,' in *Engendering Violence in Papua New Guinea*, ed. Margaret Jolly, Christine Stewart with Carolyn Brewer, Canberra: ANU E Press, online: http://press.anu.edu.au?p=182671, accessed 31 March 2014.
95   Marilyn Strathern, 1988, *The Gender of the Gift: Problems with Women and Problems with Society in Melanesia*, Berkeley: University of California Press.
96   Mark Mosko, 2010, 'Partible penitents: dividual personhood and Christian practice in Melanesia and the West,' *Journal of the Royal Anthropological Institute* 16(2): 215–40. This article elicited much debate, see Joel Robbins, 2007, 'Afterword: possessive individualism and cultural change in the Western Pacific,' *Anthropological Forum* 17(3): 299–308; Karen Sykes, 2007, 'Interrogating individuals: the theory of possessive individualism in the Western Pacific,' *Anthropological Forum* 17(3): 213–24; and other articles in this collection; and see Joel Robbins, 1994, 'Equality as a value: ideology in Dumont, Melanesia and the West,' *Social Analysis* 36: 21–70.
97   Alphonse Gelu, 2000, 'The emergence of a non-liberal democratic political culture in Papua New Guinea,' in *Politics in Papua New Guinea: Continuities, Changes and Challenges*, ed. Michael A. Rynkiewich and Roland Seib, Goroka, PNG: Melanesian Institute, 87–119, especially 91.
98   Deborah B. Gewertz and Frederick K. Errington, 1999, *Emerging Class in Papua New Guinea: The Telling of Difference*, Cambridge and New York: Cambridge University Press, 3.

claim to be reluctant to embrace global culture for fear of being labelled elitist and westernised and of antagonising men and destabilising the community.[99] Nevertheless, women activists, particularly those operating at the national level, may take up an appeal to 'women's rights as human rights' to further their aims, and reject the assumptions of men that women as the custodians of tradition are primarily responsible for the stability of the community.[100]

To convert the soul: Mission to church

> Pacific churches, fundamental as they are to Pacific societies, are powerful social institutions. *Christianity is interwoven into almost all aspects of Pacific societies and daily life* [emphasis in original].
>
> Commission on AIDS in the Pacific, 2009.[101]

This observation holds as true for PNG as it does for other Pacific countries. The Christian message has been received, appropriated, varied, sometimes distorted,[102] but despite diversities, the religious discourse of these 'powerful social institutions' has supported and been supported by the legal and regulatory discourse of PNG.

Something of a storm

> The Christian evangelism of Melanesia has often (for those involved, from earliest times) constituted something of a storm.
>
> Terry Brown, former Bishop of Malaita, Solomon Islands, 2008.[103]

For many villages, the missions provided their first experience of outsiders. The first missionaries, European and Polynesian, arrived well before the government; they went where officialdom did not; they were frequently the most sedentary of settlers, and exerted the most continuous influence, learning the local languages

---

99   Dickson-Waiko, 'The missing rib,' 99; Macintyre, '"Hear us, women of Papua New Guinea!"' 153.
100 Stivens, 'Gender politics and the reimagining of human rights in the Asia-Pacific,' 7–8, 20; Orovu V. Sepoe, 2000, *Changing Gender Relations in Papua New Guinea: the Role of Women's Organisations*, New Delhi: UBS Publishers' Distributors Ltd.
101 Commission on AIDS in the Pacific 2009, *Turning the Tide: An OPEN Strategy for a Response to AIDS in the Pacific*, 80–81.
102 See for example Peter Worsley, 1970, *The Trumpet Shall Sound: A Study of 'Cargo' Cults in Melanesia* [2nd ed], London: Paladin; Joel Robbins 2004, *Becoming Sinners: Christianity and Moral Torment in a Papua New Guinea Society*, Berkeley: University of California Press; Roger Ivar Lohmann, 2007, 'Moral and missionary positionality: Diyos of Duranmin,' in *The Anthropology of Morality in Melanesia and Beyond*, ed. John Barker, Aldershot and Burlington: Ashgate, 131–47.
103 Post by Terry Brown to Oceanic Anthropology Discussion Group ASAONET@LISTSERV.UIC.EDU, 20 September 2008.

and acquiring much deeper knowledge of the peoples among whom they lived;[104] and they actively and consciously intervened for change.[105] Assisted by wives, nuns and lay brothers and sisters,[106] they established schools and clinics, trade stores and plantations, introduced new goods, skills, crafts and crops, and often compiled excellent records of customs and languages.[107] The missions were also partly responsible for introducing the concept of a specialised social class—teachers, evangelists—which produced no material goods, but provided novel services instead and in return often required feeding or the land on which to produce food.[108] Education, 'disciplining the body in order to convert the soul,'[109] was a prime concern from the outset, with far-reaching consequences for its effect on indigenous sexuality. Schooling was essential to the evangelisation of the people: schools with a standardised curriculum were established at mission stations,[110] and the extent of social change in the villages depended in large part on the length of time of exposure to mission influences.[111] Nearly all the pre-war schools for Papua New Guineans were provided by missions.[112] The education process was often achieved by concentrating on the conversion of children, who were sequestered away from the village, first in fenced compounds, later in boarding schools.[113]

Along with traders, labour recruiters, planters and administration officers, the missions and their converts instigated great changes to traditional village culture. Some of the earliest white missionaries were somewhat appalled by what they found in the South Seas, for example interpreting refusal to convert to

---

104 Christine Weir, 2008, '"White man's burden," "white man's privilege": Christian humanism and racial determinism in Oceania, 1890–1930,' in *Foreign Bodies: Oceania and the Science of Race 1750–1940*, ed. Bronwen Douglas and Chris Ballard, Canberra: ANU E Press, 283–303, 284–86, online: http://press.anu.edu.au?p=53561, accessed 31 March 2014.
105 Franco Zocca, 2007, *Melanesia and its Churches: Past and Pesent*, Gorokoa, Melanesian Institute.
106 Different missions took different attitudes to the appointment of women assistants, wives and even female missionaries. See D. Langmore, 1982, 'A neglected force: white women missionaries in Papua 1874–1914,' *Journal of Pacific History* 17(3): 138–57.
107 Margaret Jolly and Martha Macintyre, 1989, 'Introduction,' *Family and Gender in the Pacific: Domestic Contradictions and the Colonial Impact*, ed. Jolly and Macintyre, Cambridge: Cambridge University Press, 1–18, 6–7; Dickson-Waiko, 'The missing rib, 103.
108 Ian Willis, 1974, *Lae: Village and City*, Melbourne: Melbourne University Press, 58.
109 Wayne Fife, 2001, 'Creating the moral body: missionaries and the technology of power in early Papua New Guinea,' *Ethnology* 40(3): 251–69, 260.
110 Ibid., 253–55.
111 Oram, *Colonial Town to Melanesian City*, 133. This is reflected in the form of the pre-Independence Antecedent Report provided by police in criminal cases, which asks, after questions about proximity to Administration station and Supreme Court town, how close is the nearest mission and the extent of mission influence on the accused: See Appendix 2.
112 Nelson, Taim Bilong Masta, 152.
113 Fife, 'Creating the moral body'; Martha Macintyre, 1989, 'Better homes and gardens,' in *Family and Gender in the Pacific*, ed. Margaret Jolly and Macintyre, Cambridge and Melbourne: Cambridge University Press, 156–69; David Wetherell, 1996, *Charles Abel and the Kwato Mission of Papua New Guinea 1891–1975*, Melbourne: Melbourne University Press; Michael Young, 1989, 'Suffer the children: Wesleyans in the D'Entrecasteaux,' in *Family and Gender in the Pacific*, ed. Jolly and Macintyre, Cambridge and Melbourne: Cambridge University Press, 108–34.

Christianity as stubbornness, ignorance and lack of morality.[114] They are famous for having insisted on the abolition (or at least concealment) of traditional sacred practices, particularly fertility ceremonies which often involved activities and display which were considered by the missionaries to be scandalously lewd, and the destruction of sacred objects perceived as evidence of satanic practices and cannibalism.[115] Later however, many missions were more concerned to preserve traditional ways than were the officials of the fledgling colony. Like other London Missionary Society (LMS) missionaries, James Chalmers, who worked in British New Guinea from 1877–1894, engaged sometimes intensely with the local villagers, and kept detailed diaries and records of what he saw and learnt.[116] His editor wrote,

> It is open to hope that for once we may not exterminate a race in the process of ruling it … the young colony has not readily admitted that the savage has any rights, and it is altogether too fond of the doctrine that the day of the savage has gone, and it is time that he made way for the robuster, so-called civilised race. The Australian pioneer of the nineteenth century had more faith in physical than in moral suasion, and it will need careful watching to see that England's annexation promises are not like pie-crust, made only to be broken.[117]

Unlike the other two main categories of colonist, administrators and trader/planter settlers, missionaries usually brought their womenfolk with them—even the celibate Catholic priests were accompanied by missionary nuns, and mission health services attracted nursing sisters.[118] Whereas only men were being educated 'in the broadest sense' by the opening of mines and the indentured labour system, the missionaries directed their education towards entire societies, men and women, and therefore had greater impact for cultural change in the long term.[119]

---

114 Elisabetta Gnecchi-Ruscone, 2010, '"A school of iron, vexation and blood, but a school nonetheless": the writings of the first PIME missionaries to Oceania in the 1850s,' paper presented at the Race, Encounters, and the Constitution of Human Difference in Oceania Conference, The Australian National University, Canberra, Australia.
115 Jolly and Macintyre, 'Introduction,' 10; Lamont Lindstrom and Geoffrey M. White, 1994, *Culture, Kastom, Tradition: Developing Cultural Policy in Melanesia*, Suva: Institute of Pacific Studies, 58; Macintyre, 'Better homes and gardens,' 162–63; Nelson, Taim Bilong Masta, 154, 162.
116 Collected, somewhat repetitiously, in James Chalmers and W. Wyatt Gill, 1885, *Work and Adventure in New Guinea 1877 to 1885*, London: Religious Tract Society; James Chalmers, 1887, *Pioneering in New Guinea*, London: Religious Tract Society; James Chalmers, 1895, *Pioneer Life and Work in New Guinea 1877–1894*, London: Religious Tract Society.
117 Religious Tract Society Editor, in 'Preface,' to Chalmers, *Pioneering in New Guinea*, iii.
118 Maria Lepowsky, 2001, 'The Queen of Sudest: white women and colonial cultures in British New Guinea and Papua,' in *In Colonial New Guinea: Anthropological Perspectives*, ed. Naomi McPherson, Pittsburgh: University of Pittsburgh Press, 125–50, 127.
119 Reed, *The Making of Modern New Guinea*, 234.

Missions aspired to effect far-reaching fundamental changes to the family structure and sexual relations of traditional societies—significantly, kinship, marriage, patterns of sexual segregation, the division of labour and the care of children and the sick. Their project of 'civilisation' involved a transformation of daily life, and the promotion of an idealised domesticity centring on a home whose preferred inhabitants were a nuclear family, where women's agricultural labour was denigrated, and the emphasis was on conjugal rather than sibling and kin relations.[120] The monogamous procreative couple was essential to the stability of society, the 'precocious' Papuan child was to be purified and the irresponsible mother condemned and retrained.[121] This project effected some far-reaching changes in village life, but ultimately failed in its goal of 'domesticating' village women, who have continued to carry out the work associated with subsistence living, to which many burdens of modernity, such as participation in church work, have now been added.[122] Another effect of the mission project was in the regulation of marriage itself.[123] Opposition to polygyny and insistence on monogamy in some areas resulted in many wives being discarded by their husbands and even killed, with drastic consequences for children and the wider kin networks which had been involved in the initial brideprice payments.[124] In some cases, this insistence by the missions that extra wives be divorced actually introduced the concept of divorce to the area, although the indissolubility of marriage was preached.[125]

Other more indirect changes were visited on PNG culture. A residential feature of many Melanesian communities, the men's house (often the focus not just of male kin-group cohabitation and communal work and eating, but also of secret ritual and association with departed ancestors) was replaced by smaller dwellings occupied by individual nuclear family units, a monogamous married couple and their children.[126] Associations between white men and village women were condemned as evidence of promiscuity and prostitution on the part of the

---

120 See Margaret Jolly, 2003, 'Epilogue,' *Oceania* 74(1/2): 134–47, 137, and the references there.
121 Adam Reed, 'Contested images and common strategies,' 66–70. The horrified fascination with traditional abortion practices, real and supposed, is reflected to this day in a steadfast refusal on the part of policy-makers to countenance decriminalising abortion.
122 Margaret Jolly, 2010, 'Divided mothers: changing global inequalities of "nature" and "nurture,"' in *The Globalization of Motherhood: Deconstructions and Reconstructions of Biology and Care*, ed. Wendy Chavkin and JaneMaree Maher, Abingdon, Oxon: Routledge, 154–79, 156–58.
123 Jolly and Macintyre, 'Introduction,' 2–18; Rowley, *The New Guinea Villager*, 150–51.
124 Cyndi Banks, 1993, *Women in Transition: Social Control in Papua New Guinea*, Canberra: Australian Institute of Criminology, 154–55. I can recall a visit I made in 1969 to noted Simbu parliamentarian, the late Yauwe Wauwe Moses, in his village high on the slopes of Mt. Elimbari, when he recounted proudly how he had had ten wives before the (Anglican) mission came, but when he converted he 'threw out' [*mi bin rausim*] nine of them and only kept the youngest. I do not know what effect this may have had on the kinship relations or the women involved.
125 Willis, *Lae: Village and City*, 56.
126 E.g., Macintyre, 'Better homes and gardens'; Holly Wardlow, 2006, *Wayward Women: Sexuality and Agency in a New Guinea Society*, Berkeley: University of California Press, 53.

latter,[127] and this was later reinforced by the law.[128] Mission activity provided support and reinforcement for the laws which the secular colonial administrators brought with them, particularly as those laws related to and governed sexuality.

However, the missionaries themselves were not solely responsible for all these changes. Missionaries could not have succeeded without willing compliance, even eager acceptance, on the part of their converts.[129] And in the process, Christianity has undergone some conversions of its own, as people continually reinterpret Christian themes, forms and practices within their own cultural traditions.[130] The missions moreover helped people to extend their social bonds beyond the narrow confines of the village, even if they were still bounded by the dominion of the particular church to which they belonged. Both Nigel Oram and Alan Rew noted the importance of church groups in providing a basis for urban association in Port Moresby of the 1960s, and this process continues today.[131] Many early converts went on to become local leaders who passed on what they had learnt, and some graduates went on, often via Australian high schools and local seminaries, to become some of the first of the national élite.[132] Most of the first University of Papua New Guinea students were the children either of police or of mission workers.[133] Many Papua New Guineans were, and still are, closer to the church than to government. By the mid-1960s, when the first national census was taken, over 90 per cent of those polled claimed to be Christian.[134] As government health care services decline, mission and church involvement in health care continues to increase. Today, some 50 per cent of health care is provided by the churches which are funded by the government to this effect.[135]

---

127   Jolly and Macintyre, 'Introduction,' 4.
128   Wolfers, *Race Relations and Colonial Rule*, 81, 107.
129   Margaret Jolly, 2002, 'Introduction: birthing beyond the confinements of tradition and modernity?' in *Birthing in the Pacific: Beyond Tradition and Modernity?* Ed. Vicki Lukere and Margaret Jolly. Honolulu: University of Hawai'i Press, 1–30, 11; John Garrett, 1992, *Footsteps in the Sea: Christianity in Oceania to World War II*, Suva: Institute of Pacific Studies, University of the South Pacific, xi; Robert W. Robin, 1982, 'Revival movements in the Southern Highlands Province of Papua New Guinea,' Oceania 52(4): 320–43, 336–37.
130   John Barker, 1990, 'Introduction: ethnographic perspectives on Christianity in Oceanic societies,' in *Christianity in Oceania: Ethnographic Perspectives*, ed. Barker, Lanham: University Press of America, 1–24, 5–8.
131   See Oram, *Colonial Town to Melanesian City*, 137–39; and Rew, *Social Images and Process in Urban New Guinea*, 229.
132   Rowley, *The New Guinea Villager*, 129.
133   Gammage, 'Police and power in the pre-war Papua New Guinea Highlands,' 163.
134   Rowley, *The New Guinea Villager*, 155.
135   Catholic Health Services, for example, operates some 160 health facilities throughout the country. See Lawrence Hammar, 2009, 'There wouldn't even be a national response without the churches: faith-based responses in Papua New Guinea to HIV and AIDS,' unpublished, 7; and see Vicki Luker, 2003, 'Civil society, social capital and the churches: HIV/AIDS in Papua New Guinea,' paper presented at the Governance and Civil Society Seminar in Symposium Governance in Pacific States: reassessing roles and remedies, University of the South Pacific, Suva, Fiji, 30 September–2 October.

The foundation of a (Christian) nation

In its Preamble, the *Constitution* affirmed the Christianisation of PNG, when it acknowledged Christian principles together with customs and the traditional wisdom of the ancestors as the foundation for the new society.[136] Today, approximately 96 per cent of Papua New Guineans claim adherence to one or other of the 300-odd Christian denominations and sects in PNG.[137] But the Christian message has been transformed in the process. Most Papua New Guineans have a holistic world view which melds the empirical and the non-empirical; the sacred and the secular; dreams, visions, rituals, spells, public professions of faith, with power and politics.[138] The Christian message has been 'indigenised' in many and varied ways, assisted by the advent of a multitude of churches, some of them strongly charismatic, which were admitted into the Territory by the administration even before Independence.[139] Since then, the constitutional guarantee of freedom of religion, conscience and thought in *Constitution* Section 45 has ensured the continuity of this open access policy, with only very few rejections or ejections. The result has been an 'entanglement of custom and Christianity in modern Melanesian identity politics,' presenting apparent paradoxes to anthropologists and indigenous peoples alike.[140]

There are radical divisions between the multitude of churches and denominations. The original mainstream churches—Catholic, Lutheran, United and Anglican—have joined with the Baptist Union and the Salvation Army in the Papua New Guinea Council of Churches.[141] The Seventh-day Adventists constitute their own powerful bloc, and a growing number of Pentecostal and charismatic churches form a loose alliance in distinction from the rest.[142] It has been claimed that the teachings of some fundamentalist churches may have promoted cults and revivalist movements, which in some instances have even led to ill health, psychiatric disorders and general disruption of village life.[143] And from an initial religious colouration of the village view of the world,[144] appeals are

---

136 This has often been interpreted as a declaration that Christianity is the national religion, and several attempts have been made to entrench this principle in law. See Philip Gibbs, 2002, 'Religion and religious institutions as defining factors in Papua New Guinea politics,' *Development Bulletin* 59 (October): 15–18, 16.
137 Philip Gibbs, 2004, 'Growth, decline and confusion: Church affiliation in Papua New Guinea,' *Catalyst* 34(2): 164–84; Hammar, 'There wouldn't even be a national response without the churches,' 7.
138 Gibbs, 'Religion and religious institutions as defining factors in Papua New Guinea politics,' *Development Bulletin* 59 (October): 15–18, 15.
139 Rowley, *The New Guinea Villager*, 153.
140 Bronwen Douglas, 2000, 'Introduction: hearing Melanesian women,' in *Women and Governance from the Grassroots in Melanesia*, ed. Douglas, Canberra: State Society and Governance in Melanesia Discussion Paper No. 2 of 2000, 3–7, 4.
141 Dickson-Waiko, 'The missing rib,' 109.
142 Gibbs, 'Religion and religious institutions as defining factors in Papua New Guinea politics,' 16.
143 Nelson records some *kiap* and missionary accounts of the divisive effects of some 'revivalist movements' and the ways in which cargo cults took people away from gainful garden work: Nelson, *Taim Bilong Masta*, 160; and Robin, 'Revival movements in the Southern Highlands Province of Papua New Guinea,' 327.
144 Rowley, *The New Guinea Villager*, 158.

frequently made to Christian precepts, both those filtered through the belief systems of many of these fundamentalist and charismatic denominations and those emanating from the mainstream churches,[145] in today's public discourse on the relationship of law and morality. Laura Zimmer-Tamakoshi noted in the 1980s that 'while many Christian missions promote a type of family life in which husbands and wives are partners, others preach fundamentally misogynist views that urge women to be subservient and mindful at all times of their husband's wishes.'[146] Whichever way the message is received and promulgated, the image of the good modern respectable middle-class person in PNG, a member of the *elites*, is strongly linked with being Christian.[147]

These patterns persist and have intensified with the spread of HIV in PNG. The following example is taken from a presentation prepared by a medical practitioner in the Public Health Department for use during World AIDS Day 2004 (Figure 2.2).[148] This presentation combined statistics and scientific data on HIV with religious messages such as:

> **SEX** IS **SACRED** AND **SPECIAL** FOR ALL HUMAN BEINGS **BECAUSE** IT IS BY THIS ACT THAT WE ARE BROUGHT INTO THIS WORLD   [**3S** - **S**EX IS **S**ACRED AND **S**PECIAL].
>
> SEX SHOULD NOT BE FOR SALE AND USED FOR MONEY SINCE IT **DEHUMANISED** ITS SACREDNESS.
>
> SEX BEFORE MARRIAGE [**FORNICATION**] AND OUT OF MARRIAGE [**ADULTERY**] ARE SINS AS IT WAS NOT INTENDED TO BRING FORTH LIFE AND MUST NOT BE ENCOURAGED. THESE ACTS ARE DEFINED AS " **PROMISCUOUS**' WHICH I WILL DEFINE AS THE **ROUTE OF TRANSMISSION OF HIV** IN MY PRESENTATION

Figure 2.2. Thomas Vinit, 'Sex is Sacred and Special.'

Source: Thomas Vinit, 'Sex is Sacred and Special'. Thomas Vinit, 2004, 'HIV/AIDS Control – The PNG Way: World AIDS Day 2004,' Oilsearch Ltd., Powerpoint presentation.

---

145 It is important to recognise that mainstream churches are equally implicated in sin-based messages such as those relating to HIV and condoms. See Holly Wardlow, 2008, '"You have to understand: some of us are glad AIDS has arrived": Christianity and condoms among the Huli, Papua New Guinea,' in *Making Sense of AIDS: Culture, Sexuality, and Power in Melanesia*, ed. Leslie Butt and Richard Eves, Honolulu: University of Hawai'i Press, 187–205, 195.
146 Laura Zimmer, 1990, 'Sexual exploitation and male dominance in Papua New Guinea,' in *Human Sexuality in Melanesian Cultures*, ed. Joel F. Ingebritson, Goroka; Melanesian Institute, 250–67, 259; but see Anna-Karina Hermkens, 2008, 'Josephine's journey: gender-based violence and Marian devotion in urban Papua New Guinea,' *Oceania* 78(2): 151–67; Anna-Karina Hermkens, 2012, 'Becoming Mary: coping with gender-based violence in urban Papua New Guinea,' in *Engendering Violence in Papua New Guinea*, ed. Margaret Jolly, Christine Stewart with Carolyn Brewer, Canberra: ANU E Press, online: http://press.anu.edu.au?p=182671, accessed 31 March 2014.
147 Wardlow, '"You have to understand: some of us are glad AIDS has arrived,"' 198–99.
148 Thomas Vinit, 2004, 'HIV/AIDS Control—The PNG Way: World AIDS Day 2004,' Oilsearch Ltd., Powerpoint presentation. The formatting of the original has been retained.

Meanwhile, the role of church groups in providing a basis for urban association has persisted and strengthened, both in town and in rural areas. Women's fellowship groups function both as guardians of morality, Christian and traditional, as conduits for modernity and as catalysts for women's activism. They provide a counter to male dominance in preaching which tends more towards the prescriptive and proscriptive message and have been described as the missing link in an evolving indigenous feminism.[149]

Medicine and sexuality

Foucault asserts that, along with religious discourse, the scientific and medical discourse which developed from the eighteenth century was a significant factor promoting self-regulation of the body and of populations.[150] Insofar as it related to sex work and male-male sex, the medical discourse was supported in Anglo-Australian law by 'contagious diseases' Acts,[151] further legislation governing surveillance and management of sexually transmitted infections (STIs), and the 'sodomy' laws.

Medicine as a practice and a discourse separate from other aspects of traditional PNG cosmology[152] was purely a colonial import, by both administration and mission. *Lawfare* was conducted in the colony from the outset not just through sexuality laws per se but also through its interaction with colonial medical policies and practice, which themselves were linked to religious discourse via the body/soul connection. Public health controls of the time, involving the direct approaches of surveillance, testing, notification, contact-tracing, treatment (when available) and quarantine, were enshrined in legislation and thinking.[153] Even after Independence, the *Constitution* has permitted the restriction of human rights in law for the purpose of protecting public health.[154]

---

149 Dickson-Waiko, 'The missing rib,' 99; Bronwen Douglas, 2003, 'Christianity, tradition, and everyday modernity: towards an anatomy of women's groupings in Melanesia,' *Oceania* 74(1/2): 6–23, 8.
150 Foucault, *The Will to Knowledge: The History of Sexuality Vol. 1*, 116–19, 136–39.
151 Judith R. Walkowitz, 1982, *Prostitution and Victorian Society: Women, Class, and the State*, Cambridge and New York: Cambridge University Press, 1.
152 For illustrations of traditional healing and the place of medicine in traditional societies, see Josephine Abaijah and Eric Wright, 1991, *A Thousand Coloured Dreams*, Mount Waverley, Vic: Dellasta Pacific, 46–51; Chilla Bulbeck, 1992, *Australian Women in Papua New Guinea: Colonial Passages 1920–1940*, Cambridge: Cambridge University Press, 111–12.
153 John Ballard, 1998, 'The constitution of AIDS in Australia: taking Government at a distance seriously,' in *Governing Australia: Studies in Contemporary Rationalities of Government*, ed. Mitchell Dean and Barry Hindess, Melbourne: Cambridge University Press, 125–38.
154 *Constitution* Section 38(1)(a)(i)(E).

Very serious diseases

> Venereal diseases are very serious diseases which cause loss of both health and strength, and sometimes end in a horrible death. Both men and women are liable to contract these diseases. They also injure the children of persons who are infected.
>
> Opening passage of Regulation 91, *Native Regulations* 1923 (Papua).

The health of villagers was a major concern in the two Territories. In addition to Native Regulations aimed at promoting village hygiene and suppressing disease, specific Ordinances were enacted in each Territory to govern a multitude of public health matters. These laws were eventually incorporated into the current *Public Health Act*, with an entire Part V devoted to the management of 'venereal diseases.'[155] This management includes the establishment of specialised hospitals and clinics, mandatory reporting and medical consultation on the part of persons 'suffering'; the powers of medical personnel; and a range of offences and restrictions, including prohibitions on the employment of an infected person in the food industry, and marriage while knowingly infected; and an offence of knowingly infecting another person. The Act also signals its particular concerns by criminalising the use of certificates of cure for, or in connection with, prostitution, and creating an offence of:

> *Permitting infected prostitute to occupy house, etc.*
>
> (1) The owner or occupier of a house, room or place who knowingly permits a female suffering from a venereal disease to occupy or resort to the house, room or place for the purpose of prostitution is guilty of an offence.[156]

This places female sex workers squarely in an outclass condemned by medical discourse.

The history of Part V (Venereal Diseases) is intriguing. The Native Regulations of both territories included requirements of reporting cases of venereal disease and compelling sufferers to attend hospital.[157] But there were differences between the two territories, brought about by their differing histories. In Papua, the health of villagers had been regulated almost from the outset of colonial control

---

[155] In 2006, when I was preparing the first draft of *Enabling Effective Responses to HIV in Pacific Island Countries: Options for Human Rights-Based Legislative Reform*, UNDP Pacific Centre and UNAIDS, 2009, I encountered much the same form of public health legislation for all sixteen Pacific countries surveyed.
[156] *Public Health Act* 1973 Section 67.
[157] Wolfers, *Race Relations and Colonial Rule*, 22, 31–32, 94–95; Reed, 'Contested images and common strategies'; and Katherine Lepani, 2007, '"In the process of knowing": making sense of HIV and AIDS in the Trobriand Islands of Papua New Guinea, Ph.D. thesis, Canberra: The Australian National University, 193–94, for a description of these lock hospitals in the Trobriands. The irony is that the regulations shifted the blame and the onus of control from the colonisers who introduced the diseases to the colonised who contracted them.

in the late-nineteenth century by means of the *Native Regulations*. Regulation 91, entitled simply *Venereal Diseases*, was adopted in 1904, and proceeded on from the provision above to require a person infected to

> keep himself clean by washing with water every day and ... abstain from all sexual intercourse while so diseased. He is also to be very careful that anything that touches his diseased parts is not to touch any other person, nor to come into contact with his own eyes lest they become blind.[158]

The person must report to the Village Constable, who was to take him (or her) to the Magistrate, who upon medical certification (if available) could order a period of custody in hospital. Unless released from custody upon a doctor's certification, the Magistrate could order repeated inspection. Sub-regulation (5) specifically applied the regulation to 'women and girls as well as men and youths,' and disobeying a requirement of the regulation could result in a fine or imprisonment.

In the Territory of New Guinea, the *Native Administration Regulations* 1924 included a much terser regulation on venereal disease, which simply required the village officer, the *luluai*, to take the native concerned to the nearest Government hospital, or if none was easily accessible, then to the nearest plantation or mission, for forwarding to a Government hospital. But there was a difference. New Guinea also had a specific Ordinance, the *Venereal Diseases Ordinance*, which had been enacted by the military administration in 1920, even before the *Native Administration Regulations*. No equivalent ordinance was ever enacted in Papua.

Why did the Territory of New Guinea have a venereal diseases ordinance while Papua did not? Why did it need an ordinance when native regulations would do? And why was the New Guinea ordinance enacted so swiftly, before Native Regulations, even before general civilian legislative powers were assumed in May 1921, while the Military Administration was still in control of the former German territory and the existing laws and customs of the colony were by practice and by the terms of the capitulation left undisturbed? Part of the answer, I believe, lies in the recital in the Preamble to the Ordinance:

> WHEREAS owing to the exigencies of the British Military Occupation of the Colony of German New Guinea and in the interests of public health it is expedient to make provision for the treatment of Venereal Diseases and to prevent the spread of such diseases and for the purposes consequent thereon or incidental thereto: Now therefore I Thomas

---

158 *Native Regulations* 1922 (Papua) Regulation 91(2).

Griffiths *Brigadier-General British Military Administrator of the Colony of German New Guinea* by virtue of the powers me thereunto enabling do hereby order enact and proclaim as follows [emphasis added].[159]

The territory at the time was under the control of the military. It may have been that venereal disease was already appearing in the barracks, and it was decided that measures should be taken. Native Regulations could not apply to expatriates, so an ordinance was needed. But even if no actual cases occurred, troops were believed liable to avail themselves of local prostitutes and thereby contract venereal disease; British law and policy was to enact legislation to control the prostitutes who were believed to spread venereal disease; in the absence of argument to the contrary, it would probably be a good idea to enact similar legislation in New Guinea (as had been the policy in many other British territories) in order to protect the troops.[160]

Judith Walkowitz points out that the Contagious Diseases Acts of the late-nineteenth century in England reinforced existing patterns of class and gender differentiation, as Foucault observed. Illicit extramarital sex involving soldiers of the realm became a matter of national significance. The Acts located control measures onto the female body, identifying prostitutes rather than their clients as vectors of disease, and creating an outclass of sexually deviant females.[161] So, in the enactment of the *Venereal Diseases Ordinance* 1920 during the military occupation of New Guinea, the legal discourse of sexuality was being supported by general principles derived from biomedical discourse, with its strong gender and class presumptions. The Ordinance was retained on the statute books even after the making of the *Native Administration Regulations*.

The Territory of Papua, however, never legislated for specific control of venereal diseases amongst expatriates and continued to rely solely on the controls over villagers in the *Native Regulations* until 1974. By that time, self-government was in place and the Crown Law Department was working frantically to rationalise and amalgamate the laws of the two Territories. Urban centres were expanding at a rapid rate and venereal diseases were spreading. The *Venereal Diseases Ordinance* 1920–1947 of New Guinea, although old, was considered to be capable of providing legal control measures, so it was applied to the Territory of Papua as well[162] and, re-titled the *Venereal Diseases Ordinance (Amalgamated)* 1973, became a law of what was already known as Papua New Guinea.[163]

---

159 Preamble to the *Venereal Diseases Ordinance* of New Guinea, 1920, made under the Military Occupation of New Guinea 1914–1921, and notified in the *Rabaul Gazette*, 31 July 1920.
160 Walkowitz, *Prostitution and Victorian Society: Women, Class, and the State*; Richard Phillips, 2006, *Sex, Politics and Empire: A Postcolonial Geography*, Manchester and New York: Manchester University Press.
161 Walkowitz, *Prostitution and Victorian Society*, 4–5.
162 R. Taureka, 1973, 'Venereal disease and the law,' paper presented at the Law and Development in Melanesia Waigani Seminar, Waigani, 1–2. Taureka, a medical doctor, was at the time Minister for Health.
163 *Statute Law Revision (Amalgamation of Laws) Ordinance* 1973, Section 6.

Further major law revision after Independence saw a reorganisation and complete amalgamation of public health legislation in 1986. The original health and sanitation laws were joined by those governing infectious diseases, malaria control measures, mental disorders, Hansen's Disease (leprosy), and venereal diseases, and all were incorporated, virtually unchanged in principle and content, into one lengthy *Public Health Act*.

It is probable that no specific venereal diseases legislation to govern both villagers and expatriates was enacted in the Territory of Papua because there was no military presence there until World War II. Such matters involving expatriates would have been dealt with quietly throughout most of the colonial era without the need for legislative intervention. New Guinea's venereal disease legislation may well have been adopted in Papua in 1974 due to increasing concerns about the spread of disease nation-wide. Specialist venereal disease clinics had been established in Port Moresby by the Department of Health,[164] and I can recall posters from an active awareness campaign undertaken around 1973–74. Much of the rhetoric in the 1970s and 1980s surrounding the criminalisation of prostitution revolved around the prostitute as vector of venereal disease, a view which has persisted until today.

Medical discourse continued to impact on outgroups in other ways too. Joan Johnstone was aided in her study of Highlands sex-sellers in Moresby in the late colonial period by Dr Burton-Bradley, government psychiatrist, who was interested in testing a theory in vogue at the time to the effect that there existed a specific psychological type of socially deviant person, the 'prostitute.' In her Ph.D. thesis, researched in the late 1960s but not written up until the 1990s, Johnstone concluded that her findings neither supported nor contradicted this theory, preferring to situate her conclusions regarding the choice of sex work in the forces and effects of the socio-economic climate of Port Moresby of the 1960s.[165]

The advent of AIDS

Since the late 1980s, the HIV epidemic has become well established in PNG where, as elsewhere in the world, it has focused attention on gender and sexuality—highlighting social problems, prompting legal reforms, and transforming gender activism into AIDS activism.[166] The top levels of the PNG government were slow to accept the reality of the epidemic in the 1980s, but

---

164 Joan Drikoré Johnstone, 'The Gumini *Bisnis-Meri*: a study of the development of an innovative indigenous entrepreneurial activity in Port Moresby in the early 1970s,' Ph.D. thesis, Brisbane: University of Queensland, xiv, 7.
165 Ibid., xiii–xiv, 291–94.
166 Jolly and Manderson, 'Sites of desire and economies of pleasure in Asia and the Pacific,' 4–5; Cindy Patton 2002, *Globalising AIDS*, Minneapolis and London: University of Minnesota Press, 3.

the Department of Health established a National AIDS Committee in 1986 to advise the Departmental Secretary. However, early attempts in the 1990s to introduce legislation for a National AIDS Council met with total government disinterest and denial. In 1997, however, the new Prime Minister Bill Skate, whose Port Moresby electorate was characterised by a high level of 'settler' or *grassroots* residents, took up the challenges of the issue. A National AIDS Council was established,[167] a *National Health Plan 1996–2000* identified priority areas for HIV/AIDS prevention, and a *National HIV/AIDS Medium Term Plan 1998–2002*, developed in conjunction with WHO, was endorsed in 1998.[168] Subsequent action (much of it prompted by large infusions of foreign aid) has led to increased awareness and an atmosphere of highly contested discourse on prevention, origin, and management, and high levels of stigmatisation and discrimination.[169]

The impact of HIV on political and moral thinking and practice, in the 'violent, vexed and contested political world in which we now live,' has been enormous.[170] The epidemic has served to emphasise the division of society into the 'general population' and the perverse 'other' of homosexuals and prostitutes. Gays (to be distinguished and divided from the true heterosexual man, who is presumed not to be infective) and prostitutes (who are seen as permanently contaminated)[171] have both been constructed as locales of high incidence of infection.[172] The epidemic perpetuates colonialism, as the health of aid-client state populations remains contingent on donors;[173] it plays into existing socio-cultural divisions world wide, and reinforces entrenched class and gender stereotypes.[174] Social research all too often ends up reproducing punitive stereotypes about sexuality that place blame on sexual 'deviants.'[175] In PNG, a nation of low literacy levels and poor mobilisation of civil society, popular wisdom, urban myths and

---

167 By the *National AIDS Council Act* 1997 (No 30 of 1997). I drafted the Bill in 2003 when working with the Health Department's National AIDS Committee, but the Bill's introduction into Parliament was rejected by previous governments.
168 Christine Stewart, 1993, *Law, Ethics and HIV/AIDS: Existing Law of Papua New Guinea*, Law Reform Commission of Papua New Guinea and Papua New Guinea Department of Health Joint Working Paper, 5.
169 John Ballard and Clement Malau, 2009, 'Policy-making on AIDS to 2000,' in *Policy Making and Implementation, Studies from Papua New Guinea*, ed. R.J. May, Canberra: ANU E Press, 369–78, online: http://press.anu.edu.au?p=78541, accessed 31 March 2014.
170 Nancy Scheper-Hughes, 1994, '"AIDS and the social body,"' *Social Science & Medicine* 39(7): 991–1003, 991.
171 Paula A. Treichler, 1999, *How to have Theory in an Epidemic: Cultural Chronicles of AIDS*, Durham: Duke University Press, 20.
172 Patton, *Globalising AIDS*, 68–69. The 'high risk settings strategy' was foisted upon PNG by donor countries and focused principally on the risks involved in prostitution, not marriage or companionate relationships. The terminology has been severely criticised e.g., in Lawrence James Hammar, 2010, *Sin, Sex and Stigma: A Pacific Response to HIV and AIDS*, Wantage, UK: Sean Kingston Publishing, 130–31. See also UNAIDS, *UNAIDS Terminology Guidelines (2011)*. The programme's name was changed to Tingim Laip [Think about your Life] later that year. But the stigma remains.
173 Patton, *Globalising AIDS*, 27.
174 Treichler, *How to have Theory in an Epidemic: Cultural Chronicles of AIDS*, 7.
175 Ibid., 113. When this occurs in the context of HIV, Ballard suggests that the infection itself is constituted as deviant. See Ballard, 'Sexuality and the state in time of epidemic,' 112.

received stereotypes are accepted at all levels of society.[176] Conservative views of divine retribution, claims of miracle cures accomplished by prayer, church preaching which encourages the rejection of condoms and the attribution of AIDS illness to sorcery or divine retribution are prevalent; persecution, banishment, even murder of those infected or presumed to be infected have been reported.[177] Along with many other countries which have just discovered the concept of 'homosexuality' as a discrete socio-sexual phenomenon, PNG has tried to dismiss it as a western import, or explain away evidence of 'ritual homosexuality' as a description of something different to the homosexuality of the West.[178]

Thoroughly conditioned by decades of imported processes of public health regulation, PNG's *elites* have readily accepted and preached the power-based control methods of mandatory and repeated testing,[179] immigration restrictions on foreign nationals entering for employment,[180] the focus on 'hotspots' prompted by the high risk settings strategy, and the imposition of provider-initiated testing, particularly at ante-natal clinics, with little regard for the caveats sounded in the *WHO Guidance*.[181] The concept of 'high-risk groups' was eagerly taken up by those who wished to immure themselves within the safety of a *cordon sanitaire*.[182] The later restyling of this as a concern with 'high-risk settings' made little difference, simply shifting the overt focus to stigmatised locales rather than stigmatised persons. HIV awareness has meant that for the first time, public health initiatives have focused on the infective dangers of sex between males, usually casting it, in public discourse at least, in terms of sodomy

---

176 I recall in 2002 having to listen to a woman outreach worker recount to me a number of such myths, all recast into an appropriate PNG context and mainly concerning infection of innocent citizens by evil foreign white women.
177 Nicole Haley, 2008, 'When there's no accessing basic health care: local politics and responses to HIV/AIDS at Lake Kopiago, Papua New Guinea,' in *Making Sense of AIDS*, ed. Leslie Butt and Richard Eves, Honolulu: University of Hawai'i Press, 24–40; Wardlow, '"You have to understand: some of us are glad AIDS has arrived"'; Hammar, *Sin, Sex and Stigma*, 358–60.
178 Patton, *Globalising AIDS*, 111.
179 Despite hours of training of high-level public servants in a workshop I conducted in 2002, participants still insisted that the entire public service workforce should be tested and the results divulged to top management 'for planning purposes.' It was only when confronted with estimates of the cost of this proposal that they fell silent: PNG National HIV/AIDS Support Project (NHASP), 2002, *Workplace Policy Development Workshops Report*, report prepared for PNG National HIV/AIDS Support Project, Port Moresby, 4.
180 The Immigration Division of the Department of Foreign Affairs and Trade established a policy in 1988 of requiring expatriates intending to enter for work purposes to provide proof of HIV-free status before being granted a visa. See National AIDS Council of Papua New Guinea, 2001, *Review of Policy and Legislative Reform Relating to HIV/AIDS in Papua New Guinea*, National AIDS Council of Papua New Guinea, 26.
181 World Health Organization and UNAIDS, 2007, *Guidance of Provider-Initiated HIV Testing and Counselling in Health Facilities*, Geneva: World Health Organization. To my knowledge, no research has yet been done on the adverse effects of implementing this policy in PNG, but anecdotal evidence which I and others have gathered indicates that it is resulting in highly gendered forms of discrimination and abuse.
182 Catherine Waldby, Susan Kippax and June Crawford, 1993, '*Cordon Sanitaire*: "clean" and "unclean" women in the AIDS discourse of young heterosexual men,' in *AIDS: Facing the Second Decade*, ed. Peter Aggleton, Peter Davies and Graham Hart, London: Falmer Press, 29–39, 31.

in prisons.[183] It is only very recently that society has been confronted with the reality that the epidemic has reached all sectors of society[184] but stigmatisation persists along gendered and class lines.[185]

I have outlined how the three significant colonial discourses (law, religion and medicine) have influenced the construction and regulatory control of the sexuality of the colonised by the colonisers. At Independence, some moves were made to create a new society based on 'Melanesian' ideals and customary law principles. But ultimately, elements of an already-stratified society developed and maintained their power base, in part through the perpetuation of sexual regulation.

Race, class and social stratification

> 'White prestige' is the concept, doctrine, and slogan which caps the caste structure in New Guinea today; any act or practice judged as tending to lower that prestige is regarded as a peril to white supremacy … now that rights have been freely parcelled out to the natives and the use of armed force is condemned, the white man resorts to caste rules—taboos, prescriptions, and juridical sanctions—to assure his continuing superiority.
>
> Stephen Winsor Reed, 1943.[186]

I have referred earlier in this chapter to writers such as Stoler who transposed Foucault's theories on the management of sexuality to the non-European world. In Stoler's later work, she took issue with the students of colonial history who ignored Foucault's thinking on race, while observing how Foucault himself, despite acknowledging that 'the social body is basically articulated around two races,'[187] largely neglected the possibility that racial thinking may have been constitutive of the bourgeois order in Europe itself.[188]

'State racism' is, for Stoler, an indispensible technology of rule in any kind of state, as biopower's operating mechanism. The rhetoric of race is a tool for a wide spectrum of political agendas, as the epigraph above demonstrates, and

---

183   'High risk sexual activities at Bomana,' *National* (online), 18 May 2007; 'Gay sex rife in jails,' *National* (online), 26 October 2007.
184   See e.g., 'More HIV infection in the rural areas,' *National* (online), 6 July 2009.
185   'Sex workers learn,' *Post-Courier* (online), 12 November 2009.
186   Reed, *The Making of Modern New Guinea*, 245.
187   Michel Foucault, 1997 [2004], "Society Must be Defended": *Lectures at the Collège de France, 1975–76*, London: Penguin Books, 60.
188   Richard Phillips, 2002, 'Imperialism and the regulation of sexuality: colonial legislation on contagious diseases and ages of consent,' *Journal of Historical Geography* 28(3): 339–62; Stoler, *Carnal Knowledge and Imperial Power*, 144.

can animate many different political themes.[189] And in fact, the present-day creation in PNG of outgroups based on criminalised sexualities does depend on an indigenous *élite* determined to defend itself through self-scrutiny and societal policing. This section tracks the deployment of racial discourse in the maintenance of colonial power in pre-independent PNG, and the part it played in underpinning the development of PNG's *elites* of today. This is true no matter how nearly or otherwise the discourse represents the realities of PNG societies past and present—discourses tend to lean towards simplistic binaries, and those of race, caste and class probably do so more than most.[190]

Innate racial differences

> The world of Papua's expatriate settlers before [World War II] was a dusty, lower middle class, Australian version of the British Raj. It lacked the grace and magnificence of the Empire at its zenith. Its security derived less from a sense of pride in its technological superiority and splendour than from a mean and pedantic insistence on the importance of innate racial differences.
>
> Ted Wolfers, 1975.[191]

Ted Wolfers studied race relations in colonial Papua New Guinea because he considered that 'a knowledge of race relations in the past provides invaluable insights into the roots of the present tensions.'[192] His book provides a comprehensive overview of the native regulations and other laws through which he traces the history of class, caste and discrimination in colonial PNG.

While considerations of race and ethnicity, class and caste, have underpinned studies of power relations in colonies, they have been largely disregarded in research into sexuality and gender, which, as Margaret Jolly and Lenore Manderson remind us, have until very recently been dominated by western traditions of thought—only the global threat of the HIV epidemic has prompted consideration of 'ethnicity and class as central to the terrain of gender and sexuality.'[193]

---

189 Stoler, *Carnal Knowledge and Imperial Power*, 159–60.
190 I am reminded of excellent lessons to be learnt from Kalpana Ram's critique of 'western' sociological writing on 'the Indian' subject. See Kalpana Ram, 1992, 'Modernist anthropology and the construction of Indian identity,' *Meanjin* 51(3): 589–614.
191 Wolfers, *Race Relations and Colonial Rule*, 45.
192 Ibid.
193 Jolly and Manderson, 'Sites of desire, economies of pleasure,' 6.

The subtleties of division, definition and description of race and ethnicity are manifold and ultimately arbitrary.[194] But this did not concern the early European colonists of PNG, who experienced first-hand a glaringly evident racial divide and needed to deal with it on the spot. One of the initial tasks of their law was to define the 'other' whom they had come to rule. From the governing laws of the metropole down to the native regulations in the field, the Australians in PNG grappled with the definition of 'natives' as subjects juxtaposed to themselves, but were forced to resort to the assumed meanings and tautological, non-exhaustive definitions, for example: the '"Indigenous inhabitant of Papua New Guinea" includes a person who follows, adheres to or adopts the customs, or lives after the manner of, any of the indigenous inhabitants of Papua New Guinea.'[195]

The peoples of the eastern half of the New Guinea island were as foreign to one another as were the newly arrived Europeans. More conflict usually erupted between colonised Melanesian groups than between them and the colonisers.[196] Nevertheless, European colonisers of the Pacific created the general category of 'the native' and attributed inferior qualities, needs, wants and habits to this invention.[197] In Papua, this approach was wholeheartedly embraced by Administrator Murray; and to a large extent was adopted in New Guinea when Australia assumed its administration, albeit somewhat tempered by the mandate/trusteeship arrangements.

After World War II, the assimilationist system was perpetuated by Paul Hasluck, Minister for Territories from 1950 to 1965, who asserted a right to determine all policy in the finest detail. Although 'most Australians are very sure that Australian administration in New Guinea has been of outstanding quality, partly because governments have so often said so,'[198] policies in reality promoted contempt for the colonised peoples. So Charles Rowley in 1966 was prompted to remark on

---

194 Wolfers, *Race Relations and Colonial Rule*, 1–2; John Ballard, 1979, 'Ethnicity and access in Papua New Guinea,' unpublished, 1–2; Christine Jennett and Randal G. Stewart, 1987, *Three Worlds of Inequality: Race, Class and Gender*, South Melbourne: Macmillan, 1–2; Stoler, *Race and the Education of Desire*, 45–47; Bronwen Douglas, 2008, 'Foreign bodies in Oceania,' in *Foreign Bodies: Oceania and the Science of Race 1750–1940*, ed. Douglas and Chris Ballard, Canberra: ANU E Press, 3–30, 3, online: http://press.anu.edu.au?p=53561, accessed 31 March 2014. The chapters in this volume challenge the concept of 'race' as an ontological category, and chart the shift from a stress on climatic determination to innate biological difference in western thinking. See also Stewart Firth, 1997, 'Colonial administration and the invention of the native,' in *The Cambridge History of the Pacific Islanders*, ed. Donald Denoon et al., Cambridge and New York: Cambridge University Press, 253–88 on the construction of the colonised 'native'; and Geoffrey Clark, 2003, 'Shards of meaning: archaeology and the Melanesia-Polynesia Divide,' *Journal of Pacific History* 38(2): 197–215 for constructed regional divisions.
195 *Papua New Guinea Act* 1949 (Cth).
196 Firth, 'Colonial administration and the invention of the native,' 244–46.
197 Ibid., 262–63.
198 Rowley, *The New Guinea Villager*, 7.

the inhumanity of the plural society, where each racial group uses the other for economic and political purposes of its own, with social contacts at the minimum.... '[N]atives' ... are partly a picturesque setting, and partly a vague but ever-present menace.... [E]xcept for a small minority, relationships are those of employer to employee, or are basically paternal in some other way.[199]

As well as the division along racial lines, colonisation created new categories of the colonised. The extension of administration to a slow-moving frontier created artificial geographical boundaries and ethnic divisions more suited to the colonists' regime but irrelevant to the colonised thus divided. Patterns of migration attendant upon mine and plantation labour recruitment produced identities based on district or area of origin. But, as urban migration increased in the 1950s and 1960s, more complex social identities soon emerged. Formal associations such as churches and sporting groups tended to aggregate along ethnic lines of varying degrees of bandwidth (district, region, and at the highest internal level, Papuan versus New Guinean). Differentiation and ethnic stereotyping developed, based on perceived success or failure in achieving Australian-determined norms, a status-ranking of district and regional identities in positive or negative terms ('the educated Tolai,' 'the aggressive Chimbu,' etc.).[200] Dinnen notes that even today, the police often use constructed cultural group attributes as justification for retribution, but when it suits, 'non-cultural stereotypes are simultaneously used to legitimate coercive actions against culturally heterogeneous marginal groups in the urban setting.'[201] And the police are not alone. A *Post-Courier* online editorial 'Motuan clash has surprised us all,' commenting on a violent inter-village fight near Port Moresby which saw five villagers dead, observes that

> it sounds like the battle report from some other parts of the country, where such group clashes are part of the culture and fully expected when there is a row over valuables.... However for it to come from the traditional villages near to Port Moresby, it is entirely out of character. These people are renowned for their love and respect for a peaceful life and are generally law abiding citizens.[202]

In a colonial situation it is the externally imposed state, rather than market forces, which sets the boundaries and the parameters for success in access to these resources. In the PNG colony, qualifications for access to resources were determined by the Australian coloniser in terms of European concepts of the state. So the race-based social divide of colonial PNG ensured that the colonised

---

199 Ibid., 13.
200 Ballard, 'Ethnicity and access in Papua New Guinea.'
201 Dinnen, 'Criminal justice reform in Papua New Guinea,' 261.
202 'Motuan clash has surprised us all,' editorial, *Post-Courier* (online), 3 February 2010.

were excluded almost entirely from state activities and economic benefits. This was less evident in the towns, where ethnic identities were more complex and boundaries less distinct; where education started to establish the conditions for the conversion of racial caste divisions into those of class; and where indigenous entrepreneurs began to emerge and stake their claims to access to new tools, technologies and above all, cash.

Before World War II, the prospect of an indigenous *élite* in PNG was totally abhorrent to the colonial authorities. Higher education should not be made available until the colonised were capable of assuming a measure of responsibility equivalent to that of the colonisers, and that for the moment was 'out of the question.'[203] But in the late colonial period, commentators noted the emergence of an élite, as 'the old discrimination along racial lines is being replaced by economic and other, subtler forms of social differentiation.'[204] Class, which had for the most part been based on race in the colonial period, was beginning to emerge as the major division in indigenous society. The personnel may have changed, but the principles did not: the same systems of access were perpetuated, favouring those with education, urban residence and white-collar employment—positions increasingly filled by Papua New Guineans. A new ruling class was emerging, of those 'who had learned to play by Australian rules.'[205]

Many factors converged to produce this structural shift. Colonial legal and administrative policies emphasised individual rights at the expense of group solidarity. They also de-emphasised education, so that only a small minority had achieved anything resembling tertiary education by the time of Independence.[206] Zoning and urban regulations initially excluded PNG immigrants and peri-urban villagers from towns. When they were allowed access, different standards of housing were implemented, firstly along racial lines and then according to occupational status. This emphasis on social and economic differences has increasingly stratified post-colonial society.[207] Macintyre has noted how

> the existence of a highly paid educated élite, fiercely protecting its jobs and urban living standards, perpetuates the division between haves,

---

203 Sir Hubert Murray, *Papua Annual Report for 1937*, quoted in Jinks, Biskup and Nelson, *Readings in New Guinea History*, 135–36; and see Reed, 'Contested images and common strategies.'
204 Wolfers, *Race Relations and Colonial Rule*, 146; see also Rowley, *The New Guinea Villager*, 202–03; Oram, *Colonial Town to Melanesian City*, 145–46; and particularly Narokobi, *The Melanesian Way*, 108, discussed in Gewertz and Errington, *Emerging Class in Papua New Guinea*, 3.
205 Ballard, 'Ethnicity and access in Papua New Guinea,' 13.
206 Meek, *The University of Papua New Guinea*, 65–68; Bulbeck, *Australian Women in Papua New Guinea*, 180–84.
207 David King, 1998, 'Elites, suburban commuters, and squatters: the emerging urban morphology of Papua New Guinea,' in *Modern Papua New Guinea*, ed. Laura Zimmer-Tamakoshi, Kirksville, MO: Thomas Jefferson University Press, 183–94.

have-nots, and hopefuls ... the villagers in areas remote from towns and the services or facilities linked to them see themselves as having failed in crucial ways.[208]

Writing in 1985, Epeli Hau'ofa, an intellectual of Tongan ancestry who grew up in PNG, was already describing the emergence of a 'South Pacific' society, of privileged groups across the region who shared economic, social and cultural ties. This social group emerged from the regional capitalist consumer economy promoted by the former colonial powers Australia and New Zealand, which promoted consumerism and the metropolitan way of life. By separating themselves from the struggling poor, they secure their own privileged access to the resources of this economy. This, he declared, is a very important development, because it is they who guide the destinies of island communities, while blaming the culture-bound and lazy underprivileged classes for their own straitened circumstances, telling them to preserve their traditions, and even obliging them to adopt 'the dead weight' of other traditions (such as chiefly systems and Christianity) in order to maintain social stability and preserve their own privileges.[209] But, warned Hau'ofa, 'there is a strong reluctance on the part of the regional privileged, including academics, to recognise the emergence of modern classes in the island world.'[210] In fact, there was a strong reluctance by anybody to recognise Hau'ofa's warning.

Ten years later, American anthropologists Deborah Gewertz and Fred Errington studied the emergence of class in a small provincial PNG town, Wewak, where they found a number of representatives of a highly educated, comparatively affluent group who presented themselves as 'fundamentally superior' to their rural kin.[211] This, Gewertz and Errington claimed, evidenced a middle class, juxtaposed to the remote 'international owners of capital' on the one hand and a lower class of both rural and urban poor, from whom they sought to distance and distinguish themselves, on the other.[212] In the context of urban Port Moresby, David King describes them as *elites*, suburban commuters, and squatters, but cautions that the emerging middle class is by no means entrenched in its superiority.[213]

But this tripartite hierarchical model has been challenged: a recent publication points to the absence of a 'middle class' in Melanesia able to promote democracy

---

208 Martha Macintyre, 1998, 'The persistence of inequality: women in Papua New Guinea since Independence,' in *Modern Papua New Guinea*, ed. Laura Zimmer-Tamakoshi, Kirksville, MO: Thomas Jefferson University Press, 211–30, 215.
209 Epeli Hau'ofa, 2008, *We Are the Ocean: Selected Works*, Honolulu: University of Hawai'i Press.
210 Ibid., 22.
211 Gewertz and Errington, *Emerging Class in Papua New Guinea*, 1.
212 Ibid., 7–11.
213 King, 'Elites, urban commuters, and squatters,' 193.

in the region.²¹⁴ Other writers, while perceiving various forms of sub-categories, nevertheless confirm the emergence of concepts of socially stratified groups, known in popular PNG parlance as *elites* and *grassroots*.²¹⁵

These emerging *elites* have become leaders in PNG politics, government, business and even in the underworld. They have led the nation towards forging a national identity,²¹⁶ and a citizenry focused on self-improvement along the lines of local adaptations of global modernity, increasingly nuanced by local versions of Christianity.²¹⁷ They assert their rights to own their own persons and capacities, make their own economic and social choices of action, immerse themselves in a growing consumer culture,²¹⁸ resist the claims of less fortunate kin. They are becoming, to an extent, the 'possessive individuals' of the Western Pacific.²¹⁹ But they are not merely turning their backs on 'custom' while still espousing the rhetoric.²²⁰ The performance of this 'incipient individualism'²²¹ may be only partial, their position of advantage still 'fragile.'²²² Competing and conflicting demands from kin on their property, their labour, their right to the private consumption of the commodities they have striven for, even their religious beliefs, may mean that at various points individualism must yield, or at least adapt to some form of co-existence.²²³ Customary social relations persist

---

214 Pacific Institute of Public Policy, 2011, *Youthquake: Will Melanesian Democracy be Sunk by Demography?* online: http://www.pacificpolicy.org/, accessed 23 March 2011.
215 Gewertz and Errington, *Emerging Class in Papua New Guinea*; M. Goddard, 2001, 'From rolling thunder to reggae: imagining squatter settlements in Papua New Guinea,' *Contemporary Pacific* 13(1): 1–32, 22–23; Anastasia Sai, 2007, '*Tamot*: masculinities in transition in Papua New Guinea,' Ph.D. thesis, Melbourne: Victoria University; Robbins, 'Afterword: possessive individualism and cultural change in the Western Pacific'; Sykes, 'Interrogating individuals'; Andrew Lattas and Knut M. Rio, 2011, 'Securing modernity: towards an ethnography of power in contemporary Melanesia,' *Oceania* 81(1): 1–21.
216 Countryside, 2010, 'Opportunity generation: *Time Blo Yumi*,' *ActNOW!* Blog, 13 July 2010, online http://www.actnowpng.org/content/opportunity-generation-time-blo-yumi, accessed 31 July 2010.
217 Robert J. Foster, 1992, 'Commoditization and the emergence of "kastom" as a cultural category: a New Ireland case in comparative perspective,' *Oceania* 62(4): 284–94; Robert J. Foster, 1992, 'Take care of public telephones: moral education and nation-state formation in Papua New Guinea,' *Public Culture* 4(2) 31–45; Hank Nelson, 2003, 'Dear Sir, … Evidence of civil society in the media of Papua New Guinea,' paper presented at the USP/ANU/FDC Suva Symposium, Suva, 30 September–3 October; Christine Stewart, 2010, 'The courts, the churches, the witches and their killers,' paper presented at the Law and Culture: Meaningful Legal Pluralism in the Pacific and Beyond Conference, Port Vila, Vanuatu, 30 August–1 September.
218 Robert J. Foster, 1999, 'The commercial construction of "new nations,"' *Journal of Material Culture* 4(3): 263–82; Robert J. Foster, 2002, *Materializing the Nation: Commodities, Consumption, and Media in Papua New Guinea*, Bloomington and Indianapolis: Indiana University Press.
219 Foster, 'The commercial construction of "new nations"'; Foster, *Materializing the Nation*; Keir Martin, 2007, 'Your own *buai* you must buy: the ideology of possessive individualism in Papua New Guinea,' *Anthropological Forum* 17(3): 285–98; Robbins, 'Afterword: possessive individualism and cultural change in the Western Pacific'; Sykes, 'Interrogating in dividuals.'
220 Peter Sack, 1989, 'Law, custom and good government: the Derham Report in its historical context,' in *Papua New Guinea: A Century of Colonial Impact, 1884–1984*, ed. Sione Latukefu, Port Moresby: National Research Institute and University of Papua New Guinea, 377–97, 396.
221 Wardlow, *Wayward Women*, 19.
222 King, 'Elites, urban commuters, and squatters,' 193.
223 Wardlow, *Wayward Women*, 19–22.

and co-exist, and strategies for compromise, the privileging of one over the other, or the creation of new coping mechanisms, are adopted according to the needs of the situation.²²⁴

Conclusion

> When Europeans settled in Papua New Guinea, they did not find a political vacuum on the shores and plains, and in the mountains of our islands. Our ancestors had well-organised, self-sufficient communities or *wanples*, clans and tribes, to meet the needs of their times. The price of the impact of Western colonisation has been the sapping of the initiative of our people.
>
> Constitutional Planning Committee, 1974.²²⁵

In this chapter I have offered some theoretical and historical context to the materials on sex work and sodomy which I will present in subsequent chapters. I have outlined aspects of Foucault's work upon which Goodman based his research: namely, that power has come to be exercised through disciplines of the body which develop and maintain a moral stance, shaping modern society by a process of exclusion—of the criminal, the insane, the sexually deviant and so on. Of the four sexual objects of discursive knowledge, only the heterosexual procreative couple is the norm—such abnormal outcasts as the hysterical (or in the case of sex-sellers, wanton and amoral) woman and the psychotic pervert (the abominable homosexual) are constructed as criminals.

I argue further that this process is not restricted to western societies, but was exported to many non-western colonies. I describe how 'civilisation' along western lines was introduced into the former territories of PNG through administrative practice, supported by the introduction and adoption of discourses of Christianity and of western medicine. These discourses crystallised the concepts of licit and illicit sexual relations along Foucauldian lines, criminalising non-heteronormative sexuality in the state legal system. Post-Independence, Christianity has come to play an increasingly strong role in moulding social regulatory mechanisms, as has the bio-medical discourse, now fuelled by the impact of HIV. PNG police culture is mainly concerned with punitive law enforcement and the assumption of a modern version of the warrior-

---

224 Martin, 'Your own *buai* you must buy,' 288–95; Mary Patterson and Martha Macintyre, 2011, 'Introduction: capitalism, cosmology and globalisation in the Pacific,' in *Managing Modernity in the Western Pacific*, ed. Patterson and MacIntyre, Brisbane: University of Queensland Press, 1–29, 13–17; Wardlow, *Wayward Women*, 19–20.
225 *Final Report of the Constitutional Planning Committee* 2/12, quoting from the Second Interim Report.

protectors of the community rather than the individual.[226] The post-colonial era has seen the emergence of a form of privileged class which has embraced western modernity, consumerism, individualism and, to an extent, such globally accepted discursive principles as human rights and the backwardness of traditional culture. They define themselves in contradistinction to the poor, persuading them to observe cultural practices and norms, including imported traditions, which serve to secure their own privileges and access to resources, while simultaneously upholding persistent patterns of customary socio-economic relations, and developing a myriad of differing, mutable forms of subjectivity.[227] It is this privileged class of *elites* which constructs and promulgates the social norms of PNG society today, including norms of sexual behaviour, and which controls the fashioning of the nation's laws, including sexuality laws. So in the next chapter, I describe how these laws have been introduced, constructed and modified.

---

226 Nancy Scheper-Hughes and Margaret M. Lock, 1987, 'The mindful body: a prolegomenon to future work in medical anthropology,' *Medical Anthropology Quarterly* 1(1): 6–41, 7–8.
227 Patterson and Macintyre, 'Introduction: capitalism, cosmology and globalisation in the Pacific,' 16.

3. In the Courtroom

> The colonial law was part of the colonial wave which came without invitation and without warning, toppling Papua New Guinean societies, destroying its laws and institutions.
>
> Bernard Narokobi, lawyer, philosopher.[1]

In Chapter 2, I introduced Michel Foucault's arguments concerning the connection between law and other normative discourses, and how writers on colonialism have highlighted the effective use of introduced sexuality norms and laws in governing colonised populations. In the colonial territories, a completely new paradigm of norm, boundary and discipline was established through the imposition of colonial laws. I described how the system of Native Regulations, which governed the intimate lives of villagers in minute detail, was supported by the discourses of medicine and Christianity, and how decolonisation and modernity have seen the emergence of the social groups who support the imposition of these discourses onto the social body.

Meanwhile, the introduced Anglo-Australian legal system, technically supreme from the outset, was mainly concerned with governing the colonists themselves, and only intruded into the lives of the colonised in situations of serious crimes and land disputes vis-à-vis the colonists. As I describe in this chapter, the introduced system gradually took over, and the Native Regulations were eventually abandoned.[2]

Policing the boundaries: The modern role of law in society

The classic interpretation of Foucault's thinking on law has been termed the 'expulsion thesis.' It holds that pre-modern law was identified with a repressive form of power exercised by the sovereign over transgressors, but was later displaced by the regulatory schemes of modern 'bio-power,' exercised over

---
1   Bernard Narokobi, 1980, *The Melanesian Way: Total Cosmic Vision of Life*, Boroko: Institute of Papua New Guinea Studies, 144.
2   David Weisbrot, 1988, 'Papua New Guinea's indigenous jurisprudence and the legacy of colonialism,' *University of Hawai'i Law Review* 10(1): 1–45, 2; and see *R v Womeni-Nanagawo* [1963] PNGLR 72.

whole populations by surveillance and self-discipline. Modern individuals become self-regulating, law's role is diminished, and it is 'expelled' from modern society.[3]

This classic 'expulsion thesis' of law has recently been challenged.[4] Ben Golder and Peter Fitzpatrick argue that far from vanishing, law has merely retreated to identify and police the boundaries which divide the normal from the abnormal, the licit from the illicit. But law cannot be given once and for all.[5] While it seems deterministic when it punishes transgressions and renders all within the boundary as legitimate, at the same time its illimitable capacity to be open to change puts it constantly into negotiation with resistance and transgression.[6] It can affirm the boundary between the normal and the abnormal, the legitimate and the illegitimate. Or it can adjust the boundary, either outward to render normal and legitimate that which previously was not, or inward, to create new abnormality and illegitimacy. This process of response is at the heart of each case decided by judicial process, each alteration to the statute book made by the legislature, each law reform initiative undertaken at society's behest. It is a process powerfully evident in the development of sexuality laws in Papua New Guinea (PNG), which I describe and discuss in this chapter.

Civilising the primitive: Colonial criminal law

> Except where modifications have been made as the result of the coming of Europeans, New Guinea is still almost unbelievably primitive … at the present time, the world would be acting in ignorance if it did not appreciate the primitive and unique character of the conditions in the Territory and the size of the basic civilizing tasks to be completed.
>
> Commonwealth Minister for Territories Paul Hasluck, 1960.[7]

PNG's state legal system is based on that of the administering colonial power, Australia, which in turn was based on that of its colonial power, Britain. Australia introduced versions of this legal system into both territories, Papua and New Guinea, albeit with slight variations between the two which were not resolved until around the time of Independence in 1975—and some not even then. The specific system introduced was based primarily on the laws of

---

3   For the clearest exposition, see Alan Hunt and Gary Wickham, 1994, *Foucault and the Law: Towards a Sociology of Law as Governance*, London, Boulder, Colorado: Pluto Press.
4   Ben Golder and Peter Fitzpatrick, 2009, *Foucault's Law*, Abingdon: Routledge.
5   Ibid., 78–80.
6   Ibid., 64.
7   Commonwealth of Australia, *Parliamentary Debates*, House of Representatives, 23 August 1960: 259 (Paul Hasluck, Minister for Territories).

Queensland, because during the early part of the colonial era, Australian policy tended towards a hope that the two territories might one day become part of Queensland.[8]

This Anglo-Australian legal system is known as the common law system, and is one of the two great legal systems of the West, the other being civil or Continental law.[9] Civil law systems are aimed at formulating prospective rules of conduct, usually written out fully in a 'code.' By contrast, the English common law is formed primarily by judges. The general principles of the common law are believed always to have existed. Each individual case examines closely the particular situation of facts before it, and by minute inspection and construction 'discovers' the law in ever-increasing clarity, thereby elucidating and illustrating these general principles. Written laws or 'statutes' (known as Acts, Ordinances, Regulations etc., depending on which legislating body makes them and their position in the legal hierarchy) are usually drawn up to vary old rules which are no longer satisfactory or appropriate, or to fill gaps in the common law. For many decades, the common law system of PNG has relied increasingly on statutes.

The criminal law

> The *Criminal Code* was drawn up and enacted in the light of many centuries' experience in the English community, during which time the community was thereby enabled to advance to a much higher social status. The *Code* inevitably expresses concepts of social responsibility in terms known to an advanced and civilized society.
>
> P&NG Chief Justice Mann, 1963.[10]

The common law is usually conceived of as being divided into two streams: criminal and non-criminal (the latter known, confusingly, as 'civil'). Civil law in the common law system is concerned with adjudicating and adjusting relations between parties, while the criminal law concerns itself with matters considered so serious and disruptive of social order that the state must step in and exact penalty from the perpetrator of the injustice.

The division of law into criminal and civil law has a long history reaching back for centuries in England.[11] Serious interpersonal wrongs offended the entire realm, and were punished either by the king, as sovereign of his subjects, or the

---

8   John Ballard, 1979, 'Ethnicity and access in Papua New Guinea,' unpublished, 10.
9   Continental law is followed in the Pacific only in French territories.
10 *Regina v Kauba-Paruwo* [1963] P&NGLR 18, 20.
11 R.P. Roulston, 1975, *Introduction to Criminal Law in New South Wales*, Sydney: Butterworths, 1–4; Harvey Wallace and Cliff Roberson, 2001, *Principles of Criminal Law*, 2nd ed., Boston: Allyn and Bacon, 11.

church, which had powers over all matters ecclesiastical and adjudicated such matters as defamation, witchcraft and drunkenness, and the whole range of matters arising from the relations between the sexes: incest, marriage, bigamy, abortion, sexual assault, 'fornication' and unnatural sex.[12]

The Enlightenment of the late-eighteenth century prompted the incorporation of individual rights into English criminal law. These rights acted largely as a safeguard for the middle class against the aristocracy,[13] and included the concept that justice should be done to individuals and the law should be clearly stated and known in advance, without the need for recourse to textbooks and law reports.[14] And so began a move towards codification, or the total restatement by statute of the English criminal law, resulting in a model which was exported to most English colonies and territories, starting with India in 1860.[15]

In Australia, the states of Queensland, Tasmania and Western Australia adopted a form of this code. The Queensland *Criminal Code* was then exported to the territories of Papua and New Guinea. Along with other statutory sources of criminal law, such as the former Police Offences Ordinances now replaced by the *Summary Offences Act* 1977, and the detailed Native Regulations which applied only to the indigenous population, this Code formed the bulk of the criminal law system by which the colonised were kept in order.

This system, based as it was on a concept of a superior authority vested with the power (and the wisdom) to adjudicate and punish serious wrongs, was completely alien to PNG societies.[16] Despite their diversity, areas of uniformity could be discerned in traditional legal systems: mediation, self-regulation, self-help and compensation redressed wrongs and restored harmonious relations according to the needs of the moment rather than past precedent.[17] But these processes were ignored by the colonists in their 'civilising' project, while much of the criminal law remained incomprehensible or inimical to the colonised.[18] Even in German New Guinea, where the colonists displayed no desire to transform

---

12 Sir James Fitzjames Stephen, 1883, *A History of the Criminal Law of England Vol. 2*, London: Macmillan; Roulston, *Introduction to Criminal Law in New South Wales*; Bruce L. Ottley, and Jean G. Zorn, 1983, 'Criminal law in Papua New Guinea: code, custom and the courts in conflict,' *American Journal of Comparative Law* 31: 251–300; Wallace and Roberson, *Principles of Criminal Law*, 2nd ed.
13 Alan W. Norrie, 1993, *Crime, Reason and History: A Critical Introduction to Criminal Law*, London: Weidenfeld and Nicolson.
14 H.F. Morris, 1974, 'A history of the adoption of codes of criminal law and procedure in British Colonial Africa, 1876–1935,' *Journal of African Law* 18(6): 6–23, 6.
15 Sir James Fitzjames Stephen, 1883, *A History of the Criminal Law of England Vol. 3*, London: Macmillan; Norrie, *Crime, Reason and History*.
16 Peter Lawrence, 1969, 'The state versus stateless societies in Papua and New Guinea,' in *Fashion of Law in New Guinea*, ed. B.J. Brown, Sydney, Melbourne, Brisbane: Butterworths, 15–37.
17 Cyndi Banks, 1993, *Women in Transition: Social Control in Papua New Guinea*, Canberra: Australian Institute of Criminology, 143–45; Ottley and Zorn, 'Criminal law in Papua New Guinea', 255–58.
18 Law Reform Commission of Papua New Guinea, 1977b, *Report No 7: The Role of Customary Law in the Legal System*, Waigani: Law Reform Commission of Papua New Guinea, 47.

existing cultures by absorbing them into their own introduced administrative and legal systems,[19] the first criminal regulations extended to the colonised were simply an extension of German criminal law, and no attempt was made to adapt them to local circumstances.[20]

Reforms

Laws and courts

> Although the system for the administration of justice in the Territory has probably been reasonably adequate for times when the dominating aim was to bring order, and the benefits of European administration, to a primitive and dispersed people without greatly disturbing their existing ways of life, it is not adequate to aid the achievement of the aims for the Territory to which the Commonwealth of Australia appears to be presently committed.
>
> *Derham Report*, 1960.[21]

The early colonial view that the 'primitive' way of life of the colonised should be left undisturbed gradually gave way to a goal of advancement towards self-government at some time in the foreseeable future, and the 1960s saw significant legal as well as political development. In 1959, the Australian Government appointed David P. Derham, Professor of Jurisprudence, to enquire into the system of the administration of justice in the Territory and make suggestions for its improvement.[22] As a result of his report (*Derham Report*),[23] the Courts of Native Affairs were abolished from 1963 and a unified system of law was to be applied to all.[24] The court system was revised into a single-line hierarchy, from the 'inferior' Local and District Courts, presided over by magistrates, up to the first 'superior' court, the Supreme Court, usually in the person of a single judge.[25] One of the main tasks of the Supreme Court was to try serious criminal

---

19   Alan M. Healy, 1987, 'Monocultural administration in a multicultural environment: the Australians in Papua New Guinea,' in *Colony to Coloniser: Studies in Australian Administrative History*, ed. J.J. Eddy and J.R. Nethercote, Sydney: Hale & Iremonger, 207–24, 216–17.
20   Edward P. Wolfers, 1975, *Race Relations and Colonial Rule in Papua New Guinea*, Sydney: Australia and New Zealand Book Company, 65.
21   David Plumley, 1960, *Report on the System for the Administration of Justice in the Territory of Papua and New Guinea*, Melbourne: report to the Minister for Territories, Melbourne (*Derham Report*), 5.
22   Ibid., 1.
23   Ibid.
24   For a fascinating view on this process, see Rachel Cleland, 1984, *Pathways to Independence: Story of Official and Family Life in Papua New Guinea from 1951 to 1975*, Cottesloe, WA: R. Cleland, 218–28; and for analysis, see Peter Sack, 1989, 'Law, custom and good government: the Derham Report in its historical context,' in *Papua New Guinea: A Century of Colonial Impact, 1884–1984*, ed. Sione Latukefu, Port Moresby: National Research Institute and University of Papua New Guinea, 377–97.
25   L.K. Young, 1971, *Outline of Law in Papua and New Guinea*, Sydney, Melbourne, Brisbane: The Law Book Company Ltd., 56–63. The terms 'inferior' and 'superior' refer to the courts' extent of jurisdiction and place in the court hierarchy.

cases. Parties dissatisfied with the decision of the Supreme Court could appeal to the highest court in the Territory, the Full Court, usually constituted by three judges together. A further appeal lay in special cases to the Full Court of Australia.[26]

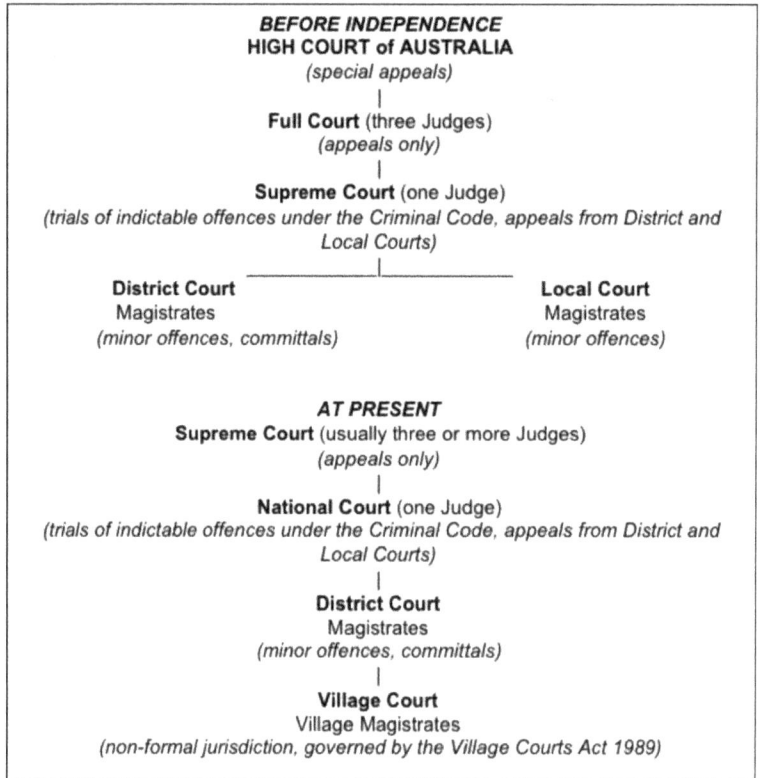

Table 3.1. Formal court system in PNG before and after Independence.

Source: Image created by Christine Stewart.

At Independence, the PNG Supreme Court was renamed the National Court and the Full Court was named the Supreme Court,[27] but otherwise their functions and form remained largely the same. A system of 'Village Courts' was established outside the formal court hierarchy and subject only to the *Constitution*, to adjudicate on specified customary issues.[28] The Village Courts have continued to mediate and adjudicate customary matters and disputes, although their relationship to the formal legal system has sometimes exceeded, or varied greatly, from that originally intended.[29]

---

26 The special right of appeal to the High Court of Australia was not abolished until Independence: *Papua New Guinea Act (No.2) 1974* (Cth) Section 9.
27 *Constitution* Part VI Division 5.
28 *Village Courts Act 1974*.
29 For background see Jean G. Zorn, 1990, 'Customary law in the Papua New Guinea Village Courts,' *Contemporary Pacific* 2(2): 39–66. For analysis and discussion of the performance of Village Courts, see

Paul Hasluck's initiatives following the *Derham Report* also established the current institutional framework of criminal justice. The western law concept of 'crime' relies on the premise that crimes are committed against the state in general rather than against individuals. They should therefore be dealt with by agents of the state: police with a monopoly over the use of legitimate force to maintain internal order; centralised courts which focus only on individual rights and responsibility and ignore the social context of crime; and a penal system designed to punish the offender but ignore the victim.[30]

Independence and law reform

The many liberation movements of the 1960s and 1970s emerging in Australian political life—espousing decolonisation and the civil rights of ethnic, gender and sexual minorities, opposing the Vietnam War, and so on—also impacted on the emerging intelligentsia of PNG in its decolonisation era.[31] Self-government and Independence were imminent, and a political system was to be set in place which would best suit the needs of a new nation.[32] Legal transformation was seen as crucial to this process. The law was no longer to be imposed from outside. The new nationalists, including Chief Minister Michael Somare, called for 'a system of laws appropriate to a self-governing, independent nation … it must respond to our own needs and values. We do not want to create an imitation of the Australian, English or American legal system.'[33]

---

e.g., Melissa Demian, 2003, 'Custom in the courtroom, law in the village: legal transformations in Papua New Guinea,' *Journal of the Royal Anthropological Institute* 9: 97–115; M. Goddard, 2005, *The Unseen City: Anthropological Perspectives on Port Moresby, Papua New Guinea*, Canberra: Pandanus Press; David Lipset, 2004, '"The Trial": A parody of the law amid the mockery of men in post-colonial Papua New Guinea,' *Journal of the Royal Anthropological Institute* 10: 63–89; Jean G. Zorn, 1994–95, 'Women, custom and state law in Papua New Guinea,' *Third World Legal Studies*, 169–205; Zorn, 2003, 'Custom then and now: the changing Melanesian family,' in *Passage of Change: Law, Society and Governance in the Pacific*, ed. Anita Jowitt and Tess Newton Cain, Canberra: Pandanus Books, 95–124.

30 Sinclair Dinnen, 1998, 'Criminal justice reform in Papua New Guinea,' in *Governance and Reform in the South Pacific*, ed. Peter Larmour, Canberra: National Centre for Development Studies, The Australian National University, 253–72, 254–55.

31 I recall a UPNG classmate intently reading Dee Brown's classic *Bury My Heart at Wounded Knee*; a student march to protest the overthrow of the Allende regime in Chile; an emerging student leader starting a Black Power movement; and my many woman friends urging me to join their women's action movement. Much of this activity was confined to the academic and political circles of Port Moresby, but these friends and students were nevertheless the Papua New Guineans destined to become future leaders in many walks of life; and see Jean G. Zorn, 2010, 'In memory of Bernard Narokobi,' *Pacificurrents* 1.2 and 2.1, online: intersections.anu.edu.au/pacificurrents/zorn_memorial.htm, accessed June 2010.

32 Donald Denoon, 2005, *A Trial Separation: Australia and the Decolonisation of Papua New Guinea*, Canberra: Pandanus Books, 70–83.

33 Abdul Paliwala and David Weisbrot, 1982, 'Changing society through law: an introduction,' in *Law and Social Change in Papua New Guinea*, ed. David Weisbrot, Abdul Paliwala and Akilagpa Sawyerr, Sydney, Melbourne, Brisbane, Adelaide, Perth: Butterworths, 3–12, 4.

This new system, part of what was sometimes dubbed the 'Melanesian Way,'[34] was in reality a mixture of local customs, the principles of Christianity, the ideals of human rights, and 'tradition' as conceived for various socio-political purposes. Custom was to be researched, constructed and where necessary formulated *ab initio* to provide a basis for this new system. Village Courts were established and directed to apply custom, not law, to a specified range of matters at village level.[35] The PNG Law Reform Commission commenced operations shortly before Independence, when it received a statutory mandate to 'make recommendations in relation to the development of new approaches to and new concepts of the law in keeping with and responsive to the changing needs of Papua New Guinea society and of individual members of that society.'[36]

Even before the establishment of the Law Reform Commission, the Crown Law Department, soon to become the Department of Justice, began work in 1973, proposing a review of the criminal law with a view to undertaking a thorough reform in order to bring the laws more into line with people's perceptions of unacceptable behaviour. In 1974, the reform process commenced by replacing the adopted criminal code of each territory with a unified *Criminal Code*.[37] Part of the review process was a review of sexual offences, already under way.[38] The report was completed in 1975, with a note that it could be of use to the Law Reform Commission, which had already commenced operations with reviews of the minor offences found in the Native Regulations and the Police Offences Ordinances.[39] A comprehensive overhaul of these laws was recommended by the Commission to Parliament and reforms were enacted.

Soon after Independence however, the PNG government lost interest in law reform, especially as it related to social issues. It appeared more preoccupied with roads and bridges, schools and hospitals, and the march towards 'development.'[40] Bernard Narokobi describes the slow demise of successive

---

34 Narokobi, *The Melanesian Way*; Narokobi, 1989, *Lo Bilong Yumi Yet: Law and Custom in Melanesia*, Suva: Institute of Pacific Studies of the University of the South Pacific and the Melanesian Institute for Pastoral and Socio-Economic Service.

35 These courts however appear to have developed in many places into a system based on principles of justice developed in an ad hoc manner, with little regard to accepted customary norms: see Demian, 'Custom in the courtroom, law in the village'; Michael Goddard, 2009, *Substantial Justice: An Anthropology of Village Courts in Papua New Guinea*, New York and Oxford: Berghahn Books.

36 *Law Reform Commission Act* (Chapter 18) Section 9(1)(e).

37 Schedule to the *Criminal Code Act* 1974.

38 Marilyn Strathern, 1975, *Report on Questionnaire Relating to Sexual Offences as Defined in the Criminal Code*, report prepared for New Guinea Research Unit, Boroko, Papua New Guinea.

39 Law Reform Commission of Papua New Guinea 1975a, *Report No.1: Report on Summary Offences*, Waigani: Law Reform Commission of Papua New Guinea; Law Reform Commission of Papua New Guinea 1975b, *Report No. 2: Report on Abolition of Native Regulations*, Waigani: Law Reform Commission of Papua New Guinea.

40 Peter King, Wendy Lee and Vincent Warakai, 1985, 'Editors' Introduction,' in *From Rhetoric to Reality? Papua New Guinea's Eight Point Plan and National Goals after a Decade*, ed. Peter King, Wendy Lee and Vincent Warakai, Waigani, Papua New Guinea: University of Papua New Guinea Press, 1–14, 2; Bernard Narokobi, 1982, 'History and movement in law reform in Papua New Guinea,' in *Law and Social Change in Papua New Guinea*, ed. David Weisbrot, Abdul Paliwala and Akilagpa Sawyerr, 13–24, 20.

governments' interest in reforming the law and introducing custom into the legal system, which was still dominated by the 'Eurocentric prejudice' that, in the absence of an indigenous legal system, the only choice was to introduce 'the legal system of civilization.'[41]

The proposed review of the *Criminal Code* was never completed,[42] despite some further comment and work.[43] In 1992, when I was working for the Law Reform Commission, Commissioners directed the re-commencement of work on the review of sexual offences in the *Criminal Code*, which led to the coordination of Commission activities with the National AIDS Committee, a committee operating at the time to advise the Secretary for Health on HIV/AIDS matters.[44] This strategy proved successful but sidelined the Commission's criminal review work.[45]

The only other significant reform of relevance in PNG is contained in the recently enacted *Criminal Code (Sexual Offences and Crimes Against Children) Act* 2002 which made extensive amendments to the *Criminal Code*, mainly in order to accord with PNG's international obligations under the *Convention on the Rights of the Child* (CRC).[46] This amendment was the result of extensive work on family and sexual violence which started in 2000,[47] and replaced much of the archaic wording of the original Code; rendered gender-neutral many of the offences previously associated only with women and girl victims; introduced major reforms relating to child sexual abuse (including child prostitution and child pornography); and criminalised rape within marriage.[48] The Bill was

---

41 Narokobi, 'History and movement in law reform in Papua New Guinea,' 22. He was echoing the words of Justice Gore, long-time colonial judge.
42 See Law Reform Commission, *Report No. 1: Report on Summary Offences*: 7.
43 Marilyn Strathern, 1976, 'Crime and correction: the place of prisons in Papua New Guinea,' *Melanesian Law Journal* 4(1): 67–93.
44 The term 'HIV/AIDS' is no longer internationally acceptable: UNAIDS, 2011, *UNAIDS Terminology Guidelines (January 2011)*, online: http://www.unaids.org/en/media/unaids/contentassets/documents/document/2011/jc1336_unaids_terminology_guide_en.pdf, accessed 8 June 2011.
45 I was the Commission's representative on the Committee. My preliminary work on HIV management law at that time resulted in several publications. See Christine Stewart, 1993, *Law, Ethics and HIV/AIDS: Existing Law of Papua New Guinea*, report prepared for Law Reform Commission of Papua New Guinea and Papua New Guinea Department of Health, Boroko, Papua New Guinea: Law Reform Commission of Papua New Guinea and Papua New Guinea Department of Health; Stewart, 1993, 'Existing law on HIV/AIDS in Papua New Guinea,' in *Law, Ethics and HIV: Proceedings of the UNDP Intercountry Consulatation, Cebu, Philippines 3–6 May, 1993*, ed. Robert A. Glick, New Delhi: United Nations Development Programme, 133–50; Christine Stewart and Pascoe Kase, 1993, 'Law, custom and the AIDS epidemic in Papua New Guinea,' in *Law, Ethics and HIV: Proceedings of the UNDP Intercountry Consulatation, Cebu, Philippines 3–6 May, 1993*, ed. Robert A. Glick, New Delhi: United Nations Development Programme, 63–76, and eventually led to the production of the *HIV/AIDS Management and Prevention Act* 2003 under the AusAID-funded programme NHASP.
46 *Convention on the Rights of the Child*, GA res 44/25, annex, 44 UN GAOR Supp (No 49) at 167, UN Doc A/44/49 (1989), entered into force 2 September, 1990.
47 See Christine Bradley, 2001, *Family and Sexual Violence in PNG: An Integrated Long-term Strategy*, Institute of National Affairs, Discussion paper no. 84.
48 For a detailed description and discussion, see John Y. Luluaki, 2003, 'Sexual crimes against and exploitation of children and the law in Papua New Guinea,' *International Journal of Law, Policy and the Family*

brought to Parliament as a private Member's Bill by the Minister for Social Welfare and Development Dame Carol Kidu M.P., widow of former Chief Justice Sir Buri Kidu. She was in the anomalous position of having promoted much of the work which produced the Bill but was unable to move it as a government Member as it was outside her portfolio, and she was unable to secure the official approval of an almost completely male-dominated Cabinet for it to be moved by the Minister for Justice. However, once it reached the floor of Parliament, it was successfully passed.

A further law, the *HIV/AIDS Management and Prevention Act* 2003, prohibits discrimination against people presumed to be infected or affected by HIV. The law was crafted to ensure that criminalised groups were afforded this protection. Again, the scope of this law was restricted by similar Westminster principles of Ministerial portfolio responsibility. HIV matters were the responsibility of the Minister for Health at the time, while responsibility for the laws criminalising sexual activity came within the portfolio of the Minister for Justice.[49] Hence a law dealing with HIV could not directly decriminalise either sex work or sodomy, but at least some measure of protection against discrimination has been provided.

To sum up, the only major response to the call for reform to accord with 'our own needs and values,' as Chief Minister Somare put it in the epigraph above, was in the establishment of Village Courts, set up to dispense customary justice. But their jurisdiction was seriously circumscribed by the law which established them.[50] Otherwise, the state legal system has remained unchanged in any major way. Most of the criminal law reforms proposed by the Law Reform Commission were never completed or implemented.

Foreign laws criminalising sexuality were introduced into PNG by direct legislative action, but recent reform initiatives have so far failed to remove them from the statute book. Changes to the law however can come about in another way: through reliance on case decisions which interpret that legislation or prior principles of common law. Both these routes have been taken in defining and setting parameters for the criminalisation of prostitution and sodomy in PNG. I deal first with the criminalisation of the sex trade, or prostitution, as the law prefers to name it.

17(3): 275–307.
49 While preparing the Bill for this Act (see n45), I was dismayed at the limitations which the portfolio system of government placed on our ability to take any initiatives towards decriminalisation.
50 *Village Courts Act* 1989 Part V. Excesses of jurisdiction occurred frequently, sometimes to the extent of infringing constitutional rights. However they could be, and often were, corrected by appeal to the formal courts, as I have discussed above.

Defending public decency: Criminalising the sex trade

> The two pillars upon which our society is founded are the Christian principles and the fountains of wisdom and good sense of our people: our customs.... Looking at custom in general, it is plain that it was a matter of a very serious affront to the dignity of the family if a woman was to sell her body for reward. In many communities such a thing was not heard of.... However, it was a custom in some Melanesian communities for men to lend their wives or daughters or sisters as part of hospitality package [sic] to a visitor.
>
> Acting Justice Narokobi, Lae 1980.[51]

The law and the prostitute: From Victorian England to modern PNG

Helen Self traces the beginnings of prostitution legislation in England to mediaeval ecclesiastical control of sexuality.[52] From the sixteenth century, the break-up of the monasteries saw massive displacement and increased marginalisation and poverty of the peasantry. Single and pregnant women were a burden on the community, so domestic service was pauperised and prostitution was subsumed with vagrancy as a potential cause of disorder. Women selling sex for survival were cruelly punished. In the nineteenth century, the Industrial Revolution instigated further population movements and a penalisation of 'vagrants,' including single women. For the first time, in 1824, the term 'common prostitute' was deployed to distinguish a group of women as separate and identifiable legal subjects. Its vagueness meant that any poor woman was suspect.[53] The 1860s saw the introduction of the UK Contagious Diseases Acts, designed to prevent the spread of venereal disease among troops quartered in garrison towns by acknowledging the necessity of prostitution and subjecting it to regulation.[54] These Acts were repealed not long afterwards, but this did not result in the decriminalisation of prostitution. Rather, moves towards social purity and the fear of white slave trafficking made soliciting in public places

---

51   *Monika Jon and Others v Dominik Kuman and Others* (Unreported) N253, 8 August 1980 (*Monika Jon's Case*).
52   This account is based on Helen J. Self, 2003, *Prostitution, Women and Misuse of the Law: The Fallen Daughters of Eve*, London and Portland OR: Frank Cass Publishers.
53   Ibid., 37–40.
54   Walkowitz, 1982, *Prostitution and Victorian Society: Women, Class, and the State*, Cambridge England; New York: Cambridge University Press.

an offence from 1885 onwards.[55] This drove prostitutes off the streets and into the arms of pimps, so an offence of 'living on the earnings of prostitution' was created at the end of the nineteenth century.

Although some writers consider that the regulation and criminalisation of prostitution and associated activities have been the norm throughout the English-speaking world,[56] others challenge this view, arguing that the system was limited and site-specific, and pointing among other instances to the many African colonies which failed to introduce such regulation.[57] Australia itself was originally a heterogeneous collection of colonies, with varying attitudes to the regulation of sexuality and sex work. For example South Australia, never having been a penal colony and therefore having no garrison to protect from disease, did not introduce prostitution regulations, while Queensland and New South Wales, the states from which much of early PNG law derived, did. Various factors underpinned the readiness by the administration of the PNG Territories to accept the criminalisation of prostitution: concern about the apparent licentious behaviour of some villagers, for example;[58] and most noticeably, the Wau gold rush of 1926, which occasioned a regulation preventing single white women from entering the Territory of New Guinea in an effort to exclude prostitutes—a prime example of the deployment of colonial law to regulate the (female) colonists rather than the colonised.[59]

However, it was not the letter of the law so much as the desire to proscribe prostitution which governed the colonial Administration's attitude to the growing sex trade. In 1960, a District Officer in Papua wrote to the Director of the Department of Native Affairs, pointing out that the repeal of the *Prisons Ordinance* (Papua) had inadvertently effected a repeal of Regulation 85 of the *Native Regulations* (Papua) which had hitherto prevented 'female natives' from engaging in prostitution.[60] He explained that he had encountered 'a fairly flagrant case of prostitution' and wished to proceed against the woman. He opined that there was a need to maintain some measure of sanction over prostitution, particularly on stations where there are collections of 'single men with money to

---

55 Self, *Prostitution, Women and Misuse of the Law*, 42–44, 53.
56 Philippa Levine, 2003, *Prostitution, Race, and Politics: Policing Venereal Disease in the British Empire*, New York: Routledge; Christine Harcourt, Sandra Egger and Basil Donovan, 2005, 'Sex work and the law,' *Sexual Health* 2(3): 121–28, 121.
57 Richard Phillips, 2005, 'Heterogeneous imperialism and the regulation of sexuality in British West Africa,' *Journal of the History of Sexuality* 14(3): 291–362.
58 Jan Roberts, 1996, *Voices from a Lost World: Australian Women and Children in Papua New Guinea before the Japanese Invasion*, Alexandria, NSW: Millenium Books, 97.
59 Maria Lepowsky, 2001, 'The Queen of Sudest: white women and colonial cultures in British New Guinea and Papua, in *In Colonial New Guinea: Anthropological Perspectives*, ed. Naomi McPherson, Pittsburgh: University of Pittsburgh Press, 125–50, 144; Roberts, *Voices from a Lost World*, 55, 198. Wau is the name of a township and colonial subdistrict in the mountains to the south-west of Lae, in Morobe Province.
60 The wording of the corresponding offence in the *Native Administration Regulations* (New Guinea) Section 87 was considerably broader: 'Any native woman who practices prostitution …'

spare.' The Secretary for Law advised the Director that there was no suggestion that a new regulation should be brought into operation, and agreed that there was no offence of soliciting in Papua which could be used (although there was a soliciting offence in New Guinea). He did however conclude that 'it may be noted that under Section 4 of the *Vagrancy Ordinance* a person in fact a common prostitute and who wanders in any place of public resort (inter alia) and behaves in an indecent manner may be convicted of an offence.'[61]

Prosecutors appear to have taken the hint. Joan Johnstone in her study of Gumini sex work in Port Moresby in the late 1960s noted that women were regularly prosecuted under the Territory of Papua's *Vagrancy Ordinance*. She attended several District Court hearings, and noted that 'the Court cases involving *bisnis-meris* which I observed each lasted approximately ten minutes. The woman accused was brought in by a policeman who stood before the magistrate. The police prosecutor then said to the woman in Tok Pisin, abruptly: "You got work? You got house? You got money?" to which the women almost invariably answered, "No," to each question.' The police prosecutor would then address the magistrate, still speaking in Tok Pisin, 'This woman has no work, no house and no money. She is a vagrant,' and the magistrate would convict her.[62]

Despite the fact that the law of the Territory of New Guinea had both a soliciting offence in the *Police Offences Ordinance* Section 38 and a prostitution offence in the *Native Administration Regulations*, it seems that vagrancy legislation was used there as well in prostitution cases. A newspaper report from 1969, for example, tells of a Rabaul woman who was imprisoned for two weeks 'for having insufficient means of support,' the wording of the charge under vagrancy legislation, upon her admission that she received $20 from an act of prostitution.[63] Vagrancy was also the charge used in Lae in an attempt to control the growing numbers of women arriving in the town via the Highlands Highway to sell sex.[64] It is understandable that the use of vagrancy legislation might have been convenient when proof of selling sex could not easily be adduced, but its use in this instance, where a confession was forthcoming, is surprising. Whether they realised it or not, the prosecutors involved were actually echoing the vagrancy control processes of the sixteenth to nineteenth centuries in the UK, as described above. The incongruity of a conviction in the Territory of New Guinea for insufficient means of support of a woman who admitted to receiving $20 (a good deal of money in 1969) seems to have escaped the officers involved in this particular instance of the dispensation of justice.

---

61   PNG National Archives Accession No.64 Box 1316 File N1-6-7, letter W.A.Tomasetti, District Officer, to Director, Department of Native Affairs, Konedobu, 23 May 1960.
62   Johnstone, 'The Gumini *Bisnis-Meri*,' 227.
63   'Tolai woman gaoled for two weeks,' *Post-Courier*, 19 November 1969, 20. It can be inferred from the report that this woman sold sex regularly, but her (known, named) pimp was acquitted of any wrongdoing.
64   E.g., 'Get out of town, court tells 4 vagrants,' *Post-Courier*, 4 April 1975, 9.

Prosecuting prostitution in an independent nation

At Independence, the new state attempted to follow emerging trends to law reform world-wide. The PNG Law Reform Commission took just three months to prepare and present its first report, on 'the appropriate means of restating and modernizing the law relating to Summary Offences.'[65] The Commission noted the need for such laws to enable people 'to live together harmoniously in the Papua New Guinea of today.' The police offences laws of Papua and New Guinea were written decades earlier, and adopted virtually unchanged from countries whose culture differed greatly from the cultures of PNG. A new summary offences law was recommended, which should be 'written very carefully to include only those offences which most of the Papua New Guinea people think are wrong. Care must also be taken to limit the powers of the policemen and the courts and protect the rights of the people.'[66]

Regarding prostitution, the Commission said that the present laws were 'most unsatisfactory.' It recommended the retention of offences relating to brothels, and living off the money made by prostitutes, but saw no point in retaining the offence of soliciting found in the New Guinea law, or extending that offence to Papua. It considered that sufficient laws already existed to control prostitutes who were causing trouble in public places, and to control the spread of venereal disease.[67]

The Commission also recommended the repeal of the 'lawful means of support' provisions of the Papuan *Vagrancy Ordinance* and the equivalent provisions of the New Guinea *Police Offences Ordinance*,[68] although the fact that these vagrancy laws were used to prosecute prostitution was not mentioned in the Commission Report. Instead, reference was made to their use in attempting to curb urban migration and rising unemployment in the formal employment sector, but the majority, with only one dissenting voice, held the view that, using the criminal law to control social and economic problems is not only ineffectual but also inappropriate and unnecessary.'[69] The Commission concluded by requesting the retention of the summary offences reference, in order to investigate whether any further measures should be taken regarding prostitution.[70] But this work was never completed.

---

65 Law Reform Commission, *Report No. 1: Report on Summary Offences*, covering letter to the Minister for Justice. 'Summary offences' or 'police offences' are minor offences prosecuted in inferior courts.
66 Ibid., 6.
67 Ibid., 22.
68 Ibid., 14.
69 Ibid., 15.
70 Ibid., 22.

The Tale of Anna and Monika

The Summary Offences Bill prepared by the Commission was enacted by the National Parliament in 1977. But the reforms which abolished soliciting and vagrancy laws did not daunt the police, who started charging women under Section 55(1) of the new *Summary Offences Act* 1977, which reads: 'A person who knowingly lives wholly or in part on the earnings of prostitution is guilty of an offence.'

In 1978, just one year later, the new law was tested before the National Court in Rabaul in *Anna Wemay's Case*.[71] Four women, through the Public Solicitor,[72] appealed against their conviction and sentence for 'living on the earnings of prostitution.' The women had admitted to 'being prostitutes' and having sex for money. The Australian judge, Justice Wilson, reasoned that he had to decide whether, 'the prostitute herself, as distinct from the madam, the tout, the bully, the protector, or the pimp, may be convicted of a breach of s. 55(1).'[73] Common sense would seem to say: no. The Law Reform Commission had already said: no. And the wording of the Act itself seems to support an answer of: no. Section 55 goes on to state

(2) The fact that—

   (a) a person lives with, or is constantly in the company of a prostitute; or

   (b) a person has exercised some degree of control or influence over the movements of a prostitute in such a manner as to show that that person is assisting her to commit prostitution,

is prima facie evidence that that person is knowingly living on the earnings of prostitution.

This can be taken to indicate that the section is concerned with criminalisation of pimping (the other two sections of Part VII deal with keeping a brothel and suppression of brothels). On the whole, then, the preferable view would seem to be that the prostitute herself does not commit an offence.

In support of this interpretation, the appellants asked the judge to consider what the Parliament may have intended when passing the Act. They urged him to consider the report of the Law Reform Commission. He was asked to take into account the fact that the repealed *Police Offences Ordinance* (New Guinea)

---

71 *Anna Wemay and Others v Kepas Tumdual* [1978] PNGLR 173 (*Anna Wemay's Case*).
72 An Office established to provide legal aid, mainly in criminal matters: *Constitution* Sections 175–6.
73 *Anna Wemay's Case*, at 174.

had contemplated three classes of offender: the prostitute who solicits, the male persons living off the earnings of prostitution, and the keeper of a brothel or a 'house of ill repute.' He was asked to agree that the first of these offenders, the prostitute, had been omitted from the 1977 Act.

But the judge would have none of it. He declared: 'It is beyond question that a prostitute who is paid money for services rendered by her as a prostitute which money she would not otherwise have available to her for living purposes but for the fact that she was a prostitute is living at least in part on the earnings of prostitution.'[74] He did not consider that the word 'male' might have been omitted from the new Act so as to conform to the constitutional guarantee of freedom from discrimination on the grounds of sex, as it is termed in the *Constitution*, or to bring the female 'madam' into the purview of the Act. He did not consider the possibilities of male prostitution and the effect of the wording of both the old and the new law. He did not acknowledge that the ordinary meaning of words in a statute is only to be taken where there is no ambiguity. He did not even acknowledge the possibility of any ambiguity at all in Section 55. He simply followed a process of strict, literal interpretation of the law, which, he decided, led him to conclude that a woman living on the earnings of her own prostitution was committing an offence under Section 55(1). Even if he were to consider the history of the legislation of police or summary offences, he thought that

> it might be argued that, when the legislature repealed and did not re-enact the section dealing with prostitutes who solicit and when the legislature widened the scope of the provisions regarding those who live on prostitution (by deleting the word 'male'), it intended that prostitutes who, by virtue of the very nature of their occupation or 'profession,' make a living or seek to make a living by having sexual intercourse with men for reward, fall within the ambit of s. 55(1).[75]

If the challenge had been successful, it would have legalised prostitution. A challenge two years later almost succeeded, when a similar case, *Monika Jon and Others v Dominik Kuman and Others* came before the National Court.[76] Again, the women involved admitted to receiving money, or money was found on them, so they were convicted in the District Court under Section 55(1). This time, however, the presiding judge was Acting Justice Narokobi, Papua New Guinea's leading proponent of the development of an autochthonous jurisprudence,[77] and formerly Chairman of the Law Reform Commission when its *Report No. 1* was prepared. Naturally enough, he considered that 'it would be useful in ambiguity and if it would help to discern the will or intent of the legislature,

---

74 Ibid., at 177.
75 Ibid.
76 *Monika Jon's Case*.
77 Fully expounded in Narokobi, Lo Bilong Yumi Yet.

to look to the report of the Commission.... It would be a chase after a soulless intent if courts were to restrict their inquiry to the four corners of a statutory enactment, in cases of uncertainty.'[78]

He was now invited to distinguish *Anna Wemay's Case*, and that is what he did. He noted that each woman had admitted to a single act of sex for which she received money. There was no evidence of any intent to sell sex on an ongoing basis, no course of conduct. He held that a person making a living out of prostitution would be committing a crime, but not the 'so called "K2.00 bush" lady,' and acquitted all three appellants.

But he was not invited, nor did he attempt, to overturn Wilson J's decision in *Anna Wemay's Case*, although he could have done so, as the National Court is not bound by its own prior decisions. Today, women continue to be charged under Section 55(1) of the *Summary Offences Act*.[79] Moreover, Narokobi AJ's reasoning is not followed. It seems to have escaped both police and prosecutors that *Monika Jon's Case* requires proof of a 'course of conduct.'

Gendering prostitution

Another point that has largely escaped law-enforcers is that of the gendering of the offence. From the outset, the legal system assumed that it was a woman selling (or being sold for) sex—the Native Regulations of both territories are specific in this regard.[80] The *Police Offences Ordinance* of New Guinea at Section 38 refers simply to a 'common prostitute who solicits, importunes or accosts,' but the related offences of pimping and brothel-keeping at Section 79 refer to use of a house 'by a female for purposes of prostitution' and 'any male person ... living wholly or in part on the earnings of the prostitute.' It was this gendering which so concerned the Law Reform Commission in its review, and which produced the carefully crafted gender-neutral language of the *Summary Offences Act*, one result of which enabled prosecutions of male prostitutes. But it seems that this never happened, despite the courts already being aware of male prostitution around the country. One such example is Siune Wel.

---

78   *Monika Jon's Case*.
79   See discussion of *Monika Jon's Case* above, and my discussion of the Three-Mile Guesthouse Raid in Chapter Five. In 2004, the charges in the raid prosecutions were all laid under this provision.
80   *Native Regulations* 1922 (Papua), Regulation 79(6) and (7), in which latter sub-regulation she is termed an 'abandoned and dissolute woman'; *Native Administration Regulations* 1924 (New Guinea): Regulations 86 and 87, where the terminology is more direct: 'any native woman who practices prostitution.'

The Tale of Siune Wel[81]

In 1972, Siune Wel of Simbu District in the Highlands was fifteen years old. He had already spent time in prison in Lae the previous year for 'permitting acts of carnal knowledge' (sodomy) and for vagrancy, and possibly other minor offences too. Now he was back in Kundiawa, the Simbu District headquarters, and back to hustling. He had sold sex on several occasions to Yawi, a prison warder. One night he also offered sex to Yawi's friend Sitai, another warder. It seems that Sitai informed the police, and all three were arrested.

Charge sheets drawn up for both Yawi and Sitai noted that each 'appeared to have been the victim of a male prostitute.'[82] This apparently was the subjective opinion of the police who drew up the charge sheet, but was then reflected in the decision of the court. Yawi and Sitai, the sexual penetrators in each case, pleaded guilty and were discharged on recognisance of $50 to be of good behaviour for one year. Wel, on the other hand, who originally claimed rape and then pleaded guilty, was sentenced to nine months in hard labour.

***

In similar vein, *Kausigor's Case*,[83] related and discussed in detail below, opens with two men meeting in a Wewak tavern in 1969, and agreeing to have sex. Money was exchanged before the two left together. It would not have been possible at the time to lay a charge of selling sex in either case, as the law still applied to prostitution by females only. But the case shows that the courts and the police were not unaware that males were involved in prostitution. Other cases refer to the purchase of sex by expatriates,[84] and Robert Aldrich notes that in 1959 the then Chief Justice of PNG was expressing concern about 'more than a suggestion' of male prostitution.[85] So even the court record extending back before Independence showed that males sold sex. Nevertheless, the prostitute, whether a submissive victim or a transgressing agent, continued to be gendered female.

It is at this point that an overlap between the criminalisation of selling sex and homosexual activity becomes apparent, so it is appropriate that I now examine the criminalisation of sodomy in the received law of PNG.

---

81 Based on *R v Siune Wel* PNG National Archives Accession 454 Box 14625 Crown Prosecution File 5-9471; *R v Hugh William Sitai* PNG National Archives Accession 454 Box 14625 Crown Prosecution File 5-9468; *R v Yawi Huaimbore* PNG National Archives Accession 454 Box 14625 Crown Prosecution File 5-9474 (*Siune Wel cases*).
82 A poor-quality photocopy, made by the PNG National Archives, is in my possession.
83 *R v Clemence Mandoma Kausigor; R v Piki Piliu* (Unreported) FC3, 7 November 1969 (*Kausigor's Case*).
84 E.g., *R v Bates* (Unreported) SC255, 9 October 1962.
85 Robert Aldrich, 2003, *Colonialism and Homosexuality*, London and New York: Routledge, 252.

Enforcing sexual morality: Criminalising sodomy

The Tale of Frank and Johnny[86]

You entered a [hotel] room with an adult European ... [and] started having sexual intercourse with each other ... the Hotel security members ... upon seeing you through the louvres naked ... alerted the management and the police.... Your lawyer has specifically ask[ed] that I consider ... that it was a consented act of intercourse between two adults and no one sustained any injury.... Carnal knowledge against the order of nature is a serious and heinous offence ... it is ... 'the behaviour of animals and must be stopped' ... as a result of your action you have placed you, your parents and members of your immediate family vulnerable to ridicule, shame and sexual advances.... I now commit you and sentence you to two years imprisonment in hard labour.

Acting Justice Pitpit to Johnny Mala, 1996.[87]

Frank, the 'adult European' in this case, had always been careful. He grew up knowing he was 'different,' knowing what he liked, but he had formed no relationships. He knew male-male sex was illegal in his home country, he had heard occasional reports of men being caught, so when he first went to work in PNG, he avoided the gay set around town. He was too scared.

Frank was responsible for the financial and accounting matters of a large business enterprise with branches country-wide, and his work took him to several of these locations. He was keenly aware that his sexuality made him an excellent target for blackmail, even kidnapping. But he had never heard of anyone being arrested.

It was in PNG that he had his first sexual experience, formed some life-long friendships, even met 'the love of his life.' Apart from that, he established many good friendships among the Papua New Guineans he met at work and after hours. In small provincial towns, there was nothing else to do in the evenings but to go to the local club. 'Nice people, no complications, good times,' he recalls. Some of these relationships were sexual, some were not. His partners were usually older men, with reason to hide. Many were married—Frank knew that

---

86 Compiled from interview 12 November 2005 and the text of a letter Frank (not his real name) wrote to friends on 6 December 1996, shortly after he fled Papua New Guinea.
87 *The State v Johnny Mala*, (Unreported, Unnumbered) National Court; CR 96 of 1997; 25–26 February 1997 (*Johnny Mala's Case*). I acquired a copy of the case decision from friends. However, the file was missing from the National Court Registry when I searched during fieldwork 2006–07, although the case appeared in the Register.

the pressure on PNG men to marry and maintain a semblance of 'respectability' was enormous. Many of his friends were from the armed forces. In fact, the only hint of blackmail he ever encountered came from a policeman he entertained one night. 'I can have you arrested for this,' the man said afterwards. Frank paid him off and left town. 'Who would I report it to?' he asked wryly.

For nearly twenty years, Frank lived worked and travelled in PNG, maintaining his caution, enjoying his friendships and his relationships. He still doesn't know why it went wrong when he met Johnny. He was near the end of a regular visit to a provincial town. He dined at his hotel with some PNG friends. Johnny was among them, and indicated that he wanted to spend the night with Frank. Frank recalls that Johnny claimed to be twenty, although the sole daily newspaper report elected to put his age at nineteen, thereby setting up the somewhat sensational headline: 'Teenager jailed for sex "against the order of nature."'[88]

Frank is sure that he closed the curtains, and thinks the breeze from the ceiling fan must have blown them aside. Still, it could not have been easy for the lurking security guard to spy on them. In his subsequent statement, the security guard claimed he suspected a drugs or arms deal. But that is not what he saw. However, he knew enough of the law to call the police anyway.

A total of six policemen and three security guards burst into the room, and the pair was taken off to the local police station, where after some banter and deliberation, the sergeant decided not to hold them overnight, joking that the cells were already full with about seventeen of 'the *real* perpetrators of crime.'[89] The pair returned next morning to be charged. Even then, the police assured them that prison would not be involved. More probably they would face a hefty fine, but Frank might be deported. Johnny himself was laughing off the whole incident, and saw no reason to dissemble. But Frank was concerned. He paid the K500 bail for himself and Johnny, and returned to Port Moresby with his committal hearing still not completed. There he was advised quietly by lawyers, employers and friends to 'do a runner.'

He took their advice, packed lightly and was taken to the airport by a friend next morning, 'a nervous wreck.' Would the police be there? What if his name was already on the Immigration list? But by an amazing stroke of good luck, it was the very day Michael Jackson arrived in Port Moresby in his 707 jet, and all attention was focused on this big event. Frank boarded his flight safely and fled.

Nearly ten years later, back home, Frank still has not fully recovered. The police had asked so many questions, and wanted full disclosure of all his income, assets and liabilities, all taken down on police forms. He was too frightened even to

---

88 'Teenager jailed for sex "against the order of nature,"' *Post-Courier*, 23 April 1997, 12.
89 Frank's account of the sergeant's words.

start his own business, so found a job and spends his time going to work, coming home—and communicating as best he can with friends in Papua New Guinea. He is very concerned about Johnny, but has been unable to contact him. He was horrified to learn of the two-year prison sentence imposed on Johnny.[90] Maybe it was greatly reduced with parole?

Frank still doesn't know why the police came down so hard on him and Johnny. He has only a few vague ideas, but no real theories. Perhaps the police were just bored stiff in a little provincial town, and looking for something to occupy themselves? He wishes that the security guard had taken the opportunity to make some fast money—Frank would gladly have paid him off. He wishes that Johnny had not urged complete honesty in the first place. If Johnny had left town as well, surely the police would not have bothered chasing him—they probably only persisted with Johnny's case, Frank surmises, because they had missed out on him, the wealthy expatriate. His feelings of loss have been compounded by guilt.

Law, rights and morality

Johnny Mala's Case is one of the very few recent sodomy cases which involve consenting adults in private.[91] It raises but does not question the law's continued right to intrude 'into the bedroom,' to the extent of imprisoning one of those involved, and requiring the other to abandon his career, his friends and much of his identity and personal security.

In PNG, the English-law crimes of same-sex activity were imported in the Native Regulations of both Territories, and the *Criminal Code*. The New Guinea Regulations from 1936 contained an offence of 'Indecent Practices':

> Any native who, whether in public or private, commits an act of indecency with another male native, or procures another male native to commit an act of indecency with him, or attempts to procure the commission of any such act by any male native with himself, shall be guilty of an offence.
>
> Penalty: Imprisonment of six months.[92]

The Papuan Regulation was less explicit:

> Any native who indecently assaults any other native shall be liable on conviction to imprisonment for any period not exceeding Six months.[93]

---

90 See *Johnny Mala's Case*.
91 For a summary of cases of forced sodomy or cases involving under-aged participants, see Appendix 4.
92 *Native Administration Regulations* (New Guinea) Regulation 105.
93 *Native Regulations* (Papua) Regulation 87.

The Regulations applied only to 'natives.' The *Criminal Code* was employed to prosecute sodomy by male colonialists. For all of the twentieth century, the Code offences were:

208. Unnatural offences.

(1) A person who—

(a)   has carnal knowledge of any person against the order of nature; or

(b)   has carnal knowledge of an animal; or

(c)   permits a male person to have carnal knowledge of him or her against the order of nature,

is guilty of a crime.

Penalty: Imprisonment for a term not exceeding 14 years.

210. Indecent treatment of boys under 14.

(2) A person who unlawfully and indecently deals with a boy under the age of 14 years is guilty of a crime.

Penalty: Imprisonment for a term not exceeding seven years.

211. Indecent practices between males.

(1) A male person who, whether in public or private—

(a)   commits an act of gross indecency with another male person; or

(b)   procures another male person to commit an act of gross indecency with him; or

(c)   attempts to procure the commission of any such act by a male person with himself or with another male person,

is guilty of a misdemeanour.

Penalty: Imprisonment for a term not exceeding three years.

These sections were renumbered Sections 210, 211 and 212 by the *Criminal Code Act* 1974 which amalgamated and revised the Codes of the two Territories. The subsequent 2002 amendments to the *Criminal Code* altered the wording but not the substance of (now) Section 210, replacing 'carnal knowledge against the order of nature' with 'sexually penetrates.'[94] Section 211 was repealed altogether, as 'indecently dealing' with an underage boy is now covered by gender-neutral offences of child sexual abuse which appear elsewhere in the Code. A person who sexually penetrates a child under sixteen is liable to imprisonment for a maximum twenty-five years, or life if the child is under twelve years, or if a relationship of trust, authority or dependency existed between the offender and the child (Section 229A). Section 212, 'Indecent practices between males,' remains unchanged.

Laws such as the sodomy law may or may not be enforced, as Ryan Goodman has discussed. When in 2005 the Fijian High Court declared its sodomy law to be unconstitutional, churches and even the Attorney-General were appalled.[95] By contrast, Nauru has a legal system very similar to and sometimes derived directly from that of PNG, as the two former colonies were both administered by Australia. The Queensland *Criminal Code* was adopted there also, but to my knowledge there has never been any prosecution under Code Section 208. In my experience, Nauruans are highly 'tolerant' of gays and transvestites, seeing nothing unusual in their behaviour.[96] Greg Dvorak reports the same 'tolerance' in the Marshall Islands, although he does not discuss the legal situation there.[97]

But tolerance of this nature has not been the case in PNG. Robert Aldrich describes how mission and administration combined in PNG to stamp out such 'immoral behaviour … inherent in the barbarity of Melanesia.'[98] His exhaustive survey of cases of homosexuality before the colonial courts revealed that, nearly every year, at least a few cases came to court, mainly involving indigenes until the mid-1950s. This he attributes both to opportunity for such activity in PNG, and the increasing vigilance of the courts, particularly in the immediate post-World War II years.[99] Cases may well have been heard under the Native Regulations of both territories.

Aldrich gleaned much of his information from newspaper reports and the casebooks of Justice Gore covering the years 1948 to 1953, a period before official case reporting started in 1963, providing further details of homosexuality

---

94   This term is defined in a new Section 6 as the introduction to any extent of a penis, other body part or object into the vagina, mouth or anus, and is used generally throughout the 2002 amendment.
95   'Fiji AG disagrees with court's view on homosexuality,' *Fiji Times* (online), 30 August 2005, http://www.fijitimes.com, accessed 1 September 2005. And see Nicole George, 2008, 'Contending masculinities and the limits of tolerance: sexual minorities in Fiji,' *The Contemporary Pacific* 20(1): 163–89.
96   I worked in Nauru drafting legislation from 1997 to 2000.
97   Greg Dvorak, 2014, 'Two sea turtles: intimacy between men in the Marshall Islands,' in *Gender on the Edge: Transgender, Gay and other Pacific Islanders*, in Niko Besnier and Kalissa Alexeyeff, Hong Kong: Hong Kong University Press, 184–209. But see critique of language of 'tolerance' therein.
98   Aldrich, *Colonialism and Homosexuality*, 247. Aldrich's materials—archival documents, court records and other sources, published and unpublished—reach back far earlier than those I accessed independently, limiting myself mainly to the period from 1963, the year when official case reporting commenced.
99   Ibid., 251–52.

cases.[100] Summaries of carnal knowledge cases in the National and Supreme Courts appear at Appendix 3. A considerable number of cases of consensual homosexual activity, often involving expatriates, came before the courts in this late colonial era. By contrast, most such encounters coming before the courts in recent times have involved underage boys;[101] and the forced sexual encounters recorded all occurred in prison.[102] *Johnny Mala's Case*, involving neither forced sex nor sex with minors, is a notable exception.

An analysis of some of these cases of consensual sex between males, together with the two National Court prostitution cases, reveals much about the ways in which legal discourses of sexuality were developed and employed in PNG, before and after Independence, to create outgroups in contrast to which the lawmakers could measure and regulate themselves.

Creating the rules

> The people who are dominant in society, who really have the means of social control, are those who dictate the laws.
>
> Margaret Davies: law professor, feminist and legal theory critic.[103]

How were rules of the law developed in PNG's colonial and post-colonial contexts? Despite the professed impartiality of legal decision-making, the introduced system contained processes which assisted the expatriate judges of the colonial era to make decisions based on their own moral views.[104] These rules and processes became so thoroughly embedded in the legal discourse that after Independence, despite some efforts directed to change, they were strengthened rather than diminished or altered. Judges were able to ignore customary beliefs. They were even able to collude with administrative processes to name and condemn entire categories of sexual offenders.

Laws are 'dictated,' as Margaret Davies puts it above, in two ways: through direct legislative intervention, and through the process of judicial decisions in cases brought before the courts. These two processes differ in certain basic respects. Legislation is passed by the legislature, on the basis of laws prepared

---

100 Ibid., 254.
101 The most recent record of conviction appears in a report by Annette Sete, 'Sodomist gets 21 years jail term,' *Post-Courier*, 20 May 2008, 6, telling of the imprisonment of a man in East New Britain for a total of twenty-one years for acts of oral and anal sex with thirteen boys.
102 Summaries of Reported and Unreported cases, and of plea and trial decisions extracted from judges' notebooks, appear at Appendices 3 and 4.
103 Margaret Davies, 2008, *Asking the Law Question*, Sydney: Law Book Co., 101.
104 For discussion of the 'hidden' sexism of judges revealed in rape case judgements, see Zorn, 2010, 'The paradoxes of sexism: proving rape in the Papua New Guinea courts,' *LAWASIA Journal* 2010: 17–58.

in general terms by the executive to implement predetermined government policy. The decisions of judges in individual cases determine the actual efficacy or otherwise of the general legislative prescription. It may be confined to a limited set of fact situations leading to a narrow interpretation, or it may be applied widely to a range of circumstances and subjects, some of whom may not even be aware that they have broken the law.

Legislature and judiciary are both representative of those 'dominant in society.' But they may also be in conflict.[105] Legislation may be drawn up to counter a court decision which conflicts with government policy. Courts may not like to be told how to decide cases, and strive to find ways to circumvent legislative provisions. This conflict was less evident when PNG was a colony and the colonists comprised both legislators and judiciary. The content of laws was determined according to colonial ideas of social regulation. The right to impose alien norms through the introduction of foreign laws, including norms pertaining to the control and management of sexualities, was barely questioned. The social norms of the colonised, in the form of their customary laws, were rarely taken into consideration.

At Independence, legislative power and the right to devise policy passed to the citizens of the new state, who immediately initiated moves to bring existing law into line with indigenous social norms by various law reform initiatives.[106] Law reformers proposed new laws, legislators approved them, and lawyers tested them before the courts. But reform was not always successful, and it was inevitable that tensions and conflicts would arise. Political power may have been handed over, but judicial power continued to be exercised by expatriate judges, aided by expatriate (and expatriate-trained) lawyers who appeared before them. Although these practitioners were now to be guided by indigenous constitutional principles rather than Australian policy, they were not able to throw off their own cultural beliefs and biases overnight. Meanwhile, the normative systems of the formerly colonised were in the process of undergoing their own changes.

---

105 Roscoe Pound, 1908, 'Common law and legislation,' *Harvard Law Review* 21(6): 383–407; R.S. Geddes, 2005, 'Purpose and context in statutory interpretation,' *University of New England Law Journal* 2005(2): 5–48.
106 As proposed in Constitutional Planning Committee, *Final Report of the Constitutional Planning Committee* and mandated in the *Constitution* (particularly the Preamble and Schedule 2).

Custom and law

> The first requirement of a sound body of law is, that it should correspond with the actual feelings and demands of the community, whether right or wrong.
>
> Oliver Wendell Holmes Jr, American jurist, 1881.[107]

In order to achieve this correspondence, the 'actual feelings and demands of the community' should be understood and taken into account in legal proceedings. For PNG, it could be assumed that these feelings and demands should include reference to the customary laws adhered to, if not by the whole society, then at least the societies of the disputants. But when the colonial courts and legal systems and the 'native' regulatory and court systems were combined in 1963, this is not what happened. The law, in content, form and process, was the state law of the metropole, modified only marginally to suit local circumstances. The Tale of Kausigor and Piliu illustrates one of the few attempts to take account of customary perceptions of sexuality.

The Tale of Kausigor and Piliu

In 1969, Clemence Kausigor and Piki Piliu met in a tavern in Wewak, headquarters of the East Sepik District. Kausigor was drinking with friends, Piliu was working with a construction gang nearby. A deal was struck whereby Kausigor paid Piliu ten shillings and the two men retired to some bushes by the beach,[108] where they were observed by a passer-by who immediately told Piliu's brother. The brother called the police, both were charged, pleaded guilty and were each sentenced to three years' imprisonment.[109]

The Public Solicitor immediately arranged an appeal on their behalf against the severity of the sentence.[110] One matter relied upon by the trial judge in sentencing was a statement by the arresting officer in the court documents that homosexuality was 'completely against local custom.'[111] But at the appeal

---

107 Oliver Wendell Holmes Jr, 1881 [1968], *The Common Law*, London, Melbourne: MacMillan, 36.
108 In 1969, Australian pre-metric currency was being used in the Territories.
109 *R v Clemence Mandoma-Kausigor and Piki Piliu* PNG National Archives Accession No. 454 Box 8139 Crown Prosecution File 5-8019 (*Kausigor's Trial*).
110 PNG National Archives Accession No.957 Box 13774 Crown Prosecution File No. PA 20 (*Piliu's Appeal*); PNG National Archives Accession No.957 Box 13775 Crown Prosecution File No. PA 21 (*Kausigor's Case*) Appeal Book 20-21.
111 Antecedent reports on the two accused in *Kausigor's Trial*. The antecedent report is part of a case file compiled by police: see Appendix 2.

hearing, Father Heineman, a priest with sixteen years' experience in the Sepik area, made a lengthy written statement and then was cross-examined on it.[112] The court summarised his evidence as follows:

> He expressed the view that before European contact homosexual behaviour between males may have been contrary to the customs of the people of the Sepik District. However, since the introduction of the contract labour system which involves men moving away from their wives and families for long periods and the housing of them together in large dormitories with no organised recreation nor recreation facilities this type of behaviour has become very common and widespread in areas where there are large labour lines. Sepik men returning to their villages at the end of their contracts of employment on plantations have introduced homosexual behaviour into the villages with the result that such behaviour has become quite common. It is not approved by those who do not indulge in it and in his opinion the people think it deserving of punishment but would consider it amply punished by sentences of two to three months imprisonment. He went on to opine that the Sepik people regard such behaviour between consenting males to be less serious than sexual intercourse between unmarried girls and men. The latter behaviour is disapproved as it interferes with brideprice and exchange arrangements and prior arrangements made in relation to the girl's marriage and with other family interests involved in the customary methods of negotiating marriages. Homosexual behaviour between males is not seen as a serious offence because the people do not see it as a threat to their society and its traditions.[113]

Others however took a different view. An expatriate Superintendent of Police deposed that in his experience

> in certain areas of the Sepik, mainly the River Sepik area, homosexual behaviour between males is frowned upon, and in the majority of areas it is not accepted as being part of the native custom. I do agree that the homosexual behaviour does occur to some degree because of the fact that many Sepik are being employed as single labourers on plantations.[114]

A Police Constable from Kausigor's village stated in his affidavit that what Kausigor did 'is against the custom of the people of my village. It is regarded as a wrong in the eyes of the people and it is a big shame.'[115] And a District

---

112 *Kausigor's Case*, transcript of cross-examination. Try as I would, I could not locate a copy of the actual affidavit, although I found a letter referring to the fact that it had been attached.
113 Ibid.
114 Ibid., affidavit of Bryan Alan Beattie, 25 June 1969.
115 Ibid., affidavit of Jimu Kunare, 25 June 1969.

Officer, hastily contacted through the Department of District Administration in Port Moresby,[116] denied claims of homosexuality on plantations, explaining that after a hard day's physical labour, workers preferred to relax with friends, and if they sought sex, the local women would oblige for a fee. He contended, somewhat surprisingly in the light of the ongoing anthropological and legal evidence to the contrary, that the Administration was aware of only one case of plantation homosexuality.[117]

The appeal court took these arguments into account. The evidence showed that any previous abhorrence of local custom, if indeed this had been the situation, had been dissipated. The three-year sentence was reduced to eighteen months.[118]

Custom in the law

In the colonial era, some attempts were made both by the courts and the legislature to admit evidence of custom.[119] But overall, any suggestion of a sympathetic approach to custom by the Australian colonists is challenged. Alan M. Healy describes the Australian method of colonial legal administration in its colony as the antithesis of the British approach in Africa, which was one of 'indirect rule' aimed at including indigenous peoples and their decision-making practices and the melding of custom with the state legal system. Healy considers that from the beginning of Australian rule

> the entire bent of Australian policy—well illustrated in the legal system—amounted to an attempt at decreed grassroots assimilation, grounded in entirely ethnocentric postulates, and ignoring or overriding indigenous tradition.[120]

It was an outcome of 'unrelieved paternalism, predicated on the antique notion of a natural hierarchy of peoples and cultures.'[121] He considers that, even after World War II, native courts and the development of laws based on custom were strongly resisted, and systems were imposed from Canberra:

---

116 *Kausigor's Trial*, letter from Acting Crown Solicitor to Director, Department of District Administration, 25 June, 1969.
117 *Kausigor's Case*, notes on discussion with District Officer Harley Rivers Dickinson.
118 Ibid.
119 Peter Bayne, 1975, 'Legal development in Papua New Guinea: the place of the common law,' *Melanesian Law Journal* 3(1): 9–39; David Weisbrot, 1982, 'Integration of laws in Papua New Guinea: custom and the criminal law in conflict,' in *Law and Social Change in Papua New Guinea*, ed. Weisbrot, Abdul Paliwala and Akilagpa Sawyerr, Sydney, Melbourne, Brisbane, Adelaide, Perth: Butterworths, 59–103; Ottley and Zorn, 'Criminal law in Papua New Guinea.'
120 Allan M. Healy, 1997, 'Colonial law as metropolitan defence: the curious case of Australia in New Guinea,' in *European Impact and Pacific Influence: British and German Colonial Policy in the Pacific Islands and the Indigenous Response*, ed. Hermann J. Hiery and John M. MacKenzie, London: Tauris Academic Studies, 214–30, 216.
121 Ibid., 218.

In fact, the legal system has been inherently dysfunctional from the early days of administration, with its motive forces being extraneous objectives, fear and paradigms—in defence of Australian interests— rather than the need to develop law and legal structures having intrinsic cultural meaning.[122]

In New Guinea, the establishment of the western legal system included the principle that

> the tribal institutions, customs and usages of the aboriginal natives of the Territory shall not be affected by this Ordinance and shall, subject to the provisions of the Ordinances of the Territory from time to time in force, be permitted to continue in existence in so far as they are applicable, apply to the Territory.[123]

The *Derham Report* discussed the inclusion of custom in the court system at some length, in its deliberations upon the desirability or otherwise of 'Native Courts.'[124] The author expressed concern that local customs would not be adequate to meet the needs of a developing society, and that the customs of a multitude of different communities, although they would be around for a long time yet, could not be known and applied in court. The report's concern with the relationship of 'law' and 'custom' should be viewed in the context of the political and ideological climate of the time, based in social Darwinist theory and setting privileged concepts like 'law,' 'justice' and 'good government' against a vague notion of 'custom,' but the result of this 'Hasluck/Derham' approach was to dismantle the *kiap* system of justice and replace it with 'proper' courts dispensing 'law' rather than justice.[125] Courts specifically concerned with 'native matters' should be established as part of the general judicial system, and so the now-defunct Local Courts were born. Matters to be decided by custom should be clearly specified, as should the matter of what is meant by custom, and how a custom is established. But 'in criminal matters where all offences are created by central legislative act and, it must be assumed, are created for the benefit and protection of all, the determination of whether an offence has been committed will not ordinarily be affected by local custom; but the appropriate penalty to be imposed may well be determined in the light of such custom.'[126]

The *Derham Report* also referred to a draft Bill which would direct all courts to take judicial notice[127] of native institutions, customs, usages and rights and to

---

122   Ibid., 226–27.
123   *Laws Repeal and Adopting Ordinance 1921–1939* (New Guinea).
124   *Derham Report*, 34–37.
125   Sack, 'Law, custom and good government,' 377–79, 388, 395.
126   *Derham Report*, 36.
127   '*Judicial notice*: The courts take cognisance or notice of matters which are so notorious or clearly established that formal evidence of their existence is unnecessary.' P.G. Osborne, 1964 [Fifth ed.], *A Concise*

give effect to them.[128] So in 1963, the Native Customs (Recognition) Bill, based in part on similar legislation in Ghana and the British Protectorate of Solomon Islands,[129] was presented to the Legislative Council. Section 4 of the Bill provided a definition of custom as, 'the custom or usage of the aboriginal inhabitants of the Territory obtaining in relation to the matter in question at the time when and the place in relation to which that question arises, regardless of whether or not that custom or usage has obtained from time immemorial.'

In introducing the Bill, J.K. McCarthy, Director of Native Affairs, had explained that this definition was necessary, as

> in ordinary English law custom is considered to be something which has existed from time immemorial. It is quite obvious that such a concept would not adequately describe the state of native custom at any given stage in the territory. Circumstances are continually occurring which were never before envisaged and accordingly custom is, to some extent at least, continually changing and adjusting itself to fit these changing circumstances.[130]

However, the *Derham Report's* suggestion that judicial notice be taken of custom (a process which would have entrenched customary rules in the legal system) was omitted from the Bill as presented, on the grounds that custom's natural development would thereby be stifled.[131] Overall, McCarthy claimed, the Bill was designed to 'regularize the position of native custom in the laws,' to assist 'a gradual development towards uniformity and the development of truly national rather than a village or clan sentiment.'[132] Custom was to be pleaded as a question of fact, necessitating the production of witnesses to explain and attest to it, rather than as a question of law, to be argued by counsel.

The Bill had a stormy passage, opposed by many expatriate Members on the grounds that it was a retrograde step:

> If you are to have social and economic progress the conflict between stone age customs and modern civilization must be minimized, not given increasing importance … [t]here should be a desire to get forward to English Common Law rather than cling to the shackles of the stone age (Mr Hurrell).[133]

Law Dictionary, London, Sweet & Maxwell, 178.
128 *Derham Report*, 35.
129 C.J. Lynch, 1968, 'Aspects of political and constitutional development and allied topics,' in *Fashion of Law in New Guinea*, ed. B.J. Brown, Sydney, Melbourne, Brisbane: Butterworths, 39–69, 63.
130 Territory of Papua and New Guinea, *Legislative Council Debates* VI:7, 26 February 1963: 665 (Mr. McCarthy).
131 Ibid.
132 Ibid., 666.
133 Ibid., 666 (Mr Hurrell).

> It would certainly rob the law of one of its most important aspects and that is consistency…. Most people will agree that within quite a short space of time very few, if any, of these customs will be important … an insane Bill (Mr Downs).[134]

Attempts were made by the Bill's opponents to limit the operation of the proposed law, but these were defeated.[135] Predictions that customs would or should soon die out were still being made five years later (in 1968, not long before *Kausigor's Case* was heard and decided) by Geoffrey Sawer, Head of the Department of Law, Research School of Social Sciences, The Australian National University. He considered that 'education, economic development, the breakdown of traditional group-boundaries, and the growth of towns will erode the "custom consciousness" of the people, especially the young, and make necessary other rules of social order.'[136]

The Ordinance contained three notable features. Firstly, the definition of custom contemplated its fluid and changing nature, a definition to be repeated in the *Constitution*.[137] Secondly, no suggestion was made, as had been the case in British colonies in Africa, that custom should be codified. It was generally considered that PNG custom was too changeable, too much a matter of 'an influence on action … rather than … a principle,' as C.J. Lynch the Legislative Draftsman put it.[138] But this view was challenged, not least by Lynch himself,[139] and then far more stridently by the Constitutional Planning Committee and particularly Narokobi, one of the Committee's legal advisers, who wrote, some years after Independence:

> My personal position then (as it is now) was that custom should form the basis of our unwritten law. Common law and equity should be available only as subsidiary sources of law to be drawn upon to supplement the already rich customary laws, values and practices of PNG.
>
> My position was that if Independence was to mean anything, we must free ourselves from the imposed web of laws, built up over the years, based on social conditions in England and Australia.[140]

The third and most significant feature of the *Native Customs (Recognition) Ordinance*, from the point of view of ordinary Papua New Guineans who for

---

134   Ibid., 666–67 (Mr Downs).
135   Ibid., 733, 777, 778 (Mr Downs).
136   Geoffrey Sawer, 1968, 'Introduction,' in *Fashion of Law in New Guinea*, ed. B.J. Brown, Sydney, Melbourne, Brisbane: Butterworths, 9–13, 12.
137   *Constitution* Schedule 1.2(1): definition of 'custom.'
138   Lynch, 'Aspects of political and constitutional development and allied topics,' 62.
139   Lynch's opposition to former Minister for Territories Paul Hasluck's insistence on the wholesale adoption of common law is discussed in Healy, 'Colonial law as metropolitan defence,' 223.
140   Narokobi, 'History and movement in law reform in Papua New Guinea,' 17.

many years, even after Independence, appeared in court only as defendants in criminal trials, was that it severely limited the application of custom in criminal matters:

> Subject to this Ordinance, native custom shall not be taken into account in a criminal case, except for the purpose of—
>
> (a)   ascertaining the existence or otherwise of a state of mind of a person;
>
> (b)   deciding the reasonableness or otherwise of an act, default or omission by a person;
>
> (c)   deciding the reasonableness or otherwise of an excuse;
>
> (d)   deciding, in accordance with any other law in force in the Territory or a part of the Territory, whether to proceed to the conviction of the guilty party,
>
> or where the court considers that by not taking the custom into account injustice will or may be done to a person.[141]

The Ordinance became an Act upon Independence, and was later retitled the *Customs Recognition Act*.[142] The *Constitution* envisaged that this retention was an interim measure,[143] to be replaced eventually by a system termed the 'underlying law,' which was to be developed by the courts and the legislature based largely upon the *Constitution* itself and its underlying National Goals and Directive Principles, and on customary principles.[144] Attempts were made by the Law Reform Commission to amplify and clarify this development,[145] but the *Underlying Law Act* prepared there in 1977[146] was not passed until 2000, in a form somewhat at variance with the Commission's earlier draft.[147]

The *Constitution* had retained the definition of custom as 'the customs and usages of indigenous inhabitants of the country existing in relation to the

---

141 Native Customs (Recognition) Ordinance, Section 7.
142 All colonial Ordinances were retitled Acts at Independence: *Constitution* Schedule 2.4.6.(2). The *Interpretation (Interim Provisions) Act* 1975 provided that the expression 'native' shall be read as a reference to 'automatic citizen,' but this posed many problems. See 'Preface,' to the *Revised Laws of Papua New Guinea*, 7. The problem in relation to this law was resolved by renaming the Ordinance under the Revision of Laws process 1973–1981.
143 Jennifer Corrin Care and Jean G. Zorn, 2001, 'Legislating pluralism: statutory "develpments" in Melanesian customary law,' *Journal of Legal Pluralism and Unofficial Law* 46: 49–101, 81.
144 *Constitution* Section 9, Schedule 2.3 and 2.4. See analysis in C.J. Lynch, 1976, 'The adoption of an underlying law by the Constitution of Papua New Guinea,' *Melanesian Law Journal* 4(1): 37–66.
145 Law Reform Commission, *Report No 7: The Role of Customary Law in the Legal System*.
146 Ibid.
147 Discussed at length in Corrin Care and Zorn, 'Legislating pluralism'; and Jean G. Zorn and Jennifer Corrin Care, 2002, 'Everything old is new again: the Underlying Law Act of Papua New Guinea,' *LAWASIA Journal* 2002: 61–97.

matter in question at the time when and the place in relation to which the matter arises, regardless of whether or not the custom or usage has existed from time immemorial.' The *Underlying Law Act* also kept this definition, but applied it to a new term 'customary law,'[148] probably in the hope that lawyers and judges would be more comfortable recognising custom if it had the connotation of a 'real' system of law.[149] Peter Sack considers that such legislative initiatives as the *Native Customs (Recognition) Ordinance*, the *Village Courts Act*, Schedule 2 of the *Constitution* and the *Underlying Law Act* were merely part of the original 'Hasluck/Derham approach' intended to 'domesticate and emasculate "custom" by "legalising" it, rather than replacing it with a new form of legitimacy' and in this it was 'astonishingly successful.'[150] This process of legalising was not confined to legislative initiatives, as case law on criminalised sexualities shows.

Considering custom

The issue which so concerned the Full Court judges in *Kausigor's Case* was to determine whether homosexuality was 'customary' in the Sepik. It concerned the lawyers as well: during preparations for the hearing, when the Public Solicitor sent Father Heineman's affidavit to the Crown Solicitor,[151] the latter immediately launched several attempts to find deponents to counter this testimony.[152] But the court was not quite sure how to deal with this evidence of changing custom before it. It said, 'We have come to the conclusion that there is fairly widespread homosexuality in the Sepik area, that *there is no tribal or village custom which allows or condones this type of behaviour*, that it brings opprobrium to those deviates who are found out, but that it is not regarded as seriously as fornication [emphasis added].'

This perceived want of custom is in hindsight surprising. Nobody seemed prepared to take account of the anthropological record, available decades before 1972, of ritual practices in PNG and specifically in the Sepik involving sexual activity between males.[153] The lawyers had plenty of time to research and present this evidence, as the appeal dragged on and even required rehearing due to the illness of the Chief Justice. Instead, both sides relied upon the evidence of *kiaps*, a policeman and a priest. The court itself could have looked more carefully at

---

148 *Underlying Law Act*, 2000, Section 1, definition of 'customary law.'
149 Corrin Care and Zorn, 'Legislating pluralism,' 74.
150 Sack, 'Law, custom and good government,' 395.
151 *Kausigor's Case*, Public Solicitor to Crown Solicitor, 20 June 1969.
152 Ibid., Crown Solicitor to Director of District Administration, 25 June 1969; affidavits of Bryan Alan Beattie and Jimu Kunare, both deposed on 25 June 1969. The testimony of the District Officer Mr Dickinson referred to in the Full Court judgement has not survived.
153 E.g., Gregory Bateson, 1936, *Naven: A Survey of the Problems Suggested by a Composite Picture of the Culture of a New Guinea Tribe Drawn from Three Points of View*, Cambridge: Cambridge University Press. Although later writers emphasised the disconnect between 'ritual homosexuality' and sexual practices born of desire, as I describe in Chapter 4, at the time a submission along these lines may have carried some weight.

the definition of 'custom' in the *Native Customs (Recognition) Ordinance*, before it so readily concluded that there was in fact no such custom. Nevertheless, it did concede that

> we consider that the learned trial Judge was influenced by the statement in the antecedent report that the present offences were completely against local custom which in the context indicates an attitude approaching abhorrence and has given it special weight. The statement does not carry the implication, as the evidence now before us shows, that the force of local custom has become greatly weakened in the observance or that the offence was not regarded by the people as meriting a long term of imprisonment.

It seems that John Comaroff's claim, that part of the *lawfare* process of the imposition of colonial law involves the denigration of custom and the outright criminalisation of cultural practices which are considered 'repugnant,'[154] is borne out by the practice of the PNG courts. The sodomy laws were imported wholesale and, where they were called into question, they were staunchly upheld. The 'odious' repugnancy test has prevailed. It was enshrined in the definition of custom in the *Constitution*,[155] and it has guided the courts both before and after Independence, whether or not they have acknowledged the fact.

Ultimately even Narokobi, that staunch advocate for customary law, found himself caught in a dilemma in *Monika Jon's Case*, noting that wife-lending was customary in some traditional societies. But he also observed that

> looking at custom in general, it is plain that it was a matter of a very serious affront to the dignity of the family if a woman was to sell her body for reward. In many communities such a thing was not heard of. Our custom in general, came close to Islamic Law, the Law of Moses too, that the proper punishment for such an offence was stoning to death.

He resolved the dilemma he perceived not by recourse to custom, but in a far more legalistic way. He drew a distinction between occasional occurrences of cash-for-sex and the ongoing occupation of selling sex. To prosecute the former was tantamount to prosecuting a woman for prostitution. What the law aimed to do, he argued, was to prosecute not the individual, but the trade, the commercialisation of sex. His distinction to a large degree paralleled that described by Alan M. Wojcicki in South Africa, where brothel-based commercial

---

154 A principle which Narokobi termed 'odious.' See Narokobi, 'Adaptation of western law in Papua New Guinea,' 57; and see his comments in 'History and movement in law reform in Papua New Guinea,' 17.
155 Schedule 2.1(2). The test was done away with upon the enactment of the *Underlying Law Act* 2000, which substituted a test of conformity with Constitutional National Goals and Directive Principles, and basic constitutional rights and freedoms.

prostitution is highly stigmatised on the basis that it is western, more visible and more threatening to male prestige and power, whereas survival sex sold in shanty-town beer-taverns has far greater social acceptance.[156]

Narokobi was making another distinction, too. A staunch advocate of equality and rights for all, he nevertheless drew a line between the village and the settlement masses on the one hand and the urbanised wealthy on the other. He was supporting a class distinction, although as was his way, his support was for the *grassroots*, and his condemnation was reserved for the emerging *elites*.[157]

The maintenance of class

> Law may be the corner stone of many mighty civilizations in human history, but it has often been used as a sharp sword by the powerful to conquer, and hold subject, the powerless. Law has been used to destroy cultures, civilizations, religions and the entire moral fabric of a people.
>
> Bernard Narokobi.[158]

In Chapter 2 I discussed the ways in which PNG's society was stratified, by race initially and then by class. The division formerly manifested primarily along racial lines was gradually transformed into one divided along power and economic lines, as the PNG *elites* emerged.

Within general categories, though, further divisions were established and maintained.[159] Pre-Independence, class divisions in the metropole were exported to the colonies, as many writers have shown.[160] There, all subordinated members of the plural society—white women, the colonised—were defined in relation to the supreme position of the white male. White men who transgressed the

---

156 Alan M. Wojcicki, 2002, 'Commercial sexwork or *Ukuphanda*? Sex-for-money exchange in Soweto and Hammanskraal area, South Africa,' *Culture, Medicine and Psychiatry* 26: 339–70.
157 See Jean Zorn's delightful and heartfelt memorial to Narokobi. Zorn, 'In memory of Bernard Narokobi.' She relates many instances of his irreverence, his belief that every Melanesian should live the simple village life, and how he exemplified this by maintaining dress of bare feet and laplap, and napping on the carpeted floor of his Waigani office.
158 Narokobi, 'History and movement in law reform in Papua New Guinea,' 13.
159 Foucault, 1997 [2004], *'Society Must be Defended': Lectures at the Collège de France, 1975–76*, London: Penguin Books: 60–62.
160 E.g., Aldrich, *Colonialism and Homosexuality*; Bulbeck, *Australian Women in Papua New Guinea*; Philip Howell, 2004, 'Sexuality, sovereignty and space: law, government and the geography of prostitution in colonial Gibraltar,' *Social History* 29(4): 445–64; Richard Phillips, 2002, 'Imperialism and the regulation of sexuality: colonial legislation on contagious diseases and ages of consent,' *Journal of Historical Geography* 28(3): 339–62; Ann Laura Stoler, 1995, *Race and the Education of Desire: Foucault's History of Sexuality and the Colonial Order of Things*, Durham and London: Duke University Press; Stoler, 2003, *Carnal Knowledge and Imperial Power: Race and the Intimate in Colonial Rule*, Berkeley: University of California Press.

boundaries, by such means as 'going native' or displaying outrageous behaviour, were liable not only to ostracism but also to physical ejection from colonial society. And this is what happened to Christopher Leech.

Tale from a *Boihaus*[161]

Leech was a British ex-RAF intelligence officer stationed at the army barracks near Lae. Early in 1972, Leech met a former boyfriend, Peter Yaku, at a hotel in Lae. They re-established the relationship, liaising at Yaku's place, a room in a *boihaus* [domestic quarters] in the backyard of a house in the town. The *boihaus* had three rooms in all, one Yaku's, one apparently a laundry/bathroom, and the third occupied by a collection of Buang people from the mountains south of Lae, including one Gwakarum. Gwakarum had left his home village as a teenager and, now aged thirty, had a wife and young child living with him in the single room, along with two relatives and their families.[162] Gwakarum had had no formal schooling, although he was assessed as 'comparatively civilised and intelligent.'[163] As was later revealed, he had had several brushes with the law, and had been imprisoned briefly on a few occasions.

On the second or third occasion that Gwakarum heard Leech's car drive up, late at night, he got up to spy on them. From behind the part-open door, he saw Yaku penetrate Leech. Afterwards, Yaku emerged to fetch a bucket of water for washing, and Gwakarum quickly hid behind a hibiscus bush and went on watching. In all, he thought he was watching for about fifteen minutes, but after the excitement was over, and the two men in the room were relaxing with beer and cigarettes, he went to the police station to raise the alarm. He returned with a police Sub-Inspector, who found the pair sitting on the concrete floor of the room in their underwear and arrested them both.[164]

This all took place in February 1972. Both were committed for trial in March, but for various technical reasons, the trial itself did not take place until September. Yaku failed to appear in court, so Leech was tried alone.[165] Despite his lawyer's

---

161 *R v C.E.C. Leech and Peter Yaku*, PNG National Archives Accession 454 Box 14619 Crown Prosecution File 5-9354; PNG Supreme Court Archives Box 2038 SCRA Prentice J Notebooks 1972, 37–38 (*Leech Trial*).
162 PNG National Archives Accession 454 Box 14648 File Nos. 9956, 9958 (*Gwakarum Trials*). This multiple occupancy was and still is not uncommon. In the decade before Independence, indigenous migrants were pouring into Lae, and their impact in the town provided material for several anthropologists of the time. See John Lucas, 1972, 'Lae—a town in transition,' *Oceania* 42(2): 260–75; Lorraine Zimmerman, 1973, 'Migration and urbanization among the Buang of Papua New Guinea,' Ph.D. thesis, Detroit, MI: Wayne State University; Ian Willis, 1974, *Lae: Village and City*, Melbourne: Melbourne University Press. The migrants included a large cohort of Buang people from the mountains to the south-west who often found work as domestic servants.
163 *Gwakarun Trials*, Antecedent Report George Gwakarun 11 July 1973.
164 Statements of George Gwakarum and Sub-Inspector Anton Daniel at Committal hearing, 16 March 1972, *Leech Trial*.
165 Backing Sheet, *Leech Trial*.

attempts to show inconsistencies in Gwakarum's evidence, reminding the court that it was uncorroborated, and even hinting at untoward motives, Leech was convicted and sentenced to three months in hard labour. The judge said,

> I find distress and distaste in this kind of case. It is tolerated in many communities. It carries a maximum penalty of 14 years, in most cases for debauchery of the young. I am aware that in some parts of the Territory it is looked upon with great distaste, while there is less disfavour in other parts.... I think the neighbour acted reasonably.[166]

The judge in this case was a comparative newcomer to the Territory bench. Two years earlier, in February 1970, William James Prentice, a Sydney barrister and devout Catholic,[167] joined six other expatriate judges on the Supreme Court bench. In December of that year, while on circuit in Wewak, he heard the case of John Passum, a young married man, well-educated, who was in prison for assault. There he had anal intercourse three times with another inmate who eventually resisted and complained to the prison authorities. On a guilty plea, Justice Prentice sentenced Passum to a mere one extra month's imprisonment.[168]

The Crown Prosecutor sought to differ from the fledgling judge. In his subsequent Circuit Report, he commented that he considered the sentence 'totally inadequate.' After summarising the mitigating factors, he proceeded to make much of Passum's prior convictions for drunkenness, stealing and assault. He referred to the Full Court decision the previous year in *Kausigor's Case*, compared the backgrounds of the two convicts and then the two sentences. Passum was the better-educated man (and by implication, more 'civilised'), was married and had worked as a broadcaster, whereas Kausigor had no education, was a villager and the crime was said to be against local custom. The Full Court on appeal had only reduced Kausigor's sentence to eighteen months.[169]

The Acting Crown Solicitor agreed and wrote to the Acting Chief Crown Prosecutor, recommending that a copy of the judgement in *Kausigor's Case* be given to the judge's associate with a request that it be brought to His Honour's attention.[170] So Justice Prentice was warned, but nevertheless he handed down a comparatively light sentence to Leech. However, this was still enough to destroy the Englishman. Even before he was released from prison, the Police Commissioner wrote to the Secretary for Law, recommending deportation. He claimed that

---

166 Crown Prosecutor's Notes, *Leech Trial*.
167 Pers. Comm. G.R. Stewart, September 2006, Stewart, my father, shared chambers with Prentice when both were at the NSW bar in the 1950s and 1960s.
168 *R v John Passum*, PNG National Archive Accession No.454 Box No.9621 File No.8596.
169 Ibid., Crown Prosecutor's Circuit Report.
170 Ibid., Letter from Acting Crown Solicitor to Acting Chief Crown Prosecutor, 29 December 1970.

at the time of passing sentence Mr. Justice Prentice expressed the view that LEECH was an undesirable person to remain in Papua New Guinea … it is believed he will have difficulty in obtaining employment in this country. It is anticipated, he will soon become a destitute person. There is also no doubt that LEECH will continue to offend in this manner and will corrupt other local persons…. His deportation from Papua New Guinea is strongly recommended.[171]

Leech was deported early in 1973.[172] Meanwhile, his partner Yaku was recaptured, and preparations were made for his trial. But then the star prosecution witness, the spy Gwakarum, disappeared. He was finally located in June the following year—in prison in Lae, charged with stabbing an expatriate to death during a burglary.[173] The case against Yaku was crumbling fast. On 5 July 1973, the Public Solicitor (who provided defence counsel in most Supreme Court trials against indigent Papua New Guineans) wrote to the Secretary for Law requesting that the case against Yaku be dropped.[174] The Acting Crown Prosecutor, in a Minute to his Prosecutors, opined that, 'consideration should still be given as to whether or not this prosecution should proceed on the grounds that acts of sodomy between consenting adults ought not generally to concern the state. Without expressing any definite opinion on the matter, my view is that our time and that of Defence Counsel could be more profitably employed.'[175]

Other government lawyers agreed. A Senior Crown Prosecutor responded that he understood Leech had been convicted principally because of the inexperience of his private practitioner defence counsel, and that Leech was 'probably the principal offender.'[176] The Crown Solicitor said that he thought it likely that the witness Gwakarum was prompted to go to the police because a European was involved, and did not anticipate that Yaku should be prosecuted.[177] The case against Yaku was eventually dropped,[178] but that was too late for Christopher Leech.

An undesirable person

The irony of this case was that if Leech had not been spied upon by someone alleged to harbour anti-European sentiments,[179] it is likely that nothing would have come of the matter. By the late colonial period, homosexual encounters

---

171 Ibid., Letter from Commissioner of Police to Secretary for Law, 4 December 1972.
172 Ibid., Letters from Director, Trade and Industry, to Secretary for Law, 15 December 1972, and from Comptroller of Customs to Legislative Draftsman, 13 February 1973.
173 *Gwakarun Trials*.
174 *Leech Trial*, Letter from Acting Public Solicitor to Secretary for Law, 5 July 1973.
175 Ibid., Minute of Acting Crown Prosecutor, 25 July 1973.
176 Ibid., Minute of Senior Crown Prosecutor of 30 July 1973.
177 Ibid., Minute of Crown Solicitor to Secretary for Law, 31 July 1973.
178 Ibid., Notation on Cover Sheet shows the *nolle prosequi* was entered at Lae, 13 August 1973.
179 According to the Crown Solicitor's comments described in the *Leech Trial*.

were tacitly accepted, provided they were kept relatively discreet and did not involve clearly under-aged boys.[180] But as this case shows, social divisions in the colony were still resisting attack. Liaisons between white men and native women in the Territory were not disapproved of, although marriages were.[181] White women were still to be protected and discouraged at all times from sexual contact with native men.[182] Sex between a white and a native man was in some ways even worse: it offended both racial and gender taboos.[183] But it happened and, as Aldrich notes, was 'frequent enough to require vigilance.' The views of homosexuality in colonial PNG implicit in records of the time had it that 'Europeans bore some responsibility for corrupting "natives". The appropriate treatment for those involved, it appeared, was to make certain that the white man left the territory speedily, and to pay off the "native".'[184]

It was easy to deport undesirables from the post-war colony. Gloria Chalmers describes how, in the 1950s, a £30 bond was required from all expatriates, male and female, to cover the fare out of the country should they be required to leave for inappropriate behaviour, such as homosexual advances, a drinking problem, even a 'questionable role in the German Army.'[185] Chilla Bulbeck too refers to the deportation of immigrant whites who did not come 'up to the mark'—in other words, those who threatened the status of white men.[186] Leech had met with his lover in the cramped space of a *boihaus*, was discovered sitting on the floor wearing only his underpants, and was accused of permitting a black man to sodomise him. He had clearly crossed the divide, and had to go. The speed with which the police responded to Gwakarum's alarm was remarkable. The state of undress of the couple and the fact that they were sitting on a bare concrete floor were considered to amount to sufficient corroborative evidence. The judge was prepared to find that the witness Gwakarum (soon to be convicted of murdering an expatriate) was credible and had acted reasonably. The Crown Solicitor thought that Gwakarum was motivated to go to the police by distaste at the conduct of a 'European.' And the Police Commissioner had already imagined a dismal future of destitution and continued depravity for Leech before he was even released from prison. Nobody involved in the deportation process contradicted this. But once he was out of the country and out of the way, and the matter of his partner Yaku was under consideration, the story changed.

---

180 Aldrich, *Colonialism and Homosexuality*, 260–62; Nelson, Taim Bilong Masta, 181.
181 Nelson, Taim Bilong Masta, 168–69; Bulbeck, *Australian Women in Papua New Guinea*, 198; and see Andrew W. Lind, 1969, *Inter-Ethnic Marriage in New Guinea*, New Guinea Research Bulletin No. 31, Port Moresby: New Guinea Research Unit.
182 See the *White Women's Protection Ordinance* 1929.
183 See Aldrich, *Colonialism and Homosexuality*, 250–52 for details of convictions.
184 Ibid., 252–53.
185 Gloria Chalmers, 2006, *Kundus, Cannibals and Cargo Cults: Papua New Guinea in the 1950's*, Watsons Bay, NSW: Books & Writers Network Pty Ltd., 25.
186 Bulbeck, *Australian Women in Papua New Guinea*, 196.

Suddenly, the 'consenting adults in private' theme emerged. The witness was motivated by anti-white sentiments. If Leech was the principal offender, this made Yaku virtually an innocent party.

This 'innocent victim' theme of colonial times could not be sustained after Independence, as the conviction of the Papua New Guinean Johnny Mala in *Johnny Mala's Case* shows. But the threat of deportation of expatriates still remains—Frank, Johnny Mala's lover, was threatened with it.

In support of the grassroots

Monika Jon's Case shows a different road but a similar imperative around class construction. In it, Narokobi described the Law Reform Commission's initiative as a 'middle-of-the-road' attempt to decriminalise prostitution.

> What was legislated against were brothels and making a living out of prostitution. If a person makes a living out of prostitution he or she would be committing a crime.... Neither the Law Reform Commission which tried to canvass the views of all sections of the community before it made its recommendations, nor the Parliament which consists of elected representatives ever intended this legislation to punish the so called 'K2.00 bush' lady.[187]

He affirmed this stance in interview in 2005, although he may well have 'refreshed his memory' before the interview.[188] At any rate, I suggest that what he seemed to be attempting was a recasting of the Law Reform Commission's equality standpoint into a kind of reverse elitism. The *elites* should stick to legitimate ways of earning wealth (and status): the *grassroots* were entitled to glean whatever they could by any means available, including some questionable sexual practices.

Narokobi was clearly sympathetic to all three of the women in *Monika Jon's Case*. Two were arrested following a tip-off at the main wharf in Lae after a night spent on board ship with some Filipino seamen, who paid them for their services. But Kuragi Ku was arrested by police who saw her receiving money for sex, and then publicly strip-searched her to find monetary 'evidence' of prostitution. She claimed it was an act of defiance against her husband.

> On Friday my husband did not give me money, he was drinking and slept elsewhere drinking beer, one of my friend told me. I was angry, I left [took off] all my clothes and followed him into the bush my husband saw me and ran away with some beer. I was angry and I took three men

---

[187] *Monika Jon's Case* at 9.
[188] Interview B. Narokobi, Wellington, NZ, 16 November 2005.

into the bush, and they paid me K2.00 each and after that, I returned and was eating betelnut near Eriku Store and they arrested me [I was arrested].... I want to make him angry so I got [took] the money.[189]

Narokobi often tried to find the 'middle road' between customary perceptions and principles, and the strictures of the imported law.[190] Hence he took great care to claim that he did not intend to convict the three 'so called "K2.00 bush" lad[ies],' while at the same time condemning the 'professional' prostitute. It is unfortunate that his fine distinctions were not observed in future arrests and convictions. It is even more unfortunate that he did not uphold in their entirety the recommendations of the Law Reform Commission in decriminalising all acts of selling sex, regardless of the status of the seller and whether or not the acts were occasional or continuous. If he had done so, the Commission's decision would finally have been implemented, prostitution would have been decriminalised, and much of the present-day police power over sellers of sex, which I describe in Chapter 5, would never have existed.

Text or context

> Sex is placed by power in a binary system: licit and illicit, permitted and forbidden ... power's hold on sex is maintained through language, or rather through the act of discourse that creates, from the very fact that it is articulated, a rule of law. It speaks and that is the rule.
>
> Michel Foucault, 1978.[191]

It is not only the content of the law that has impacted upon the colonised of PNG. Many of the basic principles and processes of the law as practised in PNG have led judges to conclusions which make little or no sense to a lay person. This is illustrated in several ways through the *Mama Kamzo* cases.

The Tale of Mama Kamzo[192]

In the early 1970s, the practice of drafting plantation labour on a two-to-three-year contract basis was still thriving, although recruiters were ranging further

---

189   *Monika Jon's Case*, 3–4. For more extensive discussion of forms of negative agency exercised by wives angry at their husbands or male relatives, see Holly Wardlow, 2006, *Wayward Women: Sexuality and Agency in a New Guinea Society*, Berkeley and Los Angeles, CA: University of California Press, 75–89.
190   In *State v Luku Wapulae* (Unreported) N233, 4 June 1980, a case of witch-killing, Narokobi AJ devised a defence of 'diminished responsibility,' a compromise verdict which did not meet with the Supreme Court's approval: *Acting Public Solicitor v Uname Aumane, Aluma Boku, Luku Wapulae and Piope Kone* [1980] PNGLR 510.
191   Michel Foucault, 1978 [1976], *The Will to Knowledge: The History of Sexuality: Vol. 1*, London: Penguin Books, 83.
192   Taken from the unreported trial decision *R v Mama Kamzo* (Unreported) SC 671, 17 February 1972, (*Mama Kamzo's Trial*); reported appeal case *R v M.K.* [1973] PNGLR 204 (*Mama Kamzo's Appeal*); and Crown Prosecution file CP File Mama Kamzo: PNG National Archives Accession 454 Box 14,612/5-9218 (*Mama Kamzo File*).

afield. The previous year, a young Wabag lad, Mama Kamzo, was recruited from his home village in the far west of what was then the Western Highlands District to work on the Lolorua rubber plantation outside Port Moresby. He was not alone—a number of clansmen or *wantoks* were working there already. One at least was closely related enough to be called 'brother.' Kamzo was around seventeen years old, and had no formal schooling. This was his first paid employment.[193]

His foreman, or *bosboi*,[194] on the plantation was one Debozina.[195] Kamzo's file showed references to previous sexual advances by Debozina to Kamzo, and to other young men as well.[196] One day in October 1971, Debozina sought out Mama Kamzo. The lad had failed to tap one or more of the rubber trees at the end of his line, apparently because they were infested with ants.[197] When they both went to inspect the trees, Debozina told Kamzo to bend over, took down both their shorts, and penetrated Kamzo. Afterwards, Kamzo grabbed both pairs of shorts and fled across the plantation to tell his brother, who advised him to go to the European manager. The manager told him to go back to work and the matter would be dealt with later.

Next day the police arrived, questioned both men, and arrested them both. Nobody was more surprised than Mama Kamzo. At the committal hearing in Port Moresby District Court, his statement was translated thus:

> At my own village we do not have sexual intercourse with male persons but we do have sexual intercourse with females. I came with [cooperated with?] the police to lodge my complaint to the police about the man who had sexual intercourse with me but the police turned around and they placed me in the lock-up for nothing. I wait for a period of 2 months to have my trial.[198]

Debozina tried to claim that Kamzo had initiated the sex. Kamzo on the other hand said he had submitted because he knew Debozina had a knife, and he feared that it would be used. And in fact Kamzo's *wantoks* had searched Debozina's shorts and found a pocket knife.

Although the prosecution tried to find ways to support Debozina's claim that Kamzo had initiated the encounter, then fled afterwards for no apparent reason

---

193 Antecedent Report Mama Kamzo in *Mama Kamzo File*. An Antecedent Report is usually prepared by the interviewing officer on arrest, and presented to the Court upon conviction or upon a plea of guilty.
194 For a description of the role of the *bosboi*, see D.C. Lewis, 1996, *The Plantation Dream: Developing British New Guinea and Papua, 1884–1942*, Canberra: The Journal of Pacific History, 270–71.
195 Unfortunately, Debozina's archive file was empty, so I was not able to learn where he came from.
196 *Mama Kamzo File*, Crown Prosecutor's Circuit Report.
197 Ibid., Statement Debozina Karawa to police.
198 Ibid., committal hearing 21 December 1971 in the Port Moresby District Court. It appears that he had spent the two months in custody on remand.

and only grabbed Debozina's shorts to be used as evidence,[199] the trial judge was having none of it. He did not believe Debozina. On the other hand he did not believe that Kamzo submitted out of fear of personal violence, though he did acknowledge that Debozina was older, was Kamzo's superior, and Kamzo was clearly afraid of him. Kamzo had done little more than submit, and after spending more than four months in prison, he was acquitted early in 1972, with a warning to stay away from men like this in future.[200]

But the Crown lawyers did not let the matter rest there. They were concerned that permitting this decision to stand would allow all receptive partners to sodomy to plead spurious coercion, as women were then alleged to do in rape cases.[201] The Chief Crown Prosecutor wrote urgently to the Crown Solicitor proposing a Full Court appeal against the decision.[202] He was extremely worried that mere 'submission' meant that 'an adult person may escape responsibility for what otherwise would be a crime carrying a maximum penalty of 14 years hard labour.' This made it a serious matter, and stringent tests should be applied. 'There must be some reasonable proportion between the seriousness of the offence and the steps that must be taken to prevent it by this [sic] whose duty is to not "permit" it.'

But this argument only makes sense if certain legal presumptions are taken into account, chiefly that which says that ignorance of the law is no defence: every person is presumed to know the law.[203] It did not matter that Kamzo was a young, uneducated man from a remote village, in an alien environment. He was presumed to be aware that sodomy was not just a wrong but a crime in the eyes of the law; that both parties to an act of sodomy were committing a serious crime; that he had a duty to prevent its commission, no matter who was attempting to perpetrate it; that he could only escape responsibility if the offending act had occurred independently of his will or he had been coerced by real fear of violence; and that his view of his position relative to his older superior was immaterial.

The Chief Crown Prosecutor not only presented four pages of legal argument in his letter, he also suggested the terms by which the trial judge should refer the matter to the Full Court. Handwritten notations on the letter indicate that this

---

199   Ibid., Crown Prosecutor's Circuit Report.
200   Ibid., Prosecutor's notes on trial.
201   But see Zorn, 'The paradoxes of sexism,' 55–58; Jean G. Zorn, 2012, 'Engendering violence in the Papua New Guinea Courts: sentencing in rape trials,' in *Engendering Violence in Papua New Guinea*, ed. Margaret Jolly, Christine Stewart with Carolyn Brewer, Canberra: ANU E Press, online: http://press.anu.edu.au?p=182671, accessed 4 April 2014.
202   *Mama Kamzo File*, Chief Crown Prosecutor to Crown Solicitor, 21 March 1972.
203   Currently Section 23, *Criminal Code*.

course of action was approved, the referral was duly processed, and three judges of the Full Court sat to decide this crucial point of law: the true meaning of the word 'permit' in Section 208.

The judgement is the sort of text which greatly interests lawyers but very few other people, apart of course from those intimately involved. Their Honours discussed the issue at length, drawing on precedent from English, Irish and Australian cases for their decision. Eventually they decided that the term 'permits' means nothing more than 'allows.' Mere fear of harm is not enough to avoid the charge of permitting the offending action. If Kamzo had resisted, he would not have 'allowed' the act to be committed upon him. But he did not resist. However, at least the law provided a happy outcome for Mama Kamzo. Upon his release, he had apparently headed home, and there, presumably, he stayed. The law does not permit anyone to be tried twice for the same offence.[204]

***

Mama Kamzo may have escaped conviction (though not several months' incarceration as a remandee awaiting trial), but the legal principle was established in PNG law. This was created through the decision-making processes employed by PNG's colonial lawyers and judges, which were coloured by their Anglo-Australian legal heritage. They took an approach to law which is based on the premise that all law is man-made, by sovereign or legislature, and only awaits discernment by judges from general basic principles in increasingly refined detail. This approach severely restricts the courts' discretion and requires minutely detailed inspection of the meaning of words.[205] The approach is known as 'positivism,' which is based on the idea that legal systems are 'posited' by people. Law is separated from social and political contingencies, must have an identifiable origin to be valid, and must be applied as written by judges.[206] In the interpretation of statutes, a 'literalist' or 'plain meaning' approach is adopted, whereby the words in a statute must be given their plain and ordinary meaning, no matter how improbable that may be.[207]

But anti-positivism was emerging in the 1970s. In the USA, a pragmatic approach which focused on the logic of experience, rather than principles and rules, was

---

204 Known as the double jeopardy or *autrefois acquit* rule: *Criminal Code* Section 17.
205 Davies, *Asking the Law Question*, 47; Geddes, 'Purpose and context in statutory interpretation'; Jean G. Zorn, 1992, 'Common law jurisprudence and customary law,' in *Legal Issues in a Developing Society*, ed. R.W. James and I. Fraser, Port Moresby: University of Papua New Guinea, 103–27, 104.
206 Davies, *Asking the Law Question*, 47, 58, 100. See also Jean G. Zorn, 2006, 'Women and witchcraft: positivist, prelapsarian, and post-modern judicial interpretations in PNG,' in *Mixed Blessings: Laws, Religions, and Women's Rights in the Asia-Pacific Region*, ed. Amanda Whiting and Carolyn Evans, Leiden: Martinus Nijhoff, 61–99, 80n67, where she explains that positivism was originally intended as 'a safety measure, keeping aristocratic judges from picking "laws" out of thin air and applying them so as to send unlucky members of the thieving classes to Australia or worse,' but soon became a stringent process.
207 Catriona Cook et al., 2001, *Laying Down the Law* [6th ed.], Sydney: Butterworths, 229.

gaining ground.[208] It was termed then 'legal realism,' or more recently 'legal pragmatism,'[209] and was first developed by the American jurist Oliver Wendell Holmes Jr in 1881, in his famous book *The Common Law*. It permitted courts to discover the law in the real lives of those before them and in the social conditions pertaining beyond the courtroom door.[210] This approach actually has an ancient and honourable lineage, from an English case of 1584.[211] However, it was read down to apply only in situations of ambiguity or inconsistency of meaning. It made little impression on Anglo-Australian common law theory of the time, though,[212] and was only adopted in Australia in the 1980s.[213]

The colonial judges were nevertheless aware of the movement towards legal realism. In *Kausigor's Case*, the Full Court made an attempt to take local sentiments into account, although it concluded that

> we must confess to some difficulty in this sphere of human behaviour in this Territory in determining what are the 'felt necessities of the time, the prevalent, moral and political theories' which Oliver Wendell Holmes Jr speaks of as having a good deal more to do than the syllogism in determining the rules by which men should be governed…. What then should be done in this case which is one of sexual intercourse between two adult consenting males for all practical purposes in private. There is no question of corrupting or seducing youth and no element of force. We have accepted what is said about the attitude of the people.[214]

Such attention to legal realism was rare, though. By and large, Australian judges in PNG, both before and after Independence, were clearly of positivist bent. This is clear in the way the Supreme Court ruminated at length on the meaning of the single word 'permit' in *R v M.K*. It is clear also in the way Justice Wilson came to his decision in *Anna Wemay's Case*. He chose to ignore the history of the legal reform, and the possible purpose behind it. He decided that there was no ambiguity in the wording of the Act, and he therefore needed to look no further than 'the ordinary and natural meaning' of the words. By doing so, he decided that 'it is beyond question that a prostitute who is paid money for

---

208 Davies, *Asking the Law Question*, 32.
209 Susan Haack, 2005, 'On legal pragmatism: where does 'the path of the law' lead us?' *American Journal of Jurisprudence* 50: 71–105. In the interpretation of statutes in Australia, the approach was termed 'purposive': Cook et al., *Laying Down the Law*, 229.
210 Oliver Wendell Holmes Jr, 1881 [1968], *The Common Law*, London and Melbourne: Macmillan, 32.
211 *Heydon's Case* (1584) 3 Co Rep 7a, 7b; 76 ER 637, 638 (*Heydon's Case*).
212 Davies, *Asking the Law Question*, 34.
213 Cook et al., *Laying Down the Law*, 236–37. See also Mark Tunick, 2002, *Ethics, Morality, and Law*, Oxford Reference, online: http://www.oxfordreference.com/views/ENTRY.html?subview=Main&entry=t122.e0313, accessed 3 October 2006; Elizabeth A. Martin and Jonathan Law, 2006, *legal positivism*, Oxford Reference, online: http://www.oxfordreference.com/views/ENTRY.html?subview=Main&entry=t49.e2224, accessed 3 May 2007.
214 *Kausigor's Case*.

services rendered by her as a prostitute which money she would not otherwise have available to her for living purposes but for the fact that she was a prostitute is living at least in part on the earnings of prostitution.'[215]

It was not only the Australian judges who embraced positivism. The first PNG lawyers were educated in this mode, or at least were greeted in the courtroom by positivist judges. They had little choice but to bow to their superiors and permit themselves to be engulfed in lengthy debate as to literal meanings, so that by the time their vanguard came to the bench in the early 1980s, the positivist approach to the law was firmly entrenched in PNG jurisprudence. The outstanding exception was Narokobi, who endeavoured to incorporate a consideration of custom, and the 'real world' of PNG at Independence, into his judgements. But he received scant support from his brother judges, both expatriate and Papua New Guinean.[216]

The positivist approach also led the Full Court to dismiss any suggestion that customary beliefs and principles should be taken into account, even though the trial judge had observed that 'Debozina was the "boss-boi," that the accused was a much younger man, and that Debozina had discovered the accused in a neglect of duty, so that it would be natural for the accused man to be afraid that he would be reported to the manager and thus get into trouble.'[217]

The reference here to the age difference between the two may well have been an acknowledgement that the court was aware of the extent of power of an older over a younger man in the PNG village context (and Kamzo was fresh from a remote village). But the implications of this observation on custom are overlooked in the appeal court's lengthy and might I add somewhat tedious deliberations on the implications of the word 'permits' in the *Criminal Code*. Considerations of customary norms played no part in their decision. Detailed analysis of English and Australian cases, referring to the use of the word 'permits,' did.

Why was no appeal made to custom in order to establish Kamzo's state of mind and the reasonableness of his actions? Yes, he had been acquitted by the trial court and could not therefore be rearrested. But even so, one might have thought that the defence team, in this case the Public Solicitor, could have made some effort to raise the application of the *Native Customs (Recognition) Ordinance*, if only on principle. We know that the Crown instigated the appeal because its lawyers considered that the trial judge had made 'an error of law in a matter of principle of such importance that the judgement should not be permitted

---

215   *Anna Wemay's Case*, 177.
216   For an outstanding exposition of the treatment of Narokobi's judicial forays into legal realism, see Zorn's discussion of the Supreme Court's treatment of Narokobi AJ's judgement in *Aumane's Case*. Zorn, 'Women and witchcraft.'
217   *Kamzo Trial*, 4. The term *boss-boi* refers to a foreman or overseer.

to stand as an authority.'²¹⁸ But we do not know what the Public Solicitor's opinion was. There is no record in the Crown Prosecutor's file and no reference in the case decision to defence counsel's argument. We can only surmise that it never occurred to the latter to raise the issue of customary norms which require obedience to elders and superiors to show, for example, the 'state of mind of the accused' when his superior began forcing sex on him.

As well as the issues created by the positivist approach, and the application of a legal 'presumption' such as that which provides that ignorance of the law is no defence (even for a totally uneducated Engan lad experiencing colonial 'civilisation' for the first time), other legal processes give rise to strange outcomes. Problems arose with the form of the *Criminal Code*. A Code is not just a law setting out general principles which are then applied (or not) to the facts of each case, it is intended as a complete statement of the law, and it limits courts and judges somewhat more than a body of criminal law dispersed through various Acts.²¹⁹ Chief Justice Mann in his 1963 judgement in *R v Kauba-Paruwo*,²²⁰ in upholding the supremacy and relative fixity of the *Criminal Code*, said that if he were free to evolve the law according to common law principles, he would be able to apply it somewhat differently and indeed more leniently. But he was bound to follow the provisions of the *Criminal Code* as they stood, and hence could not adapt its definitions to suit the circumstances of the Territory.

The same principle was applied in the case of *R v John Bomai*,²²¹ though with a slightly better outcome for the accused. Bomai killed a man who had accused him of sodomy, was charged with wilful murder, and claimed a defence of provocation. This defence appears twice in the *Criminal Code*, with somewhat different parameters in each place. The judge carefully dissected both sections, again applying the positivist approach.

> In my opinion the word, where it appears in [Section 304] should be read in its ordinary dictionary meaning. If a person is suddenly induced to do an act which causes death, and if the inducement causes him to act in the heat of passion and before there is time for his passion to cool, then I consider that such inducement constitutes provocation.²²²

A successful defence of provocation under one section leads to complete exculpation, but under the other, only reduces a murder charge to one of

---

218 CP File Mama Kamzo above, letter of Crown Prosecutor to Crown Solicitor of 21 March 1972.
219 As in the United Kingdom, NSW, Victoria and South Australia.
220 *Regina v Kauba-Paruwo* [1963] PNGLR 18. In this case, His Honour opines that the Code 'expresses concepts of social responsibility in terms known to an advanced and civilized society.'
221 *R v John Bomai* [1964] PNGLR 278.
222 Ibid., 281.

manslaughter. And this latter, the judge decided, was the only one available to the accused, 'regarding him as "a reasonable Chimbu" I am satisfied that his self-control was overborne and the crime committed in "the heat of passion".'

There is an anomaly here, however. Judges may have claimed to espouse positivism, and the ordinary dictionary meaning of the word, and the belief that the law is and always has been there for all to discern. But they were nevertheless affected by extraneous factors. Firstly, whether they consciously realised it or not, they were guided by social morals: their own, or those of the colony (or ex-colony, in the case of Justice Wilson). Through court decisions, they constructed their own legal discourse, and obliged the populace to adhere to it. It then became a matter of numbers. Narokobi tried to persuade the judges to accept his view of PNG law as a living, growing thing, guided by custom and common sense, PNG-style. But he was alone, and ultimately could not prevail.

Using the rules

> Before rules, were facts; in the beginning was not a Word, but a Doing. Behind decisions stand judges; judges are men; as men they have human backgrounds. Beyond rules, again, lie effects: beyond decisions stand people whom rules and decisions directly or indirectly touch.
>
> Karl Llewellyn, scholar of legal realism, 1931.[223]

One major defect in the positivist approach to judicial decision-making is the assumption that there can be only one plain meaning to a word. Implicit in this is the assumption that the meaning is informed by a uniform social system, with shared moral and political values. This has hardly been the situation in PNG, where the application of the metropole's legal system to every person within the entire country created a huge political and ethical chasm, foregrounding the mores of the colonists and marginalising the diverse customs, principles and beliefs that constitute PNG societies. It was inevitable that the values of the colonists should predominate at the outset. *Lawfare* was waged spectacularly well in sexuality cases in the colonial courts—its weapons were the processes of the law and the beliefs of the expatriate judges. As the founder of legal realism, Oliver Wendell Holmes Jr points out,

> The life of the law has not been logic: it has been experience. The felt necessities of the time, the prevalent moral and political theories, intuitions of public policy, avowed or unconscious, even the prejudices

---

[223] Karl Llewellyn, 1931, 'Some realism about realism—responding to Dean Pound,' *Harvard Law Review* 44(8): 1222–64, 1222.

which judges share with their fellow-men, have had a good deal more to do with the syllogism [sic] in determining the rules by which men should be governed.[224]

Felt necessities

Justice Wilson in *Anna Wemay's Case* was clearly proud of himself when he proclaimed that

> it is likely that these four appellants are the first four prostitutes ever to be prosecuted in Papua New Guinea under this section. They may indeed hold the doubtful distinction of being the first prostitutes ever to be prosecuted in this country for any offence directly appertaining to their calling or, as it is sometimes called, their 'ancient profession.'[225]

The judge himself may well hold the 'doubtful distinction' of being the only judge anywhere in the common law world, so far as I can ascertain, to have used this standard provision, intended to criminalise pimping, to apply to the prostitute herself. I can only surmise that it was personal bias on his part which led him to take such an emphatically adverse stand on the matter. It was 1977, Independence had arrived and the *Constitution* had established that in interpreting statues and principles of common law, the circumstances of the country and other relevant matters should be taken into account.[226] But this was a judge particularly renowned for advancing his personal opinions on a range of matters. He came to PNG from the South Australian Bench, first for a brief term as Acting Judge in 1973, and then to a substantive appointment at the commencement of the 1978 legal year on 1 February. In South Australia, he had charged that the Dunstan Government, renowned for its progressive approach to law reforms including the reform of sodomy laws, had attempted to interfere with his judicial independence. The incident gave rise to a Royal Commission, which in its Report in December 1976 completely exonerated the government. Rather, it took an unfavourable view of Justice Wilson's proclivity to attribute improper motives to those who opposed him, his inability to appreciate an opposing point of view and his insistence in maintaining his own, and his prevarication as a witness.[227]

Justice Wilson decided *Anna Wemay's Case* in May of 1978, not long after he took up his PNG appointment, and soon followed it with another innovative

---

224 Holmes, *The Common Law*, 5.
225 *Anna Wemay's Case*, 178.
226 *Constitution* Schedule 2.
227 Account and quotations taken from David Weisbrot, 1980, 'Judges and politicians Pt II: the Wilson affair,' *Legal Service Bulletin* 5(5): 214–17, 216–217. Weisbrot was at the time a lecturer in law at UPNG.

decision in August,[228] a cannibalism case where the accused were charged with 'improperly interfering' with a dead body. To decide whether the action was 'improper,' the judge had to measure the action against what he decided were the current standards of common propriety of the community. In doing so (and in finding the accused guilty) he advanced the proposition that the modern 'reasonable man'[229] in PNG was no longer an ordinary person in his environment and culture, but a new creation, the 'moderate Melanesian.'[230] The 'reasonable man' standard in English law is actually an objective legal test: how would any reasonable man, not just the particular individual on trial, act and react in these circumstances?[231] Justice Wilson's standard of the 'moderate Melanesian' has been considered by one commentator, at least, to be 'a giant step backward' in determining the impact of custom in criminal charges.[232]

The following year, 1979, Justice Wilson became involved as an appeal judge of the Supreme Court in what has been termed PNG's first constitutional crisis, the 'Rooney Affair,' which revolved around an exchange of letters between Nahau Rooney, then Minister for Justice, and Justice Prentice, by then Chief Justice. The judges considered that the Minister's letter impugned the integrity and impartiality of the court, the judges, the justice system and the *Constitution*, and imprisoned Rooney for contempt of court,[233] an incarceration from which Prime Minister Somare released her the following day. Thereupon, five judges including Chief Justice Prentice and Justice Wilson tendered their resignations.

There followed what has been called the 'Wilson Affair.' After the Somare government was toppled in a vote of no confidence in March 1980, Justice Wilson, who had not formalised his resignation, wrote to the new Prime Minister, Julius Chan, offering to reconsider his decision to resign; to assist in a confidential manner in the preparation of a report on the state of the judiciary and the constitutional crisis; to advise on 'the attitudes of past and present judges of the Supreme Court and the motivations and allegiance of the proposed

---

228 *The State v Aubafo Feama & Ors* [1978] PNGLR 301.
229 In the common law, the 'reasonable man' personifies the objective standards of the community, against which individual actions and beliefs are tested. See J.F. Hookey, 1968, 'The "Clapham Omnibus" in Papua and New Guinea,' in *Fashion of Law in New Guinea*, ed. B.J. Brown, Sydney, Melbourne, Brisbane: Butterworths, 117–35.
230 'The average contemporary Papua New Guinean will be one with average attitudes to matters of life and death and to matters relating to food which is good to eat. He will not be a man given to histrionics or extreme abhorrent reactions, but, on the other hand, he will not be lacking in some emotional feeling and he will have the ability to think. He will be affected by the traditions of his ancestors and he will be aware that he is living in a changing world. He will be a villager in heart and in practice—a moderate Melanesian man.' *Anna Wemay's Case*.
231 See Hookey, 'The "Clapham Omnibus" in Papua and New Guinea,' for a discussion of the difficulties in applying the English standard to the pre-Independence territories.
232 David Weisbrot, 1979, 'Judges and politicians,' *Legal Service Bulletin* 4(6): 240–45, 244.
233 *Public Prosecutor v Nahau Rooney (No.1)* [1979] PNGLR 403; *Public Prosecutor v Nahau Rooney (No.2)* [1979] PNGLR 448.

Somare appointees'; to establish a committee (on which he would be willing to serve) to advise Cabinet on the legal implications of the Rooney Affair; and to discuss these matters with the Prime Minister in person.

When this letter was eventually leaked later that year and tabled by the Somare-led Opposition in Parliament, Prime Minister Chan swiftly gagged debate. Justice Wilson officially remained on the Bench until the end of 1980, 'retiring' on 1 February 1981,[234] but his last known bench appearance pre-dated the leaking of the letter.[235]

Weisbrot comments that the suggestions contained in Justice Wilson's letter 'would seem to bind the judiciary to the political scene in a way that neither Mrs. Rooney nor any other politician would ever dare suggest, and to present a far more serious threat to the independence of the judiciary than Rooney's public criticisms.'[236]

What Justice Wilson did was 'definitely completely outside established judicial ethics then and now,' to quote another government lawyer of the time (later to became a judge himself). It seemed at the time, even to those who did not know of his South Australian background, that he was simply trying to look after himself because he had nowhere else to go.[237]

It is sad to reflect that this was the judge who presumed to create new law in relation to prostitution, while presenting himself as dispensing impartial justice in the form of a positivist approach which refused to contemplate the background to the making of the *Summary Offences Act*. I can only speculate on the reasons for his hard-line positivist decision in *Anna Wemay's Case* which refused to take current circumstances into account. I believe however that he was greatly influenced by his version of the Australian middle-class (which at that stage still meant 'professional expatriate') view of what form the new society ought to take. As Jean G. Zorn puts it,

> The predominant myth common to almost all formal legal systems is that judges decide cases based solely on reason and logic. Emotion, bias, prejudice and the judge's own personal values are presumed to play no part.... [t]here is no place for emotion, bias or prejudice in that process;

---

234   As the legal year starts at the beginning of February each year, it is probable that Justice Wilson had already departed PNG before the end of 1980.
235   *Smedley v the State* [1980] PNGLR 379, in which hearings concluded on 13 June 1980.
236   David Weisbrot, 1980, 'Judges and politicians Pt II: the Wilson affair,' *Legal Service Bulletin* 5(5): 214–17, 215.
237   Pers. Comm. by email from Justice R.K. Woods, 21 November 2007.

there is no place for personality: the applicable rules are supposed to be applied equally to everyone, regardless of power relations based upon socio-economic class, or race, or gender.[238]

But as legal realists suggest, by contrast,

> Judges are men and therefore, their political and moral convictions inevitably influence their decisions ... law must be seen as connected to existing political processes and institutions ... because judges, lawyers, legal academics and others associated with the law *are* predominantly privileged in terms of gender, race and class, law is not only not separate from politics, it is also not separate from the power which its personnel have over less privileged people.[239]

Justice Wilson's 'political and moral considerations' and the power he exercised have contributed much to the present situation and the current popular view of those who sell sex in PNG today. His refusal to admit highly relevant evidence and his insistence on a blinkered application of positivist principles were manifestations of his own belief that the criminal status of prostitution should be maintained, regardless of any wishes to the contrary expressed by the emerging nationalists of the Independence era. A chance offered to the National Court, in the person of Narokobi AJ, slipped by, and no other challenge has since been mounted. Justice Wilson's judgement stands.

Consenting, adults, in private

The tale of Frank and Johnny illustrates how PNG law can intrude upon the sexual conduct of adult individuals conducted in private, harming no-one, but nevertheless leading to disastrous consequences. The element of consent was debated at great length in *R v M.K.*, which decided that lack of consent, unless expressed vociferously, was no defence. The question of adulthood has never been seriously in contention. Mama Kamzo was probably under eighteen. Siune Wel was clearly under-aged. But until 2002, the *Criminal Code* in Sections 210 and 211 only countenanced an age defence for a boy under fourteen. *Kausigor's Case* and *Leech's Case*, as well as *Johnny Mala's Case*, all concerned acts in private, and the right to privacy is guaranteed under the *Constitution*. But this has never been raised in the PNG courts, although it has been used to effect decriminalisation elsewhere, for example in Fiji.[240]

The fact that prostitution also involves these three elements seems to have escaped the lawmakers entirely. Criminalisation both in PNG and elsewhere

---

238 Zorn, 'The paradoxes of sexism,' 24.
239 Davies, *Asking the Law Question*, 163.
240 *Nadan v The State* [2005] FJHC 1 (Fiji Islands).

has been based largely on the harm done to society in general, by disturbing public order through street soliciting;[241] offending Christian principles;[242] and by constructions of the prostitute as 'vectors of disease.'[243] No objection has ever been raised to a prosecution or other police action on the grounds that sex has taken place between consenting adults in private.

The behaviour of animals

> Carnal knowledge against the order of nature is a serious and heinous offence. It is ... the behaviour of animals and must be stopped.
>
> Pitpit AJ in *Johnny Mala's Case*

In 1975, immediately before Independence, the Full Court sat to decide whether the pre-Independence Supreme Court had imposed an adequate sentence on Kabua Dewake.[244] Dewake, while visiting with *wantoks* in Port Moresby, had taken a three-year-old boy to the beach and there effected a minimal penetration of the child's anus. The Supreme Court judge imposed a sentence of four months, and the prosecution appealed to the Full Court, which increased the sentence. The Chief Justice, delivering the judgement, said that the judge should have given consideration to 'the impressions a forcible incident such as this might have on a child's mind ... [and] the strong concern ... of the people of Papua New Guinea not only for the general care of children, but that young children should not be exposed to sexual treatment such as this which is regarded throughout the country as a matter of gravity.'

Many years later, two National Court judges tried separate cases of sodomy in prisons. In the first, Justice Brunton heard that a man serving a sentence for rape of a woman had forced himself on another prisoner.[245] The accused claimed that such sexual activities were common in prisons, and that he had 'lost control of himself.'[246] The judge, while not endorsing this claim, nevertheless acknowledged that 'homosexuality is a personal disposition, not a medical condition or a social affliction,' and considered that no purpose would be served by extending the prisoner's sentence: it might even 'aggravate his antisocial tendencies.'

---

241 *Wolfenden Report*: §229; Self, 2003, *Prostitution, Women and Misuse of the Law*, 24, 37; *Police Offences Ordinance* (New Guinea) Section 38.
242 Self, *Prostitution, Women and Misuse of the Law*, 22; *Monika Jon's Case*.
243 Walkowitz, *Prostitution and Victorian Society*.
244 *Secretary for Law v Kabua Dewake* [1975] PNGLR 100.
245 *State v John Puwa Bui* (Unreported) N944, 14 December 1990.
246 See Adam Reed, 2003, *Papua New Guinea's Last Place: Experiences of Constraint in a Postcolonial Prison*, New York and Oxford: Berghahn Books, 116-119.

The following year, Justice Jalina tried a case of sodomy in another prison.[247] It appeared that the accused had 'threatened the victim into submission.' But this judge took a different view of the incident. 'This kind of behaviour must be stopped,' he declared. 'It is the behaviour of animals.' He referred to *Secretary for Law v Kabua Dewake* to support his decision.

This is the case from which Acting Justice Pitpit derived his language and his approach in *Johnny Mala's Case*. It is hard to follow his line of reasoning, other than to assume that he was in general agreement with Justice Jalina as to the repugnance of sodomy in general. But otherwise, the two cases had little in common—and even less in common with *Secretary for Law v Kabua Dewake*, which concerned inappropriate dealing with a three-year-old child. *State v Pos* involved non-consensual sex. But Johnny Mala was an adult (although reported as a 'teenager'); he was engaged in an act of consensual sex; and it was most definitely being conducted in private. The judge added that he had rendered his family and relatives 'vulnerable to ridicule, shame and sexual advances,'[248] which he seemed to think increased the heinousness of the offence, although the last threat is a little hard to understand as a consequence of his actions. These two judges appear to have been greatly affronted by occurrences of homosexual activity, and despite attempts at reasoned judgement, seem to have allowed their prejudices to dictate their reactions and reasoning.

The conflation of consensual and forced sex, of sex between adults and sex with children, into the one crime of 'sodomy' when it involves anal penetration of one male by another, has been greatly assisted by the widely diverging penalties provided under the *Criminal Code*. Section 210, forbidding 'carnal knowledge against the order of nature,' carries a maximum penalty of fourteen years imprisonment, whereas 'Indecent treatment of boys under 14' provides only seven years. 'Indecent practices between males' at Section 212 is a mere misdemeanour with a penalty of only three years. If anal penetration can be proved, prosecutors will naturally indict for the offence with the greatest penalty. Hence 'sodomy' charges involving forced sex or under-aged 'victims' incite public outrage, while consensual sex between adults in private, which can only come to the attention of the law if a spy witnesses the occurrence or a confession is forthcoming, is tarred with the same stigmatising brush, as the utterly evil 'sodomy.'

---

247 *State v Pos* [1991] PNGLR 208.
248 *Johnny Mala's Case* above, 3.

Conclusion

> The law operates more and more as a norm, and ... the judicial institution is increasingly incorporated into a continuum of apparatuses (medical, administrative, and so on) whose functions are for the most part regulatory.
>
> Michel Foucault.[249]

Foucault's history of the law's control of sexuality in Western Europe claimed that mediaeval ecclesiastical law's control of sin and power over death became transformed from the eighteenth century to the state's power over life. Laws which criminalise sexual conduct represent an exercise of social power through the control of human bodies. Those who have the power in society make the rules, as Margaret Davies observes. The laws that they make regarding sexuality are based in the moral rules they have devised or adopted.

An illustration of this is provided by the English jurist Lord Devlin's argument[250] in opposition to the proposal in the United Kingdom in 1957 to decriminalise sodomy.[251] Lord Devlin argued that there is a 'public morality' which determines the principles of law, and enables the criminal law to intervene when the social fabric is threatened. Constructing a public morality and creating a threat to the social fabric are done by processes that operate largely by exclusion—of the criminal, the insane, the sexually deviant and so on. Prostitution and sex between males were criminalised in the Anglo-Australian law which was introduced into the PNG colony. Despite subsequent reforms overseas, and attempts at reform in PNG at Independence, the expatriate and expatriate-influenced legal practitioners used the forms and processes of the law to support their own views on these matters, and no reform has yet been effected. In post-colonial society, the legal discourse of proscription has been taken up by the dominant *elites* of society, and developed even further than in the former metropole.

We can draw several conclusions from this survey of the legislation and the case law interpreting it. The criminalisation of selling sex has persisted, despite reform attempts at Independence, because an expatriate judge used techniques of interpretation to preserve the moral regime established by the introduced legal system—his legal system. He dismissed the attempts at reform, and even congratulated himself on pioneering a 'new' principle of law which maintained the status quo. The irony of his using an apparently positivist approach is that the positivism/realism divide is not entirely true for PNG. Judges of the colonial

---

249 Foucault, *The Will to Knowledge: The History of Sexuality: Vol. 1*, 144.
250 Patrick Devlin, 1960, *The Enforcement of Morals*, London: Oxford University Press.
251 *Wolfenden Report*.

and immediate post-colonial era claimed to espouse positivist principles, but whether they knew it or not, they were affected by normative standards—the standards of their own communities of the metropole, of the colonists rather than the colonised. Through their decisions, they obliged the colonised to adhere to an introduced normative regime. Meanwhile, the true pioneer of reform, former Law Reform Commission Chairman Narokobi, was apparently not sufficiently sure of himself to overturn a more senior judge's ruling (he was only an acting judge) or alternately was drawn by the popular rhetoric of the 'prostitute' as a glamorous seductress to make his careful distinction between that character and the PNG reality of the *tukina busmeri*.

Another reality overlooked by those who dispense the law is that sex has been sold by males as well as females, but still the prostitute is gendered female in the eyes of those who administer and dispense the law, and males selling sex are penalised for the sexual act, not the commercial transaction. This may be due to the larger penalty attaching to sodomy, or to the fact that male judges find the thought of the male-male sexual acts concerned more abhorrent than that of women indulging in commercial (and therefore, wanton, casual) sex. The criminalisation of consensual sex between adult males in private has also persisted, despite reforms overseas. The law, in the persons of judges and legislators, has retained the right to intrude into the realm of private morals in PNG. Customary principles, practices and attitudes are ignored. Legal pronouncements and manipulation of legal language have succeeded in removing almost entirely the distinction between consensual, private sex and brutal force. No participant is spared.

The situation now at law is that if you are selling sex, and can be proved to be living to a reasonable extent on your earnings, you can be arrested, prosecuted and fined up to K400 or imprisoned for up to a year. If you are male, and unlucky enough to be spied upon and caught in the act of sex with another male, you can also be prosecuted, with far worse consequences: up to fourteen years in prison, and possible deportation for non-citizens.

But this is not all that criminalised outgroups can suffer. As I explained in Chapter One, Goodman demonstrates that the very fact of criminalisation can affect society's opinions and treatment of those criminalised. It may not be enough to look only at the operation of the law. In order to understand the historical antecedents of sexualities which fall outside the norms of today, and the lived experiences of those criminalised by those norms, we must step out of the courtroom and onto the streets of Port Moresby today.

4. On the Streets

> Disciplinary power is constitutively linked to the knowledge of the individual and society and the way in which the 'reversal of the procedures of individualization' rendered necessary the giving of every person (not just the politically powerful or the socially significant) a distinct individuality, a discrete place in the great social continuum of abnormal to normal.
>
> Ben Golder and Peter Fitzpatrick, 2009.[1]

Introduction

In this chapter, I describe the placing, on this 'great social continuum of abnormal to normal' as the epigraph above has it, of subjects whose sexual activities are criminalised in PNG. The ethnographic record includes some accounts of homosexuality but fewer of the sale or exchange of sex,[2] and I refer to some accounts in Chapter 2 and summarise them below. Chapter 3 has described the engagement of the formal law before and after Independence, and also refers to Aldrich's historical overview of homosexuality. But scholarly attention only really began to focus on these matters with the arrival of the HIV epidemic, which prompted a wealth of sexual behavioural research and reporting. One of the earliest truly comprehensive studies was the landmark *National Study of Sexual and Reproductive Knowledge and Behaviour in Papua New Guinea* (*National Study*) conducted under the auspices of the Papua New Guinea Institute of Medical Research (IMR) in the early 1990s.[3] This quantitative study surveyed sexual behaviours, attitudes and issues at rural community level, focusing specifically on the full range of sexual behaviours and knowledge, not just as practised in traditional village settings but also as affected by the influences of urbanisation and modernity. So it included studies of a range of sexual behaviours which included same-sex practices and the commercialisation of sex.[4] Researchers found that although the influences of

---

1   Ben Golder and Peter Fitzpatrick, 2009, *Foucault's Law*, Abingdon: Routledge, 63.
2   Notable exceptions are the work of Joan Drikoré Johnstone, 1993, 'The Gumini *Bisnis-Meri*: a study of the development of an innovative indigenous entrepreneurial activity in Port Moresby in the early 1970s,' Ph.D. thesis, Brisbane: University of Queensland; and of Holly Wardlow, especially her 2006 book, *Wayward Women: Sexuality and Agency in a New Guinea Society*, Berkeley and Los Angeles, CA: University of California Press.
3   National Sex and Reproduction Research Team and Carol Jenkins, 1994, *National Study of Sexual and Reproductive Knowledge and Behaviour in Papua New Guinea*, Papua New Guinea Institute of Medical Research (*National Study*).
4   Ibid., particularly, 24–36 and 76–122.

church, state, the cash economy and greatly increased communication, both nationally and internationally, have had deep and often homogenising effects, the range of cultural practices, ideologies and beliefs remains 'extraordinary.'[5] Further studies of sexual behaviour have continued to appear, many penned by Carol Jenkins and Lawrence Hammar, medical anthropologists working with the IMR. In 2008, the National Research Institute conducted an intensive behavioural surveillance study in a group of coffee plantations in an area of high HIV prevalence in Western Highlands Province.[6] Findings show that both male and female workers sell and exchange sex, including the purchase of sex by men from men and by women from men.[7] At the end of 2010, the *Askim na Save* [Ask and Understand] Report, a quantitative mapping survey conducted jointly by the IMR and the University of New South Wales (UNSW) appeared.[8] The study was designed to fill gaps in knowledge and provide a better understanding of the sexual networks of those who sell and exchange sex in Port Moresby, from a socio-cultural as well as a behavioural perspective.[9] Nearly 600 women, men and transgenders aged nine years and older who had sold or exchanged sex in Port Moresby during a six-month period in 2010 were sampled.

A crucial point of entry for my research, although by no means my only source of information, has been the Poro Sapot Project. This Project is the successor to the Transex Project of 1996 and the Transex-Plus Project of 1996–2000.[10] The Poro Sapot Project provides HIV awareness, clinic facilities and para-legal assistance for what it terms 'female sex workers' (FSW) and 'men who have sex with men' (MSM) in several PNG centres. So I commence with a snapshot of the Project as it was at the time of my project fieldwork, in the mid-2000s.[11]

The Poro Sapot Project

In a Boroko street, behind the usual high tin fence, is a colonial bungalow converted for use by Poro Sapot. Outside the gate are the ubiquitous *buai-*

---

5 Ibid., 5.
6 Holly Buchanan et al., 2010, *Behavioural Surveillance Research in Rural Development Enclaves in Papua New Guinea: A Study with the WR Carpenters Workforce*, Port Moresby: National Research Institute.
7 Ibid., xii, 38–42.
8 Angela Kelly et al., 2011, Askim na Save *(Ask and Understand): People Who Sell and/or Exchange Sex in Port Moresby*, Sydney, Australia: Papua New Guinea Institute of Medical Research and the University of New South Wales.
9 Ibid., 9.
10 Described in detail in Carol Jenkins 2000, *Female Sex Worker HIV Prevention Projects: Lessons Learned from Papua New Guinea, India and Bangladesh*, UNAIDS Best Practice Collection, Geneva: UNAIDS, 19–56. These projects mainly targeted sex and transport workers, police and security guards in Port Moresby, Goroka and Lae, and along the Highlands Highway.
11 This section was written before the Project was required to vacate the premises by the landlord in 2010. A new location was eventually identified nearby, and the Project moved at the beginning of 2011. I took most of these photos in 2006–07.

sellers, where passers-by, including students from the nearby Christian college, stop to purchase and chew Port Moresby's drug of choice. The security guard operates an electric gate to admit vehicles, while people pass constantly in and out of the small pedestrian gate beside it.

Figure 4.1. Poro Sapot outreach workers leave the Project yard to conduct site visits.

Source: Photo by Christine Stewart, 18 January 2006.

Inside, the former front garden is now a gravelled parking lot. Extensions and additional buildings crowd around the original building, to house a reception area, offices, a kitchen, a conference room. To one side, shadecloth screens the clinic's 'waiting room.' There are two *hauswin* [roofed sitting platforms] in the grounds, which function as drop-in centres.

Figure 4.2. MSM drop-in centre in Poro Sapot's front yard.

Source: Photo by Christine Stewart, 28 August 2007.

Figure 4.3. FSW drop-in centre at the rear of the building. A literacy class, conducted by a teacher funded by Dame Carol Kidu, is in progress.

Source: Photo by Christine Stewart, 2 September 2007.

Gays live with family, relatives or friends around town and come to the Project to find a safe space and involve themselves in the various meetings and activities which are constantly taking place there. By contrast, the street women who base themselves at their drop-in centre do so as a matter of survival. For those who sell sex in the evenings, this is the only place where they can store their meagre possessions, sleep undisturbed during the day, bathe, do their laundry and cook themselves decent meals.

The Project centre is open during office hours on weekdays only, so on weekends they are left to their own devices. The reasoning behind this policy is that otherwise, they would simply move in—and as it is estimated that there are several hundred such women in the Boroko area alone,[12] this would place an impossible strain on the Project's facilities.[13]

---

12 Interview, Scarlet Alliance Project Officer, 15 April 2006.
13 The Project is already plagued by high water and electricity bills. Staff have, however, taken the initiative to purchase in bulk and sell, at cost, such items as toilet rolls and sanitary wear.

Figure 4.4. Many women sleep, dress and prepare themselves for work at the FSW drop-in centre. Their only possessions are stored in bags in the rafters.

Source: Photo by Christine Stewart, 4 September 2007.

Figure 4.5. Laundry at the tubs.

Source: Photo by Christine Stewart, 2 September 2007.

The clinic offers treatment for sexually-transmitted infections (STIs) and voluntary counselling and testing for HIV. It is probably unique in the Pacific for providing these services to men who have sex with other men and for women who sell and exchange sex, and for their partners.

Through a system of outreach volunteers (OV) who travel around town and to clubs and guesthouses, meeting and talking with sex sellers, clients, gays, club and guesthouse staff and outreach workers in other areas and so on, the Project spreads word of its work, gives advice on HIV and sexual health, distributes male and female condoms and lubricant and provides demonstrations of their use, and encourages and organises visits to the clinic.

The emphasis is on one-to-one interaction, and on changing behaviour rather than simply passing on information, and the Project runs a variety of training sessions for this purpose. When a new nightclub opens, for example, OVs quickly arrange a visit to talk with the women there and encourage them to visit the clinic. The OVs have been issued with blue 'Poro' shirts, with lettering saying in Tok Pisin 'FRIEND, if you want to know more, talk to me…' which makes them more easily identifiable. More and more people are accosting them to ask questions and seek advice. On occasion, they encounter negative reactions, or forms of sanctimonious preaching, but this does not deter them.[14]

Another part of Poro Sapot outreach work involves working with the police. In 2006, I attended an awareness session for police held at the Poro Sapot centre. In response to much phoning-around, organisers were promised thirty-six police participants, but only six actually attended. I was told that this was usual. Those who attended were presented with sessions on sexuality, sexual health and human rights awareness conducted by various presenters. The participants at this session urged the removal of the session locale to the police stations—at that time, with tales of police abuse of sex sellers and gays abounding, this proposal seemed somewhat alarming, but outreach workers were undeterred, and started work on establishing processes for this. By early 2007, the project was able to run a lengthy (nearly week-long) workshop at the Bomana Police Training College for new police recruits. Liaison Officers began to visit police stations regularly for awareness sessions with the different shifts. Before long, police sensitisation sessions were taking place regularly in all the urban centres where Poro Sapot works.[15]

The emphasis in awareness sessions is on the human rights of all to protect themselves from infection: those selling sex, instead of being accused of spreading HIV, should be allowed and encouraged to insist on condom use, and police themselves should also use condoms consistently. Additionally, the Liaison Officers take up matters with the police on behalf of sex sellers and gays,

---

14 When I visited the Project in August 2008, staff were preparing to interview some ninety applicants for OV positions. Interest in this work is keen, which is no surprise, it is a way for those with little formal education and no other job prospects to gain on-the-job training for a variety of skills.
15 Elizabeth Reid, 2010, 'Putting values into practice in PNG: the Poro Sapot Project and aid effectiveness,' *Pacificurrents* 1.2 and 2.1, online: http://intersections.anu.edu.au/pacificurrents/reid.htm, accessed 9 August 2013.

and where appropriate, refer cases on to such bodies as the Department for Community Development for welfare matters, or human rights NGOs for legal advice and assistance.[16] Meanwhile, OVs and Project staff had extended their activities to HIV awareness performances at nightclubs, and open participation in World AIDS Day celebrations. In the five years since the Three-Mile Guesthouse Raid, police attitudes had changed considerably. The 2009 World AIDS Day motorcade was escorted by police, whose first demand on arrival at the assembly point was for their promised 'payment' of red Poro Sapot/Save the Children T-shirts and posters to adorn their police escort vehicles.

Figure 4.6. Project workers in their condom costumes, ready for the motorcade around town. World AIDS Day, 2009, Port Moresby.

Source: Photo by Christine Stewart, 1 December 2009.

It is not always an easy road for the Project. Its work targets predominantly those with little education and no formal employment, who have the least to lose by admitting their identities and activities. This is evidenced in surveys carried

---

16 Interview, Poro Sapot outreach worker, 6 September 2007.

out in 2004–2005 and 2006–2007.[17] Their sample is confined to one particular group of sister-girls, and the Project Director considers that the sample used in the survey may have been skewed by attracting responses only from those with the least to conceal.[18]

Figure 4.7. Here the police are shown placing posters on their escort vehicles.

Source: Photo by Christine Stewart, 1 December 2009.

But Poro Sapot does more than all this. Elizabeth Reid, in a tribute to the Project and its HIV work,[19] says that the instrumentalist approach insisted upon by aid donors, with its emphasis on ascribing *numerical* values to targeted achievements, ignores the values-based and human rights-centred approach so vital to achieving success in epidemic control, and so vital to Poro Sapot. This

---

17 Geraldine Maibani-Michie and William Yeka, 2005, *Baseline Research for Poro Sapot Project: A Program for Prevention of HIV/AIDS among MSM in Port Moresby and FSW in Goroka and Port Moresby Papua New Guinea (PNG)*, report prepared for Papua New Guinea Institute of Medical Research, Goroka, Papua New Guinea; Geraldine Maibani-Michie et al., 2007, *Evaluation of the Poro Sapot Project: Baseline and End-of-Project (EOP) Studies: An HIV Prevention Program among MSM in Port Moresby and FSW in Goroka and Port Moresby*, report prepared for Papua New Guinea Institute of Medical Research and Family Health International, Asia and Pacific Department, Goroka, Papua New Guinea.
18 Christopher Hershey, 2008, 'Reflections on Poro Sapot: one model of care for men's sexual and reproductive health,' paper presented at the Men's Sexual and Reproductive Health in PNG Conference, Port Moresby, PNG, 12 June, 3.
19 Reid, 'Putting values into practice in PNG.'

Project interfaces with those most outcast by society: those whose sexuality has been criminalised. It places emphasis on the way it practises its processes as much as on evaluating and enumerating its outcomes.

As an organisation working with stigmatised men and women, Poro Sapot has itself become stigmatised. This can inhibit new contacts from accessing its premises and services.[20] The criminalisation of anal sex and prostitution adds to the negative image of the Project. For example, a 2006 Letter to the *Post-Courier* called on various agencies to do something about illegal sexual activities going on, 'just opposite the Three-Mile bus stop. Towards the end of the street on the left side as you go towards the rugby oval, there is a building where sex workers are accommodated. I doubt this illegal brothel provides condoms for sex workers and clients.'[21] The portrayal of the Project as a brothel and the completely erroneous assumption regarding condom provision (the Project's main task is to distribute condoms to high-use sites and establishments, and promote their use) is typical of public reaction.

The ancient profession

> The rate and nature of historical change in Papua New Guinea is remarkable, although not evenly experienced across all cultural domains or geographical regions.... What the effects have been on sexuality, the social contexts of sexual behaviour, complex ideologies of sex and gender, the institutions of marriage and family are not well-known. Few societies were well described early enough to have a pre-missionary ethnographic baseline; even fewer of these have had a contemporary re-study to examine effects of modernization on sex and gender issues.
>
> Carol Jenkins, 1996.[22]

Ethnographic studies and administrative reports from such widely divergent parts of the country as the Papuan Plateau (south-west), Anga (central Highlands) and Massim (south-east mainland and islands) indicate that wife- and sister-exchange (whether swapping or in exchange for food and other commodities) has been a long-standing practice.[23] In some groups, extra-marital sex and even pre-

---

20 Hershey, 'Reflections on Poro Sapot,' 7.
21 Ngalye Concerned Observer, 2006, 'Call to probe illegal brothel,' *Post-Courier* (online) letter, 4 January.
22 Carol Jenkins, 1996, 'The homosexual context of heterosexual practice in Papua New Guinea,' in *Bisexualities and AIDS*, ed. Peter Aggleton, London: Taylor and Francis, 191–206, 193.
23 C. Kowald, 1894, 'Appendix R: native habits and customs of the Mekeo District (Central Division),' in *Annual Report on British New Guinea 1892–1893*, Brisbane: Edmund Gregory, Government Printer, 63; L.A. Flint, 1919, 'Muguru at Torobina, Bamu River,' *Man* 19: 38–39; John Nilles ,1950/51, 'The Kuman of the Chimbu Region, Central Highlands, New Guinea,' *Oceania* 21(1): 25–65, 30, 48; *National Study*, 115; Lawrence

marital promiscuity were strongly disapproved and often violently punished,[24] but even there, respondents to the *National Study* stated that although sex was never actually paid for with cash, unattached women might be kept supplied with food in exchange for providing sex.[25] In societies which encourage pre-marital sexual experimentation, it may be customary for the boy to give the girl a small gift, even for a one-time-only encounter.[26]

The colonists brought new cultural influences and new ways of living, being and doing to the scattered villages of PNG. The money and goods which they exchanged for food, labour, land and other commodities transformed reciprocal exchange networks generally, and in many instances, converted a system of sexual favours into a commercial commodity exchange capable of attracting immediate payment. Transactional sex meshed with prior forms of sexual networking or introduced new ones. The expanding cash economy, no matter how meagre, promoted an increase in internal migration, the growth of towns and unequal wealth distribution, which widened the scope for such transactions.[27] Various strategies (introducing store-bought goods, the levying of a head-tax) were employed to instil in the colonised a need for cash, which could best be fulfilled by signing up for indentured labour. But cash could be acquired in other ways too.

Movement of people from villages to towns was restricted by law until the 1960s, but women were already available for sex. Of the nearby Motu/Koitabu villages, the closest was Hanuabada, the 'great village,' which has now been geographically, if not socially, absorbed into the city. In the 1950s, the main offences against public morality were considered by Hanuabada village leaders to include prostitution, mainly involving the prostitution of village women to Europeans—internal prostitution only occurred 'on a significant scale' in other

---

Hammar, n.d., 'Sex and secrecy in the South Fly: *tu kina bus* in historical perspective,' unpublished, 5; Hammar. 2010, *Sin, Sex and Stigma: A Pacific Response to HIV and AIDS*, Wantage: Sean Kingston Publishing, especially 63, 73–78; Johnstone, 'The Gumini *Bisnis-Meri*,' 202.

24 See e.g., Peter Sack, 1974, 'The range of traditional Tolai remedies,' in *Contention and Dispute: Aspects of Law and Social Control in Melanesia*, ed. A.L. Epstein, Canberra: Australian National University Press, 67–92, 82–91. Many crimes among the Tolai, including sexual crimes such as wife-stealing, could be redressed by compensation of shell money.

25 *National Study*, 115–16; and see the discussion in Lawrence Hammar, 1998, 'AIDS, STDs and sex work in Papua New Guinea,' in *Modern Papua New Guinea*, ed. Laura Zimmer-Tamakoshi, Kirksville, MO: Thomas Jefferson University Press, 257–89, pp. 275–77.

26 This is certainly true of Trobriand society today, where the custom of giving (by the boy) and receiving (by the girl) of gifts, including gifts of cash, is expected as a sign of respect, mutual pleasure and the importance of the developing relationship. See Katherine Lepani, 2007, '"In the process of knowing": making sense of HIV and AIDS in the Trobriand Islands of Papua New Guinea,' Ph.D. thesis, Canberra: The Australian National University, 106, 164–70.

27 For example Hammar, *Sin, Sex and Stigma*, 66–68; Kelly et al., Askim na Save, 9; Lae Mission Station, *Annual Report*, 1936, cited in Ian Willis, 1974, *Lae: Village and City*, Melbourne: Melbourne University Press, 107–08; *National Study*, 115; Holly Wardlow, 2004, 'Anger, economy and female agency: problematizing "prostitution" and "sex work" among the Huli of Papua New Guinea,' *Signs* 29(4): 1017–39, 1028.

nearby villages.²⁸ Nevertheless, it was the concerns of Hanuabadan village leaders which had prompted the enactment of the *Native Women's Protection Ordinance*, and occasionally a case was brought to court.²⁹ Nigel Oram also recounted in 1976 how a District Officer in 1959 evicted some Hula men from a canoe settlement on 'Koke Island'³⁰ because he considered it had become a centre for prostitution, drinking and gambling.³¹ He also wrote:

> The extent of prostitution [in Port Moresby in 1976] is unknown but compared to its incidence in towns in other developing countries it is small. It has existed in the sense of sexual associations for material gain in villages and settlements since 1945 (Belshaw, 1957: 239) and even earlier (F.E. Williams nd). In November 1967 the *Pacific Islands Monthly* observed that while sex had been available in the past in canoes and villages, groups of girls could be seen at street corners and in bars and lounges, which indicated their availability. Women provide services for people of their own and allied groups in a number of settlements and in some areas men prostitute their wives. There is no long-term organisation of prostitutes although one house near Sabama served as a brothel for a time. Gangs of three or four girls sometimes share flats for short periods and are available to young European males who are 'tourists' in the town (J. Whiteman, pers. comm.) With the increasing emancipation of women from male control, semi-professional prostitution is likely to increase.³²

An example of this 'semi-professional prostitution' was provided by Rabbie Namaliu, later to become Prime Minister, who in the early 1970s wrote and staged an entertaining play ironically entitled *The Good Woman of Konedobu*.³³ It depicted a beautiful *pamuk* [sic] drinking, dancing and demanding cigarettes, drinks and snacks (though not money) from her mainly expatriate admirers at a local tavern. She is portrayed as modern, sophisticated, in pursuit of moneyed expatriate men and having her own flat, where the final scene of the play takes place.

Meanwhile, Joan Johnstone was researching her landmark study of prostitution amongst a Highlands group, although she did not write up her findings until

---

28 Cyril Shirley Belshaw, 1957, *The Great Village: The Economic and Social Welfare of Hanuabada, an Urban Community in Papua*, London: Routledge & K. Paul, 216, 218, 237.
29 Ibid., 239.
30 Now known as Koki, to the east of Ela Beach, Port Moresby; the former island has now been linked to the mainland by a causeway.
31 Nigel Oram, 1976, *Colonial Town to Melanesian City: Port Moresby 1884–1974*, Canberra: Australian National University Press, 98. The seafaring Hula people from further east along the coast were able to circumvent the restrictions on movement by anchoring their canoes below the high-water mark, where the Administration's jurisdiction ended. See Ian Stuart, 1970, *Port Moresby Yesterday and Today*, Sydney: Pacific Publications, 117. This jurisdictional limit has been a feature of European laws for centuries.
32 Oram, *Colonial Town to Melanesian City*, 152.
33 Rabbie Namaliu, 1970, 'The good woman of Konedobu,' *Kovave* 1(2): 44–53.

nearly three decades later.³⁴ Johnstone's thesis describes an 'innovative' pattern of selling sex among one specific ethnic group in the capital, the Gumini people of Simbu, in the Highlands. She explains how the entrepreneurial Gumini wanted to start up some form of business enterprise, and found a means when significant numbers began migrating to Port Moresby in the late 1960s.³⁵ They imitated other urban migrants who had already brought their wives to town and established systematised commercial sexual services for indigenous men. First one couple, then more, set up their enterprise of *bisnismeri* (businesswoman), a form of sexual entrepreneurship which involved a woman and her male partner (husband, brother, father) setting forth each day to one of the established workplaces of the city, in the open in long grass, under trees or along the rocky harbour foreshores. The women did no active soliciting, for it was not necessary. Demand outstripped supply at the time,³⁶ and all that was needed was to await custom. The male proprietor appropriated all the earnings, as Gumini women had no control over their earnings but were defined solely by their relationship to a husband or male relative.³⁷ The exception to this near universal arrangement was the *pasinja-meri* (lit. passenger-woman), usually a divorced or single woman who for one reason or another had rebelled against society and left home, engaging in commercial sex or at least a succession of short-term serial partnerships for survival.³⁸ But this was not the case with the *bisnismeri*. Johnstone's research revealed that the behaviour resulted from the socio-economic traditions of the Guminis and their adaptation to the ways of life in Port Moresby, and as far as those involved were concerned, selling sex was a 'business' just like any other small-scale trading enterprise. Nevertheless, the behaviour of *bisnismeri* was condemned by the virtuous Gumini housewives of the town.³⁹

Johnstone also noted other types of prostitution in Port Moresby at the time; mainly young unmarried women operating in nightclubs, sports clubs and hotels, and she hinted at call-girl services.⁴⁰ She told me that Tatana, a peri-

---

34 Johnstone, 'The Gumini *Bisnis-Meri*.'
35 I recall that at that time, the Simbu people constituted the majority of Highlanders coming to the town, impelled by land shortages and lack of money-making opportunities at home. They were deeply resented by the local Motu-Koitabuans, and other peoples from the Territory of Papua. The presence of Highlanders in Moresby was one of the factors prompting Josephine Abaijah's *Papua Besena* separatist political movement in the early 1970s. See Josephine Abaijah and Eric Wright, 1991, *A Thousand Coloured Dreams*, Mount Waverley, Vic: Dellasta Pacific.
36 Rew notes the conspicuous preponderance of young unmarried men in Port Moresby in the mid-1960s. See Alan Rew, 1974, *Social Images and Process in Urban New Guinea: A Study of Port Moresby*, St. Paul: West Publishing Co., 12.
37 Johnstone, 'The Gumini *Bisnis-Meri*,' 98, 108–09, 132, 138.
38 Ibid., 94, 201. *Pasinjia-meri* are discussed in detail in Wardlow, '"Prostitution," "Sexwork," and "Passenger Women"'; Holly Wardlow, 2002, 'Passenger-women: changing gender relations in the Tari Basin,' *Papua New Guinea Medical Journal* 45(1–2): 142–46; Wardlow, *Wayward Women*.
39 Johnstone, 'The Gumini *Bisnis-Meri*,' especially 1–2, 140–42, 186.
40 Ibid., 94.

urban Motu village on an island in the harbour, was known as the village supplying sex for Port Moresby at the time, and also that an expatriate living in Hohola, a low-cost-housing suburb, imported girls from Hula village to the east on the pretext that he was going to marry them, and effectively ran a brothel there.[41] I recall a call-girl enterprise operating out of the laundry behind a block of flats in the Port Moresby suburb of Boroko where I lived briefly in the early 1970s. Taxis would arrive regularly throughout the night to collect and return the women, who spent most of the following day sleeping on the floor of the communal laundry, necessitating my stepping over them to reach the washing machines. I also recall male students at UPNG in the early 1970s mentioning the wisdom of using condoms when visiting prostitutes, as a precaution against VD (as STIs were then known). The spread of venereal disease, which was becoming a concern by the early 1970s, was being attributed to the increased prevalence of prostitution, due to mass migration to urban centres. A marked sex imbalance meant that uneducated girls in towns turned to prostitution 'almost through necessity,' although it was not necessarily viewed as a permanent state of affairs.[42] As it has turned out, however, necessity has persisted as a factor in maintaining a sex trade in PNG.

The most recent and comprehensive survey of Port Moresby's sex industry to date is the *Askim Na Save* Report.[43] Its findings challenge many popularly-held conceptions about sexual behaviour across all classes and groups engaged in the sex trade of Port Moresby, by demonstrating that: people as young as nine years were selling sex; the most common location for selling or exchanging sex was a settlement or (peri-urban) village; landowners were the most common clients, followed by company employees, public servants, businessmen and students; both men and transgenders had women as clients; the major perpetrators of violence against sex sellers were family members, police and regular partners; transgenders were more physically and sexually abused than men or women; most who sold sex also sold other items such as *buai*, cigarettes and store items, strengthening the argument that 'seller of sex' is not their primary identification.

Why do it?

Jenny's Tale

Jenny was in Year 10 at High School outside Port Moresby when a girlfriend introduced her to her boyfriend's friend, a new recruit at the Police Training

---

41 Johnstone, pers. comm., Canberra, 10 December 2004.
42 Anne MacGregor, 1972, 'VD—shame and social stigma: concern is growing at rapid spread of disease,' *Post-Courier* (Port Moresby), 5 October 1972, 5; Anne MacGregor, 1972, 'VD is not new to territory: prostitutes—should they be legalised?' *Post-Courier* (Port Moresby), 10 October 1972, 5.
43 Kelly et al., Askim na Save.

College. Every weekend, she and her girlfriend headed to town to spend time with their sweethearts. But then Jenny fell pregnant and had to drop out of school.[44]

From the outset, it was a bad marriage. Her husband drank and abused her. Her father was ill, out of work, and still had debts and traditional obligations, but her husband refused to help her support her own family. He told her in front of her two sons to 'go and sell her cunt to feed her parents.' He started having affairs with other women. Then he wanted to move one into his house.

Polygyny is not customary amongst Jenny's people, but her husband came from another part of the country, where it is. The best that can be said for him was that he did at least observe the tradition of seeking her permission, as first wife, before moving another woman into the house.[45] But these requests were preceded by drinking and accompanied by humiliation and violence so bad that Jenny's friends and neighbours told her she was a 'punching bag' and urged her to leave him. Eventually, after more than ten years of abuse, her husband beat her so badly (a police boot smashed into her face, her skull hammered with rocks) that she needed seven stitches. One night he threw all her things out of the house, and she and her two little boys were left to find their way home to her parents' place, along streets and through settlements dangerous for strangers to traverse. Somehow they arrived safely.

Even there, though, she found no comfort. The 'owner' of the family home was now her brother, who already had his own family there and resented the arrival of three more people to house and feed. Jenny found work as a female security guard, but the pay was not good, so she sold sex as well. Her brother resented her children and fought with them to the point where she decided to send them back to their father, where at least they would have a reasonable home. The elder, now nineteen, left his father's house, and Jenny is deeply concerned that he will turn to crime. She is the only one currently earning. Her parents are too old and ill, her younger sister is married to a man with no job. Her brother, the householder, is out of work too, and Jenny supports them all, despite the ill-treatment from her brother. She hands over almost all the money she earns to her mother, keeping only a bit of pocket-money for her 'beer and smokes.' She has learned to live on the streets of Boroko, paying the night-guards posted outside the stores and business houses to let her sleep on a sheet of cardboard in the shelter of a doorway or a shopping arcade.

***

---

44   Interview, Jenny, Port Moresby, 8 September 2007.
45   For some illuminating descriptions of the operation of this practice, see Alome Kyakas and Polly Wiessner, 1992, *From Inside the Women's House: Enga Women's Lives and Traditions*, Buranda, Qld: Robert Brown & Associates (Qld) Pty Ltd., 153–61.

Jenny's tale is typical of many of the street walkers in Port Moresby. Theodore Levantis, speaking from an economist's viewpoint, notes that by the mid-1990s nearly half the unemployed and under-employed female youth of Port Moresby were engaged in prostitution, which provides a better financial return than other menial jobs on offer.[46] This situation has since worsened, with respondents to a more recent report on commercial child sexual exploitation saying, 'We have to survive. The boys turn to petty crime and the girls have to sell themselves. Everybody knows that. That's why no one says anything and accepts the cash, food and other things that we can bring home.'[47]

Recent reports claim that women and girls sell sex to earn money for school fees, both their own and those of relatives; for everyday subsistence; and even for items as seemingly paltry as bus fares.[48] In mid-2006, a video store in Mt Hagen was reportedly closed because it was being used as a brothel. The girls and women working there bravely planned a protest to alert the government to their plight:

> The women claimed they have 'suffered terribly'.... A 15-year-old girl ... said they had nowhere to go since the DVD room was forced to close, as their clients (men) saw hotels and guesthouses as too expensive. The girl, who has earned a living in the area since she was 11, said she did not care if people called her names or mistreated her, as 'nobody would come and put rice and tinned fish on my plate everyday.... We are trying to make ends meet. Every time the media gives prominence to politicians and bureaucrats and forget about us. Do we have a government that will care for us, or just because we are prostitutes they will dump us like this.'[49]

But poverty is not the whole story, as Hammar points out, 'When women gave testimony [to the Parliamentary Special Committee on HIV and AIDS] about their lives in prostitution they, to a one, began with busted, violent marriages, but what the committee heard was poverty. When they mentioned sexual molestation by fathers and step-fathers, the committee mentioned nightclubs.'[50]

Jenny is by no means the only one to have suffered a 'busted, violent marriage.' Many of the street and disco workers are women who leave unhappy marriages,

---

46 Theodore Levantis, 2000, *Papua New Guinea: Employment, Wages and Economic Development*, Canberra: Asia Pacific Press, 67–69.
47 HELP Resources Inc., 2005, *A Situational Analysis of Child Sexual Abuse & the Commercial Sexual Exploitation of Children in Papua New Guinea (draft)* (*HELP Resources Report*), report prepared for UNICEF, Port Moresby, PNG, 14.
48 E.g., 'Sex trade shock,' *Post-Courier*, 30 November 2005, 1; 'Social dangers in earning,' *Post-Courier* (online), 30 November 2007; 'School-girl sex news stuns,' *Post-Courier* (online) 12 January 2011.
49 'Prostitutes plan "strike,"' *Post-Courier*, 19 July 2006, 1.
50 Hammar, pers. comm. by email, 29 November 2005.

or are driven out in favour of a new 'wife.' Others face problems with families at home who do not want single mothers placing greater strains on the household. With no social security services, and a system which ensures that the husband or eldest son or brother is 'head of the house,' cast-out women have very little choice but to live on the streets and sell sex, so much so that they commonly term themselves, with some irony, 'problem mothers'—mothers with problems.[51] Some of the street-dwellers state that, due to the stigma and discrimination they know they will face, they are frightened to go back to their families after they are known to have been involved in selling sex. However, many other sex sellers still live with their families, constituting the main if not the only breadwinner, supporting an entire extended family.

Figure 4.8. Market—selling soft drinks, boiled eggs, ice blocks and vegetables—and in the background, sex, 2006.

Source: Photo by Christine Stewart, 22 January 2006.

There may be other reasons. Teenage girls in a provincial town claimed that they sold sex 'out of boredom, poverty and the desire to have some money to buy things.'[52] Transactional sex may be employed as a means of payback for ill-treatment by husbands, brothers or other kin.[53] A history of abuse is common.

---

51 It is a cruel irony that the very civil society services which sympathise with and strive to assist deserted or battered wives usually end up condemning those same women for selling sex in order to survive.
52 *HELP Resources Report*, 34.
53 Wardlow, 'Anger, economy and female agency'; and see Penelope Schoeffel Meleisea, 2008, *Gender and HIV in the Pacific Islands Region: A Review of Evidence, Policies and Strategies with Recommendations (Final*

Younger workers are often victims of sexual abuse, daughters of discarded women who have turned to selling sex themselves, or they have been rejected by a stepfather when the mother has remarried.[54] During the course of a nation-wide study conducted by the Papua New Guinea Institute of Medical Research in 2005, Hammar found in respect of the sex trade in the city of Lae that commonly, the first developmental precursor was sexual victimisation by older men, often relatives, at or near puberty; followed by being sold or otherwise transacted into sexualised relationships with other men.[55] The study found a high level of commercial sex throughout the country. Many of the women admitting to selling sex also revealed low self-esteem and a lack of autonomy. Many told of early-age rape and being introduced to the sex trade by relatives.

Some choose to sell sex. The *Poro Sapot Database* of 2006 includes an entry from an outreach worker who was approached by the mother and aunt of a girl who, they complained, was 'hanging around Boroko.' They said they tried to change her lifestyle by tying her up and beating her. To no avail.[56] Some are organised into selling sex while not necessarily seeing themselves as victims.[57] At a forum which I attended in 2006, facilitated by Scarlet Alliance to establish a PNG sex-worker community network, I observed that most of the older women told stories of being abandoned by husbands or partners, while most of the younger ones said they were introduced to selling sex by relatives.

Many factors drive women into the sex trade, with poverty and failure of family security predominating. Male violence, abuse and neglect (from husbands and kin, either in childhood or later) are factors which feature widely in research but are often overlooked in public discourse, while the woman or girl who exercises agency in the face of adversity is condemned.

Draft), UNDP Pacific Centre: §83–4. Kuragi Ku, one of the appellants in *Monika Jon's Case*, 'explained to the police that her husband did not give her some money so she sold her body' (from the judgement).

54 Lawrence Hammar, 2005, 'A different kind of "Original Sin": coitarche, commercial sex, and (non-) consent in Lae, Morobe Province, Papua New Guinea,' paper for session Gender Violence in Oceania, 2005 annual meeting of the Association for Social Anthropology in Oceania.

55 Hammar, 'A different kind of "Original Sin."'

56 *Poro Sapot Database*, 5 October 2006.

57 *HELP Resources Report*, 60. I do not intend to enter here into the 'trafficking' debate, others have done it better. See Holly Wardlow, 2001, '"Prostitution," "sexwork," and "passenger women"'; Melissa Ditmore, 2002, 'Trafficking and prostitution: a problematic conflation,' Ph.D. thesis, City University of New York; Larissa Sandy, 2006, '"My blood, sweat and tears": female sex workers in Cambodia–victims, vectors or agents?' Ph.D. thesis, Canberra: The Australian National University; Sandy, 2007, 'Just choices: representations of choice and coercion in sex work in Cambodia,' *The Australian Journal of Anthropology* 18(2): 194–206.

Figure 4.9. Up-market—freelance workers wait outside one of Port Moresby's classier hotels for security guards to summon them to work, 2006.

Source: Photo by Christine Stewart, 22 January 2006.

Who does it?

> Only the danger-loving would attempt to nail down precisely all of the forms and locations of Port Moresby's exploding sex industry.
>
> Lawrence Hammar, 2010.[58]

The IMR *National Study* referred to above was undertaken in order to determine the range of sexual behaviours in the country, both to develop strategies for preventing HIV and other STIs, and to assist those working in family planning,[59] and included a section on the commercialisation of sex.[60] Other studies soon followed, revealing the extensive and growing range of sexual networking practices in the country, and it was soon followed by others.[61] These studies

---

58 Lawrence Hammar, 2010, 'From gift to commodity … and back again: form and fluidity of sexual networking in Papua New Guinea,' in *Civic Insecurity: Law, Order and HIV in Papua New Guinea*, ed. Vicki Luker and Sinclair Dinnen, Canberra: ANU E Press, 119–39, 129, online: http://press.anu.edu.au?p=94091, accessed 7 April 2014.
59 *National Study*, vii, 4.
60 Ibid., 113–19.
61 Some examples: Carol Jenkins, 1994, *Situational Assessment of Commercial Sex Workers in Urban Papua New Guinea*, Papua New Guinea Institute of Medical Research; Lawrence Hammar, 1996, 'Sex and political economy in the South Fly: Daru Island, Western Province, Papua New Guinea,' Ph.D. thesis, New York: City University of New York; Hammar, 'AIDS, STDs and sex work in Papua New Guinea'; Hammar, 1998, 'Sex industries and sexual networking in Papua New Guinea: public health risks and implications,' *Pacific Health Dialog* 5(1): 47–53; *HELP Resources Report*; Lawrence Hammar 2008, 'Fear and loathing in Papua New Guinea: sexual health in a nation under siege,' in *Making Sense of AIDS: Culture, Sexuality, and Power in Melanesia*, ed. Leslie Butt and Richard Eves, Honolulu: University of Hawai'i Press, 60–79; Karen Fletcher and Bomal Gonapa, 2010, 'Decriminalisation of prostitution in Papua New Guinea,' in *Civic Insecurity: Law, Order and HIV in Papua New Guinea*, ed. Vicki Luker and Sinclair Dinnen, Canberra: ANU E Press, 141–52, 129, online: http://press.anu.edu.au?p=94091, accessed 7 April 2014; Lawrence Hammar 2010, '"I am an 'MSM'!… I think"': Melanesian perspectives on self, risk, and other in HIV prevention,' paper presented at the Gendered Mobility, Intimate Consumption, and HIV in Postcolonial Melanesia, American Anthropological Association Meeting Conference, New Orleans, 17–21 November; Hammar, 'From gift to commodity … and back again'; Carol Jenkins, 2010, 'Sex workers and police in Port Moresby (1994–1998): research and intervention,' in *Civic Insecurity: Law, Order and HIV in Papua New Guinea*, ed. Vicki Luker and Sinclair Dinnen, Canberra: ANU E Press, 153–64, online: http://press.anu.edu.au?p=94091, accessed 7 April 2014; Christine Stewart, 2010,

have distinguished several general categories which may be summarised as: independent sellers, who work the streets, the discos, clubs and bars; brothel and quasi-brothel sellers, operating from clubs, guesthouses, settlement houses, and so on under a variety or arrangements for payments, protection, and management; part-time sellers, often school-girls or housewives, needing money from time to time for specific purposes; *pasinjia meri* who sell sex to protest ill-treatment by relatives;[62] and opportunistic sellers who give sex for a wide variety of returns—protection from arrest, food, drink, *buai* and cigarettes, transport, better grades at school, employment, phone access or credit.[63]

Within all these categories, traditional and emergent, there may be a range of local variations throughout the country. For example, Hammar noted varying categories in the town of Daru in the early 1990s.[64] Economic enclaves throughout the country, such as logging camps, mines, plantations and fish canneries, attract sellers of sex and those who market them.[65] A considerable amount of transactional sex also targets specific areas such as major ports and the stopping places along the Highlands Highway.[66] Male-dominated corporations known generically as landowner groups have created an ever-increasing demand for sexual services in the larger towns, primarily Port Moresby. The standard method of negotiating resource deals is to round up those considered to be *papa*

'Enabling environments: the role of the law,' in *Civic Insecurity: Law, Order and HIV in Papua New Guinea*, ed. Vicki Luker and Sinclair Dinnen, Canberra: ANU E Press, 275–85, online: http://press.anu.edu.au?p=94091, accessed 7 April 2014; and most recently, Kelly et al., Askim na Save.

62   Holly Wardlow, 2002, 'Headless ghosts and roving women: specters of modernity in Papua New Guinea,' *American Ethnologist* 29(1): 5–32; Wardlow, 'Anger, economy and female agency'; and see also the testimony of Kuragi Ku in *Monika Jon's Case*.

63   See particularly *HELP Resources Report*; and Hammar, 'From gift to commodity ... and back again,' 122–24, with its well-crafted series of snapshots of sexual networking.

64   Hammar, 'Sex and political economy in the South Fly.'

65   E.g. 'Alleged sexual abuse uncovered,' *Post-Courier*, 30 June 2004; Masalai Blog, 'Government Department reports slam Rimbunan Hijau: RH workers "treated like slaves",' *Masalai i tokaut*, no. 30 (10 July 2004), online: masalai.wordpress.com, accessed 3 July 2006; group discussion with MSWs, Post Moresby, 12 September 2007; *HELP Resources Report*, vi, 13–14; Gabriel Fito, 'Sepik sex ring busted,' *National* (online), 18 February 2010; Barnabas Orere Pondros, 'Minister warns logging companies,' *National* (online), 22 February 2010; Gabriel Fito, 'Sex-for-sale case hit snag,' *National* (online), 23 February 2010; Johnny Poiya, 'Illegal activites on the rise in Hela,' *Post-Courier* (online), 22 November 2011, which tells of trucks arriving regularly from the new LNG project to collect schoolgirls from the Catholic Tari Secondary School; Deborah B. Gewertz and Frederick K. Errington, 2009, 'Jealous women of the cane,' in *Empirical Futures: Anthropologists and Historians Engage the Work of Sidney W. Mintz*, ed. George Baca, Aisha Kahn and Stephen Palmie, Chapel Hill: University of North Carolina Press, 173–95; Buchanan et al., *Behavioural Surveillance Research in Rural Development Enclaves in Papua New Guinea*; and see Nicole Haley, 2009, 'HIV/AIDS and witchcraft at Lake Kopiago,' *Catalyst* 39(1): 115–34, 118–19, where she relates that the shrinking cash economy in the Lake Kopiago area of the Southern Highlands Province has prompted young women, encouraged by male relatives, to seek out mine workers for casual sex in order to be able to buy store goods.

66   *National Study*; Jenkins, *Female Sex Worker HIV Prevention Projects*; 'Betelnut for sex rife on highway,' *Post-Courier* (online), 7 April 2005; 'PNG: health officials target HIV-AIDS hotspots,' *ABC Radio Australia Pacific Beat*, interview, 16 May 2005.

bilong graun (landowners) and treat them to a funded stay in the city. The recent negotiations for the multi-billion-dollar Liquefied Natural Gas project have produced a significant increase in this practice.[67]

Political processes, whether national or local, may provide a setting for transactional sex. In recent years, tribal fighting in the Highlands has been accompanied by the exchange of young women for guns; they may also be given by tribal leaders as payment for mercenary services in tribal fighting.[68] At election time, 'campaign houses' are set up in towns and electoral centres by candidates to distribute campaign materials and host feasts and parties. Campaign houses are also used as venues for sex with women provided by or campaigning for candidates,[69] to the point where the Electoral Commission ran newspaper advertisements prior to the 2007 general election, advising voters not to be swayed by campaigning tactics, including the free sex offered in campaign houses portrayed in an accompanying cartoon.[70]

During my fieldwork in 2006–07, I recorded interviews,[71] visited sites, took field notes of what I saw and heard around the city. I was able to get a reasonable impression of many of the forms of activity, but because my main contacts came from Poro Sapot, my picture is skewed in favour of the most disadvantaged, the ones for whom the Project provides some form of safe haven: the street walkers.

Street walkers can roam the streets and beats by day, and finish up in clubs in the evening. I was repeatedly told that they move around constantly: a woman sighted at one venue may not be there a few weeks later. On land or water, many locations provide opportunities to sell sex. A letter to the *National* in 2006, for example, described the Moresby harbour trade, where women lived aboard moored boats, coming ashore by night to work the wharf and waterfront or to be collected for parties on board visiting fishing vessels,[72] and I was shown a harbourside venue where snacks, *buai* and women were offered for sale.

---

67 Editorial, 'Use money wisely,' *Post-Courier* (online), 30 October 2009.
68 'Betelnut for sex rife on highway,' *Post-Courier* (online), 7 April 2005; 'PNG: health officials target HIV-AIDS hotspots'; 'YWCA: exchange of girls for firearms shameful,' *National* (online), 25 May 2005.
69 'Campaign houses used as brothels,' *National* (online,) 7 June 2007; Philip Gibbs and Marie Mondu, 2009, 'The context of HIV transmission during the 2007 Elections in the Enga Province Papua New Guinea,' *Catalyst* 39(1): 135–57.
70 For example, 'Campaign houses used as brothels,' *National* (online), 7 June 2007.
71 Group discussion with PSP Outreach Workers, Port Moresby, 19 January 2006; Group discussion with FSW Outreach Workers, Port Moresby, 6 September 2007; and with individuals as listed in Appendix 1.
72 'Sex on waterfront,' *National*, 24 April 2006, 24.

Figure 4.10. Harbourside sales. This landfill site has now been built over and no longer exists.

Source: Photo by Christine Stewart, 22 January 2006.

Port Moresby street walkers live an uneasy life:

> We used to get cardboards and make our beds [in the retail sector of Boroko]. It's just around the police station so we feel safer there. Sometimes men really drunk come. Come and check our pockets and pick up our money. Still happens with the girls too. The *raskols* are bigger problems than the police. They cut bags and take money. When the girls are really drunk, that's what they do … only the mobile policemen, they're the ones who come and threaten, pick us up, take our money.[73]

Guesthouses fit halfway between street work and the late-opening clubs. They are places which open through the day, where people can go and hang out, play a game of snooker, have a few beers and buy sex if they feel like it. The establishments may be licensed to sell alcohol. Or they may conduct unlicensed 'black-market' trade.

---

73 Group discussion with FSW Outreach Workers.

Figure 4.11. Typical club, with bar and snooker table.

Source: Photo by Christine Stewart.

Outreach workers estimate that they interact with some 7,000 street, club and guesthouse women selling sex in Port Moresby alone.[74] This does not include those who frequent the exclusive clubs sometimes attached to business complexes; or who seek to sell sex at the high-class hotels, either as bar visitors or as part of an operation run by hotel staff. These women, say the outreach workers, have proved very difficult to contact. But it is generally known that the hotel trade is a thriving one: 'In larger hotels, security guards, receptionists and waiters are often involved, sometimes offering to potential clients their female co-workers and sometimes the regular sex workers who congregate in nightclub bars.'[75]

Of the clubs, some feature live-in women, who may go 'home' on Sundays if their families still accept them there. The *HELP Resources Report* describes the active recruitment of young girls for live-in arrangements in various premises in Port Moresby.[76] Their ranks are swelled by others who come in on a casual basis. Other clubs have no live-in facilities, although they may provide lounges for the women. Some rent rooms to independent women, but the phenomenon of the brothel, a place where the club takes the payment and gives the woman

---

74 Ibid.
75 Alfredo P. Hernandez, 'Sex trade of Papua New Guinea,' *National*, 19 January 2007, 24.
76 *HELP Resources Report*, 57–58.

a percentage, or pays her on a bonus system according to how many drinks she can persuade a client to buy, has only recently emerged in Port Moresby.[77] These women are usually known as 'ground hostesses' and outreach workers claim this pattern of work is of Asian origin. Bargirls and waitresses are employed, and may also sell sex. Certainly, many of the classier clubs are Asian-owned, although the manager may not be Asian. They employ very young women, often under-aged girls, who are required to maintain a high standard of beauty and presentation.[78] Most of the clientele is Asian, and I was told that Papua New Guinean men claim that *'em bilong waitman tasol'* [they are only for non-indigenes].[79] Many of the workers at clubs will have regular clients, and fights can break out over theft of a client. Club rules can in some places be harsh, with women sacked if they do not satisfy a client's requirements. They may be plied with alcohol and marijuana to assist them in enduring their trade. Overall, however, there is far less male control than in the sex trade in Asia, for example.[80]

Brothels are sometimes mentioned publicly. It was alleged in 2008 for example that a 'Chinese mafia' was already operating businesses such as money-laundering, trading in counterfeit products, human smuggling, prostitution, kidnapping for ransom and illegal gambling, in collaboration with police, immigration officers, the Labour Department and the Internal Revenue Commission.[81] Occasional raids have been reported in the media: on a 'child sex ring' in Madang in 2007;[82] on a restaurant, bar and brothel compound in Port Moresby;[83] and most recently, on a brothel in a logging camp in the Sepik, where investigations were foiled when the women produced apparently valid marriage certificates, leaving police to fulminate over the prospect of future 'fatherless children' when the 'husbands' left the country.[84] A newspaper report appearing in early 2008 tells of 'Asian' prostitutes being brought illegally into PNG:

> The prostitutes, reported to be mainly from Asian countries, are part of an illegal chain of businesses operated allegedly by the Chinese mafia gang members which were confirmed to be already in the country.

---

77 By the time the *Askim na Save* survey was carried out in 2010, 46% of participants gave 'brothels' as a sex-selling location. See Kelly et al., Askim na Save, 18.
78 Group discussion with FSW Outreach Workers; personal observations at site visits 2006; *HELP Resources Report*: 58.
79 Group discussion with FSW Outreach Workers. The term *waitman* seems to have acquired an extended meaning, beyond just white men.
80 Michael Alpers, 1997, *Final Report to UNAIDS: Police and Sex Workers in Papua New Guinea*, Goroka: Papua New Guinea Institute of Medical Research, 8.
81 Asian sex racket,' *Post-Courier* (online), 20 March 2008.
82 'Cops crack child sex ring,' *National* (online), 28 May 2007.
83 'Crime ring hit,' *Post-Courier* (online), 2 April 2009.
84 *National* (online), 21 February, 22 February, 23 February, 16 March 2010.

> These prostitutes were reportedly brought into the country illegally and are engaged in prostitution behind closed doors with arranged clients....
>
> The Chinese mafia is also involved in many illegal activities like money laundering, human smuggling, prostitution, and operating illegal lottery games in the country.[85]

More recently, a study of human trafficking in the Pacific has highlighted the smuggling of Asian people into Pacific countries, including the (often illegal) importation of women and girls for purposes of prostitution.[86] There is nothing new about this: when I first joined the Department of Health's National AIDS Committee in 1992, I heard of logging ships beaching in remote provinces, and bringing with them a bevy of 'cooks' who overcame the language barrier when plying their trade by using picture-books of various positions and types of sex by number. Medical officers reported an alarming increase in some very exotic STIs, and a corresponding increase in the number of assaults on husbands by wives.

Outreach workers had already pointed out several closed-door establishments to me during my fieldwork in 2006–2007, telling me that Asian women operated there, and for a high fee, would 'do anything.' Clients, I was told, were themselves foreigners, or highly-placed PNG officials and businessmen. But outreach workers are not welcome there and detail is scant.

Another category of sex seller in Port Moresby today is termed the 'hidden sex worker.' This refers to women, usually married and often high-class, who are seeking extra money to support their households, or avenging themselves on philandering husbands. They may go to great lengths to hide the fact that they are selling sex. Many operate from their homes during the day when family members are at work or school. Some frequent clubs where they sit with beer pretending they are just enjoying the music, or go to all-day venues during daytime hours and leave before the after-work trade starts.[87] Some of the younger ones pretend that they are simply going out with their girlfriends for a good time.[88] Many of the older women purport to 'mother' the younger workers, but they will also sell sex if the opportunity presents. Certain clubs are known for their excellent security and high-class clientele, such as politicians, lawyers, doctors and landowners.

---

85 Asian sex racket,' *Post-Courier* (online), 20 March 2008.
86 Jade Lindley and Laura Beacroft, 2011, *Vulnerabilities to Trafficking in Persons in the Pacific Islands*, Australian Institute of Criminology, online: http://www.aic.gov.au/documents/C/1/9/%7BC19D723B-44B8-4B02-9FA5-CB4470207AE7%7Dtandi428.pdf, accessed 4 December 2011.
87 Interview Maggie; fieldnotes and observations at site visits, 8 September 2007.
88 *Poro Sapot Database*, 7 October 2006.

Not only 'hidden sex workers' operate out of houses. In 2009, Poro Sapot outreach workers were asked to prepare site maps of the area where they live, showing churches, stores, markets (selling *buai*, cooked food, fresh fruit and vegetables), their own houses and those of 'FSW.' Lower-class suburbs, peri-urban villages and settlements all over town were mapped in this fashion, and all clearly identifying varying numbers of women who sold sex, sometimes in close proximity to churches and missions. The *Askim na Save* Report confirms this, and lists these settlements and villages as the most common venues for selling sex, followed by hotels, guesthouses and private dwellings.[89]

These are not the only forms of the sex trade in Port Moresby today. Where the opportunity to make money from selling a family member presents, it is taken. Wives may be offered in public (sometimes unwillingly)[90] and teenage girls may be seen on weekdays at lunchtime in government and other offices, being escorted by an older female relative to what is termed a 'wet lunch.'[91]

Port Moresby's sex trade is characterised by a considerable amount of 'mixing' of ethnic groups. Jenkins told me in the mid-1990s that she could not hold joint meetings of Highlands and Motuan women at the IMR premises in Port Moresby for fear of potential conflict, echoing the sentiments of the 1960s which saw the local Papuan people developing a growing resentment of the Highlands 'invasion' of the capital on their doorsteps. But although this division persists to an extent, Moresby is fast becoming inhabited by many who call it their first and only home. They are often the offspring of parents from differing parts of the country. The melding of ethnic groups in the city is echoed in the mixed ethnic representation in groups of contemporary sex sellers. The *Askim na Save* Report shows almost equal proportions of Highlands (47%) and Southern (42%) regions of origin for participants, although 'Southern' would encompass all those born and raised in Port Moresby, irrespective of the ethnic origin of their parents. Over 40 per cent had lived in Port Moresby for fewer than ten years.[92]

Pimping is a long-standing practice. The *HELP Resources Report* describes the expectations of colonial bosses that their workers would obtain girls for them, and many local men took the opportunity to become go-betweens.[93] Johnstone's Gumini *bisnismeris* were always accompanied by their husbands on their street-rounds and, if caught, denied the involvement of their husbands in their trade.[94] Similar operational styles can be discerned in a *Post-Courier* story from 1969, which told of a Tolai man who hired a taxi to drive himself and a woman

---

89 Kelly et al., Askim na Save, 18.
90 Pers comm outreach worker April 2006, Port Moresby; and Hammar, 'Sex and political economy in the South Fly.'
91 Personal observations while working in Port Moresby during the 1990s.
92 Kelly et al., Askim na Save, 13.
93 *HELP Resources Report*, 12.
94 Johnstone, 'The Gumini *Bisnis-Meri*,' 226.

around Rabaul town and outlying villages. The woman admitted selling sex and was convicted under vagrancy laws, but denied that she had given any of her earnings to the man. An attempt to convict him for living on part of the earnings of prostitution failed.[95]

Today, pimping is commonplace, though not necessarily the norm. An entry in the 2006 *Poro Sapot Database* describes a contact simply as 'pimp.'[96] A 2005 feature article in the *National* describes it:

> In the PNG context, the term can be loosely used to refer to the hordes of young men (and in some cases women) that are now roaming the streets and arranging girls and women for one-night sexual encounters with men. These are mostly those with influence or resources at their disposal like money and cars. The PNG pimps are working for a commission. The commissions range from goods to cash and to even employment.
>
> A sad aspect of the work of the PNG pimps is that they are now arranging or as they say in Tokpisin, 'setim' even their own female relatives and wantoks to sleep around with unknown men for a night for the commission.[97]

The *HELP Resources Report* noted some pimping in Port Moresby, often by relatives or putative relatives. These may be older blood relatives, or partners who may be described as boyfriends or husbands. Such liaisons can just as readily be arranged at the behest of the client rather than the seller, most often by taxi drivers or security guards.[98]

At issue here is the connection with custom. While studying at UPNG in the 1970s, I was told by many friends that a common way of establishing a liaison with a potential girlfriend or boyfriend was to request a close friend or relative to act as go-between. Occasionally, I was approached myself to carry out such a task. The process of arranging marriages by parents often involves the prior bringing and displaying of the potential bride to the boy and his family. It is a short leap to the criminalised concept of 'pimping' as known in English law.

And despite attempts to characterise pimps as evil exploiters, the practice of pimping must be contextualised. Going through the *Poro Sapot Database* records of outreach worker site visits, I came across two particularly poignant stories related by elderly men who were respectively a security guard and a

---

95 'Tolai woman gaoled for two weeks,' *Post-Courier*, 19 November 1969, 20.
96 *Poro Sapot Database*, OV NCD 8/12/2006 record #138.
97 'HIV/AIDS and the work of pimps in PNG,' *National* (online), 23 August 2005; and see *Help Resources Report*, 60, 63–65.
98 *Help Resources Report*, 56, 64–65.

buai-seller in the downtown area. Each had befriended and assumed avuncular responsibility for a young woman in the sex trade (I was told by Poro Sapot outreach workers that this was not uncommon). One told how he had cared for his charge, bathing her and tending her open lesions as she deteriorated and passed away with AIDS. The other admitted to having had sex with his charge before she too fell ill and passed away.[99]

However sex sellers are described, viewed and categorised, there is no doubt that the sex trade is highly visible in PNG today. This is not so evident when it comes to discourse on homosexuality. It has been left largely to historians and researchers to describe and comment on manifestations of homosexual practices in PNG.

The abominable habit

> It's that bisexuality, most Melanesian men … so hard to come to terms with…. I think it would be only a tiny minority of Papua New Guinean males who would not be interested in same-sex activity at some stage in their lives, or who have probably not had same-sex relationships of some sort … and if alcohol comes in, or detention in a prison, it goes up that much higher. It really amazes me, that sexual activity is not seen really as just a male-female thing.
>
> Longtime expatriate resident, 2006.[100]

Male-male sex has long been acceptable in some Melanesian cultures, whether for pleasure or other purposes.[101] In PNG, trangenderism was accepted in some areas in the past, if not in the present:

> When I was a child [in the 1960s] … we had several of them, not in our village, from X, come on church conference-type meetings, and they would come as the women's delegates, dressed up in skirts and blouses, and absolutely wonderful human beings, very well respected, I suppose a bit like the *fa'afafines* from Samoa … the village people accepted them

---

99   *Poro Sapot Database*, 11 October 2006. Both men claimed to be feeling unwell, which was why they had approached the outreach workers.
100 Interview with Adam, Port Moresby, 12 January 2006.
101 For example, Gilbert Herdt, 1984, *Ritualized Homosexuality in Melanesia*, Berkeley: University of California Press; Tobias Schneebaum, 1988, *Where the Spirits Dwell: an Odyssey in the New Guinea Jungle*, New York: Grove Press; Bruce M. Knauft, 1993, *South Coast New Guinea Cultures: History, Comparison, Dialectic*, New York: Cambridge University Press; *National Study*, 99; Gilbert Herdt, 1997, *Same Sex, Different Cultures: Gays and Lesbians across Cultures*, Boulder, CO: Westview Press; Jenkins, 'Male sexuality and HIV.'

> ... they were men, and they would go help in the garden.... I remember one of them coming to our house ... 'she' was just an amazing person, very dignified (Steven).

However, most discussion of the historical record of non-heteronormative sexualities and gender in PNG starts with mention of what was first termed 'ritualised homosexuality.'

Sexuality, ritual or growth?

> Melanesian male sexuality does not follow a Western pattern: homosexuality is part of male socialisation, there is no clear division between heterosexual and homosexual activity and relations, and there are fewer inhibitions.
>
> Professor Clive Moore, University of Queensland.[102]

The pioneer in this field of study is Gilbert Herdt.[103] His work with the Highland group he named the Sambia revealed initiation practices designed to ensure that the innate male essence, tenuous in childhood, must be transformed and 'grown' into adult masculinity. This transformation is achieved by rituals of oral and anal homosexual inseminations which create maleness, which is then maintained by later heterosexuality in adulthood.[104] Further consideration, though, led Herdt to question the ascription 'ritual homosexuality,' renaming it 'boy insemination.' As has been discussed both by Herdt and others,[105] these practices are intended not for pleasure but for the essential purpose of growing boys into men capable of marrying and founding a family. They often involve fear, pain and violence, and were regarded as a social duty.[106] In fact, continued practice of homoerotic sex may well be regarded with as much stigma and self-loathing as in western societies, although for different cultural reasons, as Herdt describes.[107]

---

[102] Clive Moore, 2005, 'Changes in Melanesian masculinities: an historical approach,' paper presented at the Moving Masculinities: Crossing Regional and Historical Borders Conference, Canberra: The Australian National University, 29 November–2 December 2005, 12.
[103] Herdt, *Ritualized Homosexuality in Melanesia*; Gilbert Herdt, 1987, *The Sambia: Ritual and Gender in New Guinea*, Fort Worth, TX: Holt, Rinehart and Winston; Gilbert Herdt, 1992, 'Semen depletion and the sense of maleness,' in *Oceanic Homosexualities*, ed. Stephen O. Murray, New York and London: Garland Publishing, 33–68.
[104] Herdt, *The Sambia*, 6.
[105] Referred to in Bruce M. Knauft, 2003, 'What ever happened to ritualized homosexuality? Modern sexual subjects in Melanesia and elsewhere,' *Annual Review of Sex Research* 14: 137–59, 138; and see also Deborah A. Elliston, 1995, 'Erotic anthropology: "ritualized homosexuality" in Melanesia and beyond,' *American Ethnologist* 22(4): 848–67.
[106] See Carol Jenkins, 2004, 'Male sexuality, diversity and culture: Implications for HIV Prevention and Care,' unpublished report prepared for UNAIDS, Geneva, 8–9.
[107] Herdt, 'Semen depletion and the sense of maleness.'

Herdt's later work has challenged the western view of fixed sexual preferences, showing how cultural changes among the Sambia have altered sexual practices but not necessarily their gender categories.[108] In this he joins similar studies in Southeast Asia, such as Peter Jackson's on the gay/man/*kathoey* identities in Thailand and later additions and further nuancing of these categories in recent decades in the face of advancing global trends;[109] Tom Boellstorff on *gay* in Indonesia;[110] and Bruce M. Knauft's observations on the measure of change amongst the Gebusi of Western Province which has seen, in a single generation, the complete obliteration of openly proclaimed male homoeroticism in favour of 'modern' heteronormativity.[111]

As Boellstorff has argued for Indonesia, it would be a mistake to assume that such cultural practices, despite involving male-male fellatio, are direct forerunners of or indeed have any clear connection with homoeroticism in PNG today. Clive Moore considers that PNG men from areas known for ritual homosexuality in earlier times predominate in the present-day urban gay scene, but adds that this is not always the case.[112] Jenkins doubts whether earlier customs of ritualised homosexuality are essential preconditions for the entry of young men into selling sex today. Herdt describes the dilemma faced by a Sambia man who pursued his homoerotic relationships into adult life, when he should have married and turned away from such practices.[113]

I discovered scant evidence of any such historical link in the subject positions currently adopted by gays in Port Moresby. 'Ritual homosexuality' was mentioned only once, in group conversation by a gay outreach worker who, I surmise, had learned of it through his work, 'Practices from before, like the men have to go to the bush for some … manhood training…. "You are grown-up young men and you will be living with a woman, and this is what you have to do with a woman" … so they have to teach them … it's like practice' (*Palopa*).

From the earliest days of contact, colonisers' disapproval of ritual homosexuality was made clear, even in the most distant parts. The *Annual Report for British*

---

108 Herdt, *Same Sex, Different Cultures: Gays and Lesbians across Cultures*.
109 Peter Jackson, 2000, 'An explosion of Thai identities: global queering and re-imagining queer theory,' *Culture, Health & Sexuality* 2(4): 405–24; Peter Jackson, 2001, 'Interpreting "Sambia" masculine erotics: a question of sexuality or gender?' *The Asia Pacific Journal of Anthropology* 2(1): 109–13; Peter Jackson, 2009, 'Capitalism and global queering: national markets, parallels among sexual cultures, and multiple queer modernities,' *GLQ: A Journal of Lesbian and Gay Studies* 15(3): 357–95.
110 Tom Boellstorff, 2003, 'I knew it was me: mass media, "globalization," and lesbian and gay Indonesia,' in *Mobile Cultures: New Media in Queer Asia*, ed. Chris Berry, Fran Martin and Audrey Yue, Durham NC: Duke University Press, 21–51; Boellstorff, 2005, *The Gay Archipelago: Sexuality and Nation in Indonesia*, Princeton and Oxford: Princeton University Press.
111 Knauft, 'What ever happened to ritualized homosexuality?'
112 Moore, 'Changes in Melanesian masculinities,' 12.
113 Gilbert Herdt, 1992, 'Semen depletion and the sense of maleness,' in *Oceanic Homosexualities*, ed. Stephen O. Murray, New York and London: Garland Publishing, 33-68.

New Guinea of 1888 contains a summary from government officer Hugh Milman on Mowatta, in what was then the remote Western District, to the effect that a newly appointed 'chief' had been urged to 'do his best to put down the hideous practice of sodomy, which is carried on most extensively and almost openly, young boys being initiated into the practice formally at a certain season of the year. It is probable that this abominable habit is not confined to Mowatta.'[114] But only four years later, Resident Magistrate B.A. Hely wrote,

> *Admission of boys to manhood and girls to womanhood.* I cannot find that any ceremonies exist in these cases. Turi Turi, Mawatta, and other tribes say not. There are stories current of ceremonies at Kiwai and elsewhere of which there are not sufficient proofs, and which are unfit for publication, if true.[115]

It is highly improbable that the Mowatta citizenry had in fact abandoned their initiation ceremonies as instructed in the space of a few years. It is far more likely that they had quickly learned to deny and conceal their customary practices, even to point the finger at others a safe distance away.[116]

The *National Study* discovered evidence of a range of practices and attitudes throughout the country.[117] The evidence showed that among those disclosing same-sex behaviour, there was an equal division between Highlanders and lowlanders, and most of the culture areas were represented. However, the team found it difficult to elicit much information in an atmosphere of intolerance and marginalisation, and many men disguised their same-sex preferences by a presentation of bisexuality.

I learned that gays today often discuss sexual practice in ethnic context.

> Now you see … apart from the guys from Central Province and Gulf Province, you'll see people from the Highlands and New Guinea Islands. But New Guinea Islands, there are more Tolais than from any other New Guinea Island group (Len).

> Coastal areas, they understand, but … most of the 'girls' are scared of Highlanders, they get very aggressive (*Palopa*).

> Homosexual things in the Koitabuan community … all the boys from the day they were born, they are fit enough to carry a spear, they are

---

114 Hugh Milman, 1889, 'Appendix C,' in *British New Guinea, Report for the Year 1888*, Her Majesty's Special Commissioner for the Protected Territory, Brisbane: James C. Beal, 16–17.
115 B.A. Hely, 1894, 'Appendix P. Native habits and customs in the Western Division,' in *Annual Report on British New Guinea 1892–1893*, Brisbane: Edmund Gregory, Government Printer, 57–59.
116 This area of south-western Papua is well-known for these initiation rituals: Herdt, *Ritualized Homosexuality in Melanesia*, 18–22.
117 *National Study*, 98–101.

trained to fight, and in their mind is to become tough men. That's what the Koitabuan community have always maintained.... The Motuans are more open about homosexuality than the Koitabuans (Robin).

There was an Engan [Highlands ethnic group] guy, he says that he's part East New Britain and Enga, and he was living in Port Moresby and he was in drag. Every day of his life he was wearing a dress. And when I came across this guy I couldn't believe it. I said that this is the first person that I've ever seen wearing a dress, and he's from the Highlands.... [Highlanders] *hate* feminine men ... for him to be accepted by these people, that's the thing I always wanted to know about (Len).

Plantations: 'A problem of the white man's own making'

The *kiaps* and the missionaries may have brought colonisation to the villages, even in some cases drawing them to administrative or mission stations, but it was the colonial economy which prompted the mass migration of people to distant parts of the territory. One of the principal attractions of both territories to their various colonists was the prospect of commercial development, in mining[118] and plantations.[119] By the end of the nineteenth century, moves were made by the British administration in British New Guinea to attract small-scale settlers with capital to help develop the new land and defray administrative costs. But despite strenuous efforts it proved difficult to attract small-scale planters in large numbers, and plantations were eventually opened up in the new century by large trading companies operating through managers and overseers.[120] In German New Guinea, greater success was achieved. The Imperial Charter granted to the *Neu-Guinea-Compagnie* required the economic development of the colony, where plantations had developed earlier, and more successfully, along the north coast and in the more fertile offshore islands, although the company failed to show a profit.[121]

Developing-country plantations, as Hank Nelson states baldly, 'depend on cheap labour.'[122] The importation of foreign labourers was considered unfeasible in British New Guinea,[123] but not in the German colony which imported

---

118   Hank Nelson, 1976, *Black, White and Gold: Gold Mining in Papua New Guinea, 1878–1930*, Canberra: Australian National University Press.
119   D.C. Lewis, 1996, *The Plantation Dream: Developing British New Guinea and Papua, 1884–1942*, Canberra: The Journal of Pacific History.
120   Ibid., 24–25, 30.
121   B. Jinks, P. Biskup and H. Nelson, 1973, *Readings in New Guinea History*, Sydney: Angus and Robertson, 154.
122   Hank Nelson, 1982, Taim Bilong Masta: *The Australian Involvement with Papua New Guinea*, Sydney: Australian Broadcasting Commission, 75.
123   Hubert Murray, 1925, *Papua of Today: or an Australian Colony in the Making*, London: P.S. King & Son, Ltd., 107–08.

numbers of Chinese, though mainly as traders and service-providers.[124] In both Territories, colonial administration began with the regulation of internal migrant labour: British and Germans instituted an indentured labour system, subsequently inherited by the Australian administration and continued until 1950, which bound master and servant to a fixed contractual term, usually three years, after which the labourer was to be repatriated to his village of origin.[125] It was claimed that this was to prevent the development of a landless proletariat but, as Fitzpatrick argues, the policy also served the purpose of preventing the possibility of non-traditional labour organisation.[126] It also must have saved plantations a considerable amount in housing and maintaining entire villages—men were accommodated in barrack-style quarters (labour-lines). The traditional village provided the labour force, fully grown and ready to go to work, and then absorbed it back into the bush and the mountains, complete with the much-desired modern-day trade-store goods purchased with meagre pay.[127]

Entry into the plantation labour system was in theory voluntary, and recruitment became an occupation in itself for many expatriates.[128] Recruits were mainly or exclusively male. No provision was made for additional wage allowances, transport or housing for dependants, although in theory, recruits could bring their wives with them. In Papua, however, Administrator Murray opposed the recruitment of women for plantation work in Papua, saying:

> The arguments usually put forward to support the indenture of women are:-
>
> (1) That the men are more contented if they have their wives with them—of course in any case only wives accompanied by their husbands would be recruited, for the indenture of single women is merely open prostitution;
>
> (2) That the decrease of population, which is likely to ensue if a large number of men leave their villages to go to work, is prevented if the men bring their wives with them; and

---

124 Jinks, Biskup and Nelson, *Readings in New Guinea History*, 158; Charles Rowley, 1966, *The New Guinea Villager: The Impact of Colonial Rule on Primitive Society and Economy*, New York: Praeger, 193.
125 Rowley, *The New Guinea Villager*, 60.
126 Peter Fitzpatrick, 1980, 'Really rather like slavery: law and labour in the colonial economy in Papua New Guinea,' *Contemporary Crises* 4(1): 77–95, 78.
127 In 1969, I witnessed such a homeward journey in Lae: a few dozen men being returned to the Highlands were first delivered to a Chinese trade store in Ninth Street to stock up on kerosene lamps, axes, shirts, boots, brightly coloured cotton materials and the like.
128 Fitzpatrick, 'Really rather like slavery'; Lewis, *The Plantation Dream*, 47–48; Peter Sack, 2001, *Phantom History, the Rule of Law and the Colonial State: The Case of German New Guinea*, Canberra: Division of Pacific and Asian History, The Australian National University, 172, 290.

> (3) That if there are no women, unnatural vice will prevail among the labourers.
>
> As to (1) it must be remembered that this can apply only to the small number of men who bring their wives with them ...
>
> With regard to (2) and (3) it is not too much to say that these arguments are not seriously intended, and are put forward merely as an afterthought ... the numbers of these women are so small that their presence can have no effect upon the practice of unnatural vice—assuming this vice to be prevalent. In Papua it is rare.[129]

In New Guinea, wives could be recruited with their husbands and single women could be recruited for domestic service,[130] and from 1921 onward, labour recruits were to be actively encouraged to bring their wives with them.[131] But it was noted that most recruits were unmarried, and most married recruits left their wives behind in the village.[132]

The reality was that women were to remain in the village and their men were to be returned to them, in order to provide the next generation of labourers, and also to ensure some measure of social continuity.[133] All this was achieved by legislation governing not only movement of 'natives' and 'restricted areas,' but also the labour laws themselves, which provided a careful balance of economic expediency and some measure of social justice. Many of the laws were not properly observed, but the repatriation requirements were always strictly followed—it was essential to return the labourer to his village, which was responsible for the continued maintenance of him and his family.[134] It had long been acknowledged that the indenture system was 'obnoxious.'

> As for the social aspects, the less said the better. The fact that labourers must go to other divisions tells the whole story of social disruption in itself; it has been clearly proved that indenture breaks up native life and causes the spread of loathsome disease into districts untouched by

---

129   Murray, *Papua of Today*, 112–13. For all Murray supported custom and regarded his colonial charges with benevolent paternalism, the frequency of youthful homosexual practice seems to have escaped his gaze.
130   Commonwealth of Australia, 1922, *Report to the League of Nations on the Administration of the Territory of New Guinea 1914–1921*, Melbourne: Government of the Commonwealth of Australia, 12–13.
131   Ibid., 15.
132   Commonwealth of Australia, 1923, *Report to the League of Nations on the Administration of the Territory of New Guinea 1922*, Melbourne: Government of the Commonwealth of Australia, 53.
133   Rowley, *The New Guinea Villager*, 104, 109. Heavy recruiting by the Germans in some areas in the early years of their stewardship of German New Guinea had led to economic and social collapse of some villages.
134   Fitzpatrick, 'Really rather like slavery,' 82–83.

Europeans and more than a third of the criminal cases in the Territory are by 'boys' for sexual offences, even to interfering with dead female bodies.[135]

But the recruitment of plantation labour was considered essential to development.[136] Public justification for the indentured labour system in New Guinea was that, 'whether by means of the present system or in other ways, the native must be induced to work; for the experience of neighbouring islands seems to make it clear that unless the native is given both physical exercise and interest in life, to replace the occupations and excitements of his former savage life, he will surely die out.'[137]

Plantations, then, were often remote places, with a handful of whites in the form of managers, overseers and sometimes their white families, plus a large, constantly changing contingent of young, mainly unmarried village men housed in 'labour lines,' a long way from home.[138] Single white men could, and often did, avail themselves of the companionship of local women and girls, in temporary or ongoing relationships,[139] but what of the labourers themselves?

Only a small minority ever brought their wives with them. Not a lot has been written about conditions in those labour lines in PNG—the record is more detailed when it describes plantation life from the perspective of the white settlers[140] and the documentation generated by discussion between commercial interests and administrations, which viewed the labourers as a labour force rather than as individual people.[141] The official records show problems with 'marriages' by indentured labourers. The Australian administration was quick to deplore the practice, under German administration, of giving (sometimes forcing) PNG women on plantations (be they domestic servants, or sometimes widows of labourers who had died in service) to favoured workers as an inducement to sign on for a further term. This was done without regard to the possibility of different marriage customs or different place of origin of the two. Problems would arise, it was asserted, when the labourer would return to his village of origin, take a new local wife, and abandon his plantation wife who

---

135 Stephen H. Roberts, 1928, 'Racial and labour problems,' in *The Australian Mandate for New Guinea: Record of Round Table Discussion*, ed. F.W. Eggleston, Melbourne: Macmillan, 74–84, 78.
136 F.W. Eggleston, 1928, 'Record of discussion,' in *The Australian Mandate for New Guinea: Record of Round Table Discussion*, ed. Eggleston, Melbourne: Macmillan, 112–19, 116.
137 Commonwealth of Australia, *Report to the League of Nations 1922*, 52.
138 Rowley, *The New Guinea Villager*, 103.
139 Andrew W. Lind, 1969, *Inter-Ethnic Marriage in New Guinea*, Port Moresby: New Guinea Research Unit, 13.
140 For exhaustive treatments, see for example Chilla Bulbeck, 1992, *Australian Women in Papua New Guinea: Colonial Passages 1920–1940*, Cambridge: Cambridge University Press; Jan Roberts, 1996, *Voices from a Lost World: Australian Women and Children in Papua New Guinea before the Japanese Invasion*, Alexandria, NSW: Millennium Books.
141 Various documents are provided in Jinks, Biskup and Nelson, *Readings in New Guinea History*.

would then 'degenerate into the village prostitute.'[142] Stricter controls were put into place, both as regards the employment of women for domestic service and their return to their home villages.

But what of the great majority of labourers who arrived single and remained single? The main information comes from the work of those anthropologists who studied not only 'traditional' village life but also observed the impact of plantation labour on the traditional ways of the village societies they studied. J.A. Todd did fieldwork in what is now the Kandrian area of south-west New Britain in 1933–34. In his paper on the problems of 'the maintenance of law and order' among the people whom he studied,[143] he wrote:

> Although the incidence of native sodomy is much talked about by the Europeans in New Guinea, prevention rather than cure is the solution of the problem. It seems fatuous to punish it when large numbers of natives are herded together on plantations and so on away from their women and the normal outlet for their sexual energies. It is largely a product of abnormal conditions and is certainly not common, if it occurs at all, in the normal native society around Möwehafen.[144]

Shortly afterwards, Stephen Winsor Reed conducted anthropological fieldwork in the Upper Sepik in 1936–37, and followed it with what he termed a sociological study of the transformations wrought in traditional societies by culture contact. Of homosexuality in plantation labour lines, he wrote,

> The natives have a growing awareness of the extreme revulsion with which Europeans view such behaviour … and they know of the harsh prison sentences that are frequently imposed for it. In the aboriginal cultures, however, there existed no such severe sanctions on this form of conduct, and thus the native will try to get away with it when he can. Enlightened Europeans, in private life as well as in governmental service, realize that this is a problem of the white man's own making. The only sanctioned 'solution' offered to the natives so far is the sublimation preached by the missionary. It simply does not work.[145]

Peter Worsley's study of millenarian cults is prefaced by an explanation of the poor regard in which the villager held the white colonist. He claims that the stresses and strains of living in the labour lines where the labourers' companions were exclusively male manifested in 'gambling, homosexuality and

---

142 Commonwealth of Australia, *Report to the League of Nations 1922*, 53.
143 J.A. Todd 1934/35, 'Native offences and European law in South-West New Britain,' *Oceania* 5: 437–60.
144 Ibid., 445.
145 Stephen Winsor Reed, 1943, *The Making of Modern New Guinea with Special Reference to Culture Contact in the Mandated Territory*, Philadelphia: The American Philosophical Society, 220–21.

prostitution.'[146] In 1970, a report made by the Industrial Advocate of the Public Service Association of PNG into labour line conditions expressed concerns about fornication in general, and the 'unnatural vice' of homosexuality in particular, that went on in these places.[147]

Others took a more empirical view. Anthropologist Ian Hogbin, in his account of post-war Busama in the Morobe District, tells of the boring life in the labour-line compound in the post-war years, and how, in the light of the paucity of available female prostitutes, homosexuality was 'inevitable'—he describes how older men first bribed their teenage prospects, then threatened them with sorcery if they resisted or deserted.[148]

So, in response to the question: what of the labourers themselves, who were unable to bring their women with them if they were married, or to access women from local villages even if one were nearby, the answer appears to be that they resorted to relations among themselves. The criminalisation of sodomy under the *Native Administration Regulations* in New Guinea in 1936[149] was possibly a response to the growing awareness by the colonists of the prevalence of homosexual practices in plantation labour lines.[150]

Meanwhile, though, homosexuals both among the colonised and the colonists were finding companionship in other quarters.

The unmentionable vice—sex in the colony

> For right-minded Europeans, the world overseas threatened a sexual dystopia of lascivious licence, lewd dancing, polygamy, prostitution and promiscuity, the horrors of child marriage, the evils of the harem, the unbridled pleasures of the *Kama Sutra* and *The Thousand and One Nights*, the fright of foreign genitalia, the unmentionable vice of sodomy.
>
> Robert Aldrich, 2003.[151]

---

146 Peter Worsley, 1970, *The Trumpet Shall Sound: A Study of 'Cargo' Cults in Melanesia* [2nd ed.], London: Paladin, 49.
147 Rodney Magwich, 1970, *A Submission on Plantation Wages to Rural Wages Board of Industry*, 13 May 1970, National Archives of Australia, Canberra, cited in Robert Aldrich, 2003, *Colonialism and Homosexuality*, London and New York: Routledge, 247–48.
148 H. Ian Hogbin, 1951, *Transformation Scene: The Changing Culture of a New Guinea Village*, London: Routledge & Kegan Paul Ltd., 190–91; Hogbin, 1963, *Kinship and Marriage in a New Guinea Village*, London: University of London, 97–98. See also Hogbin, 1946, 'Puberty to marriage: a study of the sexual life of the natives of Wogeo, New Guinea,' *Oceania* 16(3): 185–209, where he describes how the Wogeo people of the Sepik term homosexuality by the name of another Sepik village where, they claim, it has long been common.
149 Edward P. Wolfers, 1975, *Race Relations and Colonial Rule in Papua New Guinea*, Sydney: Australia and New Zealand Book Company, 95.
150 These ethnographical references are supported by court cases which came before the pre-Independence courts.
151 Aldrich, *Colonialism and Homosexuality*, 409.

Aldrich goes on to point out that the colonial world provided many benefits for intrepid male colonists. Colonies were refuges from the constraints of Europe; they were places of sexual experimentation and of cultural inspiration; they were testing grounds for masculinities; they were sites of incredible eroticism, the lowering of inhibitions and the blurring of boundaries. For PNG,[152] he presents the results of an intensive survey not only of published literature, but also of old newspaper accounts of court cases, and the casebooks of Justice Gore of the Port Moresby Criminal Court. He concludes that it is evident that erotic encounters between males can occur and have long occurred in many situations, settings and forms in PNG, particularly in the latter part of the colonial era, describing for the 1950s and 1960s:[153]

> a range of homosexual arrangements and behaviours ... sex conceded after intimidation and sex given for money, sex between New Guineans and between Europeans and New Guineans, as well as between Europeans, sex on the beach, in a car and in a house, sex that may have been 'situational' among labourers without women companions, but also sex that fell into a regular pattern of cruising to find partners and continuing links between homosexuals, sex between men conscious of their homosexual desires or considered repeat offenders by the authorities and between men who said homosexuality was their 'fashion.'[154]

Older gays, both national and expatriate, recall the pre-Independence era with nostalgia.

> The contacts of those years ... it was a very social time too, there was a lot of bonding I think because the Europeans of that time with similar interests tended to gravitate together, because there wasn't much in the way of theatre or dances, and no TV (Adam).

> We had never any problems in those days. Never seemed to have any problems. In the 70s and that (James).

Nelson, in describing the social and sexual mixing across race barriers in colonial PNG, mentions inter-racial homosexual relations, which were 'tacitly accepted' so long as they were not paraded too obviously in public.[155] He describes what Jenkins has elsewhere called the 'patron-client' relationship, whereby an older expatriate man takes on the care, responsibility, feeding and schooling of a young man who eventually marries, whereupon the patron assumes the role of 'uncle' or 'father,' and the first-born boy is often named after him.[156] Jenkins

---

152 Ibid., 247–62.
153 Ibid., 258, 261–62.
154 Ibid., 258.
155 Nelson, Taim Bilong Masta, 181.
156 Jenkins, 'The homosexual context of heterosexual practice in Papua New Guinea,' 197.

thinks that this may have been more a feature of colonialism, although I have observed that many gay Papua New Guineans today make a point of seeking out or preferring expatriate partners, possibly for the financial benefits such a relationship may bring.

Two different worlds: Gay in the city

> I live in two different worlds. When I live in the city, I'm gay. When I go to the village, I'm like a man (Douglas).

Attention to male-male sex in the literature is often confined to reports and studies relating to sexual practices and their relationship to HIV epidemic management. There is a large ethnographic and historical literature on homosexuality in indigenous culture and the plantations referred to above. There is also some work done in recent years under the auspices of the IMR[157] and some description of child sexual abuse of boys in the *HELP Resources Report*.[158] But although gay life in PNG informs and is informed by societal attitudes to homosexuality and current law governing homosexual behaviour across the country, there has been minimal attention paid to the everyday lives and world views of PNG males today who have sex with, or are at least attracted to, other males.

Gays and transgenders were happy to be interviewed. Through the range of contacts already established in Port Moresby, I was able to connect with a wide range, from all walks of life and all social classes. As one put it,

> In PNG, we're very privileged to have [gay] people who got very high status in different sectors of society, like lawyers, doctors, even in the police, so through our network, we can easily get help from them, there are many gay people at different levels of society, they can really help us when we go through hard times, or contributing to policy and all that (Barry).

Barry himself had tertiary education, as did many others I interviewed. Others had not even finished high school, and had never been formally employed. The solidarity of outgroups here transcended class divisions.

My interviews accorded with Herdt's and Knauft's conclusions[159] in revealing a strong disconnect between 'then' and 'now.'[160] 'In the village, I was the only one like this … I was struggling … I used to think that I was the only one in this

---

157   Ibid.; also *National Study*.
158   *HELP Resources Report*. This Report seems to imply that homosexuality is derived from such abuse, which does not accord with my findings.
159   Knauft, 'What ever happened to ritualized homosexuality?'
160   Tom Boellstorff points to the fallacy of western efforts to discover the origins of today's non-normative sexualities in the past, linking 'indigenous' homosexualities and transgenderisms to present-day manifestations. See *The Gay Archipelago*, 35–38.

world' (Douglas). Many gays described feminine activities or qualities displayed early in life. Feminine dress was one (Gordon, Steven, Douglas). Girls' games at school were a big attraction (Victor). Each one came to awareness in various ways, sometimes painfully:

> In sports ... in the rugby team or soccer team ... those who weren't selected to play would have these comments, you know, *em geligeli, wai putimen i go autsait* [He's *geligeli*, that's why he was eliminated].... I tried very hard [to hide the fact that I was gay] because I didn't want to be known to be what they called me, 'cause I wanted to prove to them that ... in a men's game, I'm a man (Len).

> When I was in Grade 8, all the boys were dreaming about girls, and they were talking about it, and I was dreaming about boys, so I had to make up stories about dreaming about girls. That's when I knew that something was wrong with me (Henry).

Moving to town and the discovery of 'sisters' and networks helped. As Henry explained,

> [In Moresby] I met X [a 'sister'] and I began to fully understand myself and the world out there and all the opportunities I had, given the grim environment that is here in PNG. I always thought it was just 'life's going to be miserable' and when I met X it was okay, I had the network and the people I can talk to and they provided me that family place and that security (Henry).

Sometimes first sexual experiences were pleasant, sometimes not, and sometimes they took place during childhood.

> That's my first-first nightclub ... that white man, he got one carton of beer and he put it in front of those five gays and me ... he said: I want that little sugar-baby ... he take me out for one night ... maybe I was 13 years old, I stayed with him ... when I was 15 years old, he was 28 ... he had to go back where he belonged ... we cried and cried ... that seven years, very long time (Oscar).

My fieldwork confirms that today, whether in the bush or in town, it seems that homosexuality and transgenderism are often rejected, denied and condemned, and traditional practices sometimes totally disavowed.[161] Many of those reared in rural environments make their way to towns and cities, where at least others can be found and pseudo-families formed. But even in the city, discrimination is everywhere. 'They can tell you right in front of you ... you're a receiver from

---

161 I recall being told emphatically by a Papua New Guinean UPNG law lecturer in 2001 that homosexuality was a 'foreign import,' and had never been part of 'traditional society.'

the anals, you're a sucker … I don't open my mouth … once I open my mouth, that's the time when you are worse … you try and open your mouth, then you'll be in the shark's mouth' (Timothy).

In part, it is prompted by masculine denial. 'In PNG, it's a very shameful act that we are going through.… In our society, men, they do practise it. They like sleeping with men but they don't want it to be known or being publicised … all sorts of Papua New Guinea men … like sleeping with other guys, having a relationship, but they don't want it to be publicised' (Colin). And in part it can be attributed to church doctrine. 'I grew up in a very Christian home, Catholic, and so I knew something was wrong. That was when I became reclusive … since Grade 8 till now I've never been back to church.… I refuse to do anything to do with religion' (Henry).

Coping strategies must be developed.

> Sometimes it's bad in town. Change your way of walking and talking. What we do, we try to train ourselves to carry ourselves in public … we have calling codes, hallo, *koti*, things like that … we do sign languages, things like that. If 'she' says yes, if you feel that it is okay, you can break your wrist. If it feels okay. We try to go public, but lifestyle (*Palopa*).

And sadly, Eric explains, 'I don't go out so much … I guess because … my circle of friends is very limited, I basically just manage my business, I get home, open my wine, watch TV, dinner, I'm in bed. I really don't socialise any more, around here' (Eric).

But there are advantages in bonding with others. The pseudo-kin groupings formed amongst gays develop their own moral codes. A small group whom I interviewed together were horrified when I asked if they had sex amongst themselves. Absolutely not, they replied, 'Here in PNG, us, the sisters, even straight acting ones like me too, we don't play with each other, we play the part of the woman. We don't play with each other, we go for straight guys, who will play the part of the man. Our friends treat us as their *meris* [women, girlfriends]' (Colin). I also noticed, as I talked and mingled, that gays often formed friendships sometimes described as 'sisters' (Colin, Barry) which were clearly not sexual—they prompted each other to describe sexual exploits with partners past and present.[162]

---

162 See Niko Besnier, 2007, 'Language and gender research at the intersection of the global and the local,' *Gender and Language* 1(1): 67–78, 74–75 and Jackson, 'An explosion of Thai identities,' 416–17 for globalisation influences on languages of homosexuality and transgender.

Safe spaces

The stigma experienced by gays today means that they exercise care in selection of safe spaces. In Port Moresby, the drop-in centre at the Poro Sapot Project is one such place. But access is limited, and for those without family to turn to, 'safe space' often means living in the adjacent Motuan village of Hanuabada (HB), on the edge of the harbour downtown, where gays can be themselves, wearing:

> miniskirts, *meri* blouses, [hair] extensions, earrings, makeup....

> There's places ... to act like a girl ... the Centre, it's okay for us; Town, it's also a good place because it's also next to the village; HB ... the Motuan villages, they're okay ... mainly HB.... At HB we have all the 'girls', all the *palopas* who've already exposed, so people are exposed to us (*Palopas*).

> HB is the only village in Port Moresby that really accepts you. Only in HB in broad daylight that you can walk in skirts in broad daylight, they won't mind, they mind their own business ... before, HB gay was in secret (Oscar).

Map 4.1. Aerial view of Hanuabada (HB), beside and in the harbour, with the Yacht Club to the upper right. Each row of houses is arranged by family and clan relationships.

Source: Google Earth V7.1.2.2041. (16 October 2013). Hanuabada Village, Port Moresby, Papua New Guinea. 9° 27' 17.54"S, 147° 09' 07.76"E, Eye alt 1.28 kilometres. DigitalGlobe 2014. http://www.earth.google.com [24 June 2014].

This is true of both Motuan and non-Motuan gays. As is customary in villages, strangers received into village life are anchored by putative family structures.

> At the village [HB], we have a house, we have a sort of *giaman* [pretend] mum and dad, they don't have kids, so they have a very big house ... all the 'girls' live there ... the wife ... she treats us as her own. Graduations, course completions, we bring them along.... About seven girls in two houses (Oscar).

Some rural communities accept gays, others do not. For many Central Province villagers at least, it can be just as easy to stay at home.

> Some of them, they're in the village, they don't come to Moresby because it's a hard life in Moresby, so they stay in the village ... Central, Hula, Aroma; Kerema, Daru as well as Motuan villages.... In the village, it's safer. They come, and not long, they're gone. They come to sell their garden produce [normally a women's activity], then after market, they go back.... Sometimes if we happen to meet them ... if they come to Moresby, they know ... where we live ... more than 500 living in Moresby and in the village.... If they come to Moresby, they know HB ... more than 500 'flowers' in Moresby and in the village. Many don't come out that often. In village, you will know that if they're gay, they get a *bilum* and a knife, you will know that 'she' is a *Palopa*. You will see if they don't walk with the ladies, that is a man.... The *Palopas*, they walk with the ladies to the garden (Oscar).

And safety can sometimes mean nightclubs, although there are no specific 'gay nightclubs' in Port Moresby (Oscar). Clubs can be good pick-up places, although as I shall describe in Chapter 5, club cruising can be dangerous. The main role of the nightclubs is to provide pre-programmed sites for the increasingly popular 'drag shows.' The shows emerged in the early 2000s from an initiative started by Moses Tau, gay pop singer and MSM rights activist. As a male sex worker (MSW) explained in a group interview:

> First show ... started by Moses Tau. Twenty-two of us competing and we were competing again, and then from there we started advertising the competition. Moses put it together.... We started sending invitations out, to our 'girlfriends', telling them if you see any gays, tell them to come along, we're trying to push the gay thing out to the public ... they came from everywhere! (MSW).

News spread rapidly:

> I never thought that there were any other gays in PNG. I was at home and then one time, this friend of ours ... he walked in one afternoon:

> 'Girl, cook our dinner, and then I think I have a very exciting news for you.'… We had dinner, he goes: 'There's a ticket here, Club X, 50-50. They said it's for *geligelis*, it's for modelling or something.' We got into men's clothes, two of us walked all the way … it was our first time, we walked in and sat in a corner … ya, look at those ones, they're like us. My first time, to actually join the 'girls' (MSW).

It wasn't easy at first:

> There was a gay Mardi Gras bash … we were the only ones that dressed up … but it wasn't easy there, they were punching me and kicking me and I had to fight in the toilet, and I go into the ladies' toilet and the ladies are angry, and I go to the male toilet and wow … and security guards were accompanying us the whole time. The second time I went there, very recently, that was last year, one of those gay-organised things, and everyone was friendly, the security guards were helpful, they said, 'Oh, we know, you can go straight and change' (Henry).

Soon the shows became a focus for gay awareness and entertainment, a 'safe space.'

> I heard about the shows.… I thought it was real girls' show.… I thought, these are 'girls' sitting down! Not only PNG … but Filipinas and the Chinese … for Papua New Guineans, I can tell, but for Filipinos, just like a woman, the way they dress, the way they talk … when they walk into the club, no-one will know if they are girls or boys. The first time I went in, I thought, oh my God, I really wanted to be like them … even some of them, the ones that I know, they came up to me wearing those mini-skirts and dress and all those tight jeans and with their wigs and everything (Peter).

> I was also very much surprised.… I went the first time … my staff invited me, they said, that's right, there's a fifty-fifties night tonight, and I thought, oh yes, I like the '50s … I was really just floating when I got there, the *geligelis* were there! It was half-half, you know … all dressed up … this was about two years ago … it dawned on me, I just thought, this is accepted … that was the first time, I thought, this is good! (Eric).

Many clubs formerly catering only for male-female networking and commercial sex began setting aside specific nights for the drag shows, and ensured that security was tight. Some clubs even changed their names to reflect their new images. Complex programmes of competition 'categories' (sports, casual, dance, evening-wear and so on) are drawn up, heats, semi-finals and finals are held, with cash prizes offered. All contestants, win or lose, receive some measure of payment, and for security purposes, transport home is usually arranged. Drag shows are definitely good for business, and good for the contestants too.[163]

> Now the clubs begin to know us very well, they come to accept us, once we do a show in any club, that club makes a lot of money…. Helping us not to go out and sell yourself, get the money, hang around on the street…. Keeping 'girls' occupied, not to go out, because they're receiving one or two kina from there, when they go to the village, they have money to buy what they want (Oscar).

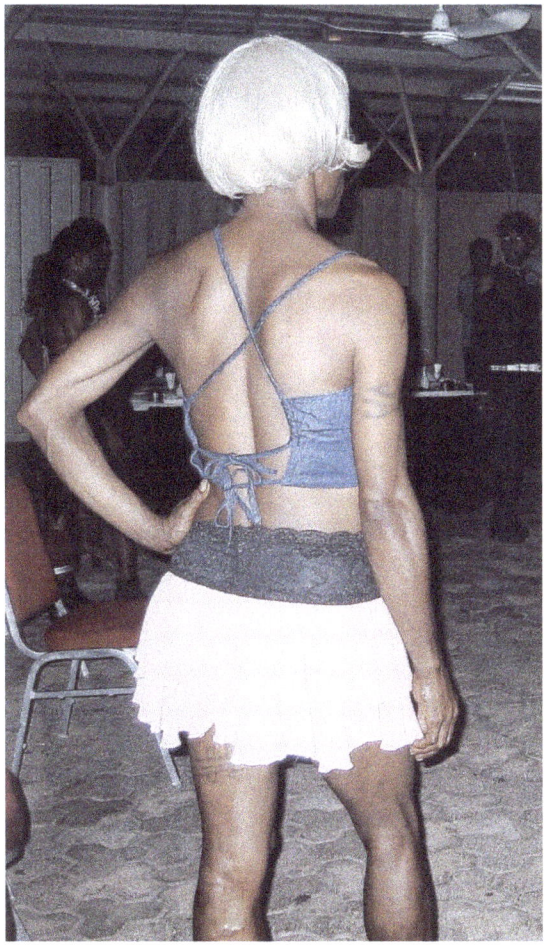

Figure 4.12. Drag show contestant.

Source: Photo by Christine Stewart, 30 March 2006.

---

163 In 2007, for example, the club hosting the current round of drag competitions paid K50 to every entrant for performing, and offered a first prize of K1,000. Security was tight at the premises, and the contestants were bussed home.

And, as I found when I was escorted to shows during fieldwork, they are a lot of fun. The second-hand clothing shops are plundered, and better-off friends (including me) are importuned to provide financial assistance towards costumes (a different one for each category). Nails are polished, hair straightened and hair-extensions painstakingly woven in, wigs and evening gowns donned, makeup carefully applied. Participants practise lip-synching to popular songs, dance routines and catwalk slinks. Even many of the audience turn up in drag, acknowledging the safety of the space. The drag shows have become a critical factor, in Port Moresby at least, for assisting in confidence-building.

Figure 4.13. Notice of MSW meeting posted on the 'notice-board' at Poro Sapot.

Source: Photo by Christine Stewart, 12 September 2007.

Males selling sex

In contrast to the focus on female sex selling in PNG in both popular and academic discourse today, scant attention has been paid to male sex selling as a category in itself.[164] It is usually conflated with men who have sex with men, but PNG is not unique in this regard. Cindy Patton notes this asymmetry in the world-wide HIV discourse, and argues that it derives from 'the active-

---

164 Kelly et al., Askim na Save, 9.

passive split that is supposed to characterize male versus female sexuality.... Whereas men sell bodies that are theirs to dispose of, women sell bodies that more properly belong to men, their families, or society as a whole.'[165]

The *Poro Sapot Evaluation Report* found evidence of the selling of sex by males in Port Moresby in 2007,[166] and Jenkins noted the activity in Lae and Daru as well in the same year,[167] but no consistent research was conducted until 2010.[168] However, there is nothing new about the selling of male sex in PNG. Examples have already been furnished in official records, such as those of *Kausigor's Case* and the *Siune Wel* cases, discussed in Chapter 3.[169] Other pre-Independence cases testify to the early identification of the purchasing of male-male sex. In 1962, for example, a drunken expatriate was convicted of an attempt to procure two 'natives' for 'acts of gross indecency' by offering them a £1 note.[170] The *National Study* includes an account of an expatriate paying village boys in the Highlands for anal sex.[171]

In 2007, I asked to meet with self-identifying male sex workers who congregate at Poro Sapot. We talked freely, no names were given, recorded or used, and as well as receiving the information they had to give, I was able to reciprocate, with information on various aspects of the law.

Some limit themselves to a few regular clients:

> At the moment, I have only one male client that I see.... I used to have ... the recent ones ... two expatriates, and another national male client ... and I found out that they also have a lot of friends ... having multiple sex partners, like clients ... so when I found about that, finished.... At the moment, that national, my client ... he gives good money, ranging from hundred, two hundred (MSW).

> Most of the men, they like to keep it discreet. They don't want to be discriminated.... They have our mobile numbers, so they give us a call when they're in town, and then give the room number, 'just go to reception, I already give your name.'... The standard price ... one or two hundred, but with drinks (MSW).

Others trawl the higher-class establishments:

---

165 Cindy Patton, 2002, *Globalising AIDS*, Minneapolis and London: University of Minnesota Press, 92.
166 Maibani-Michie et al., *Evaluation of the Poro Sapot Project*.
167 Carol Jenkins, 2007, 'HIV/AIDS, culture, and sexuality in Papua New Guinea,' in *Cultures and Contexts Matter: Understanding and Preventing HIV in the Pacific*, Manila: Asian Development Bank, 5–69, 57.
168 Kelly et al., Askim na Save.
169 *Kausigor's Trial; Kausigor's Appeal; Siune Wel Cases*.
170 *R v. Bates* (Unreported) Supreme Court No. 255 9 October 1962.
171 *National Study*, 98.

> For my clients, Asians, Filipinos, Indians, Indonesians, a few Australians, a few topshots, parliamentarians, businessmen, I go to the big hotels, I go alone just like a man. I go with some money to cover myself, take a drink, sit down, look at people playing snooker, dancing, that's how I start off. When I'm drinking I don't move around, I sit there. I call them and they speak to me. Dealing with men, they give me money. I make about four or five hundred kina in one night (MSW).

For many, it is a case of working the beats:

> We hear stories, like we have one of our friends, 'she' walks the X Park … they walk around, just as normal. When they see clients coming up towards them, they start doing their bit … if we strut our stuff, if he gives a signal like eye contact, then we know he wants it. It's up to the 'girl' to continue, take it on from there (MSW).

Some beats are exclusively male,[172] some are open to all.

Figure 4.14. The Ela Beach beat downtown.

Source: Photo by Christine Stewart, 22 January 2006.

Mine workers working on a fly-in fly-out basis are particularly good clients, as are commercial fishermen.

> Although there are sex workers around mines, they're restricted, they have fences, they don't come out, they don't bring their families. And

---

172   I was told of one outside a well-known supermarket, and had not realised until then that the lads I had noticed hanging around the carpark and entrance were offering sex rather than sizing up pickable pockets and snatchable bags—or were they?

the villagers around the mines don't come into the mines, so they are really restricted. When they come back, their pockets are really full (MSW).

I was told how many 'grew into' their profession.

> I dropped out from school, my good friend called me over and told me there's one white man, he looking for *geli*, he's going to give you money, those times I never bothered about money. He brought me over to that person's workplace, he picked me up, it was during the day, then he's trying to drop me off and he asked, do you want money. I said I don't know, he gave me K50, it was my first time to have K50, I was really happy … then I matured and knew the techniques and all that, and I started hooking men for myself, like going to the clubs … if I bump into one, and if they're good for me, then we negotiate (MSW).

> One of our sister-girls, 'she' went to Y guesthouse, now 'she' works there, bartender, they have rooms there, sometimes late in the night … men start coming in and negotiate for sex, and 'she's' got rates for wanking them or giving them a blow job or to do the full thing (MSW).

Male sex sellers contrast with their female counterparts in various ways. By and large, they are in a better negotiating position to be paid more money. This is partly due to a focus on skills-training:

> Before, when we didn't have the knowledge of approaching people and stuff, like talking in the ways, before, we just used to swing our hands…. but now we came to … the way of solving problems … they ran a workshop, training here. Communication skills, role models, stuff like that. Now I think we're more adult (MSW).

But other factors contribute to the comparative success of males in earning-power. Many have more tricks and are in a better negotiating position than most female sex sellers due to their physical strength, their ability to threaten reluctant clients with exposure, and to work *raskol* tactics such as pilfering.

> There was one time for example I was drinking in the bar, these two white people they were in the bar, they approached me and we were talking and I was already really drunk and my wrists were broken and they knew this was one *geli* and they said, do you need a lift and I said, yes please, then we went to another person's apartment, one left without giving me anything, I stayed with the other one, in the morning he only gave me K20, I was really mad, he was having his shower … looking

around, I got his camera, and I got … he dropped me, it was Friday. Then I went straight to … and I sold them, I got I think K400. He gave me K20 only, I was expecting more (MSW).

Gays and girls in the sex trade co-exist in a world of simultaneous cooperation, competition and conflict.

One place Y, the girls were staying permanently there. In 2003 I got a job down there, I heard about it but I never experienced it. There were two girls sharing a room, the rent was K150 a day. Girls were getting money from the clients, they paid the hotel room. Because of the kind of person I am, I got to get to know the girls very well, we had a very good relationship. I was duty manager at the time. When they were having problems paying their rent, they would come up to me, I would help them out with that (MSW).

These are the same clubs where the women are also trying to find.… This is where arguments start. There's a competition going on, we interrupt (MSW).

Usually ladies going with their boyfriends or husbands, if we appear, then the male client has another mentality, change their minds, the girl will get upset, say that is a male, that is a homo, 'she's' not what you think 'she' is.… But the male who has more attraction, won't even bother, he just comes straight for it, when he does that, and we want our revenge, that's when we take our revenge (MSW).

Selling sex for gays is more than a profession, more than a way of life. When I asked the group I was talking with: 'If you were offered a really good job in an office, would you give it up?' I was answered with a horrified chorus of 'No!' 'It's a game,' and 'I'm addicted.'

This contrasted strongly with the women I talked to, all of whom were seeking a way out. Jenny dreams of a sex trade centre, with a properly staffed specialist clinic, where women can do crafts as well as selling sex, and accumulate their own savings (Jenny). Angelina found a job, a good man and has borne his baby. Both or either of these alternatives is the goal of most. This illustrates a fundamental difference between males and females in the sex trade. Females in Port Moresby are engaged in a commercial activity for survival. Many of the men are enacting their sexual identities and desires—and making money at it. The selling of sex by males is a slippery concept. The kind of commercial transaction appearing in the Law Reports is understandable as male prostitution: casual encounters, the payment or the promise of money.[173] Nelson, Aldrich and Jenkins describe the

---

173 See *Kausigor's Trial, Kausigor's Appeal,* the *Siune Wel Cases,* and Aldrich, *Colonialism and Homosexuality.*

colonial situations of male 'patronage,' which involve sometimes extensive and on-going cash outlay on the part of the expatriate involved.[174] But many of these expatriates[175] view such relationships as love affairs. So also do many Papua New Guineans. On the other hand, Papua New Guinean gays may regard such relationships as pleasant but ultimately commercial transactions. Sometimes, both views may be held simultaneously: some of those interviewed individually spoke of their 'husbands,' but later joined the MSW group discussion referring to the same partners as 'clients.'

The selling of sex by men to women was touched upon briefly in my interviews: 'It's easy for the male sex workers who sell sex to women and to men' (MSW). I was assured by Elizabeth Reid some time ago that this trade certainly takes place in Port Moresby.[176] I also recall a Highlands woman telling me in 1994 how some Highlands women *elites* (for example, the widow of a wealthy businessman, the sister of a Parliamentarian) would source a likely young village lad and pay 'groomprice' for him as well as financing his clothing, education and such like.[177] I have also noted occasional mention in the press of mature women in various parts of the country 'forcing' young boys to have sex with them—possibly by offering payment.[178] Recent research however has unearthed a wealth of data on the multitude of ways in which sex is traded in Port Moresby. The *Askim na Save* report revealed that three-quarters of the men serviced women clients to some extent, a quarter of them serviced only women, and a quarter of the transgenders serviced only or mostly women. A further table shows expatriate women as constituting 16 per cent of clients overall.[179]

Conclusions

My fieldwork has revealed something of the 'discrete place in the great social continuum of abnormal to normal'[180] of the criminalised sexual subjects of Port Moresby, through time and place. Commercialised sex takes on many more forms than popular rhetoric would have it. More significantly, the sex trade is just one part of the huge informal economy in Port Moresby. Large numbers of women,

---

174 Nelson, Taim Bilong Masta, 181; Aldrich, *Colonialism and Homosexuality*; Jenkins, 'The homosexual context of heterosexual practice in Papua New Guinea.'
175 Including several of my personal acquaintances.
176 Pers. comm., Elizabeth Reid, Canberra, July 2008.
177 My informant expressed disgust at this type of behaviour. Her Highlander husband was a highly-placed professional.
178 E.g, *HELP Resources Report*, 48, 50, 52.
179 Kelly et al., Askim na Save, 17.
180 Golder and Fitzpatrick, *Foucault's Law*, 63.

girls, men, boys and transgenders sell and exchange sex as part of their daily lives, whether casually or on an ongoing basis, without necessarily admitting that what they do is part of what they are. As Hammar explains,

> In PNG 'sex worker' criteria are seldom met in terms of cohesion or consciousness. 'FSWs' and 'CSWs' are often clerks, betel-nut sellers, housewives, collectors of firewood, struggling widows, girls doing Grade 8, job applicants, and women seeking to marry expatriate boyfriends.[181]

The sale of sex is often combined with other small-scale vendor activities, selling *buai*, cigarettes, second-hand clothing, cooked food, fruit and vegetables, cold drinks and ice blocks, cheap imported goods and so on.

> Almost three-quarters [of participants in the *Askim na Save* survey of people who sold or exchanged sex] (74%; n=436) reported they had work other than selling or exchanging sex. Of the 417 participants who specified other work, the most common type of work was selling betel nut (79%), followed by selling store goods (12%).[182]

But whereas other informal economy activities are legal, although controlled by a variety of health and zoning regulations,[183] the sex trade is not. Street vendors have large sectors of the public on their side, and also speak up for themselves. Sex sellers cannot, without admitting that they are 'prostitutes,' and prostitutes are law-breakers.

Selling sex and sexual activity between males taking place in modern times both have antecedents, though not necessarily origins, in pre-colonial cultures. The introduction of the cash economy, Christianity, western medical beliefs and management practices, the growth of cities in a rural landscape of hunting, fishing and horticulture, the increasing divide between leaders and the led, between the haves and the have-nots, through colonial times and into the post-colonial era, have incidentally created groups of people whose sexuality and sexual behaviours contravene currently accepted norms, and their modern-day forms confound many popularly held views. It is not a simple matter of expatriates patronising young PNG men. Sex-selling is more than a matter of

---

181 Hammar, n.d., 'The 's' words: 'sex,' 'sex worker,' and 'stigma' in Papua New Guinea,' paper for Papua New Guinea Institute of Medical Research.
182 Kelly et al., Askim na Save, 14.
183 An attempt at management of PNG's informal economy, the *Informal Sector Act* 2004, succeeded mainly in giving wide powers to urban 'City Rangers' in Port Moresby, which they often exercised with exorbitant violence and disregard for the law: ref. my collection of newspaper clippings, and personal observations while in Port Moresby. The recent ban on selling *buai* inside Port Moresby has greatly exacerbated this situation.

women, whether helpless victims or independent agents,[184] exchanging sex for cash, goods or services. It also includes men selling sex to other men, and to women.[185]

But popular discourse relies on simplicity. Disciplinary power constructs these people as outclasses; while law, at work policing the boundary between normal and abnormal, declares their activities to be illicit. Although they have harmed none but themselves, they are treated as criminals, through legislative processes and in the courtroom itself, as I shall show in the next chapter.

---

184 Sandy, "'My blood, sweat and tears'"; Wardlow, "'Prostitution,' "Sexwork," and "Passenger Women."'
185 Kelly et al., Askim na Save, 17.

5. In Trouble

> Little is known about the collateral effects that law has in constructing individual subjects and shaping social organization through methods such as surveillance, stigma, and punishment … scholars must examine not only the instrumental, or direct, impact of laws by evaluating their transformation of social meanings, but also the indirect or collateral effects these laws have in transforming social relations and individuals' sense of themselves.
>
> Ryan Goodman, 2001.[1]

Introduction

The statutes and cases discussed in Chapter 3 demonstrate how the law, both as given by the legislature,[2] or decided by judges, can either maintain or shift the boundary between the licit and the illicit. Selling sex and male-male sexual behaviour have been placed outside the boundary, and Chapter 3 has indicated some of the direct consequences of this process of criminalisation. Punishment may cause some criminals to reform, but when others do not have this option, or are unwilling to change, they remain outside the boundary, and may become the subjects of society's victimisation.[3] In Chapter 4, I have already described some of the links between family abuse and selling sex, and some of the coping strategies gays have had to develop in order to survive in Port Moresby. But the story does not end there, and in this chapter, I examine the collateral effect of criminal sexuality laws, by describing some of the more extreme consequences of criminalisation: how the attitudes of the Papua New Guinea (PNG) *elites* support the policing of social boundaries; how stigmatisation and discrimination affect the lives of sex sellers and gays; and how the law and its enforcement agencies operate to legitimise discrimination and violence.

---

1   Ryan Goodman, 2001, 'Beyond the enforcement principle: sodomy laws, social norms, and social panoptics,' *California Law Review* 89: 643–740, 644–45.
2   The term is used here to refer both to the colonial administration and the post-Independence National Parliament.
3   Goodman, 'Beyond the enforcement principle,' 731–33.

Name, Shame and Blame: Criminalising Consensual Sex in Papua New Guinea

Pamuk Meri—sex sellers in trouble

The Tale of a raid

It was a hot Friday afternoon, 12 March 2004, in Port Moresby. Down a suburban side street, behind a high corrugated-iron fence, a live band was playing at the Three-Mile Guesthouse, and the premises were packed. The guesthouse is a converted colonial high-covenant house, with an added block of rooms behind it which are mainly let to women who sell sex and collect their own payments. Facilities include a bar, a snooker table and gaming machines; older women peddle cooked food, cigarettes and *buai* in the front yard or outside the gate; unlike many other nightclubs, it is open by day as well as in the evening, allowing housewives to drop by and augment domestic finances without the knowledge of their families.

However, not everyone at the guesthouse that afternoon was involved in the negotiation and conduct of sex. Many were there simply to enjoy a beer from the bar and listen to the band. Some of the young women were related to band members, and turned up to support their kin. Some were there for the first time, brought by a girlfriend or relative. Some were passers-by who could not even afford the two kina (then around 80¢ AUD or 60¢ USD) entry fee and peeped in through the gate to the yard. Some, men and women, were guesthouse employees: cleaners or security guards; entire families, including children, were in long-term residence.[4]

> *Mi no save raun olsem ol otherpela meri olsem ol save raun we painim moni. Mi save kukim kaikai na mi save go salim long dispela hap ... dispela em mipela save live long dispela kaikai moni* (I don't play around like all those other women, the way they go round looking for money. I cook food and sell it here ... this is how we live, by selling food) (Barbara).

> I was inside the guest house selling bettlenut and smoke [cigarettes].... I am married to a Simbu man who works in the Guest house as a security.... I sometimes stay with him at the guest house when he works but most of the time I am at Nine-mile with my in-laws who reside there (Miriam).

> I was a security at the time of the raid (Jack).

---

4   Statements were made by many caught up in the raid a few days afterwards for use in possible damages claims. Outreach workers took down most of the statements, hence some are recorded in the third person. The texts have been reproduced without alteration to grammar or spelling. Many may have been made in Tok Pisin and were either recorded thus or translated on the spot, so it is impossible to say who may have erred, the transcriber, the translator or the respondent. All those used or referred to were approved for my use by the makers, though all wished their real names to be concealed: see Appendix 1.

> She is only there waiting for her cousin brothers (band members) to finish play and go home (Meg).

> I went to the guest house to check for my husband.... I am married with a small girl aged 2 years old (Emma).

> Whilst on my way (to visit my aunty who lives nearby) I heard life band was entertaining the people ... so I decided to pip through the gate (Beth).

Then the police burst in through the gate.

> A band of policemen ... forced their way in waving, pointing guns in the air and telling everyone to freeze. Some of the policemen were with sticks bashing men and women, about 18 to 19 policemen (Jill).

People tried to escape, but the police caught and beat them. They assaulted the women with rifle butts, pool cues and lumps of wood and iron. Food was dumped over the vendors, beer over the drinkers.

> I was hit with a iron rod on my back and a wood on my head. I felt a bit dizzy as a consequence of the heavy beating. A policeman has ordered me to chew condom and swallow which I comply.... I was then ordered to sit with the girls in circle. The police pour water, beer, soft drinks and cooked food stuff all over our body (Eve).

> I was frightened but then I thought they won't do anything. This is the first time in my life to experience this kind of situation ... it was very inhuman (Susie).

Police snatched people from the rooms, looted alcohol and the till takings,[5] gaming machines and kitchen appliances,[6] rifled through people's bags and confiscated money and valuables, and raped some of the women.

> The police about 8 to 10 at the back with guns and sticks in their hands ... forced me to a room ... they had guns on my head and belted me with rubber on both of my hands and my left side of my buttock (bruised and black) and forced me onto a bed. They forced me to take my long jeans off with my pants which I did after fearing them and I was asked to open my both legs and one of them took a freshener can and pushed it into my vagina. I started to shout and they shut me down ... the same person took an empty SP bottle and began pushing it into my vagina. I shouted and another policeman came and hit me and said shut up ... then a last

---

5 Interview Poro Sapot (PSP) outreach workers, 19 January 2006.
6 Christopher Hershey, 2004, *Statement of Facts on Police Raid at 3-Mile Guesthouse 12 March 2004*, Port Moresby, Papua New Guinea.

> person came ... and pointed a pistol on my head and asked me to suck his penis. He pulled his penis out and forced me by holding a pistol on my head and I sucked his penis three times. He then told me to wear my trousers and run out. They chased me out and as I was running out they hit me with an iron bar (Jane).

They confiscated condoms from the rooms and the bar and, by continual beating, forced the women to chew and swallow them.

> A policeman who gave me the condom broke open one condom and instructed me to chew the condom. I chewed it as instructed. I chewed and felt vomiting so I started to take it out. He saw that and with his close fist hit me on my forehead and with his gun butt he hit me on my right buttock. So I swallowed the condom (Sally).

> [The police] belt me with iron on my back. They swear at us, telling us that you should get married and stay back at the house, instead of selling your body passing the virus to another people, do your vaginas get pain or not (Debbie).

Everybody present—men, women and even children—was lined up and marched at gunpoint the two kilometres through the streets to the police station. The grim procession was headed by the police vehicles and a tipper truck loaded with the gaming machines and snooker tables.[7] The women were forced to hold condoms in their mouths, or wave them like balloons above their heads as they marched. A crowd gathered quickly and, encouraged by the police, jeered at the unfortunate ones, spat on them, pelted them with stones and bottles and taunted them.

> A policeman issued 4 condom and ordered me to chew 2 of them and swallow which I did with fear. I was forced to blow 2 balloons out of the condom, hold it in the air and march with the group.... The police beat me with an iron rod and stick and booted us while on our way to the police station. The police told the public about the reasons of our arrests and the general public subsequently participate by throwing sticks, stones and rubbish at us. The public make mockery at us and used abusive words against us.... I was very embarrassed when the general public and the police alike shouted abusive words and swear at us (Anna).

> On our way, betel nut was spitted on me and beer cans was poured on me and other women. Public shouted 'see them they are AIDS carriers.' I felt really out of place (Lynne).

---

7 Interview PSP outreach workers, 19 January 2006.

I am really embarrassed about such action … but excessive force used by police does not leave any room for us to protect myself.… There was a lot of abusive words by police and the public, words like 'prostitute,' *'pamuk meri'* [slut], AIDS carriers, *'sik pulap'* [riddled with disease], *'spread sik AIDS'* [spreaders of AIDS], *'painim man o'* [man-hunters], *'raunraun meri'* [mobile/loose women], *'salim samting blong yupela tumas yupela save pilim pen tu o nogat'* [you sell your 'things' so much, I guess it doesn't even hurt you] (Beth).

At the police station, reporters from the local TV station and the three daily newspapers were waiting, presumably alerted by the police.[8] More than forty men caught up in the raid were freed, but the women and girls (a number of them aged under eighteen) were processed in batches. While they were sitting waiting on the grass outside the station, the Metropolitan Superintendent addressed them. He told them that the raid had been conducted to prevent those selling sex from contracting and spreading HIV. He claimed later that he knew that some of the women were HIV-positive and were probably infecting others through their behaviour.[9]

Some thirty-nine women and girls were charged for 'living on the earnings of prostitution' under Section 55(1) of the *Summary Offences Act* 1977, and locked in hot, crowded cells. Outreach workers from the National AIDS Council Secretariat (NACS), the National Capital District (NCD) Provincial AIDS Council, Poro Sapot, other NGOs and community organisations brought food and comfort;[10] some NGO workers managed to gain access to the station and stayed with the women in the cells. Among those locked up were a pregnant woman who was badly injured and found extreme difficulty sitting in the cramped conditions, and a woman with a new baby which was held by a friend outside and brought in intermittently for breast-feeding, as the mother was not permitted to leave the cell. That night, some young women were taken out of the cells. Miriam reported, 'whilst we were inside policeman asked six women to come out and they went and never returned.… I just want to bring my sister in to give information about what happened to her when they took her out' (Miriam).

Outreach workers reported that four were offered a lift home but once in the police vehicle, were told they had to provide sex first. Two agreed, but two

---

8 Michael Goddard mentions this tip-off process in relation to other types of raids. See M. Goddard, 2001, 'From rolling thunder to reggae: imagining squatter settlements in Papua New Guinea,' *Contemporary Pacific* 13(1): 1–32; Goddard, 2005, *The Unseen City: Anthropological Perspectives on Port Moresby, Papua New Guinea*, Canberra: Pandanus Press, 20–21.
9 Hershey, *Statement of Facts on Police Raid*.
10 Hershey, *Statement of Facts on Police Raid*; National AIDS Council of Papua New Guinea, 2004, *Statement of Facts on Police Raid at 3-Mile Guesthouse 12 March 2004*, report prepared for National AIDS Council Secretariat, Port Moresby, Papua New Guinea.

refused and were returned to the lockup.[11] The women, stinking from the beer and foodstuffs poured over them, were held for a day and a half in the hot, overcrowded cells, without food, washing facilities or medical attention for their injuries. Firstly, the Duty Officer could not be found to release them on their own recognisance. Then it was decided that they should be photographed and fingerprinted—but the fingerprinting officer was not available. After some thirty hours, the women were finally released in the early hours of Sunday morning.

The next day, Monday, both PNG English-language daily newspapers ran the story. The *Post-Courier's* front-page report included a paragraph stating that both male and female prostitutes, including a thirteen-year-old girl, had been arrested.[12] The newspaper also ran an Editorial, 'Give thought to rehabilitation,' which commenced by castigating the police for mounting such a 'public humiliation ritual … [t]hat's an interesting experiment in social reform or pre-trial processing. The defence lawyers will find it valuable in mounting a case against the prosecution. Certainly it must have been good entertainment for the street folk.'[13] The author of the Editorial then proceeded to praise the police commander for his wise words of warning to the detainees.

> The police commander who assembled the charged people on the lawn outside the police station and warned them of the perils of their so-called profession was doing the right thing.
>
> But will they listen? it asked:
>
> The only trouble is in getting those people to take note of it after they are dealt with by the courts. Looking to the future is not a thing that prostitutes are noted for….
>
> Will any of those charged people get off the bottom rung or will they be inevitable dregs of the hospital wards soon and among those anonymous carcasses to be bulldozed into a mass burial pit at Bomana cemetery one day soon, victims of HIV/AIDS?[14]

The *National's* report included a photo and a small story, relating how the Superintendent had lamented the increase in prostitution.

> It was a sad thing to see girls, as young as 14, 15 and 16 years of age sitting among the group … some of these young girls' clients were men as old as 60 … times were tough and prostitution among young women

---

11 Interview PSP outreach workers, 19 January 2006.
12 'Sex workers on parade,' 2004, *Post-Courier*, 15 March, 1.
13 Editorial, 2004, 'Give thought to rehabilitation,' *Post-Courier*, 15 March, 10.
14 Ibid.

was increasing ... [they] were risking their lives and could easily catch AIDS ... the women are drunk in most cases and do not take safety precautions like using condoms ... prostitution was the main cause of HIV/AIDS virus spreading like bushfire.[15]

The following day, Tuesday, the *Post-Courier* produced a dramatic front-page headline:

Figure 5.1. 'Males "freed" ... but 31 suspected female prostitutes charged!'

Source: *Post-Courier*, 16 March 2004, 1.

The story continued,

> FORTY-FIVE men rounded up by police for alleged prostitution walked free yesterday because there are no provisions in the law to charge male sex workers.

> However, 31 women were arrested and charged because Section 55 of the Summary Offences Act of the Criminal Code provides for female sex workers to be charged.

---

15 'Police arrest 80 in brothel raid,' 2004, *National*, 15 March, 5.

> However, a senior government lawyer yesterday said sections 55 and 57 of the law were not designed to single out women prostitutes.
>
> The lawyer said the charging of people was the discretion of the police depending on the kind of information at hand.
>
> It was not right to say that the provisions did not cater for charges being filed against male prostitutes.
>
> A prostitute is someone who earns a living from sexual favours or earns a living by providing the venue for prostitution.
>
> National AIDS Council lawyer Bomal Gonapa ... said outside court that 35 men were released from police custody because there was no provision under the current Summary Offences Act of the Criminal Code Act that covered male prostitutes.
>
> 'The release of the male suspects was not fair to their female counterparts because they were all engaged in such an activity,' Mr Gonapa said.[16]

This public reference to 'male prostitutes' seemed to come as something of a surprise, and was taken up eagerly by the media. Over the week following the raid, both newspapers solicited comments from prominent people on this topic. All commentators deplored the apparent gender bias in the police action, and explained that the law was gender neutral.[17] In fact, however, there were no male prostitutes involved in the raid. The Three-Mile Guesthouse only catered for women and girls selling sex. The males released were guesthouse employees, clients, even the band members.[18]

A few days later, the NCD Provincial AIDS Committee convened a meeting of government representatives, NGOs and churches and those caught up in the raid.[19] Among other things, court claims for damages and breach of human rights were proposed, so written statements were taken by and from many of those involved. The statements taken reflect the need to emphasise the injuries, both physical and psychological, that were visited on them. With AusAID support, a skilled criminal lawyer and former Public Prosecutor was retained to conduct their defence in the District Court.[20] The underage girls arrested had their cases

---

16 'Males "freed,"' 2004, *Post-Courier*, 16 March, 1.
17 Maureen Gerawa, 'Police wrong: NGO,' 2004, *Post-Courier*, 17 March, 4; Andrew Moutu, 2004, 'Crime to be a woman?' Letters to the Editor, *Post-Courier*, 17 March, 10; Michelle Yiprukaman, 'Kidu: probe raid on city brothel,' 2004, *Post-Courier*, 18 March, 4.
18 Hershey, *Statement of Facts on Police Raid*.
19 The National AIDS Council established these committees for each province and the National Capital District.
20 See also Karen Fletcher and Bomal Gonapa, 2010, 'Decriminalisation of prostitution in Papua New Guinea,' in *Civic Insecurity: Law, Order and HIV in Papua New Guinea*, ed. Vicki Luker and Sinclair Dinnen, Canberra: ANU E Press, 141–52, online: http://press.anu.edu.au?p=94091, accessed 8 April 2014.

removed to the Juvenile Court. But soon it became evident that all the cases would collapse. The defence asked to see a copy of the search warrant. There was none. Four weeks after the raid, the police prosecutor admitted that the raid was conducted improperly and withdrew the cases, giving the face-saving excuse that public criticism compelled it, and claiming that any further action would be delayed until an investigation could be mounted into the incident.[21] The NGO Individual and Community Rights Advocacy Forum (ICRAF) lodged a claim against the State for damages with the Solicitor-General's office, but the Solicitor General[22] stated in September 2004 that he required further particulars as to which specific policemen were allegedly involved.[23] The then Police Commissioner refused to take any disciplinary action until individual complainants appeared at a police station to substantiate their allegations.[24] Another claim for compensation for abuse of human rights was filed on behalf of the women and the guesthouse owner by the law firm which provided the defence lawyer, but it too has not been pursued.

In June 2004, the Ombudsman Commission notified the Police Commissioner that it proposed to investigate the matter.[25] However, it was five years before the Final Report was presented to the Speaker of the National Parliament on 21 December 2009, for tabling in March 2010.[26] The Commission observed that proper arrest, detention and bail procedures had not been followed, and made a number of recommendations including improvement to police operational instructions and courses for police on human rights, and urged that the police implicated should be dealt with appropriately under the *Police Act* 1998.[27] Unfortunately the Report was tabled at the same time as two other more politically significant reports, and it was never debated.

***

This tale provides a useful picture of some of the issues and problems faced by those who sell sex in PNG, and specifically in the nation's capital. Raids such as

---

21 'Police withdraw case against 40 women,' 2004, *National*, 8 April; 'Police withdraw prostitute case,' 2004, *Post-Courier*, 8 April, 3.
22 Statutory head of the Solicitor-General's Office, which is responsible for representing the State in civil actions by and against it.
23 Human Rights Watch, 2005, *'Making Their Own Rules': Police Beatings, Rape, and Torture of Children in Papua New Guinea*, New York: Human Rights Watch, 116; see also Ombudsman Commission of Papua New Guinea 2009, *Investigation Report into the Alleged Unlawful and Abuse of Human Rights by Police, Three Mile Guest House, Port Moresby, National Capital District*, Port Moresby: Report to the National Parliament, which noted that detailed evidence was not available for many of the assertions made about police conduct.
24 Human Rights Watch, 2006, *'Still Making Their Own Rules': Ongoing Impunity for Police Beatings, Rape, and Torture in Papua New Guinea*, New York: Human Rights Watch, 35.
25 Ombudsman Commission, *Investigation Report into the Alleged Unlawful and Abuse of Human Rights by Police*, 1.
26 'OC hands inquiry reports to Speaker,' 2009, *National* (online), 22 December.
27 Ombudsman Commission, *Investigation Report into the Alleged Unlawful and Abuse of Human Rights by Police*, 19–23.

this are common policing strategy in PNG towns, usually conducted in urban settlements in 'fishing expeditions' searching for stolen goods and suspected criminals and procedural accountability is poor, as shown in the lack of a search warrant in the Three-Mile Guesthouse Raid.[28] Accompanying violence, including sexual violence, is commonplace and derives partly from a perception on the part of the police and the community in general that the imported model of criminal justice is failing, and partly from a policing tradition based on early frontier-pacification strategies.[29]

Violence in the sex trade

However, police raids do not usually target commercial sex venues, apart from the Three-Mile Guesthouse, which is owned by a controversial former politician and diplomat. The brutality evidenced in these raids seems to be increasing. In a raid in 1996, reportedly the 'biggest to date,' the women were trucked to the police station.[30]

Figure 5.2. Front-page, 'Forty held in capital city brothel raid'.

Source: *Post-Courier*, 25–27 October 1996, 1.

---

28 Sinclair Dinnen, 2001, *Law and Order in a Weak State: Crime and Politics in Papua New Guinea*, Adelaide: University of Hawai'i Press and Crawford House Publishing, 64; Dinnen, 1998, 'Criminal justice reform in Papua New Guinea,' in *Governance and Reform in the South Pacific*, ed. Peter Larmour, Canberra: National Centre for Development Studies, The Australian National University, 253–72, 258; see also Goddard, 'From rolling thunder to reggae.'
29 National Research Institute (Papua New Guinea), 2005, *Port Moresby Community Crime Survey, 2005: A Report Prepared for the Government of Papua New Guinea's Law and Justice Sector's National Mechanism*, Boroko: National Research Institute, 48, 51–52, 54; Dinnen, 'Criminal justice reform in Papua New Guinea,' 260–61; Carol Jenkins, 2000, *Female Sex Worker HIV Prevention Projects: Lessons Learned From Papua New Guinea, India and Bangladesh*, Geneva: UNAIDS, 22.
30 Isaac Nicholas, 'Forty held in capital city brothel raid,' 1996, *Post-Courier*, 25–27 October, 1.

But in 1998, when police claimed that 'the problem was worsening,' the women were 'force-marched.'[31]

There is nothing surprising about the violent treatment of those caught up in the Three-Mile Guesthouse Raid. In 2005, the international NGO Human Rights Watch (HRW) published a report which documented many instances of police violence against young people in PNG, and there is no reason to believe that adult women have not been treated in the same way.[32] The following year, Amnesty International produced a report devoted solely to violence against women in PNG, in which it agreed that most of the existing long list of recommendations should be implemented and added further recommendations of its own.[33]

Figure 5.3. *Post-Courier* report of 1998 raid, referring to a 'forced march,' *Post-Courier* photo accompanying, Robyn Sela, 'Midday raid of house sees 25 behind bars'.

Source: *Post-Courier*, 17 December 1998, 3.

---

31 'Police parade suspects in the streets,' 1998, *Post-Courier*, 17 December, 3; Sela Robyn, 'Midday raid of house sees 25 behind bars,' *Post-Courier*, 17 December, 3.
32 Human Rights Watch, '*Making Their Own Rules*,' 23–43.
33 Amnesty International, 2006, *Papua New Guinea: Violence Against Women: Not Inevitable, Never Acceptable!* online: http://web.amnesty.org/library/Index/ENGASA340022006, accessed 5 September 2006.

The literature on violence against women in general in PNG is vast.[34] In addition, the daily newspapers carry regular reports of rape, gang rape, spousal rape, violence and even murder. Violence specifically towards sex sellers is not so commonly reported. And it is even less commonly acted upon. In 2009, however, the *Post-Courier* carried a report of a woman 'believed to be a sex worker' killed by alleged police brutality in Lae.[35] That night, a police ten-seater van picked up several women around the town, beat them and dropped them off again. Eye-witnesses said that the dead woman was among those picked up, although police claimed to have found her unconscious in the street.[36] Although a report was ordered by the Assistant Police Commissioner, nothing more was heard from the police, which prompted a letter-writer to question, some months later, why the police were so concerned to investigate police brutality against a businessman building the police barracks in the nearby town of Wau, in contrast to the lack of police action regarding the 'sex worker incident.' She wrote, 'What is the difference? Is it because one was a sex worker that you don't care and one is a businessman building your police barracks that you care?... I call on you … to tell PNG why one dead sex worker brutally murdered by police does not matter?'[37] Not surprisingly, no response was published.

The HIV factor

The 1998 raid was the first to be claimed publicly as having been motivated by HIV-related concerns. A report in the *Post Courier* announced, 'Supt. Gawi said apart from curbing suspected brothels, the police effort should be seen as an attempt to eliminate the spread of AIDS and other sexually transmitted diseases.'[38] By 2004, HIV prevention was claimed as the prime motivation for the Three-Mile Guesthouse Raid, as evidenced not only by the epithets hurled at the marching women by the gathering crowd or the address of the Police Metropolitan Superintendent, but also by the way in which condoms featured strongly (and symbolically) in the abuse of the women.[39]

The police had intended to use the fact that condoms were discovered at the guesthouse during the raid as circumstantial evidence of prostitution on the premises, possibly in the knowledge that this kind of evidence had already

---

34 For a good listing, see Human Rights Watch, *'Making Their Own Rules,'* 19n35; and Margaret Jolly, Christine Stewart with Carolyn Brewer (eds), *Engendering Violence in Papua New Guinea*, Canberra: ANU E Press, online: http://press.anu.edu.au?p=182671, accessed 31 March 2014.
35 'Sex worker bashed to death,' 2009, *Post-Courier* (online), 13 May.
36 'Top cop wants bashing report,' 2009, *Post-Courier* (online), 14 May.
37 Mother of one, Bumbu Compound, 'Police boss, look into businessman's attack,' 2009, *Post-Courier*, 12 October, 10.
38 'Police parade suspects in the streets,' 1998, *Post-Courier*, 17 December, 3.
39 The advocating of condoms for HIV prevention is a highly controversial issue in PNG: it has even been suggested that the State should be liable in damages for their promotion. See Avisat Nyan, 2006, 'Reconsider condom policy,' *National* (online), 7 December.

been used in New South Wales (NSW).[40] The newspapers were quick to pounce on this theme too. The *Post-Courier's* editorial quoted above spoke of mass graves of victims of HIV/AIDS; the *National's* piece of 15 March reported the Metropolitan Superintendent as saying that 'prostitution was the main cause of HIV/AIDS virus spreading like bushfire.'[41]

It is commonplace to attribute the threat of disease to women. Mary Douglas, in her classic study of pollution and taboo,[42] suggested that pollution beliefs are a way of imposing control on such chaotic phenomena as illness and desire, which threaten social boundaries. These are particularly vulnerable in sexual relations, which breach the body's boundaries and can entail fluid connections across segregated classes or races. In PNG as elsewhere, patterns of traditional beliefs of the potential dangers to men of sex and other contact with women, particularly with menstrual blood, are widespread.[43] Current fears of HIV infection through sexual contact sit well with these pollution beliefs, as well as meshing with the general attribution of pollution and disease to women.

The perceived threat posed by women increases exponentially when the woman sells sex. The view of such women as vectors of disease and infection has been well-documented in the metropoles. Maggie O'Neill describes the situation in nineteenth-century France, where one of the main concerns regarding the regulation of prostitution was the fact that its practitioners were seen as diseased.[44] In England, concerns about the spread of venereal disease in military garrisons led to the enactment of the Contagious Diseases Acts in the 1860s[45] and these Acts were often exported to the colonies.[46] 'Prostitutes' were condemned for carrying disease while their male clients were not—I term this 'the doctrine

---

40   *Bankstown City Council v Le* 2003 WL 23103843; [2003] NSWLEC 362; [2005]ALMD 2742.
41   'Police arrest 80 in brothel raid.'
42   Mary Douglas, 1966, *Purity and Danger: An Analysis of the Concepts of Pollution and Taboo*, London: Routledge & Kegan Paul.
43   Jeffrey Clark, n.d., *Huli Sexuality, the State, and STD/AIDS Prevention Programmes*, Goroka: PNG Institute of Medical Research, 191; L.L. Langness, 1999, *Men and 'Woman' in New Guinea*, Novato, CA: Chandler & Sharp Publishers Inc., 170; Wardlow, *Wayward Women*, 54–56. Such beliefs are not unique to PNG, although the attribution of pollution has been questioned elsewhere. See Alan F. Hanson, 1982, 'Female pollution in Polynesia?' *Journal of the Polynesian Society* 91: 335–81; Margaret Jolly, 2002, 'Introduction: birthing beyond the confinements of tradition and modernity?' in *Birthing in the Pacific: Beyond Tradition and Modernity?* Ed. Vicki Lukere and Margaret Jolly. Honolulu: University of Hawai'i Press, 1–30, 20–22.
44   Maggie O'Neill, 1997, 'Prostitute women now,' in *Rethinking Prostitution: Purchasing Sex in the 1990s*, ed. Graham Scambler and Annette Scambler, London and New York: Routledge, 4–28, 5–6.
45   Judith R. Walkowitz, 1982, *Prostitution and Victorian Society: Women, Class, and the State*, Cambridge and New York: Cambridge University Press, 1; Lynn Sharon Chancer, 1993, 'Prostitution, feminist theory, and ambivalence: notes from the sociological underground,' *Social Text* 37 (Winter): 143–71, 145.
46   Phillip Howell, 2004, 'Sexuality, sovereignty and space: law, government and the geography of prostitution in colonial Gibraltar,' *Social History* 29(4): 445-64; Richard Phillips, 2002, 'Imperialism and the regulation of sexuality: colonial legislation on contagious diseases and ages of consent,' *Journal of Historical Geography* 28(3): 339–62; Phillips, 2005, 'Heterogeneous imperialism and the regulation of sexuality in British West Africa,' *Journal of the History of Sexuality* 14(3): 291–362; and for Australia, see Roberta Perkins, 1991, *Working Girls: Prostitutes, their Life and Social Control*, Canberra: Australian Institute of Criminology, 73–74.

of immaculate infection.' The local sex industry was structured by regulation and policy to cater for single men,[47] a theme often repeated in the developing world, both during and after the colonial era.[48]

This view of those selling sex as vectors of disease and infection was imported into PNG through the Anglo-Australian colonisation process, both through metropolitan laws and policy and through mission preaching. Later, as the HIV epidemic spread in PNG, international organisations and aid donors moved swiftly to introduce and encourage the implementation of prevention and management strategies. Much of it was later proved to be less than perfect: Abstain, Be faithful, Use Condoms (ABC), High Risk Settings Strategy (HRSS). This Strategy was intended to enhance prevention efforts by designing and implementing behaviour change programmes 'targeted at high-risk groups, such as sex workers and men who have sex with men.'[49] It was developed in 2004 and rolled out in 2006,[50] but was extensively criticised and discontinued shortly afterwards.[51] UNAIDS soon recast the terminology involved in a less stigmatising light (terms such as 'high risk groups' should be replaced by 'key populations at higher risk'),[52] but nevertheless it is likely that 'economic and power differences make it probable that the identification of risk groups will contribute to the stigmatization of marginalized people.'[53] And this is what has happened, as indicated by the reports of the Three-Mile Guesthouse Raid, and other newspaper reportage. The 'risk' associated with sellers of sex is not *to* them but *from* them to those having sex with them. It is a further easy step to link these women with the dangerous polluter of traditional culture, as shown by the abusive names used to humiliate the marching women. Jane's account of sexual assault with an air freshener canister was more than just a tale of rape: it was the symbolic sanitisation of a source of pollution.

The stigmatisation continues. In September 2007, the *Post-Courier* ran a front-page story on the stigma and discrimination confronting some HIV-positive women selling sex in the Highlands. They had been pressured to leave home by

---

47   The irony is that impartial studies which favour investigation over judgement show that the reverse is often the case. Sex workers are aware that they are more endangered, and are more likely to develop strategies to safeguard their health. See Chancer, 'Prostitution, feminist theory, and ambivalence,' 149–50; Interview Maggi, who declared firmly that she always insists on condom use, because 'It's my life!'
48   Phillips, 'Imperialism and the regulation of sexuality,' 343; Ann Laura Stoler, 2003, *Carnal Knowledge and Imperial Power: Race and the Intimate in Colonial Rule*, Berkeley: University of California Press, 48; Larissa Sandy, 2006, '"My blood, sweat and tears": female sex workers in Cambodia—victims, vectors or agents?' Ph.D. thesis, Canberra: The Australian National University, 201, 235–38.
49   National HIV/AIDS Support Project, 2006, *High Risk Settings Strategy Report: Moving Beyond Awareness*, Milestone 90, Port Moresby, PNG: NHASP, 2.
50   Ibid., 1.
51   Bettina Beer, 2008, 'Buying betel and selling sex: contested boundaries, risk milieus, and discourses about HIV/AIDS in the Markham Valley, Papua New Guinea,' in *Making Sense of AIDS: Culture, Sexuality, and Power in Melanesia*, ed. Leslie Butt and Richard Eves, Honolulu: University of Hawai'i Press, 97–115, 113.
52   UNAIDS, *UNAIDS Terminology Guidelines (2011)*.
53   Beer, 'Buying betel and selling sex,' 98.

family and community 'because of their reputation as sex workers' or because of their HIV status. They had been obliged to sell sex for survival, and reported that despite being offered condoms, most of their customers refused to use them. The story itself was reasonable, and supported by an Editorial entitled 'Help our HIV/AIDS brothers, sisters,' but the large-font story headline, a sub-editor's creation, nevertheless blamed them, the vectors.[54]

It's a hard life — gays in trouble

The Tale of an activist[55]

Victor grew up in the provinces where both his parents worked as teachers. As a little child, he preferred to play with the girls, and was tormented by the boys at school for his effeminate looks and behaviour. When he was only ten, a man lured him into the bushes with bribes of lollies—it was his first sexual experience. Throughout his teenage years, Victor experienced a number of sexual encounters with various boys. Some were consensual, but others were forced on him by threats, usually to reveal his sexual activities to his parents. Victor was terrified of this, knowing that disclosure of his sexuality would bring shame on him and his family and lead to a beating. The stigma in rural areas was enormous, and Victor learned to be very circumspect about his sexual encounters.

Victor left home for tertiary education and a good job. His work gave him opportunities to travel on overseas trips, to experience the pleasure of meeting and socialising with other gays in the freedom of countries where there was no criminalisation of sex between males. By the year 2000, he was working in Port Moresby in awareness and intervention programmes in relation to issues such as human rights, child abuse and HIV. Gay groups in the urban centres of PNG used this work as a cover for discussion and action on gay issues. But the cover was not perfect, and on occasion, the media gave unwelcome publicity to a range of activist projects. Victor went along with it. He and his friends had already learned that the best way of achieving social acceptance as a gay was to earn respect by giving back to the community. Media coverage reinforced his status and that of his family. But it had adverse consequences too. Victor encountered abuse from strangers on the street and nuisance phone calls to his workplace. It was impossible to retaliate. He simply bore it, until one night

---

54 'Sex workers spread HIV,' 2007, *Post-Courier*, 10 September, 1; Editorial, 'Help our HIV / AIDS brothers, sisters,' 2007, *Post-Courier*, 10 September, 10.
55 As written by Victor himself. A fuller version of this story appeared as Christine Stewart, 2010, 'The tale of an activist,' *HIV Australia* 8(2): 42. *HIV Australia* is published by the Australian Federation of AIDS Organisations.

when he was returning home after a publicity event. A truck dropped him off at the short-cut track up the steep hill to his home. Half way along, a group of *raskols* ambushed him at gunpoint, dragged him into the bushes and took turns raping him. He was shaking, begging his assailants at least to use condoms, but this only aggravated them further, and they turned violent, beating and raping him to unconsciousness.

When he came to, he staggered home and sat thinking until dawn. Should he report the incident to the police? No, not in PNG. The police would insist that he had simply brought it on himself by the very fact of being gay. They would not respect any confidentiality. And should they actually investigate and make any arrests, Victor would be in great danger from the friends and relatives of the youths who raped him. The PNG 'payback' system would ensure that in retaliation for the arrests, Victor would be harmed in return.

He had never had an HIV test. Should he get one now? No, a positive result would not be treated with confidence by hospital or clinic staff. Victor was well-aware of the problems gays in PNG experienced in locating user-friendly and genuinely confidential health services.

So Victor packed his bags and fled the country. Once safely away from PNG, he felt far more comfortable about having an HIV test.

It was positive.

Now, Victor feels he can never return to PNG. He has reasoned it through. Due to his reputation as an activist, his HIV status would quickly become public knowledge, and the coupling of that with the news of his sexuality would render him extremely vulnerable to discrimination and shaming. This would reflect badly on his family and community. They would reject him.

But more significantly, he feared for his personal safety. He was already well aware of the treatment meted out to people with HIV. One of the biggest problems in addressing HIV in PNG is the issue of stigma and discrimination. Many people believe that HIV transmission is associated with transactional sex and males who have sex with other males, in the face of 'mountains of evidence' that marital fidelity poses as great a risk.[56] As a result, gays and sex sellers are targets for social stigmatisation. If the person is positive, the stigmatisation is redoubled. The community sees it as bringing great shame to all, especially the immediate family. Victor knew of instances of people being killed or buried alive due to a combination of their HIV status and their sexuality.

---

56   Hammar, *Sin, Sex and Stigma*, 1, 4 and elsewhere.

And worst of all, because HIV infection is attributed to sex sellers and gays, the youths who raped him would blame him for infecting them, not the other way around. They would hunt him down and exact their revenge. His life would be in danger. This may not be the case in an overseas country, but it is a real worry in PNG. The police would be of no help. Victor was all too aware of the many incidents involving police brutality directed against gay and transgendered people.

Victor the activist, determined to help 'all those powerless and vulnerable gays back in PNG,' coping with HIV, is now an exile from his own land.

Victor's tale illustrates a range of the problems confronting gays in PNG today. Although he grew up preferring girls' play, clothing and activities to those of the boys, he is not particularly effeminate—certainly not immediately identifiable as a 'sister-girl.' He learned early to dissemble, fearing a beating and other consequences in his family. He was coerced into sex at a young age, and threatened with exposure should he ever tell. As an adult, he had to endure stigma from total strangers, culminating in his horrific rape and the consequent HIV infection. As if that were not enough, he felt he could not seek help from the police or the PNG health services. He was even in fear of his life, expecting blame and revenge from his assailants for 'infecting them' due to his sexuality, which is associated with HIV infection, and retaliation from their kin if they were to be prosecuted.

Home and family

Victor's tale also demonstrates the importance of family approval in PNG. While some gays in PNG are welcomed and regarded well by their families and communities, many are not.

> I had an argument with my younger brother and he exposed me.... Mum was good, Dad was alright ... my other family, my own blood brothers and sisters ... it was in the village, and you know, when there is an argument, people come gathering ... that was one of the worst things that ever happened to me in my life ... when that happened, I distanced myself from the whole family ... if it's from a blood relative that is the worst (Len).

> [My sister] called me up and said 'Are you homosexual?' and I said 'Yes.' And she said 'Listen, young man' (I still remember, today) 'listen, young man, from now on you're no longer my brother, and ... as soon as I hang up here I'm going to call my Mum, and you're not going to Mum's house, and I'm going to call all your brothers and sisters in Port Moresby and in Lae' (Henry).

Fortunately for Henry, his brothers did not react as expected. They behaved no differently. One told his little girls, who had called him *geligeli* in front of him 'Uncle is not *geligeli*. He's just different from me.' And another brother is happy to let Henry's gay friends come to the house and 'hang out.'

Being thrown out of home is common.

> The worst thing was, I was rejected from my family too. I didn't have the strength to stand up to them. My mother and sisters, they do accepted me, but my dad and my brother didn't agree, they belted me badly, my dad and my brother, so I had to leave (*Palopa*).

> Me, I was rejected, so I just left without letting them know ... was fifteen. I came, I met this one in HB. I was living there, it was good, I was more safe there, then this one came, we were living together in the house, then 'she' came along, we built up a family, we shared our problems. My sisters too, sometimes come and visit to HB. I don't go to my family, I only went once, twice, with my gay friends and I didn't feel good. I had to let them know that I am a gay (*Palopa*).

Even those who manage to keep their family life intact continue to be troubled. As Henry explained, 'Your family can never be your family, if you're gay, that's it ... family will always be family, I can only live with them for a month, [but] I can live with gay men forever.'

One of the major problems for gays in PNG is the family pressure to get married. In some societies, brothers are even expected to get married in order of age, oldest first, and a failure on the part of one to do his duty will block his younger siblings.[57] Many give in to this pressure, with unhappy consequences.

> They still have this feeling, but it's how society, pressure from the family ... the society they were brought up in. Most of them [gays] still live in hiding and think there's no-one else, end up getting married. Then the marriage often lasts only a short time (Colin).

> My children's mother and I had some problems ... [then I had] my second relationship with the same sex, but then that ended a couple of years later, then I got married to my children's mother ... she told me that she had all this time known ... but she didn't care and all that, she loved me, and then we left it at that ... she got a restraining order and a maintenance order against me when I left (Fred).

> His wife was trying to counsel [a gay's wife]: 'You've got to realise that the men need to have sex with other partners, you shut up, be a good

---

57   This was the case in my adoptive Hula family in Central Province in the 1970s.

wife, look after the family, and give them the status they want, you're not going to have any problems. I've had to do that with [my husband] for years. I know he's got his girlfriends and his boyfriends, but I just ignore it, and I've got a lovely family.'… One Sunday, he got in the house and burned the house down with himself in it, so he obviously wasn't coping as well as she was coping (Adam).

Adam also tells stories of an effeminate gay who had to get married to meet family obligations, though he claimed never to have consummated it—children came along, but the wife may possibly have 'made her own arrangements.' Another gay had his boyfriend in the house and would sleep with him while the wife was there with the children—this went on for about five years until the wife gave up and divorced him. The marriage of yet another broke up when his wife found letters between him and his boyfriend in Australia (Adam).

Occasionally these marriages succeed. Peer pressure got Ned into marriage. His parents had already made two arrangements which didn't work out, so he chose his wife himself. She is supportive and he thinks she probably doesn't know about his relationships with men (Ned).

Some have managed to resist the pressure to marry, but often at the price of estrangement from their families.

> One time my mother said, I've got a question to ask you, that lady there, we're going to approach that family to pay brideprice, and … I took off. When I'm with my parents, I'm only there for about ten minutes and then I'm out. I don't want them to start talking about brideprice (Barry).

> Now, I'm not married … one of the old ladies, our grandmother, says, why aren't you getting married? So I say, no, I have to work and get money, and she says, if you don't want to get married, we'll marry you [off].… I'll just have to tell her straight off. All my life growing up, I was hiding myself.… I don't like showing it, nobody knows … I'd rather not [get married], I don't want to hurt [any woman I might marry] (Robin).

In and out of work

Employment in the formal sector is a significant feature of town life in PNG, even though it accounts for only a small percentage of the population nation-wide.[58] Because jobs are so hard to get, it is easy for employers to discriminate

---

[58] Approximately 10% according to the 2000 census. 'Labour force statistics,' in *Papua New Guinea Statistics Office*, online: http://www.spc.int/prism/country/pg/stats/Pop_Soc_%20Stats/Social/Labour%20Force/labour.htm, accessed 9 April 2014.

against gays and transgenders. 'The only jobs are in clubs. "Girls" who are over-*geli*, "open flowers", hard. I left school for that whole reason as well. Boys were hurting me' (*Palopa*).

Once employed, it can be hard to get promotion. The presence of a wife seems to be a crucial factor. Without one, sexuality is suspect, promotion is much harder, and a gay can never achieve a top position (Adam, Eric). Identity must be concealed in the workplace. As Peter explained, 'I don't come out too much. Due to work. Any "girls" who are working, hard to act themselves. At work, people are calling me boss, I have to really put on an act as a man, play a man's role. I have to control the way I'm talking.'

And then there is the ever-present threat of dismissal.

> I'm always worried that any time I could lose this job if they found out I'm gay. And it doesn't have to be me taken to the court for a real thing and be prosecuted, it could be just a story. So that's my biggest fear. I've been harassed by security guards at my workplace … and then one time I just stood up to them and I had a knife pointed at my neck and I got threatened (Henry).

Violence

More troubling even than the accounts of discrimination are the tales of violence threatened or enacted. These reinforce the sense of unease that permeates the lives of gays whenever they encounter discrimination or stigmatising behaviour—they are fully aware that insults and hatred can easily translate into action, as Victor found out. His tale of rape is an extreme example of PNG 'gay-bashing'—but for him, the consequences were far worse than they might have been in many other countries. He feared further violence from unsympathetic police, reprisals from the relatives of his assailants, breach of confidentiality from the health care services should he seek an HIV test, and further violence from his attackers who would blame him for infecting them.

For gays, danger lurks everywhere. I heard of gays walking innocently through the daytime streets, or shopping in malls, who were forced to flee, otherwise they were liable to be beaten, robbed, abducted, raped (Oscar, *Palopas*, Douglas, MSW).

> We had some really hard times, with gay-bashing … one of my friends was killed. If they know that there's a gay around, there are also other people who don't like them, decide to follow them and do stupid things, what they do, maybe just destroy their lives (Mitchell).

Expatriates are particular targets, because they have money and valuable goods, and gay expatriates living alone are vulnerable. Moresby is a small place, and word can get around.

> I've been identified as being single, you become targeted for break and entry ... there was a knock on my door about half past six, I'd been playing squash in the afternoon, I came out, there was a gun and a knife, I was taken in and tied up, a gun at my head ... they ransacked the place ... fortunately they didn't take my computer ... but everything else including half a packet of soap powder.... I was there just in my shorts, a gun at my head, the fellow with the gun at my head said, my friend wants to screw you, and I said I'd rather he didn't, and fortunately they didn't (Adam).

> I was held up outside the Z hotel at the time ... this friend came out and had a knife to my throat, made me drive ... he pulled a knife out, that's right. Anyway, I got out of it by jumping out of the car and flagging someone down and going to the [Z] police station ... they took the car and burnt it and all that ... the police were very good. I had a good police report but the guys never came back to town. It was all set up by a bad mixed-race guy (James).

As a PNG gay explained, many expatriates have developed coping strategies, such as 'family' friends (relatives of former partners), who ensure protection. They do not cruise, but stay within their familiar circle (Douglas).

Blackmail

The violence is sometimes an end in itself, but also may be used as a threat to ensure compliance with blackmail demands. Henry was blackmailed at University by his first sexual partner.

> It was at the University ... one of the students was doing final year ... he seduced me, and ... he beat me up so badly in his room ... he told me to give him all my things, and he said, every allowance day, I'll give him the K20 that I got.... I kept giving him the money, I think for two or three allowances. But the worst thing was, he started telling people about me, and so I had knocks on the door, and people were spitting at me ... the other provinces were okay, but [the people from my province] became very violent towards me, and then [they] decided to have a go at me, and they came in a group. And then after that I ran away from the University (Henry).

He was persuaded by his family to go back to University, where he was beaten up again. A friend told him that the Student Director was aware of the situation, and was threatening to call the police. So Henry went to see the Director, who immediately began 'saying all these nasty things,' like *'yu dispela man salim as long ol manki long skul na ol lektura na ol sekuriti gad'* (you are the one selling your arse to all the students, the lecturers, the security guards), and threatened to call the police unless Henry left the University immediately. The Student Counsellor also refused to help him.

Blackmail in the workplace can be an issue too.

> I was threatened when I was at B [company] by … phone calls, tell me that they are going to see my boss, reveal my lifestyle to my boss … one of those guys was a person that I had an affair with and somehow found out where I was working and he threatened me with … give me some money or *bai mipela toktok long bos bilong yu* [we'll tell your boss].… I left (Len).

As well as suffering violence, the better-off, particularly single white men, are highly vulnerable to blackmail attempts. Young men who want money set up a blackmail situation, often in organised ethnic groups. Off-duty police may also be involved. The threat of arrest is very real. Frank was not alone in his fear—many expatriates are forced to flee the country at a moment's notice. Some even commit suicide (Adam, James, Kevin).

The gradual reduction in the numbers of long-term expatriate residents has meant that PNG men of means are also targets. As Henry explained,

> I was coordinating a lot of workshops there [at a Port Moresby hotel] and I had lots of money and I had good Nike shoes … and carry a laptop and things like that, and I'm always scared about it, so mostly I tell the people working there, the securities … that I'm a volunteer with the church … and I don't have any money. The reason why we tell this story is because, like, you know about the problems with expatriates … whites equals money. Papua New Guineans, if you're a gay man, if you're on the streets, if you don't have a job, anyone can take advantage of you and have sex with you and no problem. If you're a Papua New Guinean man, especially with a degree from the University and a good job, you'll be treated like an expatriate now. So we'll make up a story … they can take me to the police station, I'll say I've finished from Grade 6 and I don't have a job, the police will probably let me go. If the police know I'm from University and I've got a good job, they'll hold me up too, because they want to get something out of me.

Apart from such dissembling, another technique is to call the blackmailers' bluff, by threatening to expose the blackmailer himself.

> The first time it happened to me, I was really terrified, and I did have to pay … he sodomised me but said you forced me, I had no idea how to handle it, I just paid the guy, 500 kina … I was happy to pay it, it really frightened me. But after talking to some other friends, they advised me how to handle the situation in the future, because I enjoy it both ways, so the next time it happened, I said okay, you go to the police, you tell them you did it to me. I said *Mi no poret* [I'm not afraid], you tell them … the law is, you fuck me … *yu iet* [it's you who did it] … you enjoyed it, I enjoyed it, it's consensual … so I've been able to successfully … are you going to go to the police and tell them I fucked you, in this case? They're going to laugh at you, say 'You're a *geligeli*!' But it does worry me (Eric and Fred).

Conversely, some gays I talked to admitted that they would try various subterfuges, including blackmail, to get money from gay clients. Again, exposure to the police, or to the man's wife, may be threatened (MSW and *Palopa*). Or trickery is employed.

> One time both of us bumped into this landowner, he wanted to take me out, so I told him, it's okay if 'she' could come with me, he agreed, and then the three of us had a couple of drinks, then he wanted us to go to his office, so we went and then, I told the guy to give 'her' the money before, and then he didn't want, he wanted the three of us to have sex … was busy with him and 'she' pinched the money … then he walked off and we went out and locked the door, he was screaming, please come and open the door. He was really rough with me, sorry, I don't do that kind of … like, I'm a human being too.… We didn't complete too, we told him to drop us, we went down [to our place], he dropped us, we told him to give us some money, when he opened the wallet, he found that there was only K25 in it.… He said who's got my money, I said I don't know … you probably wasted it all on food and beer … we pretended to call in the dark, Uncle John, but there wasn't any Uncle John around, he had to give us the K25 and drive off, we said if you don't give us the money we'll call our uncle and get him to break your windscreen.… I said: Girl, let's go shopping … we bought foodstuff for the house because we're living with this family (*Palopa*).

While in Port Moresby, I was twice asked by indigenous gays for my opinion on possible 'compensation claims' against expatriates—in reality, actions capable of being classed as extortion. One was enquiring on behalf of a friend in prison for murder, who claimed to have been acting under the influence of some strange drug given him by an expatriate; the other wanted me to write a letter 'to the Court' because he felt he had not been paid enough for a sexual encounter. I told the first that the claim had evidentiary problems in establishing an adequate chain of causality; and the second, that he was endangering himself too along the lines of *R v M.K.* Both decided to desist from seeking 'compensation,' or at least to stop trying to enlist my assistance.[59]

Moses Tau—'A very brave man'[60]

There are exceptions to this seemingly endless process of discrimination and abuse. By the late 1990s, gays were well and truly stigmatised in PNG. That was when a gay Motuan gospel singer from Central Province a little to the east of Port Moresby was wooed away from his village gospel group by the PNG recording giant CHM Supersound Studios, who urged him to go solo. He adopted a generic Pacific style of singing, using falsetto voice, and so his first song *Aito Paka Paka* was born. It was an instant hit, and was soon followed by others.[61] The accompanying video clips were all designed by Moses himself: the island-girl dancing style and costumes, lavishly replete with flowers, brightly coloured sarongs, outrageous hats and of course, the Pacific-signature swaying grass-skirt. He even managed to work a selection of tropical fruit into the dance scenes—the symbolism is obvious. It was the first public display of cross-dressing and transgenderism in the country—and it worked wonderfully. Moses became a star.[62]

Nevertheless, it wasn't all easy.

> When [the *Aito Paka Paka* clip] came out, it sort of brought this whole thing to the public, and those who were known as *geligelis* were harassed, they were called names … it came out to expose the lifestyle, and at the same time, had a negative side of it … it was sort of an awareness thing when Moses came out … he overdid that [the sarong and the flowers] … when Moses came out with his video clip, that was an issue among also the people here, and poor guy, I heard that he had a bad time too … people started stoning his car whenever they saw him, they were calling him names … very brave (Len).
>
> He's a very brave man (Adam).

---

59 Field notes August–September 2007.
60 Interview Adam, Port Moresby, 12 January 2006.
61 A compilation of Moses's video clips, headed by 'Aito Paka Paka,' was later published as Moses Tau, 2005, *The Best of Moses Tau: Beats and Dances*, DVD, Boroko Papua New Guinea: CHM Supersound Studios.
62 When a gay friend held a barbecue and invited Moses on my behalf, all the girls in the friend's office were excited and envious, claiming: 'We love his music!'

Figure 5.4. *Aito Paka Paka*, flowers, brightly coloured sarongs, outrageous hats … and fruit.

Source: Image taken from the video, Moses Tau, 2005, 'Aito Paka Paka,' in *The Best of Moses Tau*.

But Moses was more than just a new pop singer sensation. He was a gay on a mission.

> It is a very difficult thing in PNG to show your sexuality … is very scary, because it is not an accepted thing in PNG. I just want to do what I have and who I am. I also did it not for myself but for the suffering of we people through many years ago. And I told my friends: look, I'll try it out, if I fail I fail. If I go through it with success, we will all benefit. So I'm targeting to educate the people of this nation to really know that there's gays living in Papua New Guinea. So I did it. I went through it. It was very painful (Moses Tau).

Moses was invited to Cairns shortly after, for Independence celebrations.[63] Then early in 2001, he was invited by the PNG community in Sydney to take part in the famous annual Mardi Gras parade. The PNG community there was constructing a float in the form of a *lagatoi* [seafaring canoe], to feature Moses as the 'Pacific Queen,' dressed as a traditional 'Hiri Queen.' Sponsorship was offered by PNG's commercial radio station NauFM, 'because he has not only

---

63   Cairns, a north Queensland town, is less than 1½ hours' flying time away from Port Moresby, and has a large resident population of PNG people.

developed into a prominent musician but has developed a good character. He has also developed a good following and has really lifted the image of PNG music.'[64]

However, this decision was not an instant hit with many. The *Hiri Hahenamo* [celebration of Hiri culture] refers to an annual Port Moresby festival which celebrates the Papuan tradition of the Hiri trading expeditions from the Central Province north-west to the Gulf Province, returning again as the winds change towards the end of the year. Special *lagatois* are built and a feature of the festival today is the Hiri Queen competition, open to girls from all surrounding Motuan villages who dress, dance and sing in a traditional manner. The Motu-Koitabu Council, which represents the Motu and Koitabu villages surrounding Port Moresby, took offence, its Chairman saying,

> We [Motu Koitabuans] ... do not approve nor do we encourage homosexuality in our society—traditional or contemporary ... [we] are disgusted and not happy at all—to say the least—to have a very important and serious aspect of the culture portrayed at a festival for homosexuals.[65]

> We are totally against the Hiri Hanenamo [sic] concept, which promotes morals and good behaviour, being taken and abused at such a morally wrong festival ... we do not approve of or encourage such practices, and if Moses Tau wants to represent his personal beliefs and ideals, we suggest he represent himself personally by tailoring his own outfit on a theme which does not threaten to bring our name and culture into disrepute.[66]

This statement was followed by letters to the Editor and an FM-Central government radio talk-back show in which callers were divided.[67] Many Motu-Koitabuans protested the desecration of their culture but others supported Moses, praising his talent, his openness and his right to perform as he wished.[68]

Moses was very troubled. He claims a deep respect for traditions and culture, and points to his background in the church and his family's tradition as gospel singers.[69] He immediately called a press conference and denied the reports of the *lagatoi* float and the Hiri Queen costume. He said his Mardi Gras appearance was to promote his album and not to represent the PNG gay community.[70] The matter

---

64 'Moses Tau gets invited to Sydney Mardi Gras,' 2001, *Post-Courier*, 12 February, 34.
65 'Motu Koita Council offended,' 2001, *Post-Courier*, 13 February, 2.
66 'Tau's Mardi-Gras plan draws sharp rebuke,' 2001, *National*, 13 February, 1–2.
67 For example, Traditionalist, 'Please don't degrade out [sic] tradition,' 2001, *Post-Courier*, 23 February, 10.
68 Jacqueline Kapigeno, 'Uproar over singer's new "Queen" role,' 2001, *Post-Courier*, 13 February, 2.
69 Interview Moses Tau, Port Moresby, 24 January 2006.
70 Theresa Ame, 'Tau clears air over Mardi Gras visit,' 2001, *National*, 14 February, 5.

was kept in public view by a further news item showing Moses receiving his visa from the Australian Deputy High Commissioner, and relating how Sydney radio stations were carrying reports of the difficulties he was facing and the concern of the Mardi Gras organisers.[71] But in the end, Moses did not ride on a *lagatoi* float or wear traditional Hiri Queen costume—instead, he wore yet another of his 'Pacific' creations, and danced his way along the street.[72]

After Moses returned from Sydney, his success and position were assured, with club appearances,[73] sky-rocketing music sales and even a brief squabble between recording studios over him.[74] Club performances of 'Mardi Gras' nights were staged, and were so successful that when another was proposed, Moses called on his gay friends to do a 'queen' show. To his surprise, many Filipinos also took part. These shows became a great success, attracting cosmopolitan audiences and many other clubs followed suit, and became the foundation for the drag shows of today.

But it was about more than fun. Moses took the opportunity to promote awareness after every show, saying,

> We have these kind of people, this kind of community of people, that live in this country. We have no choice, we can't change them, but let's give them a chance to show their package, what they have. Give them a freedom for what they can do, for them to enjoy life. We can't keep them in a cage for them to live in fear all the time (Moses Tau).

He continues his community outreach work, travelling around villages at his own expense, distributing condoms and promoting awareness about gay rights, HIV, the dangers of consuming homebrew alcohol and marijuana. Although he receives no funding support for this work, he has achieved a strong measure of fame throughout the country, and in January 2006 was invited to sing at the funeral of Bill Skate, the first PNG Prime Minister to die in office.

Opinion is divided as to whether the recent trend towards coming out was due to Moses or not.

> One of the break-throughs I think especially in Moresby was Moses Tau's [*Aito Paka Paka*] clip. That made people talk about it. That's the turning point, it's like an awareness that there are these sort of people around (Barry and Colin).

---

71   'Tau takes off today for Sydney festival,' 2001, *National*, 16 February, 3.
72   'Floating through the Mardi Gras,' 2001, *Post-Courier*, 8 March, 1.
73   Public Notice, 2001, *National*, 13 March, 10.
74   'Studios squabble over Moses Tau,' 2001, *Post-Courier*, 5 March, 5.

> Before 'she' [Moses Tau] brought out the clip [*Aito Paka Paka*], we came out to the public before, the younger ones. As far as from what I see, those bigger ones, we've got plenty but because of the culture and the traditions ... people are still hiding and some are forced to get married, and some, they just keep themselves locked up ... like the group now we have here, like as for myself, at first I didn't come out ... but through those ones, I can see that ... it's not Moses Tau, it's these ones ... they're the ones like, coming out, all this stuff (*Palopa*, indicating others in the meeting).

Even if Moses was the catalyst, the gains have been small and there is still a long way to go, even for committed activists, as Victor's Tale above demonstrates.

The continually escalating cycle

> Papua New Guinea suffers from a culture of violence which abuses all known human rights ... [these] abuses often occur outside the accepted legal order, sometimes coinciding with wrong political and cultural practices that [are] now accepted as a way of life.
>
> Bernard Narokobi, 2000.[75]

Violence in PNG takes many forms: the violence accompanying street theft and armed robbery; spousal violence in the privacy of the home; sexual violence and rape perpetrated on both women and men; acts of sorcery and the retributive violence of witch-hunts; ethnic violence derived from customary responses to conflict situations; the structural violence wrought by poverty and urban drift; and the institutionalised violence of state agencies, sometimes the very agencies tasked to deal with violence.[76]

As can be seen above, the threat of police violence is ever-present in the lives of both street women and gays. The Three-Mile Guesthouse Raid is one of the most extreme examples of police violence, carried out in the name of protecting society. But some police violence can be no more than something for personal pleasure, taken by force from those least able to defend themselves.

---

75 Cited in Carol Kidu, 2000, 'Reflections on change, ethnicity and conflict: family and ethnic violence in Papua New Guinea,' *Development Bulletin* 53 (November): 29–33, 29.
76 Sinclair Dinnen and Allison Ley, 2000, *Reflections on Violence in Melanesia*, Leichhardt, NSW: Hawkins Press: vii–ix; Kidu, 'Reflections on change, ethnicity and conflict.'

Two Tales from the barracks

Irene's Tale[77]

One evening not long after the Three-Mile Guesthouse Raid, Irene and her girlfriend Carol were walking the Boroko beat behind the Post Office when a police mini-bus came roaring towards them. Carol saw them first and fled, but Irene was too late. The bus swerved and stopped in front of her, and the driver invited her to hop in. Irene refused, but another policeman jumped out and belted her with a piece of wire cable. Terrified, she climbed into the bus. There were seven police inside.

The bus headed to the police barracks. Two married police were dropped off at the married quarters, and then the bus stopped behind the single quarters. Another four got out, leaving Irene with the driver. He climbed into the back seat with her and started forcing her head down into his lap. Irene resisted, so he gave up on that, and started pulling her trousers down. Another struggle began, but Irene eventually gave in, fearing another belting. The driver raped her and left.

Irene started pulling her pants up, but she had no chance. One by one, the other four climbed back into the bus and raped her, until she was weak and dizzy with the roughness of their attacks. The only thing that saved her from further molestation was the arrival of a policeman friend of hers. He finally persuaded the rapists to let him take her to the safety of his room until morning. Then he escorted her to the bus stop, gave her a few coins for a bus fare home and advised her never to come back to the barracks again.

Peter's Tale[78]

Peter says he had never felt closer to death. There was a fundraiser at a newly opened club, it seemed like a 'safe' event, so he and his *Palopa* friends all put on their drag clothes and hair extensions, went along, and started enjoying themselves. A good-looking man from the Islands region approached him, saying he had a car, would Peter like to go with him?

Peter had always been a sucker for a really cute pick-up. And he had had a bit to drink, so he agreed, and out they went together. But when he saw that the promised ride was a police vehicle, he was apprehensive. However, his escort

---

77 From a statement taken at the same time as the Three-Mile Guesthouse Raid statements, following a report made to Poro Sapot.
78 Interview Peter, 21 April 2006.

reassured him, saying that police were well aware of law and order issues. He took Peter to the police barracks mess, treated him like a princess, bought more drinks, and finally seduced him.

Afterwards, Peter lay there exhausted, wondering why he could hear mumbling in the room. Then he realised that two more police had come in and watched them having sex on the bed. But that was not all. Now he was being raped! What should he do? Scream? No, it's their territory, what good would that do? And indeed word had got out that there was a 'girl' in the room, everyone wanted to join the mob. They were all coming into the room, one after the other, and taking turns, trying group sex, oral and anal, threatening him if he resisted. By the time number eleven landed on top of him, Peter was sobbing and shaking. The newcomer threatened to hit him, saying: 'Don't cry, this is nothing new to you, you are "that sort" of lady, you like it, why are you crying?'

Peter recognised the voice. It was a cousin of his! He gasped: 'Are you my cousin? Don't you know me?' His cousin switched on the light and got the shock of his life. Peter was shaking, begging him: 'Get me out of here!' The cousin offered to take him to the entrance gate of the barracks and call a cab. But when he tried to pull Peter up from the bed, the pain was too much. There was blood everywhere, Peter couldn't walk. He thought he would die. The cab rushed him to Emergency, where the doctor who came to attend to him was a Highlander. It seemed to Peter that his trials would never end—Highlanders are notorious for discriminating against gays. But true to his profession, although the doctor could see Peter's hair extensions he pulled the curtains around the bed and started treating Peter, praising his bravery.

Peter was in hospital for two days, healing. Thereafter, he vowed never to go out with any of the disciplinary forces again. Now, whenever someone comes up and says he's with the Defence Force, or he's a policeman, he gets told in no uncertain tones: 'You are totally off!'

'A routine part of policing'

Sinclair Dinnen attributes the retributive, violent nature of PNG policing first to the historical traditions of frontier pacification, reinforced after Independence by localised outbreaks of disorder, particularly 'tribal fighting' in the Highlands, and then the militarisation of the state response to the Bougainville conflict in the 1990s. Violence has long been tolerated in PNG as a strategy for resolving problems—leaders themselves tacitly support violent militaristic tactics to solve law and order problems. Police abuses are enmeshed in a continually escalating cycle.[79] Whether due to institutional weaknesses or the fact that the imported

---

79 Dinnen, 'Criminal justice reform in Papua New Guinea,' 260–62; and see also Sinclair Dinnen, 1997, 'Restorative justice in Papua New Guinea,' *International Journal of the Sociology of Law* 25: 245–62.

criminal justice system is inappropriate in PNG's circumstances, the police perform poorly and are generally regarded as incompetent at best and a threat to the personal security of the citizenry at worst.[80] Retributive police action has become an acceptable response to conflict, and no amount of money and aid poured into institutional strengthening of the police force seems to have done much to alleviate this situation.[81] A National Research Institute survey conducted in 2004, the year of the Three-Mile Guesthouse Raid, revealed that many of those surveyed at various sites around Port Moresby considered the police to be 'ineffective … inappropriately violent, corrupt, and even the perpetrators of crime.' The survey listed some of the specific concerns regarding police behaviour as violence, dishonesty, accepting bribes, theft, indiscriminate arrests, and preoccupation with alcohol and sex. Most of the crime victims surveyed did not report the incident to the police, knowing that they would not receive satisfaction. Hardly any of those who did report were satisfied with the response they received.[82]

The situation has not markedly improved. A recent *Post-Courier* Editorial, for example, complained, 'After the big pay increases awarded to police in recent years, and the millions being spent on new barracks and houses, we deserve better!'[83] And even though Poro Sapot has been in the forefront of intensive ongoing efforts to work with the police and raise their awareness of issues involving sex sellers and gays, outreach workers report that police harassment and victimisation continues.[84] The *Askim na Save* survey found that

> family members, followed by the police, were the two most common abusers in participants' experiences of physical abuse, while clients, followed by police, were the most common sexual abusers. Moreover, more transgender [sic] were forced to have sex by the police (21%), and physically abused by the police (21%) compared to women (15% for both physical abuse and forced sex) and men (both forms of abuse at 9%).[85]

---

80 Dinnen, *Law and Order in a Weak State*, 52–54; increasingly numerous newspaper reports and Letters to the Editor in my collection.
81 Dinnen, 'Criminal justice reform in Papua New Guinea,' 253, 258.
82 National Research Institute (Papua New Guinea), 2005, *Port Moresby Community Crime Survey, 2005: A Report Prepared for the Government of Papua New Guinea's Law and Justice Sector's National Coordinating Mechanism*, Boroko: National Research Institute, 48, 51–52, 54.
83 Editor, 'Crime spots: where are our police?' 2001, *Post-Courier* (online), 17 June.
84 Reid, 'Putting values into practice in PNG'; and see also the interviews and description of early interventions in Carol Jenkins, 2010, 'Sex workers and police in Port Moresby (1994–1998): research and intervention,' in *Civic Insecurity: Law, Order and HIV in Papua New Guinea*, ed. Vicki Luker and Sinclair Dinnen, Canberra: ANU E Press, 153–64, online: http://press.anu.edu.au?p=94091, accessed 8 April 2014.
85 Angela Kelly et al., 2011, Askim na Save *(Ask and Understand): People who Sell and/or Exchange Sex in Port Moresby*, Sydney: Papua New Guinea Institute of Medical Research and the University of New South Wales, 25.

Nevertheless, the report also found that some women specifically work in army barracks and police stations.[86]

The overall picture is one of police exploiting their position as the State's frontline law enforcement agency for such advantages as financial gain through bribes or as blackmail participants, or personal satisfaction through such power displays as violence and sexual abuse, all carried out in the knowledge that they would not be called to account. The HRW report sets out a long list of incidents of violence and sexual abuse,[87] calling it 'a routine part of policing in Papua New Guinea.'[88] The Ombudsman Commission's investigation into the Three-Mile Guesthouse Raid found that the entry was unlawful, the arrests and detention were unlawful, and that the excessive and unlawful force used did not constitute necessary policing activity.[89]

The fact that police are rarely if ever called to account for their actions makes this state of affairs possible. State agencies were able to fend off all attempts to bring the police to account for the violence in the Three-Mile Guesthouse Raid.[90] The Metropolitan Commander even supported the raid as a necessary part of HIV/AIDS control. Both Peter's and Victor's tales demonstrate the inability of individual outgroup members to seek redress for their assaults through normal legal processes.

Irene was in an even worse position: street workers are easy targets. The HRW notes that the most targeted are those who are the least powerful and most stigmatised, including sex sellers and gays: 'the illegality of certain acts serves as an excuse to inflict on-the-spot punishment and to deter victims from complaining.'[91] Designed as the agency responsible for front-line law enforcement, the police have become exploiters of the law they are supposed to uphold. This state of affairs persists so long as the force refuses to take responsibility for the illegal actions of its members.

Less dramatic though equally alarming for the victims is police collusion in blackmail. Some police augment their incomes by any means available, including complicity in blackmail. Adam has told of the difficulties caused by

---

86 Ibid., 19.
87 Human Rights Watch, *'Making Their Own Rules,'* 23–54.
88 Ibid., 23. Enjoyment of such benefits of power may well be a modern-day outcome of the privileges enjoyed by victorious warriors of old, but little seems to have changed despite the enormous amount of training supposedly bestowed upon the police of today.
89 Ombudsman Commission, *Investigation Report into ihe Alleged Unlawful and Abuse of Human Rights by Police*, 16–18.
90 Human Rights Watch, *'Making Their Own Rules,'* 116; Human Rights Watch, *'Still Making Their Own Rules,'* 35.
91 Human Rights Watch, *'Making Their Own Rules,'* 47. To the HRW list may be added illegitimate urban settlers. See G. Koczberski, G.N. Curry and J. Connell, 2001, 'Full circle or spiralling out of control? State violence and the control of urbanisation in Papua New Guinea,' *Urban Studies* 38(11): 2017–36, 2025.

the persistence of police intent on extortion. Expatriate Kevin tells how one of the security guards at his compound reported his 'suspicious actions' at two police stations, resulting in a visit from the police in the middle of the night. Kevin refused to admit them, fled the apartment, and laid a complaint, but he continued to be harassed by one of the police visitors until with the help of a lawyer he managed to defuse the situation.

The preceding is not always true of all police. Both Irene and Peter were rescued from their predicaments by police who knew them personally. But this may be less a matter of 'good' police taking control of the situation than of the power of kin and *wantok* networks prevailing over the less strongly cohesive group solidarity of the police. James, Fred and Eric told me how they have defused blackmail attempts by threatening to take the blackmailers themselves to the police—Henry however only feels safe from police complicity in blackmail by concealing his education and employment status. With the help of Poro Sapot outreach workers, Angelina was able to obtain redress against several police who assaulted and possibly raped her.[92]

Conclusions

In this chapter I have presented a very small sample of the types of abuse experienced by sex sellers and gays. In the years since I commenced research, other reports have appeared. HRW published a major report on a survey conducted in 2005 of beatings, rape and torture of children by police and prison guards, which included many accounts of the abuse of sex sellers and men and boys suspected of homosexual conduct.[93] This was soon followed by a further report which found little improvement in the situation, although there had been some institutional responses in the meantime.[94] At the same time, Amnesty International conducted an investigation into domestic, sexual and state violence against women in PNG, finding much the same situation— an unacceptably high level of violence, and the impunity enjoyed by state agencies, particularly the police.[95] However, participants in the recent *Askim na Save* survey reported higher levels of physical abuse from family members than from police, followed by significantly lower levels from partners, clients and other community members. Clients were the most common sexual abusers, followed by police. But the rate of physical and sexual abuse of transgenders by police exceeded that of women by police.[96]

---

92 Interview Angelina, 13 September 2007.
93 Human Rights Watch, *'Making Their Own Rules.'*
94 Human Rights Watch, *'Still Making Their Own Rules.'*
95 Amnesty International, *Papua New Guinea: Violence Against Women.*
96 Kelly et al., Askim na Save, 25.

All these findings beg the question: why is all this so? The law is there to ensure that there are limits to the exercise of individual will and boundaries to the normal. It has not retreated so far as to decriminalise physical violence. Assault and rape are crimes, so why are they not being prosecuted?

Part of the answer lies with the police culture of today. HRW refers to the 'near-total impunity for violence' of the police.[97] Other state agencies collude in this, as evidenced by the four-year delay in the production of the Ombudsman Commission report on the Three-Mile Guesthouse Raid and the glib way in which investigators and state lawyers were fobbed off when trying to call the police to account.[98]

I conclude that something else is operating to render these acts of violence invisible in certain circumstances. To identify and understand it, I turn in the next chapter to an analysis of the views expressed by PNG's citizens since the time of Independence on the vexed topics of 'prostitution' and 'homosexuality,' and then canvas a theory which offers an explanation of much that is taking place on the streets, in the courtrooms and most importantly, in the minds and hearts of the people of PNG.

---

97 Human Rights Watch, *'Still Making Their Own Rules,'* 2.
98 I do not mean to imply that the Ombudsman Commission investigators were wanting in this regard. I am well aware that the Commission is under-resourced and overstretched. The delay can probably be attributed more to a general view that the vicissitudes of a group of sex sellers ranked well below current political dramas in terms of priority.

6. At the Intersection

> Law … defines the boundaries of civic community and the expected behaviors of citizenship. In the same manner as a religious community is defined by its relation to the scriptures, the civic community in which one belongs is defined by its public laws.
>
> Ryan Goodman, 2001.[1]

My research has provided a qualitative review of the stigmatisation, discrimination, abuses and other deleterious effects suffered by sex sellers and gays in Port Moresby, both at law and in everyday life. But this research has also thrown up some perplexing conundrums, which Foucauldian theories seem inadequate to answer. Why, for example, do women leaders evince deep sympathy for abused women and go to great lengths to assist and support them, but then condemn them if they turn to selling sex for survival?[2] If the sale of sex represents performance of a commercial contract like any other, why are sellers of sex condemned and criminalised, while the buyers, their clients, are not? Why did Justice Narokobi, renowned human rights lawyer, merely distinguish *Anna Wemay's Case* when he let the women off in *Monika Jon's Case*, instead of overturning Justice Wilson's decision completely?[3] Why did public figures invoke the constitutional right to equality to justify their calls for the arrest of the alleged 'male prostitutes' caught up in the Three-Mile Guesthouse Raid, but make no mention of the highly irregular arrest procedure which clearly amounted to a breach of human rights? Why, in the face of evidence that 'ritual homosexuality' has been a feature of traditional male initiation ceremonies in many parts of the country, is homosexuality now labelled as a foreign, anti-Christian import? What about gays among the *elites*—why are they hiding? Why was openly gay musician Moses Tau chosen for the honour of singing at the state funeral of Prime Minister Skate? Why do pastors and preachers of today's Christian churches condemn certain sexualities as deviant, abominable, sinful and so on, while ignoring Christ's messages of tolerance, love and forgiveness?

---

1 Ryan Goodman, 2001, 'Beyond the enforcement principle: sodomy laws, social norms, and social panoptics,' *California Law Review* 89: 643–740, 732.
2 I have noted the rhetoric of condemnation by women leaders in various places in this work. A recent comment on this came from Sally Joseph, a PNG sex worker representative at an Australian HIV/AIDS Conference, when she identified stigma from women's groups and church groups as two major challenges to work on decriminalising the sex trade. See Sally Joseph, 2011, 'Working towards law reform for sex workers in PNG,' paper presented at the Australasian HIV/AIDS Conference, 28–30 September 2011, Canberra.
3 When a court reaches a decision in a case which differs from that reached in a previous similar case, rather than 'overturning' the previous line of reasoning, it may find that the fact situation differs sufficiently from the previous decision so that it can 'distinguish' the previous case.

To address questions such as these, I have turned to the concept of intersectionality. So far I have taken a narrative approach to my materials, describing individual experiences and extrapolating from them to form a picture of the broader social location of the individual in a range of groups.[4] Narrative-based studies of sex sellers, such as those set out in Chapter 4, identify the characteristics of the subjects which they share with other members of the group, primarily that of sexuality, and examine issues of gender, class, ethnicity and location from that perspective. But these subjects share the characteristics of only one dimension of each of the categories, which intersect to describe their social location, and this description does not explain the configurations of the stigmatisation and oppression they experience. This can be done however by comparing and contrasting the relationships between multiple dimensions of groups through the lens of intersectionality theory.

Beginning in the late 1970s, feminist scholars around the world began studying the problems of creating a space for non-white feminism.[5] Gender, no longer the sole marker of a common female identity, was problematised by a combination of race, class and gender. But this too became mired in the additive approach, the claims of 'triple oppression.' In 1989, American feminist lawyer Kimberlé Crenshaw used the term 'intersectionality' to analyse the law's treatment of employment discrimination on the grounds of race and sex claimed by black women in the USA.[6] The claims failed, because the court found that the alleged discrimination was not exclusively race or sex discrimination, and there was no combined race-sex category recognised in law. Crenshaw observed that categories such as race, class and gender are mutually exclusive, and within each of them, the subordination of one group to another (such as the subordination of women to men in the category of gender, or the subordination of black working-class women to white middle-class non-working women in that of women) becomes a disadvantage occurring within a single dimension. The simultaneous subordination of a group within two or more categories leaves those at the intersection of the categories increasingly subordinated, not necessarily cumulatively but often in qualitatively different ways. The subordinated group may not be capable of advancing one agenda (such as racial discrimination)

---

4   Leslie McCall, 2005, 'The complexity of intersectionality,' *Signs* 30(3): 1771–800, 1781.
5   Floya Anthias and Nira Yuval-Davis, 1983, 'Contextualizing feminism: gender, ethnic and class divisions,' *Feminist Review* 15: 62–75; Dorothy H. Broom, 1987, 'Another tribe: gender and inequality,' in *Three Worlds of Inequality: Race, Class and Gender*, ed. Christine Jennett and Randal G. Stewart, South Melbourne: Macmillan Company of Australia, 264–82; Gill Bottomley, Marie de Lepervanche and Jeannie Martin (eds), 1991, *Intersexions: Gender, Class, Culture, Ethnicity*, North Sydney: Allen & Unwin; and see the historical reviews in Avtar Brah and Ann Phoenix, 2004, 'Ain't i a woman? revisiting intersectionality,' *Journal of International Women's Studies* 5(3): 75–86; Nira Yuval-Davis, 2006, 'Intersectionality and feminist politics,' *European Journal of Women's Studies* 13: 193–209; and Ann Denis, 2008, 'Intersectional analysis: a contribution of feminism to sociology,' *International Sociology* 23(5): 677–94.
6   Kimberlé Crenshaw, 1989, 'Demarginalising the intersection of race and sex: a black feminist critique of antidiscrimination doctrine, feminist theory and antiracist politics,' *University of Chicago Legal Forum* 140: 139–67.

without encountering conflict with that of another category (such as gender discrimination) and because of single-dimensional frameworks, they may not be able or allowed to create a multiple identity. The existence of one category may completely deny another, and those at the intersection may even be excluded from both (or several) categories by the subordination process.

'Power is everywhere,' Michel Foucault reminds us, and it is immanent in all kinds of relations.[7] The problem, Crenshaw claims, is not the existence of the categories so much as the way in which power operates within them. It clusters around certain groups in those categories and is used against others to discriminate and oppress. A dominant group identifies and names a subordinate group and then attributes values and qualities to the subordinate group, thus creating and maintaining social hierarchies of domination and subordination.[8]

This chapter first presents data, mainly textual and spanning more than four decades, to illustrate the process of naming and constructing the subordinate groups of sex sellers and gays. The expression of the attitudes and opinions of today's Papua New Guinea (PNG) society found in the national media illustrates the range of negative values which are attributed to these groups so as to justify their stigmatisation and oppression. Then I turn to ideas of the ways by which intersectionality can illuminate dominant narratives about sex sellers and gays in PNG today, and how these stigmatised categories also intersect.

Attitudes and opinions

Sex crime studies

The Crown Law Department's 1973–75 review of the criminal law mentioned in Chapter 2 focused on attitudes to sexual offences, with a view to reform which would bring sexuality laws more into line with people's perceptions of unacceptable behaviour. Nine specific sexual offences were selected for study. One was the category of 'unnatural offences,' which included sodomy.[9] A questionnaire was circulated to all anthropologists working in PNG, and Marilyn Strathern, then of the New Guinea Research Unit, prepared a summary

---

7   Michel Foucault, 1978 [1976], *The Will to Knowledge: The History of Sexuality: Volume 1*, London: Penguin Books, 93–94.
8   Kimberlé Crenshaw, 1991, 'Mapping the margins: intersectionality, identity politics, and violence against women of color,' *Stanford Law Review* 43(6): 1241–99, 1297–98.
9   No comments were sourced directly on the issue of prostitution, possibly because urban areas were barely represented in the responses from the anthropologists polled, who worked predominantly in rural and remote areas: Marilyn Strathern, 1975, *Report on Questionnaire Relating to Sexual Offences as Defined in the Criminal Code*, Report prepared for New Guinea Research Unit, Boroko, Papua New Guinea, 8.

report, which provides probably the closest thing we have to a baseline survey.[10] Responses to queries about 'homosexual dealings' (as they were termed in the study) showed that while most PNG societies considered that intercourse should be *per vaginam*, deviations were not generally regarded as offensive perversions. 'Homosexual dealings,' in societies where they were rare, were regarded as distasteful or merely silly. Where they were normal, they were usually regarded as 'play,' and where they were institutionalised, for example in boys' initiation ceremonies, they were considered beneficial. Objections to male-male sex arose only in situations of physical assault or deliberate insult. Otherwise, as Strathern explained, even where it was considered improper, it was 'not thought to hurt anyone, nor to produce a class of perverts, nor to threaten general sexual morality or the moral fibre of society.'[11]

Another Justice Department review of the *Criminal Code* followed in 1983. Members of the University of Papua New Guinea (UPNG) Psychology Department undertook a fresh study of the level of correspondence between the Code and community perceptions of particular types of human behaviour, aiming to provide a comparison between society's perceptions of the relative seriousness of particular types of crimes and their ranking in the law. They collected data from both men and women in rural areas, and from a sample of expatriate men and women in Port Moresby. Their results showed that overall, society considered sexual offences to be more serious than did the law; but the greatest discrepancy found was not in the views of homosexuality and prostitution as they termed them, but of adultery and indecent exposure, which were felt to be far more serious than the law allowed in all areas surveyed. The study concluded by posing the question whether the laws should be changed to reflect the views of the people, or whether people should adjust their views to accord with the law.[12]

In order to determine the effects of urbanisation on traditional attitudes, the same team undertook a further study among a random selection of adult Papua New Guineans living in suburbs of Port Moresby and on the UPNG campus.[13] They found that overall, attitudes of urban dwellers to the seriousness of crimes, including the sexual crimes of homosexuality and prostitution, more

---

10   Strathern, *Report on Questionnaire Relating to Sexual Offences*. The report was circulated but never officially 'published'. Nevertheless it is widely available, as a 'large book' in the ANU library for example.
11   Ibid., 46–47. The same view was affirmed in interview with Bernard Narokobi. But contrast the sad tale of the informant in Gilbert Herdt, who evinced little or no interest in women, preferring to deplete his semen by inseminating males, and attributed his stigmatisation to the fact that he failed to fulfil his social duty to marry and produce children. See Herdt, 1992, 'Semen depletion and the sense of maleness,' in *Oceanic Homosexualities*, ed. Stephen O. Murray, New York and London: Garland Publishing, 33–68.
12   Dennis Moore, Barry Richardson and Dianne Wuillemin, 1985, 'A comparison of rural and legal ranking of seriousness of crimes in Papua New Guinea,' *Melanesian Law Journal* 12: 149–58.
13   Dianne Wuillemin, Barry Richardson and Dennis Moore, 1986, 'Ranking of crime seriousness in Papua New Guinea,' *Journal of Cross-Cultural Psychology* 17(1): 29–44.

closely approximated those of the state legal system than did the attitudes of the rural people previously studied. The question posed by the first survey, as to whether the law or the attitudes of the people should be changed, now needed no answer. As Dianne Wuillemin, Barry Richardson and Dennis Moore tell us, 'In a developing country with expanding towns and cities it appears that the people will change their values by adopting those imposed by the government and its legal system.'[14] They proposed various influences which might have contributed to these changes in attitude: weakening of traditional ties and values; changes in gender roles; greater exposure to 'global culture'; the presence of many strangers in the urban environment; changes in the likelihood or the occurrence of crime; more frequent and reliable public information about crime.[15]

The role of the media

The local media are also a rich source of public opinion in their daily news stories, their editorials, their feature pieces and their letters to the editor. In Port Moresby, the daily newspapers are purchased by people on the way to work and reading them is the first activity of the day in many offices. In bars frequented after work by the rich, the famous and the politically well placed, the music is stopped and a hush descends when the evening newscasts start on the local TV channels. Talkback radio shows are highly popular, and here the voice of the urban *grassroots* may be clearly heard. With the arrival in recent years of broadband internet and smartphones, blogs and Facebook have become popular means of disseminating opinion for those who can access the web.[16] In Australia, where in-country PNG television and radio broadcasts are not available to me on a regular basis, I have relied on a mixture of the online postings of the daily newspapers, combined with hard copy when available,[17] and more recently, several online blogs, to compile the account that follows.

Newspapers have been published in various towns in the country since the early twentieth century,[18] mainly though not entirely in English—some have appeared in Tok Pisin. The two current dailies are the venerable *Post-Courier*

---

14   Ibid., 42–43.
15   Ibid., 40–42; Dennis Altman, 2001, *Global Sex*, Sydney: Allen & Unwin.
16   Access is by no means limited to the *elites*. One popular blog is written by a medical school dropout who took to selling *buai* on the streets for a living. See the *Namorong Report*, online: http://namorong.blogspot.com.
17   The National Library of Australia has a good though incomplete collection of newspapers. I was able to fill vital gaps in my data during field trips from the excellent library of the National Research Institute in Port Moresby.
18   The earliest that I can find in the National Library of Australia holdings is the *Papuan Times*, first published in 1911 in Port Moresby. The *Rabaul Times* started in 1925 after the Australian Administration takeover, and amalgamated in 1959 with the *New Guinea Courier* (based in Lae) to form the *New Guinea Times-Courier*, which in turn amalgamated with the *South Pacific Post* in 1969 to produce the *Post-Courier* of today.

and the comparative newcomer the *National*, started in 1993 under sponsorship of the Malaysian firm Rimbunan Hijau, which had entrenched itself via a multitude of subsidiaries as the principal logging operation in the country and in the early 1990s was looking to expand its PNG investment base and to counter some of its bad press.[19]

The newspapers were originally written for and by the expatriate colonisers, but this situation was already changing before Independence, with Papua New Guinean journalists trained and writing for the *Post-Courier*, statements by national politicians being given good coverage, and Letters to the Editor being penned by future citizens.[20] These letter writers, who usually concealed their identity behind pen-names, were not and still are not representative of the entire citizenry, many of whom are illiterate, or at least not literate in English;[21] do not have regular access to the newspapers; are not interested in writing letters to newspapers or do not have the means or resources to do so. The target audience is not limited to other letter writers, but it has been suggested that writers and readers are still by no means representative of public opinion as a whole; that they mainly constitute an educated, urbanised group interested in national rather than parochial affairs, manifesting pro-capitalist and liberal views, with some measure of influence over those involved in determining national policy.[22]

Television is available only in towns, but radio is available, if sometimes only intermittently, even in the far reaches of rural areas, and is an important source of information for *grassroots* and villagers. Whereas until recently most village people lacked access to media sources other than newspapers and local radio,[23] they have now found new voices in the very recent entrants onto the media scene: the digital media, in the form of blogs, Facebook and similar internet resources. These provide a vivid alternative to the often biased information put out by the newspapers, are used more by younger people, their users do not

---

19 By comparison, the Murdoch-owned *Post-Courier* is relatively autonomous, and editorial policy is very much localised.
20 Colin Filer has estimated that by 1980 the 'great majority' of Letters to the Editor in the *Post-Courier* were received from Papua New Guineans rather than from expatriates. See Colin Filer 1985, 'What is this thing called "brideprice"?' *Mankind* 15(2): 163–83: 165.
21 The UNESCO Institute of Statistics gives basic literacy rates for PNG population aged 15 and older at around 65% in 2009. See United Nations Educational, Scientific and Cultural Organization (UNESCO), 'The official source of literary data,' *UNESCO Institute of Statistics*, online: http://www.uis.unesco.org/Pages/default.aspx, accessed 11 April 2014.
22 Filer, 'What is this thing called "brideprice"?' 164–65; and see the caveats in Hank Nelson, 2003, 'Dear Sir...: Evidence of civil society in the media of Papua New Guinea,' paper presented at the USP/ANU/FDC Suva Symposium Conference, Suva, 30 September–2 October 2003.
23 Vicki Luker, 2003. 'Civil society, social capital and the churches: HIV/AIDS in Papua New Guinea,' paper presented at the Governance and Civil Society Seminar, in Symposium Governance in Pacific States: Reassessing Roles and Remedies Conference, Suva: University of the South Pacific, 30 September–2 October 2003, 7.

hesitate to criticise and condemn 'the establishment,' and they have become the means by which civil society in PNG has found a strong new voice, augmenting the former limited options of churches, sporting groups and *wantok* systems.[24]

The media are by no means impartial and can also be very inaccurate, as the erroneous *Post-Courier* report about the males freed in the Three-Mile Guesthouse Raid shows. The newspaper never checked, and was never called to account. Although the newspapers purport to represent all sectors of society, in reality they mainly express the opinions of the *elites*, are politically biased towards their owners and can be very selective in what they print. Dame Carol Kidu cites the 'moralist negative response' of the media as one of the three main challenges to her decriminalisation initiative, along with that of sectors of the religious community and 'concerned individuals from the society at large.'[25] But for information on the development of PNG's 'public opinion' on the topics of selling sex and homosexuality, they provide an enduring record. By studying newspaper reports and letters back to the decolonisation era of the early 1970s, I have been able to construct the development of these opinions.

The sex trade

Selling sex always makes good headlines in PNG. Discussion of the pros and cons is abundant, and the newspapers often carry alarmist headlines, for example: 'PNG prostitute has AIDS,'[26] 'Betelnut for sex rife on highway,'[27] 'Sex workers spread HIV,'[28] 'Children into sex for fees,'[29] 'Floating brothels,'[30] and 'Sex trade shock.'[31] Headlines such as these appeal to readers' preconceived reactions of horror and disgust. How did such views develop?

Papua New Guinean *elite* opinion regarding prostitution has been largely but not exclusively informed by many of the shifts and changes in opinion occurring internationally throughout the twentieth century. In the colonial era, the Administration through the minutely detailed Native Regulations of both Territories sought to control every aspect of 'native' life, including prostitution which was opposed in any form.[32] But at the same time, colonial economic policy

---

24 Ibid.
25 Carol Kidu, 2011, 'A national response to the HIV epidemic in Papua New Guinea,' *UN Chronicle* XLVIII (1) May, online: http://www.un.org:80/wcm/content/site/chronicle/home/archive/issues2011/hivaidsthefourthdecade/nationalresponsetohivpapuanewguinea, accessed 20 August 2011.
26 'PNG prostitute has AIDS,' 1987, *Post-Courier* (online), 6 July.
27 'Betelnut for sex rife on highway,' 2005, *Post-Courier* (online), 7 April.
28 'Sex workers spread HIV,' 2007, *Post-Courier* (online), 10 September.
29 'Children into sex for fees,' 2008, *Post-Courier* (online), 14 March.
30 'Floating brothels,' 2008, *Post-Courier* (online), 26 September.
31 'Sex trade shock.' 2004, *Post-Courier*, 17 August, 1.
32 Chilla Bulbeck, 1992, *Australian Women in Papua New Guinea*, Cambridge: Cambridge University Press, 190; Jan Roberts, 1996, *Voices from a Lost World: Australian Women and Children in Papua New Guinea before the Japanese Invasion*, Alexandria, NSW: Millennium Books, 55; Edward P. Wolfers, 1975, *Race Relations and*

created a need for cash in an opportunity-poor environment (particularly for women). It also created new opportunities for women to escape some of the worst strictures of traditional village life.[33] All this encouraged a burgeoning sex trade. Its practitioners may not necessarily have seen prostitution as anything very shameful,[34] but divisions of opinion were already apparent even before Independence, with 'good housewives' disapproving of their relatives selling sex.[35] In the decolonisation era, Papua New Guineans were participating in media discussions around prostitution, and this has continued to the present, although attitudes and opinions have changed with other changes in post-colonial society.

The legalisation debate

The most heated discussion of the sex trade appearing in the media revolves around the question of legalisation and occasionally, the establishment of brothels.[36] Legalisation was an issue which arose even before Independence, and an examination of the debates and the arguments for and against which have appeared in the newspapers over the years reveals much about public attitudes to selling sex.[37] Opinions and comments may be classified into three categories: disease control, socio-economic factors and moral/social arguments.

Sexually transmitted infections (STIs) were a concern of the colonial administration from the outset. In the decolonisation era, writers of letters and articles were debating the need for control of prostitution to prevent the spread of these diseases. Some blamed prostitution, while others urged legalisation as a control measure. The debate continued sporadically after Independence, until HIV arrived in PNG. In 1987, a PNG citizen living overseas was reported to have died of AIDS; an expatriate actually in the country was diagnosed with the virus; and so was a sex seller, who was immediately accused of 'spreading AIDS.'[38] From then on, the legalisation debate was inextricably linked to the epidemic, and the language began changing, as donor aid found its way into the country and epidemic control measures demanded the investigation of social

---

Colonial Rule in Papua New Guinea, Sydney: Australia and New Zealand Book Company, 55, 98–100.

33   For example, the need to escape from intolerable situations created by the lack of respect and support shown by male kin in certain circumstances: Holly Wardlow, 2006, *Wayward Women: Sexuality and Agency in a New Guinea Society*, Berkeley and Los Angeles, California: University of California Press.

34   For example Joan Drikoré Johnstone, 1993, 'The Gumini *Bisnis-Meri*: a study of the development of an innovative indigenous entrepreneurial activity in Port Moresby in the early 1970s,' Ph.D. thesis, Brisbane: University of Queensland, 124, 139–40, 186.

35   Ibid., 185.

36   The distinction between 'legalisation,' 'decriminalisation' and 'regulation' is discussed in Chapter 7. Public confusion has led to the frequent use of the conflating term 'legalisation.'

37   The opinions that follow are drawn from a multitude of articles, editorials and letters appearing in the *Post-Courier*, 1972–2011, and the *National*, 1993–2011.

38   'PNG prostitute has AIDS,' 1987, *Post-Courier*, 6 July, 11.

behaviours.³⁹ Arguments supporting legalisation included: criminalisation drives it underground; legalisation will ensure access to proper medical and health facilities; legalised prostitution will reduce the incidence of rape. Arguments against were more numerous, though often less well reasoned: prostitution spreads disease; nightclubs promote prostitution which spreads disease; prostitutes don't use condoms, which prevent disease; condoms spread disease; legalisation will not prevent the spread of HIV, which can only be checked by mandatory testing of the entire population.

After the health arguments comes a long list of what can best be described as social and moral arguments. Before Independence, Highlands leaders expressed concern with urban drift, particularly of uneducated and unemployable women, and particularly down the Highlands Highway to settlements in Lae: they claimed that this brought shame to the status of the Highlands region.⁴⁰ The Administration was willing to cooperate and prosecute prostitutes under vagrancy laws. Shortly after Independence, church and women's group leaders expressed concern that a legalised sex trade would adversely affect the new nation's image on the world stage, and called for stronger control measures.⁴¹ Reflecting PNG concerns to begin crafting a new society, one letter writer argued that, 'all too often expatriates have sought to impose alien standards of morals and behaviour on dependent peoples with disastrous results. At this sensitive stage of the country's history, it appears appropriate for Papua New Guineans to begin setting their own standards.'⁴²

Employment identity cards were debated, and measures to combat the unemployment problem were called for. Social issues such as unwanted pregnancies and disruption to family life were blamed on prostitution. By 1986, the practice of seeking opinions from the man (and woman) on the street had taken hold in the PNG media, and the *Post-Courier* published three feature

---

39 For example, an article on a survey of 'high-risk settings' (nightclubs) referred to 'multiple sex partners,' 'high-risk groups' and the availability of condoms. See 'Sex study shock: 6000 unprotected sex reportedly from nightclub outings,' 2004, *Post-Courier* (online), 17 August.
40 Paul Cowdy, 1972, 'The "crime" of being out of work in a town like Lae,' *Post-Courier*, 10 March, 17; 'I-Day upstaged by prostitutes,' 1974, *Post-Courier*, 9 May, 11; Robert Famundi, 1974, 'Prostitution must stop,' *Post-Courier*, 18 October, 2.
41 'Two bishops reject legal prostitution,' 1976, *Post-Courier*, 17 August, 14; 'Women may seek world affiliation,' 1976, *Post-Courier*, 26 August, 3.
42 Ultra-Realist, 1973, 'Govts cannot legislate against sin,' *Post-Courier*, 3 October, 23. As the letter was signed 'Ultra-Realist,' it is impossible to tell whether the writer is expatriate or indigenous. However the point was an interesting one, and in keeping with the spirit of the times; and see the discussion of the 'race narrative' below.

pieces on legalisation. Elizabeth Kogomoni was struck by the reluctance of people to talk about 'it,'[43] although eventually several people were found, all of whom supported legalisation.[44]

At the same time, the rhetoric was shifting from international image to more domestic concerns: destruction of family life, destruction of cultural norms, un-Christian sinfulness. Leaders began to advise girls who sold sex to return home to the village and help their parents. The arrival of HIV prompted an upsurge of public awareness and discussion. The spread of the virus (allegedly by prostitution) was proof of a breakdown of cultural norms and a state of sinfulness, a situation which could only become worse following legalisation.

Economic factors—poverty, urban drift, inadequate schooling and the crackdown on urban street vending—have all been blamed at various times.[45] Women are pimped by relatives, girls are expected to provide for their families, mobile men with money or 'sugar daddies' are accused, and one writer even claimed that mothers who abandon their families 'force' fathers to prostitute their daughters (this was given as a rationale to make legal provision for such women to pay maintenance to fathers).[46] 'Legalisation' has been suggested as a solution to these problems because it provides greater income opportunities for women. Other suggestions however are for lazy and greedy women to return to the village and work the land, or alternatively that they be rehabilitated by teaching them income-earning skills such as sewing, cooking, and for the literate, typing.

Brothels (as opposed to freelance sex selling by individuals) have been discussed in Chapter 3. Politicians have made several proposals over the years to legalise them: in 1973, for Mt. Hagen;[47] in 1977, for East New Britain;[48] and by Dame Carol Kidu when she first started her decriminalisation campaign.[49] Arguments for brothels have included: legalising them could provide taxable income from operators; they will facilitate better health checks and disease management;

---

[43] Elizabeth Kogomoni, 1986, 'Prostitutes: we are not ashamed,' *Post-Courier*, 8 January, 3; Elizabeth Kogomoni, 1986, 'The unhappy life on the streets,' *Post-Courier*, 9 January, 3.
[44] Peter Kili, 1986, 'What the public thinks,' *Post-Courier*, 8 January, 3.
[45] When I left PNG in 1976, there were no beggars, although many people walked the city streets asking at businesses and private homes for work. When I returned in 1990, one or two beggars sat on the pavements of commercial areas. Now, beggars roam the streets throughout the city.
[46] Peter Korugl, 2010, 'Women to pay,' *Post-Courier* (online), 6 January.
[47] 'Brothel call,' 1973, *Post-Courier*, 15 August, 1; 'Brothel call "not serious",' 1973, *Post-Courier*, 17 August, 10; 'Opposition to brothels,' 1973, *Post-Courier*, 31 August, 8; 'Synod again brothel idea,' 1973, *Post-Courier*, 18 September, 3; also 'I-Day upstaged by prostitutes,' 1974, *Post-Courier*, 9 May, 11.
[48] Editorial, 'Unemployment the real issue,' 1977, *Post-Courier*, 22 April, 2.
[49] 'PNG politicians study Australian prostitution laws,' 2005, *PACNEWS* (online), 23 June; Editorial, 2005, 'Let's debate Dame Carol's proposal,' *Post-Courier*, 23 June, 10.

and they will be testing grounds for men's moral strength. Against, it has been asserted that brothels encourage exploitation and organised crime such as gambling, robbery and murder.

By the 2000s, brothel establishments began to be associated with 'Asians.' As explained to me by a UPNG classmate, the Chinese in PNG are of two kinds. The 'good' Chinese, whose ancestors were imported into German New Guinea in the nineteenth century as indentured labourers, intermarried with Papua New Guineans, formed business associations with them, provided much of the petty merchant class in both urban and rural areas, and became naturalised citizens.[50] The 'new Asians' started arriving in the 1980s, when Malaysian logging interests were beginning to extend their activities beyond Borneo. Other resource-extraction entrepreneurs followed, and 'Asian' can now refer not only to Malaysian loggers but also to Indian car mechanics, Singaporean service providers, Taiwanese fishing boat crews, Mainland Chinese miners and so on. They are often reported to display arrogance and disdain for Papua New Guineans and their land and this has earned them considerable resentment.[51] An example of the issues involved comes from a newspaper report in 2010, of the arrest of two 'Asians of Chinese origin' for the attempted murder of a (good Chinese) businessman. The two were allegedly associated with a group involved in illegal casino, nightclub and brothel operations, and there was also mention of breaches of immigration laws. Jeffrey Elapa wrote, 'Two highly placed government officers have warned since that the country was sitting on a time bomb. "We are being virtually invaded. These people will be the next biggest group in PNG."'[52]

Another report followed quickly, of the exposure of a 'sex ring' at a logging camp in the Sepik, where arrests were thwarted when the women involved all claimed to be married to the foreign loggers, and the police Inspector was left fuming that, 'these marriages only result in the poor young mothers striving daily to raise their "fatherless" children.... These foreigners are smart at this game but I will not rest this time until they learn to respect our children and women folk.'[53]

Attention had already focused on nightclubs, as part of attention to HIV management. New strategies were being introduced which focused on high-

---

50   Hank Nelson, 1982, Taim Bilong Masta: *The Australian Involvement with Papua New Guinea*, Sydney: Australian Broadcasting Commission, 29–30, 170–71, 216.
51   See for example Centre for Environmental Law and Community Rights (CELCoR) and Australian Conservation Foundation, 2006, *Bulldozing Progress: Human Rights Abuses and Corruption in Papua New Guinea's Large Scale Logging Industry*, Boroko, PNG: Australian Conservation Foundation. Numerous complaints have also been published regarding mining, fish-canning and other resource extraction enterprises in PNG.
52   Mohammed Bashir, 'Chinese duo appear in court,' 2010, *Post-Courier* (online), 5 January.
53   'Sex-for-sale case hit snag,' 2010, *National* (online), 23 February.

risk groups and involved a survey of sex-selling venues.⁵⁴ A year later, Dame Carol's suggestion that brothels be legalised for better HIV management was referred to a parliamentary committee, which commenced a nationwide study of nightclubs.⁵⁵ A proposal to close down nightclubs entirely was eventually rejected, and operators were urged to comply with existing laws.⁵⁶ In 2007, a newly appointed Justice Minister began his own anti-nightclub campaign, declaring that he would 'fight evil and any foreign practices that are brought into this country with an intention to destroy Melanesian and Christian family values.' Nightclubs, he claimed, promoted evil, contributed to family break-up and to the increase in HIV/AIDS, and should be banned outright. He deployed a range of emotive terms designed to depict the women as victims of evil nightclub owners, terms such as 'sex slaves,' 'sex objects,' 'unhealthy practices,' 'manipulate, abuse,' and 'malicious activities.'⁵⁷

Figure 6.1. Poster (carried by a man) from the 'Stop Violence Against Women' march of 2006, displaying some of the prevalent arguments against nightclubs.

Source: Photo by Christine Stewart, 2006.

---

54 'Sex study shock,' 2004, *Post-Courier* (online), 17 August.
55 Jessie Lapou, 2005, 'Prostitution issue sent to committee,' *Post-Courier*, 25 July, 2; Editorial, 2005, 'Committee set to study night clubs,' *Post-Courier*, 25 July, 10.
56 'Nightclubs urged to help enquiry,' *Post-Courier* (online), 3 February 2006.
57 'Dr Marat wants night clubs to be banned,' 2007, *National* (online) 10 December; Camillus Vovore, First Secretary to Minister for Justice and Attorney-General, 2008, 'Nightclubs promote evil, should be banned,' *National* (online), 7 January; Joshua Arlo, 2008, 'Nightclubs leading to moral decay: Marat,' *National* (online), 18 February; Michael Unagi, 2008, 'Deal with actors in sexual immorality,' *National* (online), 20 March; and various other newspaper items 2004–2009.

Christian rhetoric has increased in recent years.[58] Legalisation was most frequently opposed by appeals to Christian principles and 'family values.' Prostitution is immoral, sinful and contrary to Christian values; it is the devil's evil practice, from the time of Sodom and Gomorrah. On the contrary, it has been argued that it is a social rather than a criminal problem, politics and religion should not mix, and anyway, churches and moral preaching cannot prevent it. In 2005, the Minister for Community Development suggested amending the *Summary Offences Act* so as to prevent law-enforcing agents such as police from being legally entitled to victimise sex workers, and proposed consideration of establishing 'adult entertainment centres,' which would ensure compliance with health requirements and the prohibition on commercial sexual exploitation of children.[59] The *Post-Courier* chimed in swiftly with a remarkably sympathetic editorial:

> DAME Carol Kidu wants 'adult entertainment centres' established with the aim of reducing illegal sex activities on our streets. She told Parliament she does not want to favour the idea but due to rising illegal sex activities, Papua New Guinea must face up to reality. This is a controversial subject. Churches and other groups will oppose it while others will favour it. Whatever the arguments may be, this issue must be carefully considered before any decision is made.
>
> We have a serious problem on our streets where thousands of young women have turned to prostitution to earn a living. This is a risky behaviour which places them at a greater risk of being infected with HIV/AIDS. Many have died as a result, others now live with the virus but the numbers keep rising. Dame Carol is right. PNG must face up to reality in dealing with this problem. Our present systems and institutions are not capable of dealing with a tide that is rising right in front of our eyes.
>
> The reality facing us is that prostitution will continue to increase and no amount of force used by the state and its law enforcement organisations will end it. The Government and various state authorities can look at ways of ensuring that those involved in this behaviour as a means of survival must be protected and those who use their services are also protected. Adult entertainment centres, if these are to be legally established in PNG, must be treated with sensitivity. Strict rules of conduct must be established and enforced to ensure the interests of the

---

58 Not only in relation to sexual matters. Judicial opinion in recent times has veered away from condemning witch-killing on humanitarian grounds, and more towards claiming it is contrary to Christian principles. See Christine Stewart, 2010, 'The courts, the churches, the witches and their killers,' paper presented at the Law and Culture: Meaningful Legal Pluralism in the Pacific and Beyond Conference, Port Vila, Vanuatu, 30 August–1 September 2010.
59 'License brothels,' 2005, *Post-Courier* (online), 23 June; Damaris Minikula and Fiona Harepa, 2005, 'No legal sex: Kidu,' *National*, 5 August.

community are protected. This newspaper encourages all our readers to come forward with your views on this issue. Let's have all points of view, for and against.

The only way to reach an acceptable answer to this issue is for wider public discussion. As a nation, we have been turning a blind eye to this problem for far too long.[60]

And discuss it the public did. A flood of letters defended and opposed the proposal as if it were already law, each usually attacking the one before:

Don't forget sex workers are also important citizens of this country … as they are also human beings created by the Almighty.… Only those living in a fantasy Christian perspective seem to be having narrow notions and seem to think that they are the perfect ones and seem to marginalise the sinners.[61]

I cannot condone something that belittles another human being and dehumanises our society.[62]

It is a social problem and whether we legalise it or not will never make a difference as this activity will continue as long as we live.… If someone wants to enter prostitution to earn an easy leaving, let them be. Who are we to decide? Sex workers or not, they are still human beings, like us they too have rights.[63]

The president of the PNG National Council of Women submitted a plea for regard to Christian principles, the real value of sex, marriage and family, the norms and values of the society, PNG's strong traditional and cultural values, and the 'societal context' which regarded prostitutes as animals. She thought that legalisation would prevent an adequate HIV/AIDS response, and that 'strip tease' at hotels and nightclubs is a corrupt activity that leads to 'cvil acts of adultery and fornication.'[64]

The abomination

Lessons can be learnt from the Bible about the wrath of God when men contended that God flawed in our designs and decided to use our bodies for other purposes than those intended by the Creator. The Great Flood

---

60 Editorial, 'Let's debate Dame Carol's proposal.'
61 Kopi K. Lou, 2005, 'Dame Carol has no hidden agenda,' *Post-Courier*, 8 August.
62 Vina Mer, 2005, 'Why legalise another crime?' *Post-Courier*, 8 August.
63 Hate Me Not, 2005, 'Consider both sides on prostitution,' *Post-Courier* (online), 11 August.
64 'Women's group slams plans to legalise brothels,' 2005, *National* (online), 10 August.

during Noah's time and the destruction of Sodom and Gomorrah came about when society at large accepted unnatural, immoral and un-Godly acts.... Be warned.

Dominic Kakas, *Post-Courier*, 2010.[65]

Although PNG's daily newspapers are a rich source of information on public discourse regarding the sex trade, a similar study of newspapers for debate on homosexuality reveals very little in the way of public discourse through opinion pieces and letters. However, the norms of the colonisers were gradually being accepted in the newly independent nation, as shown by the following two tales recorded in the press.

Tale from a high school[66]

In 1980, Kerevat in East New Britain Province was one of the country's four 'National' high schools, providing Grade 11 and 12 education to selected students from around the country. It was staffed by both expatriate and Papua New Guinean teachers. That year, allegations surfaced of homosexual relations at the school involving a married expatriate teacher and a PNG student. A group of mainly expatriate teachers banded together to agitate for investigation of the allegations. The expatriate Inspector for National High Schools was accused of irregular practices in school supervision and the school chaplain was co-opted into finding evidence of homosexuality on the part of the Inspector.[67]

The Secretary for Education appointed a Committee of Enquiry in March 1981 to investigate the Inspector's conduct. By this time the teacher implicated had left the country and the student had moved on to University studies. The Committee exonerated the Inspector and condemned the teachers who called for the investigation. They were accused of stirring up trouble and were sacked. Students became upset over a radio broadcast alleging homosexuality at the school, boycotted classes and stoned school buildings. Armed police were called in, some 230 students were charged with unlawful assembly, and it was several days before order was restored.

The sacked teachers complained to the Ombudsman Commission, which is charged under the *Constitution* Section 219 to investigate 'cases where the conduct [of government officers] is or may be wrong, taking into account, amongst other things, the National Goals and Directive Principles, the Basic

---

65 Dominic Kakas, 2010, 'Throw out Dame Carol's idea,' *Post-Courier*, 25 November, 10.
66 Account derived from Ombudsman Commission of Papua New Guinea 1981, *Final Report on the Kerevat National High School Enquiry*, Port Moresby: National Parliament; as well as various *Post-Courier* reports and commentaries. I was not able to discover a copy of the original Education Department Committee Report.
67 Ironically, the chaplain himself was eventually found to have been involved in sexual relations with other men, and was forced out of town by other gays there. Pers. comm., Adam, 12 January 2006.

Rights and the Basic Social Obligations.' The Commission in its report made in October 1981[68] found the Education Department Committee's inquiry to be 'biased, dishonest and untruthful'[69] and the complaint against the Inspector to be justified, saying, 'where a public servant allows his private life to interfere with his public duties—especially where those duties touch upon the education of our children … it no longer remains a private matter.'[70]

It recommended reinstatement of the sacked teachers and dismissal of the Inspector and the Superintendent of Operations (responsible for the staffing of National High Schools). The Education Department 'vehemently' defended the Committee, but reinstated the sacked teachers. Attempts to direct the police to withdraw the charges against the students were protested by the police on grounds of the constitutional independence of the Constabulary. A test case against student ringleaders went to court and was dismissed. The Inspector resigned and left the country, claiming pressure from unsubstantiated allegations. The Superintendent protested his innocence and wrote to the Education Secretary complaining that the opinions expressed in the Ombudsman Commission report were not supported by evidence. Accusations of misrepresentation, distortions of the truth, unfair dealings and disparaging innuendo flew back and forth in early 1982, and the government was pressured to act against the superintendent. The Public Services Commission conducted an 'assessment' of the superintendent's case, and he was ultimately sacked and afforded no opportunity to appeal.[71]

***

At the time of the affair (1981–82), public comment focused mainly on condemning expatriate education officers and the Department in general.[72] A very few PNG letter writers came out for and against homosexuality in educational institutions in November and December 1981. In December 1982, however, the two teachers most prominent in agitating for action against the teacher and the Inspector (a married couple who had been sacked, reinstated and redeployed elsewhere in the country) revived the matter in a lengthy letter to the newspaper. In it they claimed that 'homosexual abuse of students by male expatriates remains widespread'; and 'during our time at Kerevat two of our students became mentally unstable and violent following interference by homosexuals.' The inspection system, they claimed, continued to be abused, and 'expatriates or

---

68 Ombudsman Commission of Papua New Guinea, 1981, *Final Report on the Kerevat National High School Enquiry*, Report prepared for National Parliament, Port Moresby.
69 Ibid., 6.
70 Ibid., 42–43.
71 'Donohue sacked,' 1982, *Post-Courier*, 20 May, 1.
72 For example, a *Post-Courier* Editorial of 18 November 1981 entitled 'Clean out the closets' proposed that 'any mess' should be cleaned up to restore public confidence in the education system, 2; subsequent letters to the newspaper argued the case for and against permitting homosexuality.

"co-operative" nationals are given posts ahead of eligible national applicants.' The problem, they said, still lay in Department headquarters, where the 'small group of senior expatriates remaining from colonial days operate as they wish.'[73]

There are two ways of viewing the affair. If the Ombudsman Commission and these two teachers are to be believed, the Education Department Committee embarked on a witch-hunt against certain teachers at the school who were simply trying to bring to the attention of the authorities a case of malpractice on the part of the Inspector. He had covered up a breach of moral duty at the school. Resentment against his actions, and allegations of homosexuality, had led to the deployment of armed police against children. The Committee itself was negligent in failing to enquire whether the Inspector's alleged homosexual involvements affected his public responsibilities, on the grounds that it would violate his right to privacy under Section 49 of the *Constitution*. It was misled by the actions of the Superintendent, who had intimidated a witness to the Committee. Subsequent public discussion unearthed the likelihood that a band of expatriate officers at department headquarters were the ones dictating policy, keeping secret files on teachers, and so on. An expatriate teacher in a provincial high school condemned the 'expatriate clique' in the Department of Education which 'function[ed] as a close knit, incestuous operation which favors and protects those loyal to it but will not hesitate to use dirty tricks to remove or disadvantage anyone who challenges or threatens its existence … an assessment system in which obsequious and scurrilous backbiting count for much more than professional competence.'[74]

Another writer claimed that, 'the problem is not simply confined to senior expatriate officers. Alliances have developed between some of these officers and some of the new national elite.… These alliances do not augur well for the health and vitality of the nation … one legacy left to PNG has been particular Australian forms of incompetence.'[75] In this view, the Ombudsman Commission had acted properly in 'put[ting] aside our normal Melanesian politeness' and speaking plainly.[76] It placed primary significance on the special role of teachers in society, and the ethical obligations therefore placed upon them, stating that 'the public has the right to be assured that its publicly funded education system does not expose the youth of this nation to sexual treatment which may damage them psychologically and permanently affect their lives by leading them into a minority life style which does not have the approval of the majority of society,' and quoted from a Circular entitled 'Simplified Interpretation of the Papua New

---

73 J. Mendzela and E. Mendzela, 1982, 'Kerevat: the lesson wasn't learnt,' *Post-Courier*, 16 December, 4.
74 'Secret files on teachers deter recruitment,' 1982, *Post-Courier*, 1 April, 4.
75 'Report gathers dust,' 1982, *Post-Courier*, 2 April, 4.
76 Ombudsman Commission, *Final Report on the Kerevat National High School Enquiry*, 6.

Guinea Teachers Association Code of Ethics' thus: 'healthy moral development relates to the child's behaviour and how he views his [sic] social relationship through the accepted social and religious values.'[77]

This is the view of the Kerevat Affair taken by the majority of letter writers, and the *Post-Courier* itself, in its implicit condemnation of the conduct of the teacher alleged to have had the relationship with the student, the Inspector who supported him and the Superintendent who allegedly supported both of them and allegedly intimidated a witness to that effect.

But there is another view: one lone voice pointed out that the Commission report and recommendations were not grounded in fact.[78] This is the view taken by the original Education Department enquiry, which was supported throughout by the Secretary for Education. The Committee Report says that neither the relationship between the student (who had not been proved to be under eighteen at the relevant time) and the teacher,[79] nor the sexual proclivities of the Inspector, ought to be a matter of public scrutiny. Rather, it claimed, the teachers who lodged the complaints about the relationship were themselves involved in a homophobic witch-hunt. There is no proof that the Superintendent intimidated anyone, and no matter how strongly he protested his innocence, he was ultimately sacrificed. There are also no proofs, only allegations, of a group of officers at Department headquarters (some of whom were supposedly themselves homosexual) protecting their own.

Either way, the report of the investigations and the public comment demonstrate how easily insinuations of homosexuality can be made, and the drastic consequences this can have for those involved. The media role was pivotal. The new nation was developing an anti-colonial reconstruction of the 'expatriate' as the villain in the piece, while paradoxically emulating colonial concepts of normative sex, with 'perverted' (expatriate) homosexuals condemned for their influence on precocious but innocent (Papua New Guinean) children.[80]

The Tale of a parliamentarian[81]

At the end of 1983, a scandal broke in the media surrounding allegations of sexual misconduct in the late 1970s on the part of two Ministers in the Somare National Government. The allegations were made by a Minister in the Morobe

---

77   Ibid., 43.
78   Concerned Resident, 'Report needs scrutiny,' 1982, *Post-Courier*, 14 April, 4.
79   Given that most children starting school before Independence were at least six or seven years old, he would have been very close to attaining his majority, if he had not already done so. The fact that the Commission did not raise the possibility, relying instead on reference to teachers' ethics and the duty of a public servant not to let his private life interfere with his public duties, seem to bear out this conclusion.
80   Foucault, *The Will to Knowledge: The History of Sexuality Vol. 1*, 146.
81   Account derived from *Post-Courier* reports of 1983–1984. The newspaper ran the story as front-page news for over two months.

Provincial Government, formerly a Deputy Police Commissioner. One allegation of sex with an under-aged girl was made against Sir Pita Lus and Boyamo Sali, Member for Morobe Province in the National Government, was accused of sodomy. It was claimed that the original cases had been covered up by the government's applying political pressure to the police involved.[82] The sodomy allegation against Sali arose in connection with a prosecution in 1978 for driving under the influence of liquor in Rabaul. The driving charge was upheld, but the allegation of sodomy was thrown out for lack of evidence.

The allegations appear to have been politically motivated. Conflicts between national and provincial governments were frequent in the twenty years following Independence. Many provincial governments were investigated and suspended, until a law revision in 1995 gave the national government greater control over them. The Morobe Premier and the Prime Minister clashed often.[83] The Premier at the time was embroiled in conflict with the National Government, resulting in a prosecution for insulting a police officer,[84] and the Provincial Minister declared he was critical of the police and supported the Premier.[85] A *Post-Courier* editorial wondered whether the nation was on the verge of an era of witch-hunts. Sali himself claimed that it was 'cheap politics,'[86] and the Commission of Inquiry which eventually sat on the matter supported the view that the whole incident was politically motivated.[87]

Despite initial attempts by the Police Minister and the Prime Minister to brush the matter off, the Opposition mounted a strong campaign against the 'cover-ups,' which included advertising for signatures to a petition to have both cases re-opened on the grounds of political interference with the course of justice. The Ombudsman Commission rapidly backed out of any involvement in the matter, but the Prime Minister bowed to public pressure and appointed a Commission of Inquiry on 13 January 1984. The two Ministers stood aside pending the outcome of the inquiry, which was conducted by (then) Deputy Chief Justice Kapi. The inquiry investigated the allegations against Sir Pita first, and then moved on to those against Sali. Various police officers allegedly or actually involved at the time gave somewhat confused evidence, but all denied

---

82 'Govt Ministers in sex case – claim,' 1983, *Post-Courier*, 21 November, 1.
83 Hartmut Holzknecht, 'Morobe Province 1978–1991,' 1997, in *Political Decentralisation in a New State: The Experience of Provincial Government in Papua New Guinea*, ed. Ronald James May, A.J. Regan and Allison Ley, Bathurst: Crawford House Publishing, 199–227, 222; Sean Dorney, 1990, *Papua New Guinea: People, Politics and History since 1975*, Milsons Point, NSW: Random House: 150–52, 164.
84 *Samana v Waki* (Unreported) N449, 23 January 1984.
85 'Govt Ministers in sex case – claim,' 1983, *Post-Courier*, 21 November, 1; Angwi Hriehwazi, 1983, 'PG to reveal names,' 1983, *Post Courier*, 15 December, 1–2.
86 Angwi Hriehwazi, 1983, 'It's Sali and Lus: Merire,' 1983, *Post-Courier*, 16 December, 1, 2.
87 'Police were not influenced,' 1984, *Post-Courier*, 5 June, 2.

any political pressure. Sali, through his counsel, claimed to be 'scandalised' by the constant use of the word 'sodomy' and objected to its use, but Justice Kapi allowed reference to both 'sodomy' and 'gross indecency.'

The inquiry report was tabled in Parliament on 4 June 1984. It ruled out any interference with police investigations, and cleared both Ministers of any alleged wrongdoing. The Prime Minister professed himself 'appalled and outraged' at the behaviour of the Provincial Minister who first raised the matter, the Opposition and the *Post-Courier*. He announced that he would recommend to the National Executive Council that the State cover any costs incurred by either Minister in libel actions against the newspaper.[88]

The matter provoked little written public comment. During the course of the inquiry, an Opposition frontbencher announced that he intended to reveal the names of some MPs and top public servants who were homosexual, and working in league with expatriates recruited to work in PNG.[89] A letter writer retaliated by calling it all a 'storm in a teacup' and suggested that it might be better to name parliamentarians and officials who had mistresses.[90] Otherwise, nothing further appeared in the press. It is worth noting, however, that Prime Minister Somare had, by then, gained a reputation for protecting his ministers, as had emerged in the Rooney Affair of 1979, resulting in the mass resignation of expatriate judges from the bench and the downfall of the Somare government of the time.[91]

***

Both these tales illustrate the many ways in which allegations of sexual impropriety can form a basis for public discussion and the construction of social mores. The Kerevat Affair gave rise to a storm of allegation and innuendo, and a public airing of the belief that it was expatriates who were 'teaching' national youth to indulge in 'it' (homosexuality). The MPs' Scandal did not provoke much in the way of letter writing, but newspaper reports ensured that it was kept well in the public view. Homosexuality was becoming entrenched in the new nation as anti-social.

'Males freed' – the gender factor

Apart from the report of Johnny Mala's conviction in 1997, very little comment on homosexuality appeared for many years, other than the occasional report

---

88 'Lus, Sali clear – Somare,' 1984, *Post-Courier*, 5 June, 1.
89 'Homosexual MPs to be named,' 1984, *Post-Courier*, 25 January, 10.
90 P.R. Sharp, 1984, 'Storm in a teacup,' *Post-Courier*, 2 February, 4.
91 David Weisbrot, 1979, 'Judges and politicians,' *Legal Service Bulletin* 4(6): 240–45; Weisbrot, 1980, 'Judges and politicians Pt II: the Wilson affair,' *Legal Service Bulletin* 5(5): 214–17.

of forced sex or sex in prisons. But in 2004, considerable public debate ensued about the freeing of alleged male prostitutes in the Three-Mile Guesthouse Raid. This reveals a lot about public perceptions of prostitutes as always being female. The gendering of the category of 'prostitute' had already been confirmed in the discourse of the colonial law simultaneously with its naming. References are made in the colonial Ordinances to prostitution by a 'female native,' a 'native woman,' or simply, a 'female.'[92] Extra emphasis is given to this female gendering by the long-standing rule in the imported legal system that 'words importing the masculine gender include females,'[93] and it is still standard legislative drafting practice in PNG to use 'he' to denote either male or female. So the use of these female terms places explicit emphasis on the gender of prostitutes. Until the reforms of 1977, the law held that only women could be prostitutes.

It was already amply clear that males had been selling sex in colonial times. Several cases from that era mentioned monetary exchange, and one file document from the *Siune Wel Cases* specifically stated that one party to consensual male-male sex was entitled to be exonerated as 'the victim of a male prostitute.'[94] However, the criminal charges laid in all such cases are those of male-male sex, which carry far higher penalties than the 'prostitution' offences which criminalise those who sell sex. This is probably the reason why no public discourse has emerged around commercial sex between males. Rather, in the case of sex between males, attention has focused on the conflation of consensual sex between adults with forced sex and sex with under-aged males, all of which are lumped together in media reportage as 'sodomy.' As Cindy Patton has stated, the global HIV discourse has assisted in conflating AIDS and selling sex, and 'sex workers were largely presumed to be women, and women at risk were assumed to be prostitutes,' while 'men who sell sex to men were lumped together as men who have sex with men.'[95]

Perhaps because of this history of avoiding reference to the selling of sex by males, it is not surprising that the comparatively novel concept of 'male prostitutes' caught up in the Three-Mile Guesthouse Raid was taken up so eagerly by the media. The *Post-Courier* had already headlined this aspect of the raid on the front page with its 'Males freed' story,[96] and reported the comments of the National AIDS Council lawyer to the effect that 'the release of the male suspects was not fair to their female counterparts.' Over the week following the raid, both newspapers solicited comments from prominent people on this topic. The *Post-Courier* on the following day reported that officials of the NGO ICRAF

---

92 *Native Regulations* 1939 (Papua) Section 85; *Native Administration Regulations* 1924 (New Guinea) Section 87; *Police Offences Ordinance* (New Guinea) Section 79.
93 *Interpretation Act* 1975 Section 6.
94 Robert Aldrich, 2003, *Colonialism and Homosexuality*, London and New York: Routledge.
95 Cindy Patton, 2002, *Globalising AIDS*, Minneapolis and London: University of Minnesota Press, 92.
96 'Males freed,' 2004, *Post-Courier*, 16 March, 1.

explained that the law 'covered both male and female prostitutes.... How can the police justify their actions by saying the law only relates to women? Where is the justice that they are supposed to be providing to the people of this land when they clearly have a prejudice against women?'[97]

On the same day, in a horrified letter headed 'Crime to Be a Woman?' a (male) writer complained bitterly about the discrimination evidenced by

> this apparent male chauvinistic ideology which stigmatises the female gender as sexual entrepreneurs. After the motley gang of both male and female sex workers were detained and interrogated, males were vindicated but the females were castigated ... if this case reveals an inherent legislative bias that privileges the male gender against moral and legal indictment, it is also a case that points to the dehumanisation of the female species. Is it a crime to be a woman?[98]

The *Post-Courier* sought comment from Minister Kidu who on Thursday condemned the police brutality and reportedly mentioned that 'the fact that only the women were victimised was unjust because both males and females were arrested during the raid.'[99] On Friday, the Minister responsible for the police, Bire Kimisopa, described the release of the forty-five male prostitutes as a 'joke' and a 'completely stupid' action by police because not all sex workers were females. He condemned the police action in forcing the shameful march to the station 'because by doing such a thing, people would lose the respect they have for the force.' He went on,

> 'I want a review on the whole incident and all male suspects to be brought in and charged appropriately,' he said ... he would be writing to Police Commissioner Sam Inguba to have the officer responsible charged for releasing the male prostitutes. 'The release of the male prostitutes is a terrible injustice to the female citizens of this country,' Mr. Kimisopa said.[100]

What is intriguing, if not frightening, is that not one voice in those newspaper reports and statements, amidst all the cries for recognition of the equal rights of males and females, all the complaints about police abuses, suggested that the women should have been freed too, along with the 'male prostitutes.' Apart from the ICRAF representatives, who complained about police violence and foreshadowed civil suits for damages, no-one expressed any opinion about the breaches of human rights in the actions of the police. I have suggested elsewhere

---

97 Maureen Gerawa, 'Police wrong: NGO,' 2004, *Post-Courier*, 17 March, 4.
98 A. Moutu, 2004, 'Crime to be a woman?' *Post-Courier*, 17 March, 10.
99 Michelle Yiprukaman, 2004, 'Kidu: probe raid on city brothel,' *Post-Courier*, 18 March, 4.
100 Michelle Yiprukaman, 2004, 'Police actions damned,' *Post-Courier*, 19 March, 4.

that 'rather than complaining about the unfair violence, or the unfair law which led to it, some preferred to ensure that all males who might behave similarly to the outclass of "prostitutes" should be re-gendered so as to deserve equal ill-treatment.'[101]

The decriminalisation furore

I have referred above to Dame Carol Kidu's first suggestion in 2005 that brothels, or 'adult entertainment centres' as she termed them, be legalised, and the flood of discussion that ensued.[102] She defused the issue by sending the matter to the parliamentary committee of Health and Family Welfare, and the whole matter evolved into an investigation of nightclubs.[103] Nevertheless, debate continued for several months.

Meanwhile, as Minister, she established a semi-formal Decriminalisation Task Force to start looking into the decriminalisation of both sex work and sodomy.[104] She tried repeatedly to take submissions to Cabinet, only to be rejected by the pre-screening committees. When she was re-elected in 2007 and re-allocated the Community Development Ministry, she moved quickly to gain endorsement by Cabinet of a proposal to refer a review of the laws in question to the Constitutional and Law Reform Commission (CLRC), with instructions to undertake widespread and lengthy community consultation. She formalised the Task Force and reconstituted it as a Decriminalisation Reference Group, to work in consultation with the CLRC and also to consider alternative strategies for decriminalisation of both sex work and sodomy. She also made a statement to the press about the CLRC reference.[105]

Whilst the discourse on decriminalisation of prostitution has been dense, that on the sodomy law has not, consisting mainly of innuendo during the Kerevat Affair regarding the 'foreign influence' of expatriate men leading innocent young PNG men astray[106] and, more recently, horror expressed at sodomy committed by force in prisons or on young boys. Stigma and shame have largely kept male-male sex from the public view, only noticed when the law steps in. But the

---

101 Christine Stewart, 2012, '"Crime to be a woman?" Engendering violence against female sex workers in Port Moresby, Papua New Guinea,' in *Engendering Violence in Papua New Guinea*, ed. Margaret Jolly, Christine Stewart with Carolyn Brewer, Canberra: ANU E Press, online: http://press.anu.edu.au?p=182671, accessed 31 March 2014.
102 Eric Tappakau, 'License brothels,' *Post-Courier*, 23 June 2005, 1; Editorial, 'Let's debate Dame Carol's proposal.'
103 Lapou, 'Prostitution issue sent to committee.'
104 Kidu, 'A national response to the HIV epidemic in Papua New Guinea.'
105 'Cabinet endorses review on country's sex laws,' 2010, *National*, 22 October, 3; H. Joku, 'PNG sex laws under review: homosexuality and prostitution may be legalised,' 2010, *Post-Courier*, 5 November, 1, 4.
106 As explained to me by a member of the National AIDS Council Legal and Ethical Committee, 2001; also, interview Ume Wainetti, Port Moresby, 20 March 2006.

Minister's decriminalisation statement unleashed a massive backlash, notable not least for the fact that for the first time, homosexuality became the subject of much public condemnation. According to those whose press statements were published, the proposal would 'contribute to moral decay in the very fabric of a nation of Christians'; she was 'legalising mass murder in PNG'; 'those practising are not fit to live as human'; 'prostitution and homosexual activities (including same sex marriages) are abominations in the sight of God'; and so on. It was even suggested that the Minister should apologise to God and the people of PNG over her moves to legalise prostitution and homosexuality.

There was little support. The *Post-Courier* of 9 November 2010 printed an explanatory letter from Dame Carol herself, together with the supporting views of the NACS Director, and the Editorial of that edition urged reason, presenting the arguments for both sides and welcoming the CLRC review. But that was all. The media appear to be highly selective in choosing what to print.[107] The anti-decriminalisation stories and letters have continued.

Categories and intersections

> [A] large and continuing project for subordinated people ... is thinking about the way power has clustered around certain categories and is exercised against others. This project attempts to unveil the processes of subordination and the various ways those processes are experienced by people who are subordinated and people who are privileged by them. It is, then, a project that presumes that categories have meaning and consequences. And this project's most pressing problem, in many if not most cases, is not the existence of the categories, but rather the particular values attached to them and the way those values foster and create social hierarchies.
>
> Kimberlé Crenshaw, 1991.[108]

The deployment of intersectionality

Kathy Davis claims that one of the reasons intersectionality theory is so popular is that it coincides with Foucauldian perspectives on power, through its focus on dynamic processes and the deconstruction of homogenous categories.[109] Those dominant in society create and maintain their superior position of power

---

107 Kidu, 'A national response to the HIV epidemic in Papua New Guinea'; field notes 12 November 2010.
108 Crenshaw, 'Mapping the margins,' 1296–97.
109 Kathy Davis, 2008, 'Intersectionality as buzzword: A sociology of science perspective on what makes a feminist theory successful,' *Feminist Theory* 9(1): 67–85, 71.

by imagining and stigmatising the outlawed. The illicit is necessary for the licit, the abnormal for normality, the unclean for the pure and moral.[110] This process must be ongoing if the dominant position is to be maintained, and when danger threatens, the dominant in society seek to expand the range of controls exerted over the outlaws who are perceived as the source of the threat.[111] Stigma and discrimination are not so much an individual practice as a social process, producing relations of power and control. Culturally constituted stigmatisation is essential to the establishment and maintenance of social order.[112]

Intersectionality theory explains how social control is produced. Cultural narratives imagine members of dominant and subordinate groups (for example, white middle-class women, being chaste and submissive, can be raped against their wills while African-American women, being sexual, autonomous and earthy, cannot). These narratives are then deployed to justify discrimination against members of the subordinate groups.

In PNG today, there is little dispute that men are dominant over women.[113] But neither of these gender groups is unitary. The understanding of each is always intermeshed with other social divisions, such as those of class, sexuality, place and so on, in a process which creates a multiplicity of understandings of manhood and womanhood.[114] To draw a comprehensive picture of the narratives of the PNG man and the PNG woman, the content and influence of these other divisions must be considered.

Class, which at its simplest is divided into *elites* and *grassroots*,[115] has emerged as one of the most significant social categories in the country today. In many ways, the *elites* are dominant, the *grassroots*, a conceptualised category created by the *elites* from a nation evincing extreme cultural diversity, are subordinate.[116] In

---

110 Richard Parker and Peter Aggleton, 2003, 'HIV and AIDS-related stigma and discrimination: a conceptual framework and implications for action,' *Social Science & Medicine* 57: 13–24, 14–17.
111 Catherine Campbell and Andrew Gibbs, 2009, 'Stigma, gender and HIV: case studies of intersectionality,' in *Gender and HIV/AIDS: Critical Perspectives from the Developing World*, ed. Jelke Boesten and Nana K. Poku, Farnham: Ashgate, 29–46, 32; following Mary Douglas, 1966, *Purity and Danger: An Analysis of the Concepts of Pollution and Taboo*, London: Routledge & Kegan Paul.
112 Parker and Aggleton, 'HIV and AIDS-related stigma and discrimination,' 17.
113 See for example the many chapters in Peter King, Wendy Lee and Vincent Warakai (eds), 1985, *From Rhetoric to Reality? Papua New Guinea's Eight Point Plan and National Goals after a Decade*, Waigani, Papua New Guinea: University of Papua New Guinea Press; and the many letters opposing the two-year-long battle for reserved seats for women in the almost totally male-dominated national parliament. First-stage legislation was finally passed late in 2011. See Eoin Blackwell, 2011, 'Activists welcome PNG women's bill,' *Sydney Morning Herald*, 23 November, online: http://news.smh.com.au/breaking-news-world/activists-welcome-png-womens-bill-20111123-1nue2.html, accessed 30 June 2014.
114 Yuval-Davis, 'Intersectionality and feminist politics,' 195.
115 See M. Goddard, 2005, *The Unseen City: Anthropological Perspectives on Port Moresby, Papua New Guinea*, Canberra: Pandanus Press, 50n8, where he explains that both terms, pluralised in Tok Pisin, lend themselves readily to singularisation, as an *elite* leader, a settlement-dwelling *grassroot*.
116 Laura Zimmer-Tamakoshi, 1993, 'Nationalism and sexuality in Papua New Guinea,' *Pacific Studies* 16(4): 61–97, 61.

2003, for example, a police officer was reported to have been 'surprised to learn from the media that a sex trade exists in Kokopo.... An SOS officer ... said there were reports of one-off incidents happening around town where women were selling their bodies for money. He said when one deals with people from the lower class, such situations occurred.'[117]

Considering that some of the earliest published reports of arrests for soliciting come from pre-Independence East New Britain, the surprise is to learn that these police officers claim to have become aware of the local sex trade for the first time. Nevertheless, it illustrates one of the predominant themes of the *elites'* constructions of the sex trade today. These women are the 'lower classes' from which a police officer wished to dissociate himself. Those involved in selling sex are somehow set apart from 'normal' people, occupying different places in society, visibly different, behaving in different ways, and automatically relegated to the 'lower class.' In the same vein, the *Post-Courier* Editorial quoted in Chapter 5 pontificated:

> prostitutes ... are often on the bottom rung of society's ladder and have few social or working skills to be able to climb higher in society.
>
> Usually, their prime task is to find money to feed and house themselves and the knowledge that they can satisfy those needs by selling their bodies comes before the 'finer things of life.'[118]

Within these class groupings, the dominant narrative of the *elites* is that of the male leader, successful in a range of enterprises;[119] that of the *grassroots* is of an honest, hardworking villager, respectful and observant of custom, a good Christian and member of his local community, the backbone of the country. Others within these groupings who fail to meet these standards are lacking in some way.

Culture is also a category of significance. Charges of lack of respect for cultural or traditional values are used in condemning 'badness' of various kinds. Culture also includes Christianity, as orator after orator, letter writer after letter writer, claim that 'PNG is a Christian nation,' ignoring the import of the precise wording of the *Constitution* which talks of 'our noble traditions and *the Christian principles* that are ours now [emphasis added].'[120] The 'good Christian' rhetoric adds a powerful dimension to the narratives of other categories. This

---

117 'Sex trade surprise,' 2003, *Post-Courier*, 28 March, 3.
118 Editorial, 2004, 'Give thought to rehabilitation,' *Post-Courier*, 15 March, 10.
119 Keir Martin, 2007, 'Your own *buai* you must buy: the ideology of possessive individualism in Papua New Guinea,' *Anthropological Forum* 17(3): 285–98; Joel Robbins, 2007, 'Afterword: possessive individualism and cultural change in the western Pacific,' *Anthropological Forum* 17(3): 299–308; Karen Sykes, 2007, 'Interrogating individuals: the theory of possessive individualism in the western Pacific,' *Anthropological Forum* 17(3): 213–24.
120 Preamble to the *Constitution*.

narrative is drawn from the perpetuation of much of the pre-Independence mission evangelisation carried out by the mainline churches, combined with the fundamentalist teachings of the 'new churches' (Pentecostal, charismatic, fundamentalist, Evangelical) which owe much of their inspiration to their largely North American origins.[121] So the dominant narrative of PNG Christianity is increasingly a fundamentalist one, of a God-fearing congregation dedicated to stamping out evil as defined by (sometimes self-ordained) church pastors and leaders. Reference is made to the Christian virtues of respect and obedience, the sinful sexuality of Sodom and Gomorrah, the abominations of Leviticus, and the decay of society's moral fabric, as it was in response to the announcement of Dame Carol's decriminalisation proposals.

With these significant features in mind, I can begin to describe the dominant, or idealised, narratives of man and woman in PNG today. Gender narratives have undergone a significant shift since Independence. In colonial times the 'native male' as constructed by the Australian colonists included features such as childishness, duplicity, laziness and lasciviousness.[122] But independence and modernity have changed that. Now the dominant group consists of PNG's political and business leaders, whether village or urban, *grassroots* or *elite*, who have reconstructed the patriarchal narrative to portray the PNG male as head of the household, prominent in the extended family and the clan, as well as in newer social networks such as work-groups and leisure activities.[123] The narrative of the PNG woman has undergone similar changes, but women today, whether *elite* or *grassroots*, remain subordinate, unable to participate fully in the construction of their own narratives. The complex intersections of race, class, kinship, culture and gender ensure that the *elites* must constantly strive to ensure that their dominant position is maintained. As Foucault reminds us, constant resistance ensures that no power relations are simple.[124] The *elites* may make the laws, determine social policies, publish the newspapers, but this power is tempered by the threat of subaltern resistance. All PNG *elites* are to varying extents obliged to assuage the jealousies of their village and urban *wantoks*, both directly through prestations and indirectly through adapting their viewpoints to reflect grassroots mores.

---

121 Franco Zocca, 2007, *Melanesia and its Churches: Past and Present*, Goroka, PNG: Melanesian Institute, 200–201.
122 Wolfers, *Race Relations and Colonial Rule;* and for a valiant attempt to the contrary, Charles Rowley, 1966, *The New Guinea Villager: The Impact of Colonial Rule on Primitive Society and Economy*, New York: Praeger; for sexuality features see, Amirah Inglis, 1974, *'Not a White Woman Safe': Sexual Anxiety and Politics in Port Moresby, 1920–1934*, Canberra: Australian National University Press; and Jean G. Zorn, 2010, 'The paradoxes of sexism: proving rape in the Papua New Guinea courts,' *LAWASIA Journal* 2010: 17–58.
123 Bruce M. Knauft, 1997, 'Gender identity, political economy and modernity in Melanesia and Amazonia,' *Journal of the Royal Anthropological Institute* 3(2): 233–59, 250.
124 Michel Foucault, 1982, 'The subject and power,' *Critical Inquiry* 8(4): 777–95.

Good mother, bad *pamuk*

Much intersectionality scholarship in the West has focused on the dominant narrative of 'woman' as white, middle-class, chaste, passive.[125] But the dominant narrative of the 'good woman' in PNG differs in some respects. White colonial women were classically constructed by their menfolk as respectable, passionless and fragile,[126] contrasted in every possible way to indigenous PNG women, who were considered at the time to be irresponsible, poor mothers, sexually unrestrained and ever-available.[127] The decolonisation period brought a shift, both in action and narratives. As the emerging PNG *elites* started to supplant such narratives, they re-cast colonial women as 'extreme racists and domestic bullies.' At the same time, progressive white women who allied themselves with nationalist political struggles and social improvement programmes were rejecting the practice of hiring black men to perform 'demeaning' domestic work, and socialising with them, even taking them as lovers. But rather than being hailed as heroines, these women often encountered hostility and abuse from Papua New Guineans.[128] The construction of these white women as loose and sexually available continued into the post-Independence era, while PNG women, as expected, 'follow[ed] their gender roles into occupying the private spaces vacated by colonial women.'[129] They have also been affected by the influences of modernity, but in contradistinction to men, whose status depends on constraining women's sexuality and limiting their access to non-traditional cultural and economic relationships,[130] women themselves were reconstructed as hardworking *grassroots* village dwellers, modest, pure, unassertive, who observe and uphold custom.[131] Age is a factor, requiring unmarried girls to be

---

125 Crenshaw, 'Demarginalising the intersection of race and sex,' especially 155–57; Denis, 'Intersectional analysis,' 679.
126 Inglis, *'Not a White Woman Safe'*, 14; Adam Reed, 1997, 'Contested images and common strategies: early colonial sexual politics in the Massim,' in *Sites of Desire, Economies of Pleasure: Sexualities in Asia and the Pacific*, ed. Lenore Manderson and Margaret Jolly. Chicago: University of Chicago Press, 48–71, 66; P. Reid, 2005, 'Whiteness as goodness: white women in PNG and Australia, 1960's to the present,' Ph.D. thesis, Brisbane: Griffith University, 74. Trish Reid notes that progressive white women in PNG's decolonising period constructed and lived disloyalty to that narrative. Amirah Inglis relates how such rebellions had taken place for decades, though not to the extent practised in the immediate pre-Independence period.
127 Inglis, *'Not a White Woman Safe'*; Adam Reed, 'Contested images and common strategies.'
128 P. Reid, 'Whiteness as goodness.'
129 Anne Dickson-Waiko, 2010, *Taking Over, of What and From Whom? Women and Independence, the PNG Experience*, Report for Deakin University, Geelong VIC: Alfred Deakin Research Institute, 8.
130 Bruce M. Knauft, 1997, 'Gender identity, political economy and modernity in Melanesia and Amazonia,' *Journal of the Royal Anthropological Institute* 3(2): 233–59, 250.
131 Pamela Rosi and Laura Zimmer-Tamakoshi, 1993, 'Love and marriage among the educated elite in Port Moresby,' in *The Business of Marriage: Transformations in Oceanic Matrimony*, ed. Richard A. Marksbury, ASAO Monograph No.14, Pittsburgh and London: University of Pittsburgh Press, 175–204; Zimmer-Tamakoshi, 'Nationalism and sexuality in Papua New Guinea.' Needless to say, such narratives bear little relation to the reality of a vast range of local, ethnic and other differences. See Martha Macintyre, 1998, 'The persistence of inequality: women in Papua New Guinea since Independence,' in *Modern Papua New Guinea*, ed. Laura Zimmer-Tamakoshi, Kirksville, MO: Thomas Jefferson University Press, 211–30, 214.

chaste virgins,[132] and grown women to be married, monogamous and maternal. Stress is laid on the core values of Christianity and motherhood—the standard term now used by the media and in everyday parlance for PNG women is 'mothers.' Elis Onda, a married Highlands village-dweller, was vilified through massive public outcry for having drowned her four children and attempting to drown herself in mid-2009 as a result, she claimed, of her husband's drug-taking and neglect. The 'shocked' local MP said, 'the mother should be put to death … she was not fit to live in this world … she is worse than an animal and should not live in our society.'[133]

Similarly, a report of young single women in desperate circumstances selling their babies at the market in Kokopo in East New Britain brought the furious response from the town mayor that it was 'illegal and against Christian teachings and principles … a cheap and fast way of getting rid of the infants.… He condemned this type of business which he described as immoral and portrayed total disrespect for the souls of the newborns.'[134]

By contrast, the fatal assault in 2009 by police on a woman selling sex in Lae barely elicited public comment;[135] reports of the sexual abuse by men of daughters, nieces and grandchildren often appear, unaccompanied by any similar outcry; while men abandon women and their children frequently and are only penalised to the extent of being required to pay maintenance, and then only if the deserted woman is able to mount a successful court case.[136]

The educated urban woman of today is having a hard time of it. She is transgressing accepted gender roles.[137] Laura Zimmer-Tamakoshi argues that (male) *elites* have created the myth of the selfless, obedient village woman to counter threats to male dominance from educated, urbanised women, many of whom come from coastal and island communities where matriliny is common and traditions of employment and education well-established.[138] Such women

---

132 Social standards for unmarried Trobriand girls are a notable exception in some respects, although girls are still expected to conform to cultural expectations. See Katherine Lepani, 2012, *Islands of Love, Islands of Risk: Culture and HIV in the Trobriands*, Nashville, TN: Vanderbilt University Press.
133 James Apa Gumono, 2009, 'Kids killed: Mum tells cops she drowned children as hubby failed to look after them,' *National* (online), 6 July; and numerous other newspaper reports from July 2009, many contributors (both men and women) lamenting the slaughter of the 'little angels' labelling it 'a heinous crime' and calling for the death penalty for Onda's 'crimes against humanity.'
134 Evah Kuamin, 2010, 'Single mothers sell newborns at Kokopo market,' *National* (online), 23 August.
135 Franco Nebas and Frank Rai, 2009, 'Sex worker bashed to death,' *Post-Courier* (online), 13 May.
136 Under the *Deserted Wives and Children Act* 1951. On 11 April 2006, while interviewing the late Lady Hilan Los, CEO of the NGO ICRAF, I watched floods of women discussing proposed maintenance cases with the one paralegal officer on duty. I was told that maintenance cases formed the bulk of ICRAF's court work. I have no idea of the success rate of these cases.
137 Ceridwen Spark, 2010, 'Changing lives: understanding the barriers that confront educated women in Papua New Guinea,' *Australian Feminist Studies* 25(63): 17–30; Ceridwen Spark, 2011, 'Educated women in PNG: who are they today?' Paper presented at the Symposium PNG Today—and Tomorrow, Deakin University, 27 May.
138 Laura Zimmer-Tamakoshi, 1993, 'Nationalism and sexuality in Papua New Guinea,' *Pacific Studies* 16(4): 61–97.

are thereby marginalised, their aspirations are suppressed, the divide between rural and urban educated women is exacerbated and women's nationalist movements are sabotaged. *Elite* men may elect to marry women of lower status simply to affirm their status and power—either way, wives must suffer husbands' infidelities and neglect.

An illustration of a woman's attempt to portray the modern woman comes from a letter in early 2009, in response to a call for applications for three women to be nominated to Parliament, which proposed that:

> Nominee must be a very well educated PNG woman. At this time and age, we need parliamentarians who can read between the lines, who can articulate issues, and who can understand the modern language of development, and are able to communicate effectively in this modern world.
>
> Nominee must be a PNG woman that is a good role model with basic understanding of the differing views of PNG cultures. In addition, she is a wife, and a mother. Select a woman who understands the importance of family and her role in the family. It is also important to select a married woman who values her matrimonial vows, whether her marriage is through customary or statutory means, and this marriage is recognised in the community.
>
> Nominee must not be a woman who has caused disharmony, pain and family problems by her acts of adultery and fornication against other women folk in local communities
>
> Nominee is a PNG woman who regards personal integrity to be of importance in society. That criteria have proven to enable individuals to be very good persons/leaders that are able to differentiate between what is right and wrong.[139]

In relation to the same issues, another woman letter writer called for, 'women with qualifications and knowledgeable, women with quality leadership, women with hearts for the people, women with good heart and intentions, strong cultural values with Christian principles and mothers at heart.'[140]

---

139   Theresa Kas, 2009, 'Give women a fair go for 2012 elections,' *Post-Courier*, 28 January. These same sentiments were later echoed in a letter by Aspiring wife politician,' 2011, 'Gender and politics are different,' *National* (online), 5 October.
140   Aspiring wife politician, 2011, 'Gender and politics – two different issues,' *Post-Courier* (online), 1 September.

The educated working woman is resented on many fronts: she is economically independent, and may be accused of taking jobs from educated male high-school drop-outs.[141] Maybe, if she is sufficiently humble and unassertive, she may gain a measure of credibility, as one letter writer opined that

> there are two kinds of women, moral and immoral.... Moral women with Proverbs 31 characteristics are ones that should enter parliament as they will be God-fearing and would have the god's given wisdom to help govern the nation. God says such women are hard to find as they work in humility unnoticed.... God's strategy is in the book of Ester, We have many Esthers busy working today in various strategic positions in Ministries, Government Department, private sector, NGOs and community levels, advising and making positive impacts unnoticed.... When these ladies go to the polls in this male dominant society in prayer and faith, God willing they will win the elections to enter parliament.[142]

The breach of almost any of the dimensions of the narrative of the multiply subordinated category of 'good' woman are capable of rendering her 'bad.' At the village and *grassroots* level, evidence of promiscuity even after the death or desertion of a husband can render her liable to imprisonment by an all-male Village Court.[143] If a PNG woman is urban-dwelling, if she asserts her autonomy in any way, if she is educated, single, employed in the formal workforce or otherwise supporting herself financially, then her degradation is inevitable.[144] The 'good village woman' narrative persists, despite signs that a critical mass of tertiary-educated women has been emerging over the past two decades.[145] The breach of the submissiveness quality is a strong factor in 'female' badness. The individualisation of modern female agency poses huge threats to male insecurities.[146] So the 'bad' urbanised, educated, financially independent, smartly-dressed woman is condemned for campaigning against domestic

---

141   Macintyre, 'The persistence of inequality,' 221.
142   Friendly & caring citizen, 2010, 'Unwise creation,' *Post-Courier* (online), 29 December.
143   Jean G. Zorn, 1994–1995, 'Women, custom and state law in Papua New Guinea,' *Third World Legal Studies* 13(7): 169–205, online: http://scholar.valpo.edu/twls/vol13/iss1/7, accessed 11 April 2014, discussing *Re Wagi Non and Section 42(5) of the Constitution* [1991] PNGLR 84; see also *Re Kaka Ruk and Section 42(5) of the Constitution* [1991] PNGLR 105; *In the Matter of Kepo Raramu and in the Matter of Yowe Village Court* [1994] PNGLR 486; *In the Matter of Kopa Kaipia and in the Matter of Constitution Section 42 (5)* (Unreported) N709(M) 10 May 1989.
144   Zimmer-Tamakoshi, 'Nationalism and sexuality in Papua New Guinea'; Rosi and Zimmer-Tamakoshi, 'Love and marriage among the educated elite in Port Moresby'; Spark, 'Changing lives'; and for the non-urbanised and uneducated woman, see Wardlow, *Wayward Women*.
145   Dickson-Waiko, *Taking Over, of What and From Whom?*; Spark, 'Changing lives.'
146   Knauft, 'Gender identity, political economy and modernity in Melanesia and Amazonia,' 250; Bruce M. Knauft 2007, 'Moral exchange and exchanging morals: alternative paths of cultural change in Papua New Guinea,' in *The Anthropology of Morality in Melanesia and Beyond*, ed. John Barker, Aldershot: Ashgate Publishing Ltd., 59–73, 73; Bruce M. Knauft, 2011, 'Men, modernity and Melanesia,' in *Echoes of the Tambaran: Masculinity, History and the Subject in the Work of Donald F. Tuzin*, ed. David Lipset and Paul Roscoe, Canberra: ANU E Press, 103–14, 105, online: http://press.anu.edu.au?p=146101, accessed 10 April 2014.

violence and rape,[147] or being so non-submissive as to advocate the provision of special women's seats in Parliament, notwithstanding the attempt to rationalise the process in the letter above.[148] Even Bernard Narokobi, champion of human rights, thought that modern Melanesian women did not need 'women's lib' because they were already liberated, in that they wore make-up and mini-skirts, but then conceded that in other respects, (the surely more important matter of political power, for example, or the right to speak out in public) they could not and should not assert themselves.[149]

Worst of all is the prostitute. Autonomy was one of the earliest features by which public discourse distinguished the prostitute from the 'good' woman. In Sir Rabbie Namaliu's play penned and performed in the 1970s, entitled with fine irony *The Good Woman of Konedobu*, the woman in question is discovered in a city bar, insisting that the men who approach her buy her drinks and cigarettes, and she lives in her own flat in town, where the final scene of humiliation of the country boy come to town takes place.[150]

The prostitute today is automatically presumed to be female, and 'from the lower class,' as the Kokopo policeman said, and as the *Post-Courier* Editor noted in his comment on the Three-Mile Guesthouse Raid, when he described those charged as being 'on the bottom rung of society's ladder [with] few social or working skills to be able to climb higher in society,' destined to become the 'inevitable dregs of hospital wards … among those anonymous carcasses to be bulldozed into mass graves.'[151] She has abandoned her village, her kin and her reproductivity to survive by taking ownership of her own sexuality. She is non-submissive and above all promiscuous. It is in the inflection of the gender narrative of woman by these dimensions of sexuality and assertiveness that I locate the answer to my question about *elite* women's reactions to the abused woman who turns to selling sex. Those who represent the dominant narrative in any group are often the most eager to assert their superior place in the social hierarchy. So women 'leaders' may be the first to condemn subordinated sex sellers. The president of the PNG National Council of Women, for example, responded to Dame Carol's 2005 proposal to legalise brothels by begging:

---

147 When the Law Reform Commission's Interim Report on domestic violence was first presented to Parliament in 1987, it created an uproar amongst male members, as I was informed when I joined the Commission in late 1989; and see Law Reform Commission of Papua New Guinea, 1992, *Report No. 14: Final Report on Domestic Violence*, Boroko: Law Reform Commission of Papua New Guinea, 9.
148 This move has been strongly promoted by Dame Carol Kidu for some years now.
149 Narokobi, *The Melanesian Way*, 70–74.
150 Namaliu, *The Good Woman of Konedobu*. I had the good fortune to see the first performance of this play at UPNG, with the Good Woman played by one of PNG's most famous women, Dame Meg Taylor, costumed in mini-skirt and bright blue eye-shadow.
151 Editorial, 2004, 'Give thought to rehabilitation,' *Post-Courier* (online), 15 March.

> Do not tolerate unchristian practices and beliefs to rot this country … the real value of sex, marriage and family will be lost forever.… PNG must be conscious about its strong traditional and cultural values … prostitutes or *'raun raun (pamuk) meri/man'* are regarded as animals.… Strip tease is against our societal norms and customs … it's a corrupt act that leads to evil acts of adultery and fornication.[152]

The outcast woman may retain society's sympathy if she is the victim of domestic violence, even if she demonstrates a lack of fidelity and submissiveness in leaving a violent marriage. But if she exercises too much autonomy, if she assumes responsibility for her body and her financial independence by selling sex, she becomes bad. She may yet be saved, but only if she leaves the sex trade, adopts a socially acceptable income-earning strategy and becomes a 'good woman.'[153] Good women—not just women leaders, but any good Christian housewife— are doubly threatened. Her own marriage and livelihood is at risk through the possibilities of her husband's infidelities of whatever kind. The family income may be applied not only to drink and gambling but to the purchase of sex as well. Little wonder that they are so vocal in retaining the criminalisation of sex selling, and of chastising those who sell it.

This good/bad narrative was reflected in both *Anna Wemay's Case* and *Monika Jon's Case*. Justice Wilson in *Anna Wemay's Case* was totally convinced by the bad woman stereotype, carried over from colonial times. His choice of language (allying 'the prostitute' with 'the madam, the tout, the bully, the protector or the pimp') was emotionally charged. He refused to accept any evidence of the newly independent state's expressed desire to alter that narrative, and constructed his own legal reasoning to ensure that the classic stereotype was continued into the post-Independence era.

---

152 'Women group slams plans to legalise brothels,' 2005, *National* (online), 10 August.
153 For example, 'Sex workers learn,' 2009, *Post-Courier* (online), 12 November. Stories such as this, which joyfully relates how thirty sex workers were trained for a week in everything from 'cooking, baking, screen printing to tie dying, flower arrangement to gender-based violence training,' often appear in the press.

Figure 6.2. 'Good or Bad? – a cartoon from 1981. The caption reads 'Yes, this brothel idea is no good. If they do start one, where will the good women like us find any men?'

Source: *Post-Courier*, 21 December 1981, 2.

In *Monika Jon's Case*, however, Acting Justice Narokobi was more restrained.[154] He agreed only partially with the bad-woman stereotype, when he created a distinction between the mythical 'real' prostitute and the good *tukina bus meri*, and exonerated the latter.[155] Narokobi was a staunch supporter of all that smacked of 'village' and custom,[156] and this is what saved the appellants. He imagined them as essentially 'good' *grassroots* village-style women (using the term *tukina bus*) who had temporarily lapsed, or in the case of Kuragi Ku, had simply carried out a quasi-customary form of protest at the behaviour of an errant husband. The real criminals are the 'prostitutes' whom he imagined as

---

154 Bernard Narokobi, 1980, *The Melanesian Way: Total Cosmic Vision of Life*, Boroko: Institute of Papua New Guinea Studies.
155 Narokobi affirmed this distinction in interview with me, Auckland, 16 November 2005.
156 Narokobi, *The Melanesian Way*.

'those who make it a habit or a regular practice of living either wholly or in part on the earnings of prostitution,' who say, 'every Friday, I would go and earn for myself.'

The 'mother' factor plays a part in the construction of sex sellers as 'bad.'[157] The dumping of a dead baby was quickly attributed to a 'known sex worker':

> The woman who allegedly dumped her new-born in a storm water drain at Erima, Port Moresby, has been identified by police as a known sex worker. Less than a week after disposing her baby with the umbilical cord and placenta still intact, police tracked her to a nightclub in Port Moresby, where she had been seen allegedly plying her trade again ... an apparent barbaric act.[158]

The rhetoric in the Sepik 'sex ring' incident described above changed very rapidly from that surrounding the prosecution of prostitutes to one of sympathy for imagined 'poor young mothers striving daily to raise their "fatherless" children,' when the foreign loggers' contracts ended and they left the country.[159]

One of the women caught up in the Three-Mile Guesthouse Raid deployed the term successfully:

> I was marketing *buai* and smoke outside of the guesthouse gate.... I brought my son to the laundry and was showering him ... they [police] brought condoms and distributed them to everyone except me as my son was all the time in my hands with me.... I joined hands with my son on my shoulders and we walked along the streets.... I was asked to swallow condom but I told the policeman I am mother and how can I swallow condom so I did not (Miriam).

Sex seller groups generally have recently attempted to reclaim the valorised status of hapless victim accorded to battered wives by styling themselves 'problem mothers'—mothers with problems. Problem mothers are laying a claim to the universality described by Crenshaw, saying, first of all, that they are one with all worthy PNG women, but they are unable to conform totally due to the problems they confront. These problems have categorised them in a way that is merely 'contingent, circumstantial, nondeterminant.'[160] They have created a name for themselves which is designed to elicit the same sympathy as the battered wives from whom they have been distinguished.

---

157 Anne Dickson-Waiko reminds us, however, that the construction of women as gendered beings has worked against their acceptance as full citizens of the post-colonial state, hence much of the opposition to reserved women's seats in Parliament. See Dickson-Waiko, 'The missing rib,' 101–02.
158 Bonney Bonsella, 2006, 'Sex worker dumped baby: Police track mum to nightclub barely a week after incident,' *National* (online), 6 February.
159 Gabriel Fito, 2010, 'Sex-for-sale case hit snag,' *National* (online), 20 February.
160 Crenshaw, 'Mapping the margins,' 1297.

The sex seller's clients however, always presumed to be male,[161] are not similarly stigmatised. It is not essential that PNG men be monogamous and faithful—rather, excessive displays of potency are excused, even admired, and their purchase of sex passes unremarked (except, probably, by their wives): 'the men who trade money for sex are protected and their involvement is not foregrounded in the discussions about prostitution. In other words, women's involvement in the trade is highlighted, but the men's involvement is almost invisible. Here women are seen as the inferior, immoral "Other."'[162]

Man tru, rabis man

The dominant narrative of the PNG man, *man tru* as Anastasia Sai terms him,[163] is productive and hardworking; has ready access to resources which he shares appropriately; he is physically and mentally strong and protective of his immediate family, extended family and other kin.[164] His prestige depends increasingly on the acquisition of cash and commodities. He is heteronormative, married, potent and paternal; sexual infidelity is permitted him to varying degrees depending on such factors as status and locale,[165] and in this he is supported by the law which recognises customary marriages including polygyny.[166]

However, a man who breaches any essential feature of the masculine norm (as constructed by successful married men) stands to be rendered worthless, a *rabis man*.[167] If he is not strong or productive, and does not share, he is *rabis man*. If

---

161 Hence the public amazement at news of research which has shown that women may also be clients of sex sellers.
162 Anastasia Sai, 2007, '*Tamot*: masculinities in transition in Papua New Guinea,' Ph.D. thesis, Melbourne: Victoria University, 61–62. Unfortunately, although Sai realised that the men netted in the Three-Mile Guesthouse Raid were set free, she continued to believe that it was because they were male sex workers. Had she realised that many were purchasing sex, it would have strengthened her argument.
163 Ibid.
164 See Kenelm Burridge, 1960, *Mambu: A Melanesian Millennium*, London: Methuen, 75, 108–11; Sai, '*Tamot*,' 160, for a more nuanced description of the urban *elite* man's view of the ideal man, whom she terms *man tru*; and Holly Wardlow, 2009, 'Whip him in the head with a stick!' in *The Secret: Love, Marriage, and HIV*, ed. Jennifer S. Hirsch et al., Nashville, TN: Vanderbilt University Press, 136–67, 146–47, 155 for a rural equivalent, which nevertheless takes the urbanised wealthy man as the ideal to be emulated.
165 Wardlow, 'Whip him in the head with a stick!'
166 The *Marriage Act* 1963 Section 3, which recognises all forms of customary marriage. Unfortunately, the proviso that the marriage must be 'in accordance with the custom prevailing in the tribe or group to which the parties to the marriage or either of them belong or belongs' and other customary conditions such as co-wives' permission (e.g., Alome Kyakas and Polly Wiessner, 1992, *From Inside the Women's House: Enga Women's Lives and Traditions*, Buranda, Qld: Robert Brown & Associates (Qld) Pty Ltd., 153–60) have become increasingly ignored, to the extent that multiple 'wives' have become the order of the day among men of all classes and locales.
167 Sai, '*Tamot*.'

he is lacking in adequate social relationships, he is *rabis man*.¹⁶⁸ Criminals are regarded (by *elite* men, at least) as *rabis man*, but may redeem themselves by sharing with their immediate community.¹⁶⁹

Male sexuality is of utmost significance. While a man loses little status through promiscuity, whether or not the sex is purchased, he stands to lose a good deal if he is found to have breached the dimension of heteronormativity. MP Sali's political career was ruined when he was publicly exposed as having engaged in homosexual activities, even though the police case was never proven and an enquiry exonerated him, while Sir Pita Lus was able to continue a long and distinguished career in Parliament despite the allegations, at the same time, of his having had sex with an under-aged girl; there is very little wrong seen in a leader having sex with a female minor. An *elite* man may even lose status from mere allegations of homosexual conduct. The students who rioted in the Kerevat Affair were reported to be protesting against the mere possibility of their being labelled gay,¹⁷⁰ even though little was actually said in the press about the sexuality of PNG students involved. The reportage of the Kerevat Affair was focused mainly on the race factor, and although debate revolved largely around the professional integrity or otherwise of expatriate teachers, it turned out that the main and enduring concern of their (expatriate) opponents, writing a year later, was the homosexual proclivities of those teachers. They wrote of the 'administrative and moral corruption in the Education Department,' and related how

> homosexual abuse of students by male expatriates remains widespread … two of our students [at Kerevat] became mentally instable and violent following interference by homosexuals—one had to be expelled, and the other had to be jailed and then went home.… The roots of the problem lie at Education Department headquarters. The small group of senior expatriates remaining from colonial days operate as they wish.¹⁷¹

So great, in fact, is the fear of exposure as a gay that *elite* gays remain firmly in the closet. Exposure can ruin a national parliamentarian's career and visit brutal punishment on an activist such as Victor. The need for *elite* gays to dissemble is even greater than for the *grassroots*. So Henry explained that gays on the streets, jobless, are not harassed, but a PNG gay with a university degree and a good job will 'be treated like an expatriate.' If he is caught by the police, he claims to be a jobless grade school dropout, otherwise 'they'll want to get something

---

168   Joel Robbins, 1994, 'Equality as a value: ideology in Dumont, Melanesia and the West,' *Social Analysis* 36: 21–70, 38–39.
169   Sinclair Dinnen, 2001, *Law and Order in a Weak State: Crime and Politics in Papua New Guinea*, Adelaide: University of Hawai'i Press and Crawford House Publishing, 79.
170   Ombudsman Commission, *Final Report on the Kerevat National High School Enquiry*.
171   Mendzela and Mendzela, 'Kerevat: the lesson wasn't learnt,' 4.

out of me' (Henry). Another gay, a teacher, told me that no gay in PNG would dare to speak out publicly for gay rights, even in the face of evidence that this would support HIV prevention efforts, for fear of retaliation. He approved the suggestion that I as a woman should support decriminalisation work. So it was *grassroots* gays who were most willing to give me interviews, while those which I obtained from *elite* gays were arranged covertly through their personal networks.

Even less comment was made to me about 'ritual homosexuality,' and in fact it is seldom discussed today, except by anthropologists.[172] A Papua New Guinean wrote from Wabag in Enga in relation to the aftermath of the Kerevat Affair scolding another writer from Goroka for claiming that homosexuality 'was not a new thing, it was not introduced, it has been part of our society.' He continued: 'All I want is the good culture of Papua New Guinea and not the bad practice of yours to be exposed.'[173]

This makes sense if ritual homosexuality is seen not as a matter of homoerotic sexuality, but as part of male bonding and the male gender narrative of deference to custom: many practices of ritual homosexuality involved practices such as the transfer of semen (and other substances) from grown men to boys to make men of them.[174]

As Justice Wilson did in describing the sex trade, Justice Prentice displayed a voyeuristic fascination with language in his judgement in the Full Court case *R v M.K.* 'Buggery,' he said, 'is traditionally hedged about with pejorative adverbs and adjectives in statutes, and in indictments alleging its achievement. I cite one old form … "did permit and suffer the said—feloniously, wickedly, diabolically and against the order of nature to have a venereal affair with him and then … to carnally know him."'

He was merely following in the footsteps of a long line of white male colonists in his choice of 'pejorative adverbs and adjectives.' But was it really necessary so to indulge himself in the course of handing down a decision on appeal? Judges are, after all, supposed to decide cases 'based solely on reason and logic. Emotion, bias, prejudice and the judge's own personal values are presumed to play no part

---

172 Bruce Knauft, 2003, 'What ever happened to ritualized homosexuality? Modern sexual subjects in Melanesia and elsewhere,' *Annual Review of Sex Research* 14: 137–59. Only one reference was made to me in interviews—the overwhelming majority claimed that, while growing up, each thought he was alone in the world.
173 'Getting a bad name,' 1983, *Post-Courier*, 17 February, 4.
174 Knauft, 'Gender identity, political economy and modernity in Melanesia and Amazonia'; Gilbert Herdt, 1984, *Ritualized Homosexuality in Melanesia*, Berkeley, CA: University of California Press; Deborah A. Elliston, 1995, 'Erotic anthropology: "ritualized homosexuality" in Melanesia and beyond,' *American Ethnologist* 22(4): 848–67; Carol Jenkins, 2004, 'Male sexuality, diversity and culture: implications for HIV prevention and care,' unpublished report prepared for UNAIDS, Geneva, online: http://www.popline.org/node/264909, accessed 7 July 2014.

... the applicable rules are supposed to be applied equally to everyone, regardless of power relations based upon socio-economic class, or race, or gender.'[175] This judge seems to have let his emotions, biases, prejudices and personal values suffuse his reasoned decision.

The alleged 'male prostitutes' caught up in the Three-Mile Guesthouse Raid posed a dilemma to political leaders. The suggestion of homoeroticism undermined their status as PNG males. But this could not be proved, only inferred from the fact that they were selling sex—presumably to other men.[176] And as they were males, the promiscuity inherent in selling sex was not a factor which could render them 'bad.' Only women could commit the offence of prostitution, and these were not women—or were they? The solution to the dilemma was to reclassify them as female, and to call for their 'equal right' to be treated as criminals, without human rights.[177]

The case of Moses Tau and the invitation to sing at the funeral of Prime Minister Skate in 2006 is also a puzzle. One explanation of the fact that his overtly gay identity did not render him 'bad' is that by the time of the funeral, several years after his solo career began, his immense popularity as a singer and his unmitigated efforts at outreach work had made of him something of a national icon, a celebrity in his own right, and this afforded him considerable protection.[178] It helped, too, that he was working at Parliament House at the time (albeit in a somewhat humble clerical position) and was well known to the leaders of the nation. And finally, it was fitting that he should publicly mourn the passing of the Prime Minister who, as representative of a Port Moresby electorate consisting largely of formal and informal settlements, had constructed himself as a 'man of the people' and emphasised his *grassroots* background in his 1997 election campaign. As Michael Goddard observes, 'The potential of the obverse, positive meaning added to those already existing in the simplistic imagery of settlements appropriated from European usage cannot be overlooked.'[179]

It seems that Moses Tau enjoyed a similar 'obverse, positive' image. Or perhaps his position is better explained as one of what Ratna Kapur terms the resistive

---

175 Zorn, 'The paradoxes of sexism,' 24.
176 At this stage, evidence of men selling sex to women had not yet been published: see Angela Kelly et al., 2011, Askim na Save *(Ask and Understand): People who Sell and/or Exchange Sex in Port Moresby*, Sydney: Papua New Guinea Institute of Medical Research and the University of New South Wales; and Holly Buchanan et al., 2010, *Behavioural Surveillance Research in Rural Development Enclaves in Papua New Guinea: A Study with the WR Carpenters Workforce*, Port Moresby: National Research Institute.
177 See also Stewart, '"Crime to be a woman?"' where I develop this argument about re-gendering.
178 In 2010, a highly placed bureaucrat shot and killed a national football star in an altercation outside a nightclub. Despite the bureaucrat's high status and strong connections to the government of the time, he was condemned by all commentators, arrested and refused bail. National icons are not to be messed with!
179 M. Goddard, 2001, 'From rolling thunder to reggae: imagining squatter settlements in Papua New Guinea,' *Contemporary Pacific* 13(1): 1–32, 19.

subject.[180] Kapur warns of the dangers of essentialising both subject positions and social groups. But a resistive subject, poised on the periphery, can challenge normative stereotypes and may open up a space for others. 'Where there is power, there is resistance,' Foucault claims, but resistances are part of power, 'mobile and transitory points of resistance, producing cleavages in a society that shift about, fracturing unities and effecting regroupings, furrowing across individuals themselves, cutting them up and remolding them ... the swarm of points of resistance traverses social stratifications and individual unities.'[181]

In participating in the Sydney Mardi Gras as a 'Pacific Queen' and in initiating drag shows Moses not only provided a safe space for gay and transgender performance. He was also challenging the dominant cultural and gender stereotypes of contemporary PNG society and opening a space for others to follow suit. Then he moved on to use his star status and his songs to promote awareness about gay rights, HIV, the dangers of consuming drugs, and other social issues. He is one of PNG's best examples of successful resistance to stigmatising norms.

Conclusions

Intersectionality theory has provided some answers to many of the questions that have troubled me throughout the process of writing this book. My survey of media and other documents through which social representations of the sex trade and male-male sex have been identified and described has displayed clear trends in the formation of the *elites'* arguments, opinions and beliefs. By delineating the categories of identity, experience and analysis formed by law, politics and social action in PNG, by identifying the narratives attaching to the social groups and sub-groups within those categories, I have reached some understanding of the ways by which those dominant in PNG society today have created and maintained the set of social norms through which members of outgroups are imagined and stigmatised—norms which are shored up by the law, and simultaneously dictate the content and direction of the law. Categories and the narratives within them are essentialised, and it is in this essentialising process that norms gain their strength.

In the concluding chapter, I sum up the results of my research: the adverse effects of society's stigmatisation of sexually marginalised groups and the theoretical approaches I have taken to try to understand the societal forces which have produced these effects. I attempt to evaluate the chances of successful

---

180   Ratna Kapur, 2002, 'The tragedy of victimization rhetoric: resurrecting the "native" subject in international/post-colonial feminist legal politics,' *Harvard Human Rights Journal* 15: 1–37, 29–34.
181   Foucault, *The Will to Knowledge: The History of Sexuality Vol. 1*, 95–96.

decriminalisation and the means by which it might be attained, and pose the crucial question: given all of the above, what are the chances of success for decriminalisation, as urged by international opinion and by reformers within the country?

7. Where to Now?

> I urge all countries to remove punitive laws, policies and practices that hamper the AIDS response.... Successful AIDS responses do not punish people; they protect them.... In many countries, legal frameworks institutionalize discrimination against groups most at risk. Yet discrimination against sex workers, drug users and men who have sex with men only fuels the epidemic and prevents cost-effective interventions. We must ensure that AIDS responses are based on evidence, not ideology, and reach those most in need and most affected.
>
> Ban Ki-moon, United Nations Secretary-General, 2009.[1]

In this concluding chapter, I turn to questioning whether law reform would make a difference to social attitudes. This is the question Ryan Goodman asked himself as he embarked on his South African work. He learned that, yes, even when punitive laws are not enforced, they affect people's attitudes to those criminalised, but that with decriminalisation these attitudes begin to change. I thought it was not too much to hope that decriminalisation might have the same outcome in Papua New Guinea (PNG).

In Chapter 3, I referred briefly to the ancient English case of 1584, *Heydon's Case*, which sets out the parameters for reform of the common law, as

> for the sure and true interpretation of all statutes in general (be they penal or beneficial, restrictive or enlarging of the common law) four things are to be discerned and considered:
>
> 1st. What was the common law before the making of the Act.
>
> 2nd. What was the mischief and defect for which the common law did not provide.
>
> 3rd. What remedy the Parliament hath resolved and appointed to cure the disease of the commonwealth.
>
> And, 4th. The true reason of the remedy;
>
> and then the office of all the Judges is always to make such construction as shall suppress the mischief, and advance the remedy, and to suppress

---

[1] United Nations Secretary-General's message for World AIDS Day, 30 November 2009, online: http://www.un.org/News/Press/docs/2009/sgsm12638.doc.htm, accessed 23 August 2011.

subtle inventions and evasions for continuance of the mischief, and *pro privato commodo*, and to add force and life to the cure and remedy, according to the true intent of the makers of the Act, *pro bono publico*.

News of the Three-Mile Guesthouse Raid first alerted me to the 'mischief.' People were suffering, and it seemed to me that one of the reasons was a defect in the law. The police and the bystanders were able to do as they did because they believed that their actions were legitimised by criminalising laws. I also recalled my regret that the PNG Law Reform Commission's research into sexual offences, particularly the sodomy offence, had never been completed. I felt it incumbent on me to 'discern and consider' the possibility of a defect in the law which, if found, might be remedied by law reform.

I posed myself several questions. Is decriminalisation necessary? Do those criminalised by such laws really suffer ill-effects? If so, how much can be blamed on criminalising laws? Do these laws have any effect at all on community attitudes, or are other influences at work? What form do the laws take and how did they achieve their present form? Given that the attitudes and sexual practices of many traditional PNG communities differed greatly from those reflected in the sexuality laws introduced by the colonists, why does the post-Independence society retain the introduced laws? Should they be retained or repealed? I needed answers to questions such as these. I needed evidence and understanding. I needed to review reform efforts both overseas and locally. I needed to understand the fundamental issues at the heart of the decriminalisation efforts. Only then could I engage with the obstacles to reform and assess the prospects for success.

Research

Finding the evidence

There have been very few comprehensive studies of the history, development or form of sexuality laws in PNG. From the little that has been compiled, and from comprehensive searches of primary materials, I have put together a picture not only of the history of the cases and statutes, but also of the legal influences on sexuality laws: influences such as the various international treaties and declarations having a bearing on human rights, the incorporation of the principles of the *International Covenant on Civil and Political Rights* (ICCPR) in the *Constitution* at Independence, the recently declared and accepted *Yogyakarta Principles* and so on.[2]

Social research however was a bigger challenge. Some work had been done on the sex trade, mainly behavioural studies in connection with HIV-related research and programming. I knew of some excellent ethnographic studies, the most notable being those of Joan Johnstone,[3] Lawrence Hammar[4] and Holly Wardlow,[5] but otherwise, there was little else on transactional sex until the appearance of the *Askim na Save* report. The broader corpus of literature dealing with the marginalisation, vulnerability and abuse of women and girls in PNG makes little or no reference to those who sell or exchange sex—'women' have been essentialised in PNG studies as elsewhere in the world. Much anthropological work has been done on 'ritualised homosexuality,' but the arguments that the semen exchange practices involved in the initiation ceremonies of certain Melanesian societies are not a matter of sexuality are convincing. In contrast, male-male sexual practices today are largely invisible, to be revealed only recently in connection with HIV prevention work. I needed to discover and reveal what goes on in PNG in the present, and for that I needed engagement with subjects in the field, supported by archival and textual studies.

My research has provided plenty of evidence to support an argument for decriminalisation. I have traced the origins of the present-day laws to the early days of the colonial rule. It was then that the sexuality laws were introduced, beginning with the paternalist Native Regulations of colonial times and developing through to the formal cases of the post-Independence appellate courts, which establish the parameters of the laws criminalising (and declining to decriminalise) prostitution and sodomy. Under this regime, the Port Moresby residents who sell sex, and those identified as gays or transgenders, live their lives and endure multiple misfortunes. They endure opprobrium not only through the processes of the law, but through the media and through the practices of a society which blames, condemns and oppresses them.

As my research proceeded, other work in the same areas began to appear. I have found very little in this recent work to contradict what I had already found.

---

2 United Nations Human Rights Council, International Commission of Jurists and International Service for Human Rights, 2007, *The Yogyakarta Principles: Principles on the Application of International Human Rights Law in Relation to Sexual Orientation and Gender Identity*, online: http://www.yogyakartaprinciples.org/docs/File/Yogyakarta_Principles_EN.pdf, accessed 15 May 2007.
3 Joan Drikoré Johnstone, 1993, 'The Gumini *Bisnis-Meri*: a study of the development of an innovative indigenous entrepreneurial activity in Port Moresby in the early 1970s,' Ph.D. thesis, Brisbane: University of Queensland.
4 Among others, Lawrence Hammar, 2010, *Sin, Sex and Stigma: A Pacific Response to HIV and AIDS*, Wantage, UK: Sean Kingston Publishing.
5 Among others, Holly Wardlow, 2006, *Wayward Women: Sexuality and Agency in a New Guinea Society*, Berkeley and Los Angeles, California: University of California Press.

In fact, some of my early conclusions were borne out and augmented by later, more intensive studies: for example, the findings of the *Askim na Save* report on the lack of clear self-definition of female sex sellers as sex workers; male sex selling; and the violence and stigma experienced by gays in the home. Together, these studies paint a picture of highly marginalised groups. Gays and transgenders suffer greatly from stigmatisation, discrimination and persecution, as my research has demonstrated. Much of this is enacted in physical violence, sexual and otherwise, from society at large and, significantly, from agents of the state, and some of the violence has had very serious and sometimes fatal consequences.

But there are differences. Females who sell or exchange sex in PNG are not doing so out of a sense of identity. It is something they do, permanently or sporadically, either willingly, or because they are forced or obliged to do so by kin, or because they have no other choice for survival. The law disapproves of the exchange of sex for gain, and hence criminalises it. Attempts to prosecute sex sellers on the grounds of identity exceed the limits of the legal process, and become acts of persecution. Nevertheless, the fact of criminalisation lends credence to society's condemnation of those so labelled, and support for police action against them.

By contrast, males engage in sex with other males for any number of motives ranging from emotional attachment to economic gain, and in doing so they may assume one of several sexual identities, including that of the heteronormative man engaged in an act of sexual penetration. There is a dissonance between perceived identity, internal subjectivity or sense of self, and actual conduct, and the law can only prosecute the last.[6] But opinions expressed in the media generally take a more simplistic view. Males having sex with other males are condemned not for what they do but for what they are. And the higher the status, the more there is to be lost by openly professing a non-normative sexual identity.[7] Professional gays, who should be best-positioned to advocate gay rights, have the greatest need to conceal their sexuality. The gay rights movement in PNG, such as it is, is so far one principally of the *grassroots*.

Understanding the sources

To understand the origins of this stigma, discrimination and persecution, I have applied the theories of Michel Foucault and his views of the relationship of law to disciplinary power, bio-power and governmentality. These regulatory processes are supported by other discourses, principally those of medicine and

---

6   Sonia Katyal, 2002, 'Exporting identity,' *Yale Journal of Law and Feminism* 14(1): 98–176, 168.
7   PNG gays are not just afraid of repercussions such as blackmail or violence, they can also be deeply concerned about shame visited on the family and community, as illustrated by Victor's story.

religion. To these, in the context of the colonial enterprise, should be added the language of race and class.[8] Writers on colonialism both in and beyond PNG have highlighted the effective use of introduced sexual norms and laws in governing colonised populations and, whether or not they acknowledge Foucault, his insights can be discerned in much of their work.

In Chapter 2, I described how 'civilisation' along western lines was introduced into the former territories of PNG through these processes of the introduction and adoption of discourses of Christianity and of western medicine. Non-monogamous, non-heteronormative and deviant sexuality was criminalised in the introduced Anglo-Australian common law system. At Independence, despite a few faltering attempts to develop non-western mores and laws, the PNG *elites* of the post-colonial era emerged as a dominant class which embraced much of western modernity and consumerism. Despite overt espousal of the principles of human rights, moves to reform the introduced colonial law and faltering attempts to recover 'tradition,' the formal legal system has been retained virtually intact, and that system includes proscription of prostitution in the form of the offence of living on the earnings of prostitution, and homosexual behaviour in the form of the sodomy law.

In Chapter 3, I described how Ben Golder and Peter Fitzpatrick developed Foucault's theories by challenging those who argue for the 'expulsion thesis': that the power of mediaeval law has been ousted by the regulatory norms of modernity. They considered that law has merely retreated to the boundaries of the socially normative, leaving society's regulatory norms as the core. But while law evokes fixity, it is nevertheless responsive to the demands of an ever-changing society, affirming the status quo or shifting the boundaries, either inward or outward, in processes of law reform. In this chapter I have demonstrated the processes by which the law determines and maintains those boundaries, through a study of the history of the criminalising process as applied to sex selling and sodomy.

Through tales of the fraught experiences of sellers of sex and gays in Port Moresby nowadays, in chapters 4 and 5 I have described the exercises of power both in maintaining and resisting the boundaries of what is normative and legal. Chapter 6 considered media representations through the lens of intersectionality theory to examine the narratives which attach to social groups, creating and maintaining powerful social norms of sexual behaviour. Social norms, which are created by and create the law, in turn are supported by and support the law.

---

8 Ann Laura Stoler, 2003, *Carnal Knowledge and Imperial Power: Race and the Intimate in Colonial Rule*, Berkeley: University of California Press, 158.

Questioning reform

In Chapter 1, I posed a central question: will law reform have any effect on prevailing social norms which stigmatise sex sellers and gays? To respond, I turned to the work of legal writers who challenge the 'enforcement principle': the belief of commentators, lawyers and courts that an unenforced criminal law is harmless. The opposing view is that as long as such laws remain on the statute books, they operate to form and inform social norms. To understand the effects of law in general, and laws which criminalise sexual conduct in particular, one must take into account the law's role in a wider social context. Goodman realised this when he took the opportunity to study South African society's attitudes to and treatment of gays and lesbians before and after the repeal there of the sodomy law. The processes of sexuality reform elsewhere offer further examples of the interaction between laws and society.

Although I believed, and continue to believe, that decriminalisation is essential if the constitutional rights of all citizens are to be recognised, some friends and colleagues disagree, pointing to the negative and emotional responses that have been made in the past to decriminalisation proposals. Some pressed what I now recognise as the enforcement principle. Many of my gay respondents, even the well-educated, displayed little if any knowledge or understanding of the sodomy law, believing that social and family attitudes or church doctrine were the cause of all their problems. But it is my firm belief that the fact of criminalisation has made a difference, especially in a country which had developed such a strong culture of violence among the police as well as the general community. I respond that it is the threat of criminal sanctions, coupled with a culture of poor internal discipline, which enables state law enforcement agents to act with increasing severity against vulnerable groups. Because they knew that prostitution is a crime, the police were able to break down the gate of the Three-Mile Guesthouse and commit the atrocities of the raid there with impunity. And because the judge in *Mala's Case* knew that sodomy was a crime, he was able to describe Mala's action as 'the behaviour of animals.' Both these incidents may have exceeded reason and legitimacy, but there has been no redress for those stigmatised and abused. Criminalised victims of law enforcement abuses are unable to resist or to enforce their human rights. The law's view that such behaviour is criminal facilitates and supports social condemnation and stigma.

Nevertheless, I acknowledge that decriminalisation is not the end of the process. On its own, legislative reform will not guarantee universal respect, dignity or better lives to those currently criminalised. Cheryl Overs and Bebe Loff argue that the fundamental issue is that of 'lack of recognition as a person before the law' and conclude that 'multi-faceted, setting-specific reform is needed,' rather than mere decriminalisation.⁹ Legislative reform must be accompanied by implementation and awareness, and by addressing the structural causes of the power imbalance which the criminalisation regime has created and maintained. But legislative reform is a start and, as Goodman has shown, it can have an immediate effect on the lives of those most closely affected before the law was changed. In my view, any initiative which can prevent or at least reduce the stigma, discrimination and violence experienced by sex sellers and gays is worth undertaking.

My final task then is to review reform initiatives to date in other countries, and the recent moves at international level to urge states to consider decriminalisation of marginalised groups. Based on this survey, I then set out the various ways and means by which decriminalisation could be achieved in PNG.

Reform initiatives

> Advancing human rights and gender equality for the HIV response means ending the HIV-related stigma, discrimination, gender inequality and violence against women and girls that drive the risk of, and vulnerability to, HIV infection by keeping people from accessing prevention, treatment, care and support services. It means putting laws, policies and programmes in place to create legal environments that protect people from infection and support access to justice. At the core of these efforts is protecting human rights in the context of HIV—including the rights of people living with HIV, women, young people, men who have sex with men, people who use drugs and sex workers and their clients.... Countries with punitive laws and practices around HIV transmission, sex work, drug use or homosexuality that block effective responses [to be] reduced by half.
>
> UNAIDS Strategy 2011–2015.

International and regional initiatives

The HIV epidemic, despite its tragedy, has had its positive side. The necessity to focus on and work with individuals and groups whose sexual activity is criminalised engenders their greater recognition and assistance.[10]

---

9   Cheryl Overs and Bebe Loff, 2013, 'Toward a legal framework that promotes and protects sex workers' health and human rights,' *Health and Human Rights* 15(1): 186–96.
10 Dennis Altman, 2001, *Global Sex*, Sydney: Allen & Unwin, 75. Although the recognition may be adverse, as in the Three-Mile Guesthouse Raid described and discussed in Chapter 5, the final outcome can sometimes be positive.

Acknowledgement of the epidemic as more than purely a health issue led to the formation of UNAIDS. In conjunction with other international partners, UNAIDS produced the *International Guidelines* and the *Handbook for Legislators*,[11] and, in 2007, *Taking Action Against HIV: A Handbook for Parliamentarians*,[12] to guide states in the development of appropriate laws and policies for HIV management and prevention. These publications urge states to adopt a human rights approach to epidemic management, an approach which includes the repeal and removal of discriminatory laws and practices. United Nations agencies have produced or supported the production of a host of other publications, all with the same message: HIV can only be managed through a human rights approach, and this is underpinned by reform of the law.

In September 2000, building upon a decade of major United Nations conferences and summits, world leaders came together in New York to adopt the *United Nations Millennium Declaration*, a set of eight targets, the Millennium Development Goals (MDGs), which embody basic human rights to health, education, shelter and security. Among other things, they combined Goal 3: 'Promote gender equality and empower women' with Goal 6: 'Combat HIV/AIDS, malaria and other diseases' to urge greater control by women over their own sexuality.[13] This was followed in June 2001 by the United Nations General Assembly Special Session (UNGASS) *Declaration of Commitment on HIV/AIDS*, the subsequent General Assembly 60th Session *Political Declaration on HIV/AIDS* 2006[14] and a further *Political Declaration* in 2011.[15] All of these Declarations urge states to enact legislation aimed at eliminating discrimination against vulnerable groups, and to overcome stigma and discrimination associated with the epidemic. None however has achieved treaty status, attempts being consistently blocked by some Middle Eastern states and the USA. The only references in the 2011 Declaration to actions regarding 'populations at higher risk' require states to define their specific populations at risk (§29), to promote human rights (§38), to target prevention strategies and data collection systems at them (§61) and to

---

11 Office of the United Nations High Commissioner for Human Rights (UNHCR) and Joint United Nations Programme on HIV/AIDS (UNAIDS), 1998, *HIV/AIDS and Human Rights: International Guidelines*, HR/PUB/98/1, report prepared for United Nations, New York and Geneva: UNHCR and UNAIDS (*International Guidelines*); Joint United Nations Programme on HIV/AIDS (UNAIDS), 1999, *Handbook for Legislators on HIV/AIDS, Law and Human Rights: Action to Combat HIV/AIDS in View of its Devastating Human, Economic and Social Impact*, UNAIDS/99.48E, report prepared for Joint United Nations Programme on HIV/AIDS (UNAIDS), Geneva (*Handbook for Legislators*). The PNG legislation which I drafted in 2001–2002 was based on these guidelines.
12 Inter-Parliamentary Union (IPU), United Nations Development Programme (UNDP) and Joint United Nations Programme on HIV/AIDS (UNAIDS), 2007, *Taking Action Against HIV: A Handbook for Parliamentarians*, Le Grand-Saconnex, New York, Geneva: IPU, UNDP, UNAIDS.
13 United Nations, 2002–2006, *Millennium Development Goals Beyond 2015*, online, http://www.unmillenniumproject.org/goals/,accessed 15 April 2014.
14 A/Res/60/262 adopted 15 June 2006.
15 Political Declaration on HIV/AIDS: Intensifying our Efforts to Eliminate HIV/AIDS, A/RES/65/277, adopted 10 June 2011.

create enabling legal frameworks for the protection of women and girls (§81), with an emphasis on 'sexual exploitation including for commercial reasons,' meaning trafficking. This may leave sex workers even more vulnerable to state-sanctioned violence and rights abuses. Nevertheless, the Declaration is ground-breaking in that for the first time it makes specific reference to sex workers and men who have sex with men (but not transgenders) as groups at higher risk of HIV infection.[16]

Meanwhile, in 2007, the International Commission of Jurists and the International Service for Human Rights produced the *Yogyakarta Principles*, a set of twenty-nine principles which address a broad range of human rights standards and their application to issues of sexual orientation and gender identity.[17] The *Yogyakarta Principles* combine the familiar civil and political rights of the ICCPR with the less justiciable social and economic rights of the International Covenant on Economic, Social and Cultural Rights (ICESCR), plus some newly expressed rights of particular significance for gender minorities and disadvantaged groups such as the right to recognition before the law, protection from all forms of exploitation, sale and trafficking of human beings, and protection from medical abuses. All actors have responsibilities to promote and protect these rights, including the UN human rights system, national human rights institutions, the media, NGOs and donor agencies.[18]

The Global Commission on HIV and the Law was launched in June 2010, to develop human rights-based recommendations for effective HIV responses.[19] It comprised eminent persons from public life and aimed to promote and develop an enabling legal environment for epidemic management, which may in some cases be undermined by the criminalisation of HIV transmission and exposure, sex work, adult consensual same-sex sexual relations, and drug use. PNG's Dame Carol Kidu was one of the Commissioners.[20]

At regional level, Pacific Island leaders at the Pacific Islands Forum Meeting of 2003 called for a regional strategy on HIV/AIDS, resulting in *The Pacific Regional Strategy on HIV/AIDS 2004–2008*.[21] The Strategy called for equitable attention to vulnerable groups, including those involved in the sex trade and

---

16 Asia Pacific Council of AIDS Service Organizations (APCASO), Civil Society Perspectives on the 2011 HIV/AIDS HLM, 2011, 'The 2011 Political Declaration on HIV/AIDS,' *infocus* 1 (August), online: http://www.apcaso.org/v2/wp-content/uploads/2011/12/APCASO-InFocus-No1.pdf, accessed 15 April 2014.
17 *Yogyakarta Principles*.
18 Ibid., 7.
19 *Global Commission on HIV and the Law*, n.d., online: http://www.hivlawcommission.org, accessed 21 March 2011.
20 'Information note,' June 2010, *Global Commission on HIV and the Law*. And see 'The Commissioners,' n.d., *Global Commission on HIV and the Law*, online: www.hivlawcommission.org/images/stories/cmsrsbios_28_sept2010_english.pdf, online: accessed 22 March 2011.
21 Secretariat of the Pacific Community (SPC), 2005, *The Pacific Regional Strategy on HIV/AIDS 2004–2008*, Noumea, New Caledonia: Secretariat of the Pacific Community.

men who have sex with men.²² In 2004, the Pacific Parliamentary Assembly on Population and Development (PPAPD) called its inaugural meeting to inform Pacific Parliamentarians on basic facts about HIV and AIDS and to urge them to become champions in leading the fight against HIV and AIDS in Pacific communities.²³ The meeting reinforced the importance of commitment by Pacific states to the Pacific Regional Strategy, and culminated in the signing by the Parliamentarians, including Dr Banare Bun Zzferio, MP of PNG, of the *Suva Declaration on HIV/AIDS*. The Declaration's commitment to legislative action was couched in general terms and made no specific mention of sex work or MSM when it discussed protection of vulnerable groups from stigma, violence and discrimination.²⁴ In 2007, UNAIDS facilitated the establishment of the Commission on AIDS in the Pacific and tasked it with providing an analysis of the status of the epidemic in the region, in order to provide policy options to Pacific countries and their development partners. In 2009 the Commission produced its report, *Turning the Tide*, which found that targeted prevention programmes with sex sellers and gays are successful, and recommended that 'countries must undertake progressive legislative reform to repeal legislation that criminalizes high-risk behaviour and promotes HIV-related discrimination. Changing the laws need not imply approval of the behaviour but would signal a greater concern for people.'²⁵

The same year, the Pacific Sexual Diversity Network, the regional network of Pacific MSM and transgender organisations, launched its Strategic Plan 2010–2013, with one of its goals to reform discriminatory laws affecting MSM and transgenders.²⁶

Reforms overseas

Long before PNG's reform attempts at the time of Independence, reform of sexuality laws was under way overseas. In the United Kingdom, as a result of social changes in post-World War II England, the government through the Home Office and the Scottish Home Department in 1954 commissioned a joint investigation of law and practice relating to homosexual and prostitution offences.²⁷ Helen J. Self considers that the primary aim was to endorse the current

---

22 Ibid., 32.
23 Pacific Parliamentary Assembly on Population and Development (PPAPD), 2004, 'The Suva declaration on HIV/AIDS by Pacific parliamentarians,' report of the *1st Conference for Pacific Parliamentarians on: 'The Role of Pacific Parliamentarians in the Fight against HIV/AIDS,'* Suva, Fiji, 11–13 October (*Suva Declaration*).
24 Ibid., 35.
25 UNAIDS, 2009, Commission on AIDS in the Pacific, *Turning the Tide: An OPEN Strategy for a Response to AIDS in the Pacific*, Recommendation 4: 6, online: http://data.unaids.org/pub/report/2009/20091202_pacificcommission_en.pdf, accessed 8 July 2014.
26 Pacific Sexual Diversity Network, 2009, *Strategic Plan 2010–2013*, 9.
27 *Report of the Committee on Homosexual Offences and Prostitution*, 1957, London: HMSO, Cmnd. 247, (*Wolfenden Report*).

situation of criminalised prostitution, and sodomy was included not because reforms to homosexual laws were considered necessary, but because of public anxieties of the time over several incidences of homosexual cases involving high-profile figures and because, at the time, homosexuality was considered to be a curable pathology.[28]

The result was the 1957 *Wolfenden Report* (so named for its Chairman). It recommended some changes to soliciting laws and the decriminalisation of male-to-male sex in private by consenting adults aged twenty-one years and over. The logic of the *Wolfenden Report*, in reconstructing homosexuality and prostitution in terms of public proscription and private freedom, was gradually adopted by other English-speaking countries of the developed world.[29] Countries such as Australia and New Zealand, motivated in part by the liberation movements which gathered momentum through the 1960s and 1970s, not only withdrew from the active policing of private consensual sex but also began to move towards decriminalisation.[30]

Prostitution

> We are concerned not with prostitution itself but with the manner in which the activities of prostitutes and those associated with them offend against public order and decency, expose the ordinary citizen to what is offensive or injurious, or involve the exploitation of others.
>
> *Wolfenden Report*, 1957.[31]

Reform of prostitution laws in the Anglo-Australian common law world has long been beset by problems. It is piecemeal, attempting to appease the conflicting aims of maintenance of public order and protection of women and children from

---

28 Helen J. Self, 2003, *Prostitution, Women and Misuse of the Law: The Fallen Daughters of Eve*, London and Portland OR: Frank Cass Publishers, 76.
29 John Ballard, 1998, 'The constitution of AIDS in Australia: taking government at a distance seriously,' in *Governing Australia: Studies in Contemporary Rationalities of Government*, ed. Mitchell Dean and Barry Hindess, Melbourne: Cambridge University Press, 125–38.
30 For accounts of reforms in Australia, see for example Roberta Perkins and Garry Bennett, 1985, *Being a Prostitute: Prostitute Women and Prostitute Men*, Sydney: George Allen & Unwin; Graham Willett, 2008, 'From 'vice' to homosexuality: policing perversion in the 1950s,' in *Homophobia: An Australian History*, ed. Shirleene Robinson, Annandale, NSW: The Federation Press, 113–127; Clive Moore, 2001, *Sunshine and Rainbows: The Development of Gay and Lesbian Culture in Queensland*, St Lucia: University of Queensland Press.
31 *Wolfenden Report*, 80 §227.

'trafficking'; an agenda which proliferated following the US Anti-Prostitution Pledge.[32] Every attempt to ameliorate perceived injustices only serves to create new issues and more social problems.[33]

As I observed earlier, the criminalisation of prostitution has had a long history in British law. The fornicating penitent of mediaeval times was transformed into the recalcitrant sinner in need of discipline by the rise of Protestantism in the Reformation period. Following first the Enclosures Acts of the sixteenth century, and then the Industrial Revolution in the nineteenth, the promiscuous woman, the female vagrant, the single mother were all cast as prostitutes—there was little else left for them but to sell themselves for survival.[34] The Contagious Diseases Acts of the nineteenth century were a means of controlling female sexuality in the interests of maintaining the health of garrisoned soldiers.[35] The panic over white slaving prompted their repeal, but police powers and vagrancy laws were tightened, pushing prostitutes off the streets and into the hands of pimps.[36] All this regulatory action succeeded in creating an 'outgroup,' deserving of both contempt and pity, although both sentiments were eclipsed by the fear of disease.[37]

In post-World War II England, women were evicted from wartime work back to 'the home' or into low-paid menial employment. Prostitution was not an offence, nor was solicitation unless it caused annoyance.[38] But concerns about the preference of Englishwomen for American servicemen, the increasing incidence of venereal disease, scaremongering about the possibility of large numbers of 'coloured' immigrants and about prostitution and street soliciting generally all played a large part in prompting the Wolfenden Committee's enquiry into 'the law and practice relating to offences against the criminal law in connection with prostitution and solicitation for immoral purposes, and to report what changes, if any, are in our opinion desirable.'[39]

The Committee was not convinced that it was primarily economic circumstances, 'bad upbringing, seduction at an early age, or a broken marriage,' which compelled

---

32 Larissa Sandy, 2007, 'Just choices: representations of choice and coercion in sex work in Cambodia,' *The Australian Journal of Anthropology* 18(2): 194–206, 197–09; Nicole Franck Masenior and Chris Beyrer, 2007, 'The US anti-prostitution pledge: first amendment challenges and public health priorities,' *PLoS Medicine* 4: 7, online: http://www.humantrafficking.org/uploads/publications/Masenior_and_Beyrer.pdf, accessed 16 May 2011; Center for Health and Gender Equity, 2008, *Implications of U.S. Policy Restrictions for HIV Programs Aimed at Commercial Sex Workers*, online: http://www.genderhealth.org/files/uploads/change/publications/aplobrief.pdf, accessed 16 May 2011.
33 Self, *Prostitution, Women and Misuse of the Law*, 293.
34 Ibid., 22–40.
35 Judith R. Walkowitz, 1982, *Prostitution and Victorian Society: Women, Class, and the State*, Cambridge and New York: Cambridge University Press.
36 Self, *Prostitution, Women and Misuse of the Law*, 40–41.
37 Ibid., 53.
38 Ibid., 74–77, 80–81.
39 *Wolfenden Report*, §1.

women to take to selling sex,[40] and opined that there must be something in the psychological make-up of certain women to predispose them to the enjoyment of this occupation. But the Committee took very little evidence from women—misogyny and the caricaturing of women were commonplace at the time, and the Committee was not really concerned to decriminalise prostitution.[41] What it found objectionable was the public display of sexual availability which street prostitution produced. So it recommended the framing of an offence which tightened the soliciting laws, designed to remove the prostitute from the streets, and incidentally, into the hands of pimps and brothel-managers.[42]

In Australia, prostitution (and pornography) were first constituted as public problems in the late-nineteenth and early-twentieth centuries.[43] Although the act of prostitution was never itself illegal, the visibility of its practice drew the attention of police and lawgivers. In the 1950s, new cultural concerns about sexual deviance (homosexuality and prostitution) began to appear and new laws to control salacious literature were enacted. By the 1970s, commercial sex became an important political and social issue, with new anti-prostitution laws enacted. During the 1970s, as sexuality was being constructed in terms of freedom, reciprocity and mutuality, sex industries expanded and traditional governmental approaches to control were questioned. Prostitution was conceptualised in terms of a private sexual activity in which state interference was illegitimate, and some states decriminalised. Currently, the legal status of prostitution varies between Australian states, while trafficking and sex-slavery are criminalised under Federal law.[44]

---

40 See Chapter 3 for my description of society's (mis-)constructions of the reasons why women sell sex.
41 Self, *Prostitution, Women and Misuse of the Law*, 76, 121.
42 *Wolfenden Report* §79–80, §87.
43 Barbara Ann Sullivan, 1997, *The Politics of Sex: Prostitution and Pornography in Australia since 1945*, New York: Cambridge University Press, 10–12. See also Roberta Perkins, 1991, *Working Girls: Prostitutes, their Life and Social Control*, Canberra: Australian Institute of Criminology; Meg Arnot, 1988, 'The oldest profession in a new Britannia,' in *Constructing a Culture*, ed. Verity Burgmann and Jenny Lee, Fitzroy, Vic: McPhee Gribble/Penguin, 46–62; Craig Johnston, 1985, 'Prostitution law reform in New South Wales: two shuffles forward, one stumble back,' in *Being a Prostitute: Prostitute Women and Prostitute Men*, ed. Roberta Perkins and Garry Bennett, Sydney, London, Boston: George Allen & Unwin, 261–73.
44 Perkins, *Working Girls*; Susanne Davies, 1995, 'Captives of their bodies: law and punishment, 1880s–1980s,' in *Sex Power and Justice: Historical Perspectives on Law in Australia*, ed. Dianne Kirkby, Melbourne: Oxford University Press, 99–115, 101–05; Sullivan, *The Politics of Sex*; and for updates during the last two decades, Scarlet Alliance, ca. 2010, *State by State Laws in Australia*, online: http://www.scarletalliance.org.au/laws/, accessed 8 July 2010.

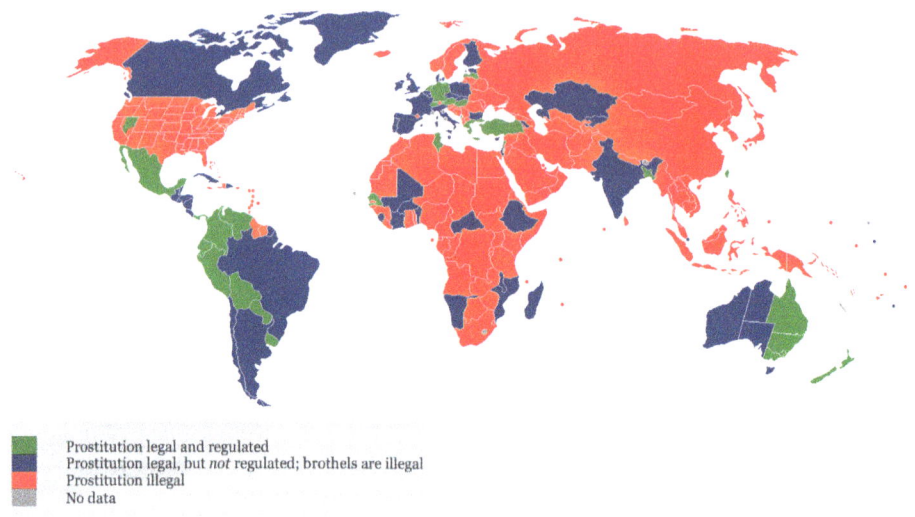

Map 7.1. Prostitution laws of the world.

Source: 'Prostitution laws of the world' by Runningfridgesrule – Own work. Licensed under Public domain via Wikimedia Commons - http://commons.wikimedia.org/wiki/File:Prostitution_laws_of_the_world.PNG#mediaviewer/File:Prostitution_laws_of_the_world.PNG, accessed 8 July 2014.

Elsewhere, New Zealand reformed its prostitution laws in 2003, retaining only offences of coercion.[45] The USA, most of the Asian continent and most African states continue to criminalise prostitution, as shown in Map 7.1. The extent and type of regulation, where it exists, varies greatly.

Sodomy

In the 1950s, while the *Wolfenden Report* was being prepared, the only countries in Europe apart from the United Kingdom which criminalised consensual sex between adult males in private were Austria, Germany and Norway. Other European countries only punished such behaviour when it involved underage boys or an abuse of a situation of dependency; offended public decency; or was conducted by means of force or coercion.[46]

The Wolfenden Committee was tasked 'to consider the law and practice relating to homosexual offences and the treatment of persons convicted of such offences by the courts; and to report what changes, if any, are … desirable.'[47] It recommended the decriminalisation of sex between consenting adults in private,

---

45 'Prostitution in New Zealand,' *Wikipedia*, online: http://en.wikipedia.org/wiki/Prostitution_in_New_Zealand, accessed 27 August 2011.
46 *Wolfenden Report*, Appendix III: 149–51.
47 Ibid., §1.

'adult' being defined as a person over twenty-one years of age.[48] However, it took ten years for a reluctant parliament to implement the recommendation, and in that period, public interest waned.[49] It took a further thirty-five years for the European Court of Human Rights to affirm that the European *Convention for the Protection of Human Rights and Fundamental Freedoms*[50] prohibits discrimination on the basis of sexual orientation.[51]

Reform movements in Australia were sparked in large part by the Wolfenden inquiry, and aided by the new liberalism of Whitlam and the Labour Party in the 1970s.[52] South Australia was the first state to decriminalise homosexuality in 1972, to be followed gradually by others, although Tasmania held out for over twenty years until the Australian Commonwealth was taken to the Human Rights Committee of the United Nations in 1994,[53] and Tasmania was obliged to capitulate.[54]

Elsewhere, in 1986 the US Supreme Court in the case of *Bowers v Hardwick* upheld the constitutional right of states to enact laws criminalising homosexuality,[55] although not their right to discriminate.[56] However, the *Bowers Case* was overturned in 2003 by *Lawrence v. Texas*,[57] which held that laws criminalising same sex activities by consenting adults in the privacy of their own homes are unconstitutional as they violate the fundamental right to privacy. In 1998, the prohibition on discrimination on the grounds of 'sexual orientation' (as opposed to 'sex') in South Africa's new *Constitution* was applied to strike down the South African sodomy law.[58] In 2005, the High Court of Hong Kong declared that the relevant sections of the *Crimes Ordinance* of the Special Administrative Region offend the rights to equality and freedom from discrimination under the Basic Law and the right to freedom from interference in privacy under the Bill of Rights.[59]

---

48   Ibid., §62.
49   Jeffrey Weeks, 1977, *Coming Out: Homosexual Politics in Britain, from the Nineteenth Century to the Present*, London, Melbourne, New York: Quartet Books, 156.
50   *Convention for the Protection of Human Rights and Fundamental Freedoms* (Europe) (ETS No. 5), 213 U.N.T.S. 222, entered into force 3 September 1953.
51   *Salgueiro da Silva Mouta v. Portugal* [2001] 1 F.C.R. 653, discussed in Jonathan Herring, 2002, 'Gay rights come quietly,' *Law Quarterly Review* 118: 31–35.
52   Moore, *Sunshine and Rainbows*; Graham Willett, 2000, *Living Out Loud: A History of Gay and Lesbian Activism in Australia*, St. Leonards, NSW: Allen & Unwin, 26–27.
53   *Toonen v Australia* (1994) 1 Int Hum Rts Reports 97, discussed in Michael Kirby, 2000, 'Human rights—the way forward,' *Victoria University of Wellington Law Review* 36(4): 703–20, 711–2.
54   Ibid.
55   *Bowers v Hardwick* 478 U.S. 186 (1986).
56   *Romer v Evans* 116 S.Ct. 1620 (1996).
57   *Lawrence v. Texas* 539 U.S. 558, 578, 123 S.Ct. 2472, 156 L.Ed.2d 508 (2003).
58   *National Coalition for Gay and Lesbian Equality & Anor v. Minister of Justice & Ors*, 1998 (12) BCLR 1517 (Constitutional Court); and see Ryan Goodman, 2001, 'Beyond the enforcement principle: sodomy laws, social norms, and social panoptics,' *California Law Review* 89: 643–740.
59   *Leung TC William Roy v. Secretary for Justice* [2005] HKCFI 713.

Closer to home, in the notable cases of *Nadan v The State* and *McCoskar v The State* in the High Court of Fiji in 2005,[60] the appeal court held that the sections of the Fiji *Penal Code* dealing with carnal knowledge against the order of nature and gross indecency between males breached the constitutionally guaranteed rights to privacy and equality, and were invalid to the extent that they applied to consensual sexual conduct between males eighteen years and over occurring in private. And then in early 2010, following the promulgation of a new constitution which prevented discrimination on the grounds of 'gender equality' rather than 'sex,' a new *Criminal Decree* repealed the *Penal Code* and thereby abolished the crime of consensual sex between adult males in Fiji.[61] This was hailed as a first for the Pacific.[62] Then in 2009 in India, in the landmark *Naz Case*,[63] the New Delhi High Court struck down the law as it related to consenting adults in private on the grounds that it infringed the human rights to privacy, equality and liberty. The positive recognition of queer people and their rights (to equality, to love) was accompanied by a 'broader acceptance in public culture.' That decision was a starting point for a nation-wide conversation in India.[64] Unfortunately, the case was overturned by the Indian Supreme Court late in 2013,[65] but public acceptance remained high and the Supreme Court's decision elicited much criticism.[66]

---

60   *Nadan v The State* [2005] FJHC 1 and *McCoskar v The State* [2005] FJHC 500.
61   Shalveen Chand, 2010, 'Same sex law decriminalised,' *Fiji Times*, 26 February, online: http://www.fijitimes.com/print.aspx?id=140812, accessed 26 February 2010. See also Editorial, 2010, 'Being happy and gay,' *Fiji Times*, 26 February, online: http://www.fijitimes.com/print.aspx?id=140824, accessed 26 February 2010, published upon the announcement of decriminalisation of sodomy in Fiji.
62   'UNAIDS welcomes Fiji decree to decriminalise homosexuality,' 2010, *PACNEWS*, 3 March, posted to AIDSTOK, 3 March 2010, online: aidstok@lyris.spc.int. This claim should more properly be restricted to the Anglophone Pacific.
63   *Naz Foundation (India) Trust v Government of ACT of Delhi and Others* WP(C) No.7445/2001, date of decision 2 July 2009, (India) (*Naz Case*).
64   Arvind Narrain and Alok Gupta, 2011, 'Introduction,' in *Law Like Love: Queer Perspectives on Law*, ed. Arvind Narrain and Alok Gupta, Calcutta: Yoda Press, xi–lvi, xi–xii.
65   *Suresh Kumar Koushal and another v Naz Foundation and others*, Civil Appeal No.10972 of 2013, 11 December 2013 (*Naz Appeal*).
66   For example Sudhir Krishnaswamy, 2013, 'Naz Foundation: reading down the Supreme Court,' *Oxford Human Rights Law*, 13 December, online: http://ohrh.law.ox.ac.uk/?p=3733, accessed 31 December 2013; Prachi Shrivastava, 2013, '7 creative (legal) reasons the Supreme Court found not to strike down Section #377,' online: http://www.legallyindia.com/201312114184/Constitutional-law/7-reasons-the-supreme-court-didnt-strike-down-377, accessed 14 December 2013; Erik Voeten, 2013, 'The recriminalization of homosexuality in India and the potential for broader backlash,' *Washington Post*, 11 December, online: http://www.washingtonpost.com/blogs/monkey-cage/wp/2013/12/11/the-recriminalization-of-homosexuality-in-india-and-the-potential-for-broader-backlash/, accessed 16 December 2013.

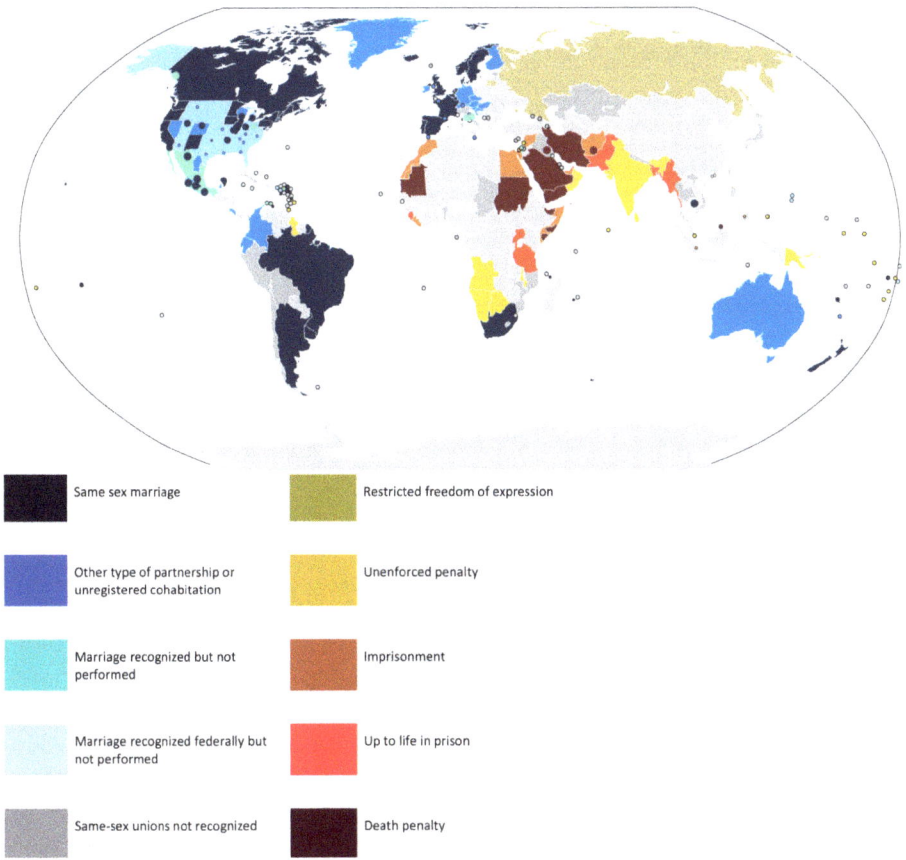

Map 7.2. 'LGBT rights by country or territory'.

Source: 'World laws pertaining to homosexual relationships and expression' by Various (Initial version by Silje) - Own work. This vector image was created with Inkscape. Other sources: Nigerian Sharia states based on File:NG-Sharia.pngMerida (Venezuela) from File:Venezuela Merida State Location.svg; Wisconsin: File:Blank US Map.svg; Law in Russia restricting freedom of expression and assembly [1] US after DOMA decision [2] Syria: [3] Moldova: [4]. Licensed under Creative Commons Attribution-Share Alike 3.0 via Wikimedia Commons - http://commons.wikimedia.org/wiki/File:World_laws_pertaining_to_homosexual_relationships_and_expression.svg#mediaviewer/File:World_laws_pertaining_to_homosexual_relationships_and_expression.svg, accessed 8 July 2014.

Map 7.2 shows that it is predominantly the Arab-speaking nations of the Middle East and northern Africa, and the former British colonies of Africa, South Asia and the Pacific, which continue to criminalise sodomy. A distinction may be drawn between the laws of Pacific countries based on the laws of the colonist or former colonist. French territories and Micronesian states whose laws are based on the American legal system do not criminalise sex between males: nearly all of those whose laws are derived from England, Australia and New Zealand do.

The exception here is Vanuatu, with a combined English-French legal heritage, which only prohibits 'homosexual acts' with a person of the same sex under eighteen years.[67]

Reform in PNG

There are two ways to reform law. One is through direct legislative intervention, by preparing and having Parliament pass legislation; and the other is by court challenge, either in the context of an appropriate case already on foot, or as a constitutional challenge on the grounds of infringement of human rights. Both have their problems.

Legislative action requires the concurrence of the government of the day, and to a large extent, of society also. If the government sponsors a Bill, it will usually pass; such is the nature of the Westminster system. Non-government-sponsored legislation may yet achieve parliamentary approval, but only if the government agrees. This was the situation in PNG with the 2002 *Criminal Code* amendments, brought as a private member's Bill by Dame Carol Kidu, which were supported by government because they were framed as protecting children from abuse.[68] The major stumbling block to legislative action is lack of political will.

Court challenges run various risks. If they arise in the course of another matter, as was the situation with the 2005 *Nadan* and *McCoskar Cases* in Fiji, they are totally dependent on the circumstances of the case, the lawyers and judge who happen to be involved, and the processes applicable in the circumstances. In Fiji, the cases came before a single judge in the appellate division of the High Court, who chose to apply human rights principles. In PNG, a clear process is set out in the *Constitution* where a question of constitutionality arises in the National Court. The matter should immediately be referred to the Supreme Court, either upon request of the lawyers involved or on the judge's own initiative.[69]

A direct court challenge may be initiated in two ways. PNG's *Constitution* at Section 57(1) provides that

> a right or freedom referred to in this Division [*Division 3.—Basic Rights*] shall be protected by, and is enforceable in, the Supreme Court or the National Court ... either on its own initiative or on application by any person who has an interest in its protection and enforcement, or in the

---

[67] Section 99 of the Vanuatu *Penal Code*.
[68] Even the title was designed with this in mind: although only an amending Act, it was entitled the *Criminal Code (Sexual Offences and Crimes against Children) Act*.
[69] *Constitution* Section 18.

case of a person who is, in the opinion of the court, unable fully and freely to exercise his rights under this section by a person acting on his behalf, whether or not by his authority.

This was the action contemplated when a case for the protection of human rights was filed in the National Court by the women in the Three-Mile Guesthouse Raid. It was the kind of action taken in *Croome's Case* in Tasmania.[70] Properly planned, it could be very effective. It relies however on a situation which has already occurred in which the rights have been infringed. And it relies on the courage of an applicant (in this context, a sex seller or gay person) to take the case, or on the court being prepared to declare that another person or body has sufficient standing to take the action on their behalf.[71]

Alternatively, a challenge to the constitutionality of a law may be taken directly by 'special reference' to the highest court in the land, the Supreme Court, by certain prescribed officers.[72] The Attorney-General, the Ombudsman Commission and the Law Reform Commission are among those entitled to take these special references. They differ from the usual case process where the court is asked to make a ruling on a set of facts—in special references, the Supreme Court may be asked to give its opinion on a hypothetical question, such as that of the unconstitutionality of the laws governing prostitution or sodomy.[73]

All cases, particularly those arising unexpectedly, run the risk of an adverse finding, so the safer course of action is to take a fully-prepared case directly to an appropriate court of competent jurisdiction under Section 19 or Section 57. There is now ample precedent overseas to provide material for a case of this kind. Further material can be sourced from international documents. The *Constitution* specifically recognises the relevance in the PNG context of determinations of the United Nations under international human rights law. Section 39 provides that when considering whether a restriction of a particular right under the *Constitution* is 'reasonably justifiable in a democratic society having a proper respect for the rights and dignity of mankind,' a court may have regard—among other things—to any decision of the United Nations concerning human rights and fundamental freedoms. This enables the courts to allow use of these international instruments 'apparently without the need for ratification.'[74] This would be relevant, in particular, to the right to privacy, because the United Nations Human Rights Committee has ruled that laws criminalising

---

70 *Croome v Tasmania* (1997) 191 CLR 119.
71 *In the Matter of an Application under Section 57 of the Constitution; Application by Individual and Community Rights Advocacy Forum Inc (ICRAF); In re Miriam Willingal* (Unreported) N1506 (10 February 1997) (*Willingal's Case*).
72 *Constitution* Section 19.
73 SCR No 5 of 1982: *Re Disputed Returns for the Kairuku-Hiri Open Electorate* [1982] PNGLR 379.
74 Pacific Regional Rights Resource Team, 2005, *Pacific Human Rights Law Digest: Volume 1, PHRLD*, Suva: Pacific Regional Rights Resource Team, xi.

consensual male-male sex amount to an arbitrary interference with privacy in violation of Article 17 of the ICCPR. So the existence of laws making male-male sex a criminal offence in PNG most probably amounts to a breach of the right to privacy under Section 49 of the *Constitution* as well as a breach of PNG's obligations as a signatory to the ICCPR.

None of these courses has yet been adopted in PNG. Despite having signed up to many of the international resolutions, and despite Dame Carol's participation at regional and international level in many HIV initiatives, the PNG government has been reluctant to follow international trends. Attempts have been made, but are largely ignored by the government of the day. The *National HIV/ AIDS Medium Term Plan 1998–2002* included the recommendation that the sex-work industry be decriminalised 'under specific conditions to enable the enforcement of appropriate health standards and to enable sex workers to access health services without fear of discrimination,'[75] and the National AIDS Council was ready to implement the Plan. But due to the Westminster system of apportionment of ministerial responsibilities, the National AIDS Council fell within the portfolio of the Minister for Health at the time when HIV management legislation was being prepared, while criminal legislation was the responsibility of the Minister for Justice. So the National AIDS Council was unable to propose that the Minister for Health take any direct action to reform the laws, either those relating to prostitution or those criminalising sodomy. Neither was the Minister for Justice (and indeed most of the government of the time) in the least interested in participating in any such reform initiative.

The one piece of legislation for which the National AIDS Council was responsible, the *HIV/AIDS Management and Prevention Act* 2003, did attempt to protect marginalised groups presumed to be associated with HIV infection from stigma and discrimination in a climate of criminalisation of non-normative sexuality. But inadequate awareness and understanding of its terms in the community, and the inability of the marginalised to access effective legal services, have left this legislation largely unimplemented.[76] The *National Strategic Plan on HIV/ AIDS 2004–2008*, although making much of the need to target prevention programmes to vulnerable groups including sex workers and gays, made no

---

75 Papua New Guinea, 1988, *National HIV/AIDS Medium Term Plan*, Port Moresby: Government of Papua New Guinea Strategy, 3.1.11: 35.
76 Work has begun to remedy this situation. In 2010, the International Development Law Organization (IDLO), an international intergovernmental organisation dedicated to promoting the rule of law and good governance in developing countries, commenced a PNG programme providing legal aid to People Living with HIV (PLHIV) and vulnerable groups: field notes and pers. comm. 2010, Port Moresby. In 2013, funding was assumed by the Australian government and responsibility transferred to the HIV/AIDS Legal Centre (HALC), a community legal centre which provides free legal aid and advice to people with HIV-related legal matters and advocates for the reform of laws and the legal system in areas that affect people living with HIV.

mention of legislative reform.[77] But, due in part at least to the participation of sex sellers, gays and transgenders in its formulation, the subsequent *National HIV and AIDS Strategy 2011–2015* does so.[78] In carefully chosen language, it acknowledges that 'laws that criminalise sex work and same-sex practices create barriers to people accessing services and reinforce vulnerability, stigma and discrimination' and urges that 'greater advocacy from all stakeholders is needed to support plans for introducing reforms to legislation that aim to reduce vulnerability and stigma and discrimination.'[79] And PNG's report to the United Nations General Assembly Special Session on HIV/AIDS (UNGASS) on PNG's progress in meeting its obligations under the 2001 *Declaration of Commitment on HIV/AIDS*[80] identified laws criminalising sex work and sodomy as presenting an obstacle to HIV prevention, treatment, care and support for sexually marginalised groups.[81]

Decriminalisation of prostitution

> TWO adults enter a room, agree a price, and have sex. Has either committed a crime? Common sense suggests not: sex is not illegal in itself, and the fact that money has changed hands does not turn a private act into a social menace. If both parties consent, it is hard to see how either is a victim. But prostitution has rarely been treated as just another transaction, or even as a run-of-the-mill crime: the oldest profession is also the oldest pretext for outraged moralising and unrealistic lawmaking devised by man.
>
> *Economist*, 2004.[82]

In Chapter 6, I identified the main arguments made in PNG for decriminalising acts of selling or exchanging sex: that decriminalisation would reduce rape and sexual violence, whereas criminalisation drives the practice underground, increases the spread of disease, and in any event cannot stop it. Arguments against are that the sex trade spreads disease and is against Christian, moral, cultural and family values. Blame is attributed to the needs of survival, women's

---

77   National AIDS Council of Papua New Guinea, n.d., *Papua New Guinea National Strategic Plan on HIV/AIDS 2004–2008*, Port Moresby: PNG National AIDS Council.
78   Carol Kidu, 2011, 'A national response to the HIV epidemic in Papua New Guinea,' *UN Chronicle* XLVIII (1) May, online: http://www.un.org:80/wcm/content/site/chronicle/home/archive/issues2011/hivaidsthefourthdecade/nationalresponsetohivpapuanewguinea, accessed 20 August 2011.
79   National AIDS Council of Papua New Guinea, 2010, *Papua New Guinea: National HIV and AIDS Strategy 2011–2015*, Port Moresby National AIDS Council of Papua New Guinea, 52.
80   United Nations General Assembly Special Session on HIV/AIDS (UNGASS), *Declaration of Commitment on HIV/AIDS*, 27 June 2001 A/RES/S-26/2.
81   National AIDS Council of Papua New Guinea, *Papua New Guinea: National HIV and AIDS Strategy 2011–2015*, 52.
82   'Sex is their business,' 2004, *Economist* (London), 372(8391), September 4: 11, online: http://www.economist.com/node/3151258, accessed 27 August 2011.

laziness and failure to 'go home to the village and work hard,' lack of discipline and more recently, the intervention of men as moneyed clients or as pimps. Solutions posited are to send the women back to the village, rehabilitate them with domestic skills training, or to legalise prostitution through registration of brothel workers accompanied by regular health checks.

Whether or not the criminalisation of the sex trade is supported or condemned, most public comments demonstrate that there is considerable confusion surrounding the terms decriminalisation and legalisation.[83] The Australian Sex Workers Association Scarlet Alliance defines them as follows:

> *Decriminalisation* refers to the removal of all criminal laws relating to sex work and the operation of the sex industry. The decriminalisation model is the favoured model of law reform of the international sex workers rights movement. Occupational health and safety and other workplace issues can be supported through existing industrial laws and regulations that apply to any legal workplaces ...
>
> *Legalisation* refers to the use of criminal laws to regulate or control the sex industry by determining the legal conditions under which the sex industry can operate. Legalisation can be highly regulatory or merely define the operation of the various sectors of the sex industry. It can vary between rigid controls under legalised state controlled systems to privatising the sex industry within a legally defined framework. It is often accompanied by strict criminal penalties for sex industry businesses that operate outside the legal framework.[84]

The regulatory aspects of legalisation do not appear to serve sex sellers well, certainly not in the developing world, at least. According to Jenkins,

> [T]he regulatory approach is government-driven and aims at monitoring impact through standard HIV surveillance. The broader public is ... considered to be at risk due to sex workers who must be controlled. This is apparent from the emphasis on commercial sex only.... Stigmatization of sex workers, discriminatory practices and activation of their rights as either workers or citizens are not issues of concern. The police and madams play a major role and gain additional power over sex workers through government (usually health department) intervention....

---

83 In 2011, Dame Carol Kidu attributed the failure of public advocacy efforts to inadequate differentiation of the two. See Kidu, 'A national response to the HIV epidemic in Papua New Guinea.'
84 Scarlet Alliance, n.d., *Terminology*, online: http://www.scarletalliance.org.au/issues/terminology/, accessed 20 March 2011.

Secondary issues, such as prevention of violence, recruitment into sex work, trafficking of girls and women, and retirement from sex work are not addressed at all.[85]

Others too consider that legalisation, with or without regulation of the sex industry, is not appropriate for less-developed countries.[86] A recent report from Fiji details severe human rights abuses at the hands of the military following the introduction of that country's new, stricter prostitution laws.[87] Any intervention by the state into the selling of sex in PNG will only open the way for further abuse, if not by police then by health officials, city rangers appointed to regulate the informal sector, and so on.[88] PNG would be better served by simple decriminalisation. This is the aim of Scarlet Alliance itself, even in a developed country such as Australia.[89]

In 2004, a paper was prepared for the National AIDS Council on decriminalisation options for prostitution.[90] It raised the possibility of a test case to challenge the reasoning of Justice Wilson in *Anna Wemay's Case*, or at least to affirm Acting Justice Narokobi's suggestion in *Monika Jon's Case* that a single act of selling sex does not constitute a crime. It then suggested various legislative amendments: first, to the child prostitution provisions in the *Criminal Code*, to ensure that prostitution by a child was not a crime in any circumstances; second to ensure that condoms did not provide evidence of prostitution. The possibility of legalisation and regulation was again canvassed, and dismissed as inappropriate in the PNG context. The paper concludes with a recommendation for simple decriminalisation.

The options for reform of sex trade laws are firstly, legislative action. In addition to the changes to the *Criminal Code's* child prostitution provisions canvassed in

---

85   Carol Jenkins and Andrew Hunter, 2005, *Empowering Sex Workers: Does It Matter?* Report for CARE, Asia Regional Management Unit 4.
86   See for example Bebe Loff, Cheryl Overs and Paulo Longo, 2003, 'Can health programmes lead to mistreatment of sex workers?' *Lancet* 361, 7 June: 1982–83.
87   Karen McMillan and Heather Worth, 2011, *Sex Workers and HIV Prevention in Fiji: after the Fiji Crimes Decree 2009*, Sydney: International HIV Research Group, UNSW.
88   The international Network of Sex Work Projects has long recognised the negative effects of mandating STI health checks, brothel registration, condom use and so on. Placing more powers of control into the hands of officials, whether police or otherwise, simply enables more harassment and abuse. See Loff, Overs and Longo, 'Can health programmes lead to mistreatment of sex workers?'; Jenkins and Hunter, *Empowering Sex Workers: Does It Matter?* 8. Even where the objects of surveillance and control are not engaging in sexual activity, abuses are frequent. Reports of rangers in Moresby harassing *buai* sellers are frequent, and in 2010, I personally witnessed a contingent of police swooping on vendors of drinks, newspapers, cheap trade goods etc., and while I saw no personal violence, I saw property smashed and confiscated.
89   As I heard declared and roundly cheered at the Scarlet Alliance National Forum, 17–19 November 2009, Canberra.
90   Eventually published in 2010. Karen Fletcher and Bomal Gonapa, 2010, 'Decriminalisation of prostitution in Papua New Guinea,' in *Civic Insecurity: Law, Order and HIV in Papua New Guinea*, ed. Vicki Luker and Sinclair Dinnen, Canberra: ANU E Press, 141–52, online: http://press.anu.edu.au?p=94091, accessed 8 April 2014.

Fletcher's paper, legislative changes should also be considered to the *Criminal Code* Section 231 (Bawdy Houses), which creates the offence of keeping a 'bawdy house': 'A person who keeps a house, room, set of rooms or place of any kind for purposes of prostitution is guilty of a misdemeanour.'

Other legislative reform initiatives should also include reforms to the *Summary Offences Act* Section 55, the law which makes 'living on the earnings of prostitution' an offence; and to Section 56 'Keeping a Brothel' and Section 57 'Suppression of Brothels'; two sections which criminalise brothel-keeping, providing financial assistance to brothel-keeping, using or permitting the use of premises as a brothel, or letting premises to be used as a brothel.

None of these provisions is much used by the formal law enforcement system. The greatest threats posed to sex sellers come from police violence, abuse and harassment, and the stigma and abuse associated with them in PNG. This is profoundly disempowering, undermining any sense of self-esteem and self-worth of those involved, and reduces their ability to come out into the open to access counselling, information about HIV prevention, condoms or necessary health and social services, or to insist on safe sex practices with their clients. Repeal of Section 55 at least could reverse these negative effects, uphold the human rights of sex sellers, and assist greatly in the management of the HIV epidemic.

The alternative to direct legislative intervention lies through the courts. A test case could be mounted whereby a person convicted in the District Court Under Section 55 appeals to the National Court to have the decision in *Anna Wemay's Case* overturned, firstly on the simple ground that it is bad law, supported by such constitutional grounds as interference with the right to privacy, and the rights of all citizens to integral human development. Success in such a case will not affect laws relating to brothels, but there is some argument for retaining these offences which criminalise the sexual exploitation, particularly of women and girls. Removal of brothel and pimping offences may encourage an increase in brothels, which may become centres for organised crime, drug dealing and trafficking. On the other hand, retention of brothel offences will maintain the sex trade as a covert activity, with its associated stigma and discrimination, and continue to restrict the access by workers themselves to health, counselling and condoms.

Decriminalisation of sodomy

> It was urged that conduct of this kind is a cause of the demoralisation and decay of civilisations ... this argument ... is often no more than the expression of revulsion against what is regarded as unnatural, sinful or disgusting. Many people feel this revulsion, for one or more of these

> reasons. But moral conviction or instinctive feeling, however strong, is not a valid basis for overriding the individual's privacy and for bringing within the ambit of the criminal law private sexual behaviour of this kind.
>
> *Wolfenden Report*, 1957.[91]

Legislative reform of the sodomy laws would be a relatively simple matter. Unlike many other jurisdictions which must rely exclusively on them to prosecute instances of forced sex and sex with boys, PNG already has laws to cover these offences, introduced as part of the *Criminal Code (Sexual Offences and Crimes Against Children) Act* 2002. By the introduction of gender-neutral language and the concept of 'sexual penetration,' this amendment made it illegal to rape a male.[92] And the new Part IV Division 2A criminalises all sexual interference with children, boys or girls. The continuance of the sodomy laws means that there are now in effect two different offences for the same act; and that the removal of Sections 210 and 212 would be a simple matter of repeal.[93] Again, success of this course of action depends on political will.

An alternative would be to take a case challenging the constitutionality of the sodomy laws to the Supreme Court under *Constitution* Section 19. This does not require the existence of a prior course of conduct, but it does require that one of the officers or bodies specified under Section 19 agrees to mount the case. Alternatively, if a person considers that his rights have been breached, for example his right to privacy if he is being prosecuted under *Criminal Code* Section 210 as Johnny Mala was, he could ask the judge during the prosecution to refer the case to the Supreme Court under *Constitution* Section 18. Or he could take a case under Section 57. There are many variations on these scenarios, but they all presume that a case will come to court in the first place, and that the person involved (as applicant or defendant) has access to legal assistance.

Decriminalisation initiatives

> Rather than analyzing power from the point of view of its internal rationality, it consists of analysing power relations through the antagonism of strategies.... For example, to find out what our society means by sanity, perhaps we should investigate what is happening in the field of insanity.... And what we mean by legality in the field of

---

91 *Wolfenden Report*, §54.
92 *Criminal Code* Sections 347, 349.
93 This of course does not take into account the many other issues raised in the area of queer law reform, such as rights to insurance, marriage etc. Those are different issues entirely, and I have not considered them in my research.

illegality.... And, in order to understand what power relations are about, perhaps we should investigate the forms of resistance and attempts made to dissociate these relations.

Michel Foucault, 1982.[94]

Resistance comes in many forms. The sex selling gays I described in Chapter 5 who stole the abusive expatriate client's wallet were resisting in a small way. So too is Peter, when he tells men from the Disciplined Forces to get lost. In Chapter 5 too, I described the activism of one of PNG's favourite singing stars, Moses Tau. I portrayed his position as a 'resistive subject,' the individual activist who challenges essentialised stereotypes and disrupts the normative framework—he demonstrates the power of the 'resistive subject' to bring about change. He is not alone, although he may be one of the most conspicuous. When Dame Carol Kidu became Minister for Community Development, she was able to further various human rights agendas, including that of decriminalisation of sex work and sodomy. In Chapter 6, I described her involvement in the public debate of 2005 on the legalisation of prostitution. When members of the medical profession informed her of their concerns about the harmful effects on HIV prevention and care of criminal laws on selling sex and male-male sex, she embarked on a multi-sectoral effort to review those laws. After reappointment following elections in 2007, she reformulated this effort into a Reference Group of public sector, private sector and civil society representatives, including representatives of criminalised groups, to further the decriminalisation initiative.[95] The Reference Group started work, canvassing possibilities for reform based on human rights and public health grounds.

In 2010, Dame Carol took a submission to the National Executive Council (Cabinet) based on the Reference Group work, requesting a review of laws on sex work and consensual male-to-male sex from a social and public health perspective, but Cabinet rejected it outright on moral, religious and custom grounds.[96] She did however succeed in obtaining endorsement of her proposal to refer a review of the laws in question to the Constitutional and Law Reform Commission (CLRC), with instructions to undertake widespread and lengthy community consultation and work in conjunction with the Reference Group. Meanwhile, her advocacy work with parliamentarians had resulted in the then Attorney-General becoming enthusiastic about the possibilities of a special reference under *Constitution* Section 19 to the Supreme Court challenging the

---

94 Michel Foucault, 1982, 'The subject and power,' *Critical Inquiry* 8(4): 777–95, 780.
95 Kidu, 'A national response to the HIV epidemic in Papua New Guinea.'
96 Ibid.

constitutional validity of laws which criminalised consensual sex between adults in private.⁹⁷ She called the 'perfect storm' meeting, on that sultry morning in late 2010, to tell us this good news.

But politics intervened. Within weeks of the Attorney-General's decision, a Cabinet reshuffle saw him replaced by a new Attorney-General known for his conservative religious views on social issues.⁹⁸ The initiative lapsed, and the CLRC did not make any apparent moves to implement the NEC direction.

Despite these political upheavals, Dame Carol Kidu continued her work, which culminated in a 'National Dialogue on HIV/AIDS, Human Rights and Law' held in Port Moresby in June 2011. Retired Australian High Court Justice Michael Kirby was guest speaker, and proceedings included satellite consultations with the faith community, civil society, the media and women's groups, panel and group discussions at the Dialogue itself, and side meetings facilitated by Kirby with parliamentarians, legal officers, religious leaders and the media.⁹⁹ Although many invited politicians, including the Minister for Health, failed to attend, Dame Carol Kidu claimed that the Dialogue had 'got people talking,' and had given a human face to the epidemic as participants from all groups in the community met and exchanged views.¹⁰⁰

In 2011, politics intervened again in a highly significant way. The Somare-led government of the day was voted out of office in August, Dame Carol lost her Ministry, and she had already announced publicly that she would not stand for election again.¹⁰¹ Following the general election of 2012, the decriminalisation initiative lost its prime parliamentary champion. The new Minister for Community Development does not appear to be interested in such matters.

What are the chances?

> If law is discourse, it plays a role in the construction of the subject. Law is constantly engaged in re-inventing and re-interpreting the subject, including the sexual subject.... When the sexual [subject] comes to law,

---

97 Field notes November 2010.
98 The new Attorney-General was sworn in on 7 December. See 'Govt in turmoil,' 2010, *Post-Courier* (online), 8 December.
99 National AIDS Council of Papua New Guinea, 2011, Press Release, 14 June, online: http://www.undp.org.pg/docs/Press%20Release%2014%20June%202011%20-%20National%20Dialogue.pdf, accessed 27 August 2011.
100 L. Fox, 2011, 'Australian lawyer calls for PNG action on HIV,' *Australia Network News* (online), 17 July, online: http://www.undp.org.pg/docs/Press%20Release%2014%20June%202011%20-%20National%20Dialogue.pdf, accessed 27 August 2011; pers. comm. friends involved in organisation of the Dialogue.
101 See for example 'Dame Carol Kidu,' 2011, *Australia Network—Pacific Pulse* (online), 8 June, http://australianetwork.com/pacificpulse/stories/3238859.htm, accessed 27 August 2011.

whether to claim rights, or to challenge a punitive regime that bounds her off as someone who is stigmatized, inauthentic or foreign, she counters the weight of sexual and cultural normativity as she transgresses the boundaries of both. In challenging these normative boundaries, she creates the possibility for the recognition of multiple sexual identities or sexual practices through redefining and redrawing the boundaries.

Ratna Kapur, 2001.[102]

Law reform is not just a matter of selecting the best course of action from the options canvassed above, writing the law or the case submissions, and letting it all take its course to a triumphant conclusion. A further essential requirement is will—political will, the will of society, the will of peripheral and resistive non-state actors—which inspires and guides the contests of power in a society. Law is inextricably linked to power, through its role in constructing and maintaining the socio-political norms which guide the exercise of that power. But society is not managed solely through regulatory norms. Resistance, the continual transgression of the boundaries of identity and community, can provoke social transformation as well as social reproduction. Because law's ever-responsive nature keeps it open to an ever-changing society, it too may be provoked into change.[103] Through successful resistance, social order can be unmade and remade, and law can respond accordingly. Resistance, capable of redrawing the boundaries, of remaking society's order, becomes a process aimed at disrupting the dominant narratives which comprise social norms.

A problem of narratives

In Chapter 6, I used intersectionality theory to analyse the nature of categories of experience in PNG, and the construction of dominant and subordinate groups within those categories which provides a matrix of power relations. This is done by the linguistic creation of labels and narratives affixed to categories, groups and sub-groups, who are then classified as 'good' or 'bad' depending on their degree of dominance or subordination. So prostitutes as a group are categorised by gender as 'woman.' The dominant narrative of 'woman' is inflected in the category of locale, by the quality of the hardworking, submissive village-dwelling woman, and in the category of sexuality by the quality of purity, so that the mobile, urbanised, promiscuous prostitute becomes 'bad' in multiple ways. By the same process, gays and transgenders, although classified by gender

---

[102] Ratna Kapur, 2000–2001, 'Postcolonial erotic disruptions: legal narratives of culture, sex, and nation in India,' *Columbia Journal of Gender and Law* 10: 333–84, 382–83.
[103] Ben Golder and Peter Fitzpatrick, 2009, *Foucault's Law*, Abingdon, UK: Routledge, 61–62, 65, 80–81, 109–10.

as 'man,' fail completely in terms of sexuality to conform to the dominant narrative of the heterosexual, married and fertile *man tru*. Like sex sellers, gays and transgenders are 'bad,' and deserving of society's punishment.

Herein lies the problem. It is not enough to argue that criminalising sexual minorities spreads HIV by driving them underground. It is not enough to argue their human rights to equal treatment before the law, and their freedom from discrimination and abuse. Those seeking reform must challenge the entire weight of the normative narratives which subordinate them. In doing so, they perforce enter the murky terrain of law's right to define, distinguish and adjudge right and wrong.

Crimes, sins and morals

> A state that recognises difference does not mean a state without morality or one without a point of view. It does not banish concepts of right and wrong, nor envisage a world without good and evil. It is impartial in its dealings with people and groups, but is not neutral in its value system. The Constitution certainly does not debar the state from enforcing morality. Indeed, the Bill of Rights is nothing if not a document founded on deep political morality. What is central to the character and functioning of the state, however, is that the dictates of the morality which it enforces, and the limits to which it may go, are to be found in the text and spirit of the Constitution itself.
>
> Constitutional Court of South Africa, 1998.[104]

Half a century after the *Wolfenden Report*, sexual reform movements are firmly on the international agenda. The United Nations and its agencies, countless international NGOs, national governments and civil society organisations, are all urging states to move towards the decriminalisation of the selling of sex and sex between males. Apart from pressing the public health issue of HIV, the main principle on which arguments are founded (briefly, lengthily, eloquently, forcefully) is the breach of human rights.[105]

---

104 *National Coalition for Gay and Lesbian Equality and Another v Minister of Justice and Others* (CCT11/98) [1998] ZACC 15, §136 per Sachs J.
105 See for example 'Objectives,' n.d., *Scarlet Alliance*, online: http://www.scarletalliance.org.au/object/, accessed 31 August 2011; Frans Viljoen, 2009, 'International Human Rights law: a short history,' *UN Chronicle* L(4) December, online: http://www.un.org:80/wcm/content/site/chronicle/home/archive/Issues2009/internationalhumanrightslawashorthistory, accessed 6 August 2011; Human Rights Watch, 2008, *This Alien Legacy: The Origins of 'Sodomy' Laws in British Colonialism*, New York: Human Rights Watch; Kirby, 'Human rights—the way forward'; and numerous international and regional documents, including those referred to above.

Opposition to decriminalisation in PNG is based largely on concerns about morality. Arguments against selling and exchanging sex are posed usually in terms of threats to the status of those involved, Christian principles, and the need to uphold family values. Arguments against condoning male-male sex are perhaps even more blatantly couched in terms of offences against morality and Christianity. As I have demonstrated in Chapter 6, publications, letters and statements propounding these arguments usually conclude with an exhortation to reaffirm criminalisation. Such views rarely if ever undertake any express consideration of the relationship of morality and law, or of law's right to intrude in matters of sexual morality.[106]

Law and morality

> The function of the criminal law ... is to preserve public order and decency, to protect the citizen from what is offensive or injurious, and to provide sufficient safeguards against exploitation and corruption of others, particularly those who are specially vulnerable because they are young, weak in body or mind, inexperienced, or in a state of special physical, official, or economic dependence ... but [not] to intervene in the private lives of citizens, or to seek to enforce any particular patterns of behaviour.
>
> *Wolfenden Report*, 1957.[107]

The *Constitution* recognises the significance of this principle. Laws may regulate or restrict fundamental rights and freedoms to the extent necessary in order to give effect to the public interest in public safety, public order and public welfare (Section 38). The right to privacy under Section 49, the right to equal treatment before the law in Section 37, the freedom from discrimination in Section 55 may all be restricted on the grounds of public interest. This was the argument taken in the *Naz Appeal*. The problem lies in the interpretation and application of these principles.

The court in *Mama Kamzo's Appeal*, and indeed the lawyers who instigated it, were deeply concerned that a precedent would be set whereby every recipient in an anal sex act would be able to claim duress, or a lack of free will. The Chief Crown Prosecutor considered it 'a matter of principle of such importance that the judgement should not be permitted to stand as an authority.' He noted that the offence charged was serious, carrying a high maximum penalty, and went on to opine that 'there must be some reasonable proportion between the seriousness of the offence and the steps that must be taken to prevent it by those

---

106 A striking exception is Bernard Narokobi's essay in the *Post-Courier* in 1977. See Narokobi, 1977, 'Should the law permit immorality?' *Post-Courier*, 27 April, 12–13.
107 *Wolfenden Report*, §13–14.

whose duty is to not "permit" it.'[108] The court agreed, declaring that the accused must do more than simply allow, in order to be not guilty of 'permitting' the act. The accused must be proactive in his opposition.[109]

But perhaps Justice Prentice, who wrote a separate but concurring opinion in the appeal case, came closest to revealing the true intentions of the law when he wrote:

> Buggery is one of the offences of sexual indecency which modern text writers see as 'not designed so much for private protection as for the enforcement of officially received opinions on particular aspects of sexual morality.'… The State, until recent times has asserted an interest against its occurrence, to the extent of constituting it an assault despite its being a consensual act.[110]

The state, he pointed out, objects to acts of sodomy, or 'buggery' as he calls it, on moral grounds. And if society decrees through its laws that its morals must be thus protected via the law, then the judges are bound to obey and protect. A similar argument had been raised, although not for the first time, before the Wolfenden Committee a decade previously. But in its report, the Committee declared that 'unless a deliberate attempt is to be made by society, acting through the agency of the law, to equate the sphere of crime with that of sin, there must remain a realm of private morality and immorality which is, in brief and crude terms, not the law's business.'[111]

These differing views of the relationship of law and morality are but one representation of a debate which has been carried on since the nineteenth century. British jurist Lord Devlin, in response to the *Wolfenden Report*, urged that it is the law's duty to protect morality, perhaps because it promotes social cohesion—even private acts should be criminalised if ordinary people feel a sufficient intensity of 'intolerance, indignation and disgust' towards a particular form of conduct.[112] Contra this view, legal philosopher H.L.A. Hart supported the *Wolfenden Report's* view that each individual has the right to act as he wants, so long as these actions do not harm others,[113] an argument based

---

108 *Mama Kamzo File*, Chief Crown Prosecutor to Crown Solicitor, 21 March 1972, Accession 452, Box 14612, Crown Prosecution file 5-9218, 1.
109 *R v M.K.* [1973] PNGLR 204 (*Mama Kamzo's Appeal*).
110 Ibid.
111 *Wolfenden Report*, §13–14, §61.
112 Patrick Devlin, 1960, *The Enforcement of Morals*, London: Oxford University Press.
113 H.L.A. Hart, 1963, *Law, Liberty and Morality*, London: Oxford University Press.

on John Stuart Mill's 'Harm Principle': 'the only purpose for which power can be rightfully exercised over any member of a civilised community, against his will, is to prevent harm to others.'[114]

Since then, new considerations have been advanced and new principles have been elaborated: those of equal rights, the right to privacy, and a clearer articulation of the morality/law divide. The *Universal Declaration of Human Rights* (UDHR) provides at Article One that 'all human beings are born free and equal in dignity and rights. They are endowed with reason and conscience and should act towards one another in a spirit of brotherhood.'[115] And at Article Twelve: 'No one shall be subjected to arbitrary interference with his privacy, family, home or correspondence, nor to attacks upon his honour and reputation. Everyone has the right to the protection of the law against such interference or attacks.'

The PNG *Constitution*, in common with the constitutions of other newly-independent nations of the time, entrenches the political and civil human rights set out in the UDHR, including the right to life, the right to privacy, the right to freedom of choice of employment, the right to equal treatment of all before the law and the right of all citizens to the same rights, privileges, obligations and duties irrespective of race, tribe, place of origin, political opinion, colour, creed, religion or sex.[116] It also requires courts to have regard to this and many other international documents regarding human rights.[117] However, as described above, PNG's legal system is characterised by tensions between this modern and detailed system of constitutionally entrenched human rights, the body of imported law which is often paternalistic, outdated and inappropriate, and many of the fundamental principles of customary law.[118]

In a lengthy newspaper article on decriminalisation of prostitution in 1977, Bernard Narokobi made reference to Mill's Harm Principle and reminded readers that, nevertheless, the English criminal law is known for its heavy encroachment

---

114 John Stuart Mill, 1992 [1959], *On Liberty*, Legal Classics Library; John Skorupski, 2005, 'Mill, John Stuart,' in *The Oxford Companion to Philosophy [2nd ed.]*, online: http://www.oxfordreference.com/view/10.1093/acref/9780199264797.001.0001/acref-9780199264797-e-1604?rskey=NAp1Zf&result=3, accessed 16 April 2014.
115 Despite being a statement of the equal rights of all humanity, the term 'brotherhood' is patently gendered. Similarly, the masculine pronoun is used in Article 12.
116 See the description in Christine Stewart, 1993, *Law, Ethics and HIV/AIDS: Existing Law of Papua New Guinea*, report prepared for Law Reform Commission of Papua New Guinea and Papua New Guinea Department of Health, Boroko, Papua New Guinea: Law Reform Commission of Papua New Guinea and Papua New Guinea Department of Health, 2–3; and the further discussion in National AIDS Council of Papua New Guinea, 2001, *Review of Policy and Legislative Reform Relating to HIV/AIDS in Papua New Guinea*, report prepared for National AIDS Council of Papua New Guinea, Port Moresby, 27–31.
117 *Constitution* Section 39(3).
118 Christine Stewart, 1993, 'Existing law on HIV/AIDS in Papua New Guinea,' in *Law, Ethics and HIV: Proceedings of the UNDP Intercountry Consulatation, Cebu, Philippines 3–6 May, 1993*, ed. Robert A Glick, New Delhi: United Nations Development Programme, 133–50, 68–70.

on matters of individual liberty. But there can be a price: 'For those who want to see law and morality merge, there is the need also to see that the policing of that law does not create even greater social and moral ills. It is all too easy for us to set up our own judgement.'[119] He warns that 'there is a limit to what we can do by way of controlling human conduct through criminal law.' Reliance on the criminal law not only might create further harm, but might not really work to address underlying social issues, for example the poverty which causes women to sell sex.[120] And how right he was!

A further dimension can be added to this argument. In the *Naz Case* which declared the Indian *Penal Code*'s sodomy law unconstitutional insofar as it related to consensual sex between adults, the New Delhi High Court drew a distinction between what it termed popular or public morality and constitutional morality:

> Popular morality or public disapproval of certain acts is not a valid justification for restriction of the fundamental rights.... Popular morality, as distinct from a constitutional morality derived from constitutional values, is based on shifting and subjecting [*sic*] notions of right and wrong. If there is any type of 'morality' that can pass the test of compelling state interest, it must be 'constitutional' morality and not public morality.[121]

Constitutional morality, the court went on to point out, is to be found in the Fundamental Rights and Directive Principles of the Indian *Constitution*—the 'conscience of the *Constitution*.'[122] The same argument can be made in relation to the PNG *Constitution*, where 'constitutional morality' is better-known as 'the spirit of the Constitution,' and its principles are to be found in the Preamble. In both jurisdictions, it is incumbent on the State to protect these principles.[123]

Contradicting these arguments, however, the Indian Supreme Court proceeded to strike down the initial *Naz Case* on the grounds *inter alia* of morality. Whereas the Delhi High Court had held that moral indignation cannot be a basis for curtailing an individual's rights to privacy and dignity,[124] the Supreme Court too found no 'compelling state interest' which would justify retention

---

119   Narokobi, 'Should the law permit immorality?' 12–13.
120   Ibid.
121   The *Naz Case*. The Indian *Penal Code* is similar to the PNG *Criminal Code*; so too are the human rights provisions of the Indian *Constitution*.
122   Ibid., §80.
123   Ibid., §81.
124   Mrinal Satish, 2013. 'Comment: breaking down the SC judgement on Section 377,' *IBN Live*, online: http://ibnlive.in.com/news/comment-breaking-down-the-sc-judgement-on-section-377/439348-3.html, accessed 14 December 2013.

of a law which infringes on fundamental human rights, but nevertheless applied the principle—or more precisely, declined to take responsibility for overturning it.[125]

The new Christianity

Lawyers may argue the legal niceties of popular, private and constitutional moralities, but it is through expressions of community opinion that social norms can be mapped. In PNG, family values and Christian morality, the latter increasingly derived from fundamentalist doctrine, are significant factors in the formulation of public opinions on sexuality, as I have described in Chapter 6. The constructs of intersectionality I developed in that chapter answered many of my questions, but failed in part to respond to one: why do many of today's Christian churches in PNG come to the aid of the state in condemning outlawed sexualities, while at the same time ignoring the Christian message of tolerance, love and forgiveness?

Allen Feldman discusses the modern state's use of visual and aural images portraying 'anthropologically threatening images of violence, terror, covert infection and social suffering' to construct a *cordon sanitaire* around its citizens, striving to protect them from danger.[126] Risks are classified using categories similar to those posited by intersectionality theory (race, class, gender, ethnicity, religion, immune system status and sexuality) to identify and construct a narrative of the 'other' as constituting the zone of danger. This danger lies not only beyond the boundary of the zone, it also lurks within, as a terrorist 'sleeper body' which carries the continual risk of violence and destruction. We are no longer able to perceive or defend ourselves from these insidious threats, and must rely on superior agency to do it for us. The globalised sleeper body within is impossible to eradicate completely but can be managed by exposure and combat. We must be eternally vigilant, and our need for protection must be continually reproduced through media techniques which enable and legitimise the state's on-going processes of security provision.

Feldman's discussions centred upon the politics of western states and the threat of physical violence from sleeper terrorists. His arguments are constructed in the context of the USA post-9/11, but they have a wider application. The same psychology may apply anywhere, and for any reason. Disease, the 'covert infection,' elicits the need for greater social control.[127] Stigmatised and

---

125 Prachi Shrivastava, 2013, 'Column inches slamming SC's ruling overwhelm but 2009 academic argues how #377 is constitutional,' *Legally India*, online: http://www.legallyindia.com/201312124187/Constitutional-law/section-377-judgment-reactions, accessed 14 December 2013.
126 Allen Feldman, 2005, 'On the actuarial gaze: from 9/11 to Abu Ghraib,' *Cultural Studies* 19(2): 203–26.
127 Catherine Campbell and Andrew Gibbs, 2009, 'Stigma, gender and HIV: case studies of inter-sectionality,' in *Gender and HIV/AIDS: Critical Perspectives from the Developing World*, ed. Jelke Boesten and Nana K. Poku, Farnham: Ashgate, 29–46, 32.

vulnerable groups such as sex sellers and gays are easily perceived as sources of covert infection, sin and social suffering and classified as risk-bearing parts of the threatening sleeper body. The processes of security-provision decrease their capacity to make visible the consequences of their stigmatisation, render invisible or marginal the violations of their human rights.

New-wave churches in PNG and elsewhere, through their fundamentalist and charismatic Christian preaching, extend to their congregations the protection of a similar spiritual *cordon sanitaire*. In place of the shock conveyed by the images of death and destruction which Feldman describes, these churches deploy often exuberant, dramatic, spirit-filled rituals to elicit ecstatic experiences; insist on strict adherence to rigid rules of living; and promise salvation to every individual who achieves conversion and the appropriate state of grace. The doctrinal message is of the damnation of sinners without and the saved within—salvation is achieved by prayer, obedience to church doctrine and constant vigilance.[128] Vulnerable groups stigmatised on the basis of their sexuality are the bearers of threat, posing risk to the utopian vision of normalcy within. The New Testament message of brotherly love is eclipsed by this exclusionary process, which declares them all as sinners, to be damned or saved but never to be accepted for their sexual identity or activity. They constitute the moral sleeper body, and it is the church, not the state, which provides the vital on-going processes of security-provision for their management and containment, through the vehement preaching and public statements by any number of pastors and congregational adherents. Reasoned appeals to the New Testament's Christian ideals of love, humility, compassion and mercy pale beside the promise of protection from threats of death and damnation.[129]

The hope of change

> Law represents a key modality of our sociality, of our continuate being-with each other. Through its ability to combine iteratively a determinate securing of limits and a responsive regard to the disruption of those limits and their re-formation, law provides an opening to futurity.
>
> Ben Golder and Peter Fitzpatrick.[130]

The title of this book is designed to emphasise the nexus between the criminal law and the opprobrium with which sex sellers and gays, as people criminalised

---

128 Tanya Luhrmann, 2004, 'Metakinesis: How God becomes intimate in contemporary US Christianity,' *American Anthropologist* 106(3): 518–28; Joel Robbins, 2004, *Becoming Sinners: Christianity and Moral Torment in a Papua New Guinea Society*, Berkeley: University of California Press, 319–24; Robbins, 2004, 'The globalization of Pentecostal and Charismatic Christianity,' *Annual Review of Anthropology* 33: 117–43.
129 Franco Zocca, 2007, *Melanesia and its Churches: Past and Present*, Goroka: Melanesian Institute, 193–95.
130 Golder and Fitzpatrick, *Foucault's Law*, 125.

for acts of consensual sex, are regarded in PNG today. They are criminalised by a system of governing laws introduced by a colonising power—laws based on the principles of the relationship between law and morality pertaining in the metropole at the time, and often greatly at odds with indigenous legal systems.

But times have changed, and as the colonised became citizens of an independent state, so too have their social mores. Laws given by the state are accepted, in principle at least, as the system of power by which society is governed. Other discourses have also become internalised in the new PNG. The colonial system of medicine was based on the control of the health status of colonised individuals, using public health models of disease control, such as identification, contact tracing, barrier nursing, isolation, quarantine and so on, measures now fixed in public health law. If the disease is connected to sex, then the sexually subordinated were subject to the most stringent forms of these controls. Medical discourse now focuses on the search for power over the HIV virus, an enterprise strengthened by constant media attention and international aid donor strategies of epidemic management.

Religious discourse is even more strongly linked to disciplinary power: 'All religions are basically concerned with power. They are concerned with the discovery, identification, moral relevance and ... the systematic orderings of different kinds of power, particularly those seen as significantly beneficial or dangerous.'[131] Both before and after Independence, religion (whether Christian or not) played a crucial role in social ordering in PNG, and people still move easily between the secular and the 'religious,' which today has become a blend of traditional beliefs and Christian piety. Today, religious narratives are an inextricable part of political discourse, right up to the level of national politics.[132] The right of religion to declare who are sinners and who are saved, as interpreted by the essentialised teachings of the 'new churches,' is increasingly accepted. Social protectionism now sits well with fundamentalist Christian doctrine and its promise of control over the sleeper body (be it the HIV virus or the sexually abnormal) within society.

But as Foucault reminds us, the sovereignty of the state, the form of the laws it promulgates and enforces, are only the terminal forms that power takes—power

---

131   Kenelm Burridge, 1969, *New Heaven, New Earth: A Study of Millenarian Activities*, Oxford: Basil Blackwell, 5.

132   Phillip Gibbs, 2002, 'Religion and religious institutions as defining factors in Papua New Guinea politics,' *Development Bulletin* 59 (October): 15–18; Gibbs, 2005, *Political Discourse and Religious Narratives of Church and State in Papua New Guinea*, State Society and Governance in Melanesia Working Paper No. 1 of 2005, 5–6. The political upheaval of December 2011 saw a coalition of most of the mainstream churches, and several Pentecostal and fundamentalist ones, organising a roundtable conference between the two contending Prime Ministers, O'Neil and Somare, to resolve the political impasse, saying that 'being the voice and the mouthpiece of the 6-point-5 million Papua New Guineans, they have made it their business to ensure there's reconciliation so that the ordinary Papua New Guineans are not unnecessarily penalized.' See 'O'Neill/Namah … In control of Government,' 2011, *Papua New Guinea Blogs*, 16 December, online: http://www.pngblogs.com, accessed 17 December 2011.

is always immanent and power relations are always unequal.[133] Despite PNG's official acceptance of global standards of human rights and their entrenchment in the *Constitution*, the PNG state today is little interested in the human rights of its citizens. Those who have the power, the *elites*, declare the norms and make the laws. Crimes, sins and morals typically focus on sexual practices as the area most subjected to unduly harsh penalties, if they fall outside the parameters of normative heterosexual, marital, monogamous, reproductive and non-commercial sexuality. Practices such as sex between males or selling sex bear the greatest social, religious and legal stigma. Any attempts to refigure 'bad' sexual practices as morally and legally acceptable are feared and resisted.[134] The sexually subordinated are at the intersection, but it is not a forgotten space; rather, the space looms large in the imagination, as it confronts dominant and predominant narratives of what is 'good' and 'bad' about sex and sexualities, what is legitimate and what is criminal, what is blessed and what is sinful.

I trust that the evidence and analysis I have set out will help those who hope and work for change in carrying on, on many fronts:[135] in challenging fear and resistance; in loosening the forces which entangle law and morality; in identifying and foregrounding those 'resistive subjects,' the champions whose social transgressions can be morally productive, like those of the *bigman* of old.[136] I hope that my research has provided evidence which can support the argument for reform of oppressive and stigmatising laws. I hope that someday, Dame Carol Kidu's perfect storm will break and PNG will come closer to achieving the respect for the dignity of the individual, the freedom for all from domination and oppression and the protection rather than the oppression of the law, as called for by the *Constitution*.

> Ultimately it is God—not human beings, legislators, courts or churches—who will decide whether the actions of the gay, lesbian and transgender community are right or wrong.
>
> We cannot judge people because of the choices they make about whom to love or live with.
>
> *Fiji Times Online*, 2010.[137]

---

133 Michel Foucault, 1978 [1976], *The Will to Knowledge: The History of Sexuality: Volume 1*, London: Penguin Books, 92–94.
134 Kapur, 'Postcolonial erotic disruptions: legal narratives of culture, sex, and nation in India,' 339.
135 Ratna Kapur, 'The tragedy of victimization rhetoric: resurrecting the "native" subject in international/post-colonial feminist legal politics,' *Harvard Human Rights Journal* 15: 1–37, 5.
136 F.G. Bailey, 2007, 'Reaching for the absolute,' in *The Anthropology of Morality in Melanesia and Beyond*, ed. John Barker, Aldershot and Burlington: Ashgate, 191–207.
137 On the announcement of decriminalisation of sodomy in Fiji the following was published: 'Being happy and gay,' 2010, *Fiji Times Online*, 26 February, online: http://www.fijitimes.com/print.aspx?id=140824, accessed 26 February 2010.

Appendix 1. Respondents

Background respondents

Name	Position	Date and place of interview, notes and comments
Sir Robert K. Woods Kt CBE	Former National and Supreme Court Judge, PNG	Interview 20 March 2005, Wellington NSW. Further information provided by subsequent emails and phone conversations
Bernard Narokobi	Formerly Chairman, PNG Law Reform Commission, Acting Judge, Attorney-General and Member of Parliament	Interview 16 Nov 2005, Auckland, New Zealand
Outreach workers	Poro Sapot	Interview 19 Jan 2006, first-hand account of the Three-Mile Guesthouse Raid
Moses Tau	Singer and activist	Interview 24 Jan 2006, Port Moresby, in relation to outreach work and career
Ms. Ume Wainetti	CEO, Family and Sexual Violence Action Committee	Interview 20 March 2006, Port Moresby
Lady Hilan Los	CEO, Individual and Community Rights Advocacy Forum	Interview 11 April 2006, Port Moresby
Dr Aly Murray	PNG Officer, Scarlet Alliance	Interview 15 April 2006, Port Moresby
Outreach worker (name withheld)	Poro Sapot Police Liaison Officer	6 Sep 2007, Port Moresby
'William' (pseudonym)	Former resident, PNG	Phone conversation and subsequent emails, July 2010

Note: All names are real unless otherwise indicated.

Sex seller respondents

Three-Mile Guesthouse Raid statements

Name	Age	Comments
Anna	23	
Barbara	40	
Beth	18	
Debbie	23	
Diane	27	
Ellen	19	
Emma	21	
Helen	32	
Gaby	37	
Jack	28	male security guard

Jane	23	
Jolene	26	
Jill	26	
Karl	-	male
Kathy	33	
Laura	17	
Lorraine	18	
Lynne	17	
Margaret	20	
Martha	34	
Meg	38	
Miriam	21	
Nana	30	
Natalie	19	
Nell	26	
Sally	22	
Sharon	21	
Susie	21	

Sex seller interviews and group discussions

Name	Age	Comments
Irene	16	Statement regarding police rape taken with raid statements above, March 2004, Port Moresby
PSP outreach workers	group discussion of Three-Mile Guesthouse Raid	19 January 2006, Port Moresby
FSW outreach workers	group discussion	6 Sep 2007, Port Moresby.
Jenny		8 Sep 2007, Port Moresby
Maggi		8 Sep 2007, Port Moresby
Angelina		13 Sep 2007, Port Moresby

Appendix 1. Respondents

Gay respondents

Name/Pseudonym	Age (approx.)	Date of interview, notes and comments*
Frank	50s	Interview, written record, 20 Dec 2005
Adam	50s	12 Jan 2006
Barry	late 30s	14 Jan 2006, interviewed jointly
Colin	30s	14 Jan 2006, interviewed jointly
Douglas	30s	14 Jan 2006, interviewed jointly
Eric	50s	14 Jan 2006
Frank	40s	2005
Fred	early 50s	16 Jan 2006
Gordon	20s	18 Jan 2006
Henry	30s	18 Jan 2006
James	50s	19 Jan 2006
Kevin	50s	20 Jan 2006
Len	40s	22 Jan 2006
Mitchell	30s	24 Jan 2006
Ned	late 40s	16 Apr 2006, (notes only)
Oscar	30s	21 Apr 2006, interviewed jointly
Peter	late 20s	21 Apr 2006, interviewed jointly
Palopas	group discussion	28 May 2006, anonymity verbally agreed*
Robin	20s	9 Sep 2007, Port Moresby
MSW	group discussion	12 Sep 2007, Port Moresby, anonymity agreed**
Steven	50s	11 April 2008
Timothy	30s	22 Aug 2008
Victor	late 30s	Email correspondence and consent May 2008

* Most interviews were conducted in Port Moresby. A small number were not, but to state place of interview could possibly lead to breach of confidentiality. I have therefore suppressed the place of interview in all cases.

** Participants drifted in and out. Some were unknown to me. Obtaining written consent from individuals was impossible, and a policy of 'no names to be used' was agreed verbally at the start of discussion, and reaffirmed occasionally thereafter.

Appendix 2. Sample Antecedent Report

Royal Papua and New Guinea Constabulary

Antecedent Report

Station...........

Date..............

Offence for which committed	Date when accused taken into custody
Baptismal name	Native name
Father's name	aliases (if any)
Village	Subdistrict

1. Age and place of birth
   District

2. How frequently is accused's area patrolled

3. Recent history and degree of Administration influence in accused's area

4. How close is the nearest Supreme Court town to accused's area (distance and walking time)
   Name of town

5. How close is the nearest mission station to the accused's village (distance and walking time)

6. Name of mission and when established

7. Has the accused come under mission influence and if so, how long and to what extent

8. Character and standing of accused's parents

9. Accused's home life, upbringing and environment

10. Accused's character whilst at school

11. Has accused received any education
    and if so, where

12. Standard of education attained by accused

    Accused's degree of intelligence, and accused's mentality (normal or otherwise)

13. Particulars of accused's employment since leaving school

14. Particulars of accused's service (if any) in the Defence Forces and conduct whilst a member of such Forces.

15. Marital Status. If married, date and place of marriage/s.

    Whether by native custom or by a mission

    Number of children and age of each child

    Whether or not accused is living with and supporting his wife/wives and family/families (if not particulars of circumstances under which living and why separate)

16. Circumstances of extenuation generally

17. Circumstances of aggravation generally

18. Accused's associates. If accused charged conjointly, particulars as to whether the accused was the principal offender or not

19. Does local custom have any special attitude to the crime charged (such attitudes may include complete indifference or abhorrence)

20. Special remarks (where special factors involving general circumstances, environment, special belief or superstitions may have bearing on the commission of the crime)

21. Has accused any other prior convictions. If so, state nature of conviction, showing date, court, charge and result

22. Brief summary of each offence of which accused has been convicted, being of a like nature to that which is the basis of the present charge

    Age when first convicted   Has accused been fingerprinted

    Have fingerprints been sent to Criminal Investigation Bureau

23. Other relevant particulars

Officer

Appendix 2. Sample Antecedent Report

Six copies of the Antecedent Report must be completed, as far as possible by the arresting officer, as soon as the accused has been committed. He will forward the report to the Criminal Investigation Bureau, Port Moresby for checking and onward transmission to the Crown Solicitor, Port Moresby or (where the offence is committed in the New Guinea Islands) to the Deputy Crown Solicitor in Rabaul.

Source: This form was copied from one of the many pre-Independence Crown Prosecution files I studied in the National Archives, Port Moresby.

Appendix 3. Review of Homosexuality Cases

For which written judgements are available

This review is compiled from that commenced in the early 1990s by Justice Woods, and continued in the Law Faculty, UPNG, until digitised case reporting commenced with the publication of *PNGinlaw* in the latter part of that decade. I have added some subsequent updates.

1957

Barker v. R [1967-68] PNGLR 204, appeal to High Court of Australia from Supreme Court No. 92 18/8/56.

Lae: Expatriate convicted of 'unlawfully and indecently dealing' (by handling private parts) an expatriate boy aged under 14 (one of several) in a swimming pool changing room.

1961

R v. John Bomai [1964] PNGLR 278

JB, from Chimbu, was convicted before a Court of Native Affairs of sodomy while in Lufa gaol on another sentence. He strenuously denied this act and claimed the charge was highly insulting to Chimbu people. It led him to murder his accuser, but on a defence of provocation, this was reduced to manslaughter.

1962

R v. Bates (Unreported) Supreme Court No. 255 9/10/62

Rabaul. Drunken expatriate attempted to procure two 'natives' for 'acts of gross indecency', offered a £1 note.

1969

R v. Kausigor, R v. Piliu (Unreported) FC3 7/11/69

Wewak. Kausigor (26, from Wewak Sub-District) and Piliu (19, from village near Vanimo) met at a tavern around midday, went to nearby bushes for sex. K. then gave P. a small sum of money. K claimed to have been solicited by P. An observer threatened to tell Piliu's brother.

Antecedent reports claimed that the crime was against 'local' (presumably Wewak) custom. New evidence at appeal rehearing, from a Catholic priest and contradicting, from the prosecution. Fr. Heinemans has 16 years' experience in 'the Sepik area' and considered that before European contact, homosexual behaviour may have been contrary to Sepik customs. But since the introduction of contract labour and plantation dormitory housing, homosexuality was 'very common and widespread where there are large labour lines. (See also Reed 1943, p. 220: where there is no normal sexual outlet in the labour lines, homosexual practices are the easiest adjustment—very common and increasing. 'The natives have a growing awareness of the extreme revulsion with which Europeans view such behaviour, and they know of the harsh prison sentences that are frequently imposed for it. In the aboriginal cultures, however, there existed no such severe sanctions on this form of conduct, and thus the native will try to get away with it when he can.') It has been introduced back to villages by returning labourers so that it was now 'quite common,' but not approved by those who do not indulge in it, though regarded as less serious than sex between men and unmarried girls, which interferes with bride price and exchange arrangements, and other family interests involved in negotiating marriages. Homosexual behaviour is not seen as serious because it is not a threat to society and traditions. A District Officer prosecution witness cast doubt on these assertions but the court believed the priest. A reference to 'six known instances before the Court.'

Appeal Minogue ACJ, Frost J, O'Loghlen AJ (Unreported) FC 3

Sentences reduced from three years to 18 months.

1970

R v. Byrne [1971-72] PNGLR 1

Accused was arrested and charged with carnal knowledge against the order of nature, committing an act of gross indecency with a male person and unlawful and indecent assault. Released on bail on his own recognisance. Disappeared.

1971

R v. Stanley Sydenham Oxenham & Hendrick Lapanga Patau

Prentice J. Kieta, Bougainville, 2nd Dec 1971

Papua New Guinea National Archives Acc 454 Box 4605 File 5-9087 (Crown Prosecutions file).

1972

R v. Mama Kamzo (Unreported, Unnumbered) No.671, 17 Feb 1972

Frost SPJ Port Moresby 17 Feb 1972

Criminal law—carnal knowledge. Not guilty; homosexual act; judge defined permitting carnal knowledge as an act of free will; he ruled accused only submitted to act; reversed in *R v M.K.*

R v. M.K. [1973] PNGLR 204

Appeal: Rubber plantation labourer permitted his *bosboi* to have sex with him under the threat that he would be reported for dereliction of duty. The trial judge acquitted on the grounds that free will permission must be proved, but referred the matter to the Full Court, which overturned the qualification.

Prentice J. quotes from Howard 176: many sex offences are designed to protect the victim. Others however, those prohibiting buggery, other deviant sexual practices between humans, and sexual contact with animals 'are not designed so much for private protection as for the enforcement of officially received opinions on particular aspects of sexual morality.' Buggery is 'traditionally hedged about with pejorative adverbs and adjectives in statutes, and in indictments.... The State until recent times has asserted an interest against its occurrence, to the extent of constituting it an assault despite its being a consensual act.' '[L]ong continuance of legislative abhorrence for this class of deed, apparently intended to be carried on into the *Criminal Code*...'

R v. Leni Gone of Tawat and Joseph Oura of Kumuki

Prentice J Kieta, Bougainville, 10 May 1972

Papua New Guinea National Archives Acc 454 Box 14619 File 5-9351

1972

R v. Siune Wel Acc 454 Box 14625 Files **5-9471**

R v. Hugh William Sitai   **5-9468**

R v. Yawi Huaimbore   **5-9474**

Frost SPJ Kundiawa, Chimbu, June 1972

1972

R v. Christopher Leech

Supreme Court Archives Box 2038 SCRA Prentice J. Notebooks 37-38 1972

Indictment of 5 May 1972

s.208 permitted Peter Yakai to have carnal knowledge 7 Feb 1972. Plea: not guilty. Reliable witness ultimately arrested for wilful murder of another European.

1973

R v. Joseph Mambiam and Raphael Warasurin

Acc 454 Box 14,654 File 10058

Wewak, Committal hearing 1/10/73, discharged. Prisoners in Boram. Evidence of another prisoner. RM R.Tovue

1975

Secretary for Law v. Dewake **[1975] PNGLR 100**

Man 20 from Morehead, Western Province, holidaying in Port Moresby, took a small child about 3 from the same area to the beach and minimally penetrated his anus. The people of PNG hold strong concern that young children should not be exposed to such sexual treatment as this, and the sentence should reflect this.

1990

State v. Bui (Unreported) N944 14/12/90

Brunton J Goroka

Eastern Highlands Province. While imprisoned for rape, the accused forced sex on another detainee. He told the Court that homosexual acts were not uncommon in prison, and usually did not get punished. Judge (Brunton) said that homosexuality is a personal disposition, not a medical condition or a social affliction. Allowed remissions because to keep him in prison would only exacerbate the situation.

1991

State v. Pos [1991] PNGLR 208

Jalina J

Man 20 from Morobe who migrated to East New Britain as a plantation labourer but is not employed. While in prison, he with others threatened another man into submitting to sex from at least 4. Judge (Jalina) considered it the behaviour of animals, awarded deterrent punishment, referred *Dewake*.

1993

State v. Kuengu [1993] PNGLR 124

Doherty J

Man 29 forced sex on 16-year old remandee in prison in Rabaul. Judge (Doherty) considered it analogous to rape 'an act of forced sexual connection without the consent of the victim.' Because of Constitution S.55, the same factors should be considered in sentencing. Community attitudes differ with regard to sodomy. Very few communities where it is totally acceptable, but in some it is more tolerated than others, in some it invokes a high degree of abhorrence. But aware of no community in which forced connection of this kind is acceptable.

1993

State v. Merriam [1994] PNGLR 104

Accused was American founder and director of a mission in Eastern Highlands Province, alleged had sex with a 7–8 year-old boy whom he and his wife took in and treated like a son. Court considered it a typical child sexual abuse case (stated that nearly all victims of paedophiles were boys).

Court notes that Sections 213(4) defilement of girls under 12, 216(3) defilement of girls under 16 and of idiots, 218(2) procuring a girl or woman and 219(2) procuring a girl or woman by drugs all require corroborative evidence, but S.210 among others in the Division does not. Rape requires recent complaint.

1997

State v. Johnny Mala (Unreported, Unnumbered) CR96 of 1997, 26 February 1997

Pitpit AJ, Tabubil, Western Province

Premeditated and consensual sexual intercourse between two male adults. Plea of guilty. Carnal knowledge *per anum*, need for deterrent sentence.

Appendix 4. Summary of Sentences

In category 'carnal knowledge'

This is drawn principally from Justice Woods's private records of sentencing practice,[1] derived annually from National Court judges' monthly diaries for the years 1982–1997, and covering a range of indictable offences, including 'Carnal Knowledge.' These are the only years he was able to discover on a return trip to Port Moresby (April 2005) after he left the PNG Bench. There may be more extant. Woods J claims to be able to deduce the location of each judge by the preponderance of types of crime he/she dealt with.

The judge's name is given in the first column. The description of each case in the second column is taken from the one-line summary of each judge's five-line summary. The 'Carnal Knowledge' category included offences of both sodomy and indecent dealing between males many offences of interference with underage girls, and it was assumed that charges relating to the former were all indicated by reference to 'boy' or prison environment, and so are the only ones shown here. Where the case has been reported its name is shown in brackets. The last column indicates whether a guilty plea was entered ('P') or the case went to trial ('T'). Plea cases are rarely reported unless there is an unusual sentencing issue.

Judge	Case description	Plea or trial
1990		
Woods	old man with young boy indecent assault	T
Brunton	forced sodomy in prison (Bui)	P
1991		
Kidu	attempted sodomy on boy	P
Ellis	sodomy	P
Jalina	sodomy, forced in gaol (Pos)	T
Jalina	sodomy, forced in gaol	P
1992–1993		
Summaries not available		
1993		
Doherty	Rabaul: man forced 16-year-old in prison (Kuengu)	T

---

1 Compiled by Justice Sir Robert Woods, commencing when he came from the Justice Department to the Bench in 1982 (photocopy documents in my possession, obtained courtesy of Justice Woods).

Sakora	Goroka: expat missionary with boy 8–9 (Merriam)	T
1994		
Woods	16-year-old and 6-year-old boy	P
Hinchcliffe	15 years indecent assault of 7-year-old boy	P
	8-year-old indecent dealing with 13-year-old boy	P
Brown	sodomy of another prisoner in gaol	P
Salika	unlawful carnal knowledge of boy	P
	unlawful carnal knowledge of boy by 13-year-old	P
1995		
Woods	with 10-year-old boy who was hospitalised	P
Andrew	33-year-old with 7-year-old boy	P
Sakora	sodomy at CIS, threatened victim	P
Samuel	sodomy	P
	sodomy	T
Pitpit	with 6-year-old boy	P
1996		
Andrew	18-year-old with 7-year-old boy	P
Akuram	with 10-year-old boy	P
Lenalia	with 6-year-old boy	P
1997		
Jalina	high school teacher sodomy with student	P
Jalina	sodomy	P
Jalina	sodomy 17-year-old	P
Batari	15-year-old sodomy with 5-year-old	P

Source: Compiled by Justice Sir Robert Woods.

Cases reported only as 'sodomy' may or may not relate to incidents between consenting adults in private. The term 'sodomy' has come to encompass all acts of anal-penetrative sex between males, as Section 210 was always charged if provable, due to its significantly higher penalty.

Bibliography

Articles, books and reports

Abaijah, Josephine and Eric Wright, 1991. *A Thousand Coloured Dreams*. Mount Waverley, Vic: Dellasta Pacific.

Adams, Michael F., 1975. 'Law versus order.' In *Lo Bilong Ol Manmeri: Crime, Compensation and Village Courts*, ed. Jean Zorn and Peter Bayne. Port Moresby: University of Papua New Guinea, 97–103.

Aggleton, Peter, Peter Davies and Graham Hart (eds), 1993. *AIDS: Facing the Second Decade*. London: Falmer Press.

Aldrich, Robert, 2003. *Colonialism and Homosexuality*. London and New York: Routledge.

Alpers, Michael, 1997. *Final Report to UNAIDS: Police and Sex Workers in Papua New Guinea*. Report prepared for Papua New Guinea Institute of Medical Research, Goroka.

Altman, Dennis, 2001. *Global Sex*. Sydney: Allen & Unwin.

Amnesty International, 2006. *Papua New Guinea: Violence Against Women: Not Inevitable, Never Acceptable!* Amnesty International. Online: http://web.amnesty.org/library/Index/ENGASA340022006, accessed 5 September 2006.

Anthias, Floya and Nira Yuval-Davis, 1983. 'Contextualizing feminism: gender, ethnic and class divisions.' *Feminist Review* 15: 62–75.

Arnot, Meg, 1988. 'The oldest profession in a new Britannia.' In *Constructing a Culture*, ed. Verity Burgmann and Jenny Lee. Fitzroy, Vic: McPheeGribble/Penguin, 46–62.

Asia Pacific Council of AIDS Service Organizations (APCASO), Civil Society Perspectives on the 2011 HIV/AIDS HLM, 2011. 'The 2011 Political Declaration on HIV/AIDS.' *infocus* 1 (August). Online: http://www.apcaso.org/v2/wp-content/uploads/2011/12/APCASO-InFocus-No1.pdf, accessed 15 April 2014.

Baca, George, Aisha Kahn and Stephen Palmie (eds), 2009. *Empirical Futures: Anthropologists and Historians Engage the Work of Sidney W. Mintz*. Chapel Hill: University of North Carolina Press.

Bailey, F.G., 2007. 'Reaching for the absolute.' In *The Anthropology of Morality in Melanesia and Beyond*, ed. John Barker. Aldershot and Burlington: Ashgate, 191–207.

Ballard, John, 1979. 'Ethnicity and access in Papua New Guinea.' Unpublished.

-------- 1992. 'Sexuality and the state in time of epidemic.' In *Rethinking Sex: Social Theory and Sexuality Research*, ed. R.W. Connell and G.W. Dowsett. Carlton, Vic: Melbourne University Press, 102–16.

-------- 1998. 'The constitution of AIDS in Australia: taking government at a distance seriously.' In *Governing Australia: Studies in Contemporary Rationalities of Government*, ed. Mitchell Dean and Barry Hindess. Melbourne: Cambridge University Press, 125–38.

Ballard, John and Clement Malau, 2009. 'Policy-making on AIDS to 2000.' In *Policy Making and Implementation, Studies from Papua New Guinea*, ed. R.J. May. Canberra: ANU E Press, 369–78. Online: http://press.anu.edu.au?p=78541m, accessed 31 March 2014.

Banks, Cyndi, 1993. *Women in Transition: Social Control in Papua New Guinea*. Canberra: Australian Institute of Criminology.

Barber, K., 2003. 'The Bugiau community at Eight-mile: an urban settlement in Port Moresby, Papua New Guinea.' *Oceania* 73(4): 287–97.

Barker, John (ed.), 1990. *Christianity in Oceania: Ethnographic Perspectives*. Lanham: University Press of America.

-------- 2007. *The Anthropology of Morality in Melanesia and Beyond*. Aldershot and Burlington: Ashgate.

Bateson, Gregory, 1936. *Naven: A Survey of the Problems Suggested by a Composite Picture of the Culture of a New Guinea Tribe Drawn From Three Points of View*. Cambridge: Cambridge University Press.

Bayne, Peter, 1975. 'Legal development in Papua New Guinea: the place of the common law.' *Melanesian Law Journal* 3(1): 9–39.

Beardmore, Edward, 1890. 'The natives of Mowat, Daudai, New Guinea.' *The Journal of the Anthropological Institute of Great Britain and Ireland* 19: 459–66.

Beaver, Wilfred Norman, 1920. *Unexplored New Guinea: A Record of the Travels, Adventures, and Experiences of a Resident Magistrate*. London: Seeley, Service & Co.

Beer, Bettina, 2008. 'Buying betel and selling sex: contested boundaries, risk milieus, and discourses about HIV/AIDS in the Markham Valley, Papua New Guinea.' In *Making Sense of AIDS: Culture, Sexuality, and Power in Melanesia*, ed. Leslie Butt and Richard Eves. Honolulu: University of Hawai'i Press, 97–115.

Behar, Ruth, 1996. *The Vulnerable Observer: Anthropology that Breaks your Heart*. Boston: Beacon Press.

Belshaw, Cyril Shirley, 1957. *The Great Village: The Economic and Social Welfare of Hanuabada, an Urban Community in Papua*. London: Routledge & Kegan Paul.

Berry, Chris, Fran Martin and Audrey Yue (eds), 2003. *Mobile Cultures: New Media in Queer Asia*. Durham NC: Duke University Press.

Besnier, Niko, 1994. 'Polynesian gender liminality through time and space.' In *Third Sex, Third Gender: Beyond Sexual Dimorphism in Culture and History*, ed. Gilbert Herdt. New York: Zone Books, 285–328.

-------- 2007. 'Language and gender research at the intersection of the global and the local.' *Gender and Language* 1(1): 67–78.

Besnier, Niko and Kalissa Alexeyeff (eds), 2014. *Gender on the Edge: Transgender, Gay and other Pacific Islanders*. Hong Kong: Hong Kong University Press.

Boellstorff, Tom, 2003. 'I knew it was me: mass media, "globalization," and lesbian and gay Indonesia.' In *Mobile Cultures: New Media in Queer Asia*, ed. Chris Berry, Fran Martin and Audrey Yue. Durham, NC: Duke University Press, 21–41.

-------- 2005. *The Gay Archipelago: Sexuality and Nation in Indonesia*. Princeton and Oxford: Princeton University Press.

Boesten, Jelke and Nana K. Poku (eds), 2009. *Gender and HIV/AIDS: Critical Perspectives from the Developing World*. Farnham: Ashgate.

Borrey, Anou, 2003. 'Understanding sexual violence: the case of Papua New Guinea.' Ph.D. thesis. Sydney: University of Sydney.

Bottomley, Gill, Marie de Lepervanche and Jeannie Martin (eds), 1991. *Intersexions: Gender, Class, Culture, Ethnicity*. North Sydney: Allen & Unwin.

Bradley, Christine, 2001. *Family and Sexual Violence in PNG: An Integrated Long-Term Strategy*. Port Moresby: Institute of National Affairs, Discussion Paper no. 84.

Brah, Avtar and Ann Phoenix, 2004. 'Ain't i a woman? Revisiting intersectionality.' *Journal of International Women's Studies* 5(3): 75–86.

Braithwaite, John, 2009. 'Foreword.' In *A Bird That Flies With Two Wings: Kastom and State Justice Systems in Vanuatu*, Miranda Forsyth. Canberra: ANU E Press, xi–xiv. Online: http://press.anu.edu.au?p=49351, accessed 10 April 2014.

Broom, Dorothy H., 1987. 'Another tribe: gender and inequality.' In *Three Worlds of Inequality: Race, Class and Gender*, ed. Christine Jennet and Randal G. Stewart. South Melbourne: Macmillan Company of Australia, 264–82.

Brown, B.J. (ed.), 1969. *Fashion of Law in New Guinea: Being an Account of the Past, Present and Developing System of Laws in Papua and New Guinea*. Sydney, Melbourne, Brisbane: Butterworths.

Buchanan, Holly et al., 2010. *Behavioural Surveillance Research in Rural Development Enclaves in Papua New Guinea: A Study with the WR Carpenters Workforce*. Port Moresby: National Research Institute.

Bulbeck, Chilla, 1992. *Australian Women in Papua New Guinea: Colonial Passages 1920–1940*. Cambridge: Cambridge University Press.

Burgmann, Verity and Jenny Lee (eds), 1988. *Constructing a Culture*. Fitzroy, Vic: McPheeGribble/Penguin.

Burridge, Kenelm, 1960. *Mambu: A Melanesian Millennium*. London: Methuen.

-------- 1969. *New Heaven, New Earth: A Study of Millenarian Activities*. Oxford: Basil Blackwell.

Butler, Judith, 1993. *Bodies That Matter: On the Discursive Limits of 'Sex.'* New York: Routledge.

Butt, Leslie and Richard Eves (eds), 2008. *Making Sense of AIDS: Culture, Sexuality, and Power in Melanesia*, Honolulu: University of Hawai'i Press.

Campbell, Catherine and Andrew Gibbs, 2009. 'Stigma, gender and HIV: case studies of inter-sectionality.' In *Gender and HIV/AIDS: Critical Perspectives from the Developing World*, ed. Jelke Boesten and Nana K. Poku. Farnham: Ashgate, 29–46.

Center for Health and Gender Equity, 2008. *Implications of U.S. Policy Restrictions for HIV Programs Aimed at Commercial Sex Workers*. Online: http://www.genderhealth.org/files/uploads/change/publications/aplobrief.pdf, accessed 16 May 2011.

Centre for Environmental Law and Community Rights (CELCoR) and Australian Conservation Foundation, 2006. *Bulldozing Progress: Human Rights Abuses and Corruption in Papua New Guinea's Large Scale Logging Industry*. Boroko, PNG: Australian Conservation Foundation.

Chalmers, Gloria, 2006. *Kundus, Cannibals and Cargo Cults: Papua New Guinea in the 1950's*. Watsons Bay, NSW: Books and Writers Network Pty Ltd.

Chalmers, James, 1887. *Pioneering in New Guinea*. London: Religious Tract Society.

-------- 1895. *Pioneer Life and Work in New Guinea 1877–1894*. London: Religious Tract Society.

Chalmers, James and W. Wyatt Gill, 1885. *Work and Adventure in New Guinea 1877 to 1885*. London: Religious Tract Society.

Chamallas, Martha, 2003. *Introduction to Feminist Legal Theory*, [2nd ed.]. New York: Aspen Publishers.

Chancer, Lynn Sharon, 1993. 'Prostitution, feminist theory, and ambivalence: notes from the sociological underground.' *Social Text* 37 (Winter): 143–71.

Chatterton, Percy, 1974. *Day That I Have Loved: Percy Chatterton's Papua*. Sydney: Pacific Publications.

Chavkin, Wendy and JaneMaree Maher (eds), 2010. *The Globalization of Motherhood: Deconstructions and Reconstructions of Biology and Care*. Abingdon, Oxon: Routledge.

Clark, Geoffrey, 2003. 'Shards of meaning: archaeology and the Melanesia-Polynesia divide.' *Journal of Pacific History* 38(2): 197–215.

Clark, Jeffrey, n.d. *Huli Sexuality, the State, and STD/AIDS Prevention Programmes*. Goroka: report prepared for PNG Institute of Medical Research.

Cleland, Rachel, 1984. *Pathways to Independence: Story of Official and Family Life in Papua New Guinea from 1951 to 1975*. Cottesloe, WA: R. Cleland.

Clifford, James, 1997. *Routes: Travel and Translation in the Late Twentieth Century*. Cambridge, MA: Harvard University Press.

Comaroff, John L., 2001. 'Colonialism, culture, and the law: a foreword.' *Law & Social Inquiry* 26(2): 305–14.

Commission on AIDS in the Pacific, 2009. *Turning the Tide: An Open Strategy for a Response to AIDS in the Pacific*. Suva: UNAIDS Pacific Region.

Connell, John, 2003. 'Regulation of space in the contemporary postcolonial Pacific city: Port Moresby and Suva.' *Asia Pacific Viewpoint* 44(3): 243–57.

Connell, R.W. and G.W. Dowsett (eds), 1992. *Rethinking Sex: Social Theory and Sexuality Research*. Carlton, Vic: Melbourne University Press.

Cook, Catriona et al., 2001. *Laying Down the Law* [6th ed.]. Sydney: Butterworths.

Corrin Care, Jennifer and Jean G. Zorn, 2001. 'Legislating pluralism: statutory "developments" in Melanesian customary law.' *Journal of Legal Pluralism and Unofficial Law* 46: 49–101.

Countryside, 2010. 'Opportunity generation: *time blo yumi*.' In *ActNow Blog*, 13 July. Online: http://www.actnowpng.org/content/opportunity-generation-time-blo-yumi, accessed 31 July 2010.

Crenshaw, Kimberlé, 1989. 'Demarginalising the intersection of race and sex: a black feminist critique of antidiscrimination doctrine, feminist theory and antiracist politics.' *University of Chicago Legal Forum* 140: 139–67.

-------- 1991. 'Mapping the margins: intersectionality, identity politics, and violence against women of color.' *Stanford Law Review* 43(6): 1241–99.

Davidson, Arnold I., 1986. 'Archaeology, genealogy, ethics.' In *Foucault: A Critical Reader*, ed. David Couzens Hoy. Oxford and New York: B. Blackwell, 221–46.

Davies, Margaret, 2008. *Asking the Law Question*. Sydney: Law Book Co.

Davies, Susanne, 1995. 'Captives of their bodies: law and punishment, 1880s–1980s.' In *Sex Power and Justice: Historical Perspectives on Law in Australia*, ed. Dianne Kirkby. Melbourne: Oxford University Press, 99–115.

Davis, Kathy, 2008. 'Intersectionality as buzzword: a sociology of science perspective on what makes a feminist theory successful.' *Feminist Theory* 9(1): 67–85.

Dean, Mitchell and Barry Hindess (eds), 1998. *Governing Australia: Studies in Contemporary Rationalities of Government*. Melbourne: Cambridge University Press.

Demian, Melissa, 2003. 'Custom in the courtroom, law in the village: legal transformations in Papua New Guinea.' *Journal of the Royal Anthropological Institute* 9: 97–115.

Denis, Ann, 2008. 'Intersectional analysis: a contribution of feminism to sociology.' *International Sociology* 23(5): 677–94.

Denoon, Donald, 2005. *A Trial Separation: Australia and the Decolonisation of Papua New Guinea*. Canberra: Pandanus Books.

Denoon, Donald et al. (eds), 1997. *The Cambridge History of the Pacific Islanders*. Cambridge and New York: Cambridge University Press.

Derham, David Plumley, 1960. *Report on the System for the Administration of Justice in the Territory of Papua and New Guinea*. Melbourne: Report to the Minister for Territories (*Derham Report*).

Devlin, Patrick, 1960. *The Enforcement of Morals*. London: Oxford University Press.

Dickson-Waiko, Anne, 2003. 'The missing rib: mobilizing church women for change in Papua New Guinea.' *Oceania* 74(1/2): 98–119.

-------- 2010. *Taking Over, of What and From Whom? Women and Independence, the PNG Experience*. Report for Deakin University. Geelong Vic: Alfred Deakin Research Institute.

Dinnen, Sinclair, 1989. 'Crime, law and order in Papua New Guinea.' *Melanesian Law Journal* 17: 10–25.

-------- 1997. 'Restorative justice in Papua New Guinea.' *International Journal of the Sociology of Law* 25: 245–62.

-------- 1998. 'Criminal justice reform in Papua New Guinea.' In *Governance and Reform in the South Pacific*, ed. Peter Larmour. Canberra: National Centre for Development Studies, The Australian National University, 253–72.

-------- 2001. *Law and Order in a Weak State: Crime and Politics in Papua New Guinea*. Adelaide: University of Hawai'i Press and Crawford House Publishing.

Dinnen, Sinclair and John Braithwaite, 2009. 'Reinventing policing through the prism of the colonial kiap,' *Policing and Society* 19(2): 161–73. Online: http://dx.doi.org/10.1080/10439460802187571, accessed 7 May 2011.

Dinnen, Sinclair and Allison Ley, 2000. *Reflections on Violence in Melanesia*. Leichhardt, NSW: Hawkins Press.

Dinnen, Sinclair, Tess Newton and Anita Jowitt (eds), 2003. *A Kind of Mending: Restorative Justice in the Pacific Islands*. Canberra: Pandanus Books.

Ditmore, Melissa, 2002. 'Trafficking and prostitution: a problematic conflation.' Ph.D. thesis, New York: City University of New York.

Dorney, Sean, 1990. *Papua New Guinea: People, Politics and History since 1975*. Milsons Point, NSW: Random House.

Douglas, Bronwen, 2000. *Women and Governance from the Grassroots in Melanesia. State Society and Governance in Melanesia, Discussion Paper no. 2.* Canberra: Research School of Pacific and Asian Studies, The Australian National University.

-------- 2003. 'Christianity, tradition, and everyday modernity: towards an anatomy of women's groupings in Melanesia.' *Oceania* 74(1/2): 6–23.

-------- 2008. 'Foreign bodies in Oceania.' In *Foreign Bodies: Oceania and the Science of Race 1750–1940*, ed. Bronwen Douglas and Chris Ballard. Canberra: ANU E Press, 3–30. Online: http://press.anu.edu.au?p=53561, accessed 31 March 2014.

Douglas, Bronwen and Chris Ballard (eds), 2008. *Foreign Bodies: Oceania and the Science of Race 1750–1940.* Canberra: ANU E Press. Online: http://press.anu.edu.au?p=53561, accessed 31 March 2014.

Douglas, Mary, 1966. *Purity and Danger: An Analysis of the Concepts of Pollution and Taboo.* London: Routledge & Kegan Paul.

Dvorak, Greg, 2014. 'Two sea turtles: intimacy between men in the Marshall Islands.' In *Gender on the Edge: Transgender, Gay and other Pacific Islanders*, ed. Niko Besnier and Kalissa Alexeyeff. Hong Kong: Hong Kong University Press, 184–209.

Eddy, J.J., and J.R. Nethercote (eds), 1987. *Colony to Coloniser: Studies in Australian Administrative History.* Sydney: Hale and Iremonger.

Eggleston, F.W., 1928. 'Record of discussion.' In *The Australian Mandate for New Guinea: Record of Round Table Discussion*, ed. F.W. Eggleston. Melbourne: Macmillan, 112–19.

Eggleston, F.W. (ed.), 1928. *The Australian Mandate for New Guinea: Record of Round Table Discussion.* Melbourne: Macmillan.

Elliston, Deborah A., 1995. 'Erotic anthropology: "ritualized homosexuality" in Melanesia and beyond.' *American Ethnologist* 22(4): 848–67.

Epstein, A.L. (ed.), 1974. *Contention and Dispute: Aspects of Law and Social Control in Melanesia.* Canberra: Australian National University Press.

Feldman, Allen, 2005. 'On the actuarial gaze: from 9/11 to Abu Ghraib.' *Cultural Studies* 19(2): 203–26.

Fife, Wayne, 2001. 'Creating the moral body: missionaries and the technology of power in early Papua New Guinea.' *Ethnology* 40(3): 251–69.

Filer, Colin, 1985. 'What is this thing called "brideprice?"' *Mankind* 15(2): 163–83.

Firth, Stewart, 1997. 'Colonial administration and the invention of the native.' In *The Cambridge History of the Pacific Islanders*, ed. Donald Denoon et al. Cambridge and New York: Cambridge University Press, 253–88.

Fitzpatrick, Peter, 1980. 'Really rather like slavery: law and labour in the colonial economy in Papua New Guinea.' *Contemporary Crises* 4(1): 77–95.

-------- 1982. 'The political economy of law in the post-colonial period.' In *Law and Social Change in Papua New Guinea*, ed. David Weisbrot, Abdul Paliwala and Akilagpa Sawyerr. Sydney, Melbourne, Brisbane, Adelaide, Perth: Butterworths, 25–55.

-------- 1984. 'Traditionalism and traditional law.' *Journal of African Law* 28: 20–27.

-------- 1992. *The Mythology of Modern Law*. London and New York: Routledge.

-------- 2000. 'Magnified features: the underdevelopment of law and legitimation.' *Journal of South Pacific Law* 4. Online: http://www.paclii.org/journals/fJSPL/vol04/5.shtml, accessed 18 June 2007.

Fletcher, Karen and Bomal Gonapa, 2010. 'Decriminalisation of prostitution in Papua New Guinea.' In *Civic Insecurity: Law, Order and HIV in Papua New Guinea*, ed. Vicki Luker and Sinclair Dinnen. Canberra: ANU E Press, 141–52. Online: http://press.anu.edu.au?p=94091, accessed 8 April 2014.

Flint, L.A., 1919. 'Muguru at Torobina, Bamu River.' *Man* 19: 38–39.

Forsyth, Miranda, 2009. *A Bird That Flies With Two Wings: Kastom and State Justice Systems in Vanuatu*. Canberra: ANU E Press. Online: http://press.anu.edu.au?p=49351, accessed 10 April 2014.

Foster, Robert J., 1992. 'Commoditization and the emergence of "kastom" as a cultural category: a New Ireland case in comparative perspective.' *Oceania* 62(4): 284–94.

-------- 1992. 'Take care of public telephones: moral education and nation-state formation in Papua New Guinea.' *Public Culture* 4(2): 31–45.

-------- 1999. 'The commercial construction of "new nations."' *Journal of Material Culture* 4(3): 263–82.

-------- 2002. *Materializing the Nation: Commodities, Consumption, and Media in Papua New Guinea*. Bloomington and Indianapolis: Indiana University Press.

Foucault, Michel, 1978 [1976]. *The Will to Knowledge: The History of Sexuality: Volume 1*, London: Penguin Books.

-------- 2004 [1997]. *"Society Must be Defended": Lectures at the Collège de France, 1975–76*. London: Penguin Books.

-------- 1982. 'The subject and power.' *Critical Inquiry* 8(4): 777–95.

Franke, Katherine M., 2004. 'Sexual tensions of post-empire.' *Columbia Law School Pub. Law Research Paper No. 04–62*. Online: http://ssrn.com/abstract=491205, accessed 12 November 2006.

Gammage, Bill, 1996. 'Police and power in the pre-war Papua New Guinea Highlands.' *Journal of Pacific History* 31(2): 162–77.

Garrett, John, 1992. *Footsteps in the Sea: Christianity in Oceania to World War II*. Suva: Suva Institute of Pacific Studies, University of the South Pacific.

Gatens, Moira, 1991. 'A critique of the sex/gender distinction.' In *A Reader in Feminist Knowledge*, ed. Sneja Gunew. London and New York: Routledge, 139–57.

Geddes, R.S., 2005. 'Purpose and context in statutory interpretation.' *University of New England Law Journal* 2005(2): 5–48.

Gelu, Alphonse, 2000. 'The emergence of a non-liberal democratic political culture in Papua New Guinea.' In *Politics in Papua New Guinea: Continuities, Changes and Challenges*, ed. Michael A. Rynkiewich and Roland Seib. Goroka: Melanesian Institute, 87–119.

George, Nicole, 2008. 'Contending masculinities and the limits of tolerance: sexual minorities in Fiji.' *The Contemporary Pacific* 20(1): 163–89.

Gewertz, Deborah B. and Frederick K. Errington, 1999. *Emerging Class in Papua New Guinea: The Telling of Difference*. Cambridge and New York: Cambridge University Press.

Gewertz, Deborah and Frederick Errington, 2009. 'Jealous women of the cane.' In *Empirical Futures: Anthropologists and Historians Engage the Work of Sidney W. Mintz*, ed. George Baca, Aisha Kahn and Stephen Palmie. Chapel Hill: University of North Carolina Press, 173–95.

Gibbs, Philip, 2002. 'Religion and religious institutions as defining factors in Papua New Guinea politics.' *Development Bulletin* 59 (October): 15–18.

-------- 2004. 'Growth, decline and confusion: Church affiliation in Papua New Guinea.' *Catalyst* 34(2):164–84.

-------- 2005. *Political Discourse and Religious Narratives of Church and State in Papua New Guinea*. State Society and Governance in Melanesia Working Paper No. 1. Canberra: The Australian National University.

-------- 2012. 'Engendered violence and witch-killing in Simbu.' In *Engendering Violence in Papua New Guinea*, ed. Margaret Jolly, Christine Stewart with Carolyn Brewer. Canberra: ANU E Press, 107–35. Online: http://press.anu.edu.au?p=182671, accessed 31 March 2014.

Gibbs, Philip and Marie Mondu, 2009. 'The context of HIV transmission during the 2007 elections in the Enga Province Papua New Guinea.' *Catalyst* 39(1): 135–57.

Global Commission on HIV and the Law. Online: http://www.hivlawcommission.org, accessed 21 March 2011.

Gnecchi-Ruscone, Elisabetta, 2010. '"A school of iron, vexation and blood, but a school nonetheless": the writings of the first PIME missionaries to Oceania in the 1850s.' Paper presented at the Race, Encounters, and the Constitution of Human Difference in Oceania Conference. Canberra: The Australian National University, 20–22 January.

Goddard, M., 2001. 'From rolling thunder to reggae: imagining squatter settlements in Papua New Guinea.' *Contemporary Pacific* 13(1): 1–32.

-------- 2005. *The Unseen City: Anthropological Perspectives on Port Moresby, Papua New Guinea*. Canberra: Pandanus Press.

-------- 2009. *Substantial Justice: An Anthropology of Village Courts in Papua New Guinea*. New York and Oxford: Berghahn Books.

Golder, Ben and Peter Fitzpatrick, 2009. *Foucault's Law*. Abingdon: Routledge.

Goldring, John, 1978. *The Constitution of Papua New Guinea*. Sydney, Melbourne, Brisbane, Perth: The Law Book Company.

Goodman, Ryan, 2001. 'Beyond the enforcement principle: sodomy laws, social norms, and social panoptics.' *California Law Review* 89: 643–740.

Gunew, Sneja (ed.), 1991. *A Reader in Feminist Knowledge*, London and New York: Routledge.

Gupta, Akhil and James Ferguson, 1997. 'Discipline and practice: "the field" as site, method and location in anthropology.' In *Anthropological Locations: Boundaries and Grounds of a Field Science*, ed. Akhil Gupta and James Ferguson. Berkeley: California University Press, 1–29.

Gupta, Akhil and James Ferguson (eds), 1997. *Anthropological Locations: Boundaries and Grounds of a Field Science*. Berkeley: California University Press.

Haack, Susan, 2005. 'On legal pragmatism: where does "the path of the law" lead us?' *American Journal of Jurisprudence* 50: 71–105.

Haley, Nicole, 2008. 'When there's no accessing basic health care: local politics and responses to HIV/AIDS at Lake Kopiago, Papua New Guinea.' In *Making Sense of AIDS: Culture, Sexuality, and Power in Melanesia*, ed. Leslie Butt and Richard Eves. Honolulu: University of Hawai'i Press, 24–40.

-------- 2009. 'HIV/AIDS and witchcraft at Lake Kopiago.' *Catalyst* 39(1): 115–34.

Hammar, Lawrence, 1996. 'Sex and political economy in the South Fly: Daru Island, Western Province, Papua New Guinea.' Ph.D. thesis, New York: City University of New York.

-------- 1998. 'AIDS, STDs and sex work in Papua New Guinea.' In *Modern Papua New Guinea*, ed. Laura Zimmer-Tamakoshi. Kirksville MO: Thomas Jefferson University Press, 257–89.

-------- 1998. 'Sex industries and sexual networking in Papua New Guinea: public health risks and implications.' *Pacific Health Dialog* 5(1): 47–53.

-------- 2005. 'A different kind of "Original Sin": coitarche, commercial sex, and (non-)consent in Lae, Morobe Province, Papua New Guinea.' Paper for the Annual Meeting of the Association for Social Anthropology in Oceania.

-------- 2008. 'Fear and loathing in Papua New Guinea: sexual health in a nation under siege.' In *Making Sense of AIDS: Culture, Sexuality, and Power in Melanesia*, ed. Leslie Butt and Richard Eves. Honolulu: University of Hawai'i Press, 60–79.

-------- 2009. 'There wouldn't even be a national response without the churches: faith-based responses in Papua New Guinea to HIV and AIDS.' Unpublished.

-------- 2010. *Sin, Sex and Stigma: A Pacific Response to HIV and AIDS*. Wantage: Sean Kingston Publishing.

-------- 2010. 'Anger management: why I wrote *Sin, Sex and Stigma: A Pacific Response to HIV and AIDS*.' Yellow Springs, Ohio. Unpublished.

-------- 2010. 'From gift to commodity ... and back again: form and fluidity of sexual networking in Papua New Guinea.' In *Civic Insecurity: Law, Order and*

HIV in Papua New Guinea, ed. Vicki Luker and Sinclair Dinnen. Canberra: ANU E Press, 119–39. Online: http://press.anu.edu.au?p=94091, accessed 7 April 2014.

-------- 2010. '"I am an 'MSM'! ... I think": Melanesian perspectives on self, risk, and other in HIV prevention.' Paper presented at the Gendered Mobility, Intimate Consumption, and HIV in Postcolonial Melanesia, American Anthropological Association Meeting Conference, New Orleans, 17–21 November.

-------- n.d. 'The 's' words: 'sex,' 'sex worker,' and 'stigma' in Papua New Guinea.' Paper for Papua New Guinea Institute of Medical Research.

-------- n.d. 'Sex and secrecy in the South Fly: *tu kina bus* in historical perspective.' Unpublished.

Hanson, Alan F., 1982. 'Female pollution in Polynesia?' *Journal of the Polynesian Society* 91: 335–81.

Harcourt, Christine, Sandra Egger and Basil Donovan, 2005. 'Sex work and the law.' *Sexual Health* 2(3): 121–28.

Hart, H.L.A., 1963. *Law, Liberty and Morality*. London: Oxford University Press.

Hau'ofa, Epeli, 2008. *We Are The Ocean: Selected Works*. Honolulu: University of Hawai'i Press.

HELP Resources Inc., 2005. *A Situational Analysis of Child Sexual Abuse & the Commercial Sexual Exploitation of Children in Papua New Guinea (draft)*. Report prepared for UNICEF, Port Moresby.

Hely, B.A., 1894. 'Appendix P. Native habits and customs in the Western Division.' In *Annual Report on British New Guinea 1892–1893*, Brisbane: Edmund Gregory, Government Printer.

Herdt, Gilbert, 1984. *Ritualized Homosexuality in Melanesia*. Berkeley CA: University of California Press.

-------- 1987. *The Sambia: Ritual and Gender in New Guinea*. Fort Worth TX: Holt, Rinehart & Winston.

-------- 1992. 'Semen depletion and the sense of maleness.' In *Oceanic Homosexualities*, ed. Stephen O. Murray. New York and London: Garland Publishing, 33–68.

-------- 1994. *Third Sex, Third Gender: Beyond Sexual Dimorphism in Culture and History*. New York: Zone Books.

-------- 1997. *Same Sex, Different Cultures: Gays and Lesbians across Cultures*. Boulder, CO: Westview Press.

Hermkens, Anna-Karina, 2008. 'Josephine's journey: gender-based violence and Marian devotion in urban Papua New Guinea.' *Oceania* 78(2): 151–67.

-------- 2012. 'Becoming Mary: coping with gender-based violence in Urban Papua New Guinea.' In *Engendering Violence in Papua New Guinea*, ed. Margaret Jolly, Christine Stewart with Carolyn Brewer. Canberra: ANU E Press. Online: http://press.anu.edu.au?p=182671, accessed 31 March 2014.

Herring, Jonathan, 2002. 'Gay rights come quietly.' *Law Quarterly Review* 118: 31–35.

Hershey, Christopher, 2004. Statement of Facts on Police Raid at 3-Mile Guesthouse 12 March 2004, and Related Incidents. Statement made on behalf of Poro Sapot Project, Save the Children in Papua New Guinea, 20 March.

-------- 2008. 'Reflections on Poro Sapot: one model of care for men's sexual & reproductive health.' Paper presented at the Men's Sexual and Reproductive Health in PNG Conference, Port Moresby, 12 June.

Hiery, Herman and John MacKenzie (eds), 1997. *European Impact and Pacific Influence: British and German Colonial Policy in the Pacific Islands and the Indigenous Response*. London: Tauris Academic Studies.

Hilsdon, Anne-Marie et al. (eds), 2000. *Human Rights and Gender Politics: Asia-Pacific Perspectives*. London and New York: Routledge.

Hirsch, Jennifer S. et al., 2009. *The Secret: Love, Marriage and HIV*. Nashville, TE: Vanderbilt University Press.

Hogbin, H. Ian, 1946. 'Puberty to marriage: a study of the sexual life of the natives of Wogeo, New Guinea.' *Oceania* 16(3): 185–209.

-------- 1951. *Transformation Scene: the Changing Culture of a New Guinea Village*. London: Routledge and Kegan Paul.

-------- 1963. *Kinship and Marriage in a New Guinea Village*. London: University of London.

Holmes, Oliver Wendell Jr, 1968 [1881]. *The Common Law*. London and Melbourne: Macmillan.

Holzknecht, Hartmut, 1997. 'Morobe Province 1978–1991.' In *Political Decentralisation in a New State: The Experience of Provincial Government in Papua New Guinea*, ed. Ronald James May, A.J. Regan and Allison Ley. Bathurst, Crawford House Publishing, 199–227.

Hookey, J.F., 1968. 'The "Clapham Omnibus" in Papua and New Guinea.' In *Fashion of Law in New Guinea: Being an Account of the Past, Present and Developing System of Laws in Papua and New Guinea*, ed. B.J. Brown. Sydney, Melbourne, Brisbane: Butterworths, 117–35.

Howell, Philip, 2004. 'Sexuality, sovereignty and space: law, government and the geography of prostitution in colonial Gibraltar.' *Social History* 29(4): 445–64.

Hoy, David Couzens (ed.), 1986. *Foucault: A Critical Reader*. Oxford and New York: B. Blackwell.

Hukula, Fiona, 2012. 'Conversations with convicted rapists.' In *Engendering Violence in Papua New Guinea*, ed. Margaret Jolly, Christine Stewart with Carolyn Brewer. Canberra: ANU E Press, 197–212. Online: http://press.anu.edu.au?p=182671, accessed 31 March 2014.

Human Rights Watch, 2005. *'Making Their Own Rules': Police Beatings, Rape, and Torture of Children in Papua New Guinea*. New York: Human Rights Watch.

-------- 2006. *'Still Making Their Own Rules': Ongoing Impunity for Police Beatings, Rape, and Torture in Papua New Guinea*. New York: Human Rights Watch.

-------- 2008. *This Alien Legacy: The Origins of 'Sodomy' Laws in British Colonialism*. New York: Human Rights Watch.

Hunt, Alan and Gary Wickham, 1994. *Foucault and the Law: Towards a Sociology of Law as Governance*. London, Boulder, Colorado: Pluto Press.

Ingebritson, Joel F. (ed.), 1990. *Human Sexuality in Melanesian Cultures*. Goroka: Melanesian Institute.

Inglis, Amirah, 1974. *'Not a White Woman Safe': Sexual Anxiety and Politics in Port Moresby, 1920–1934*. Canberra: Australian National University Press.

Inter-Parliamentary Union (IPU), United Nations Development Programme (UNDP) and Joint United Nations Programme on HIV/AIDS (UNAIDS), 2007. *Taking Action against HIV: A Handbook for Parliamentarians*. Le Grand-Saconnex, New York, Geneva: IPU, UNDP, UNAIDS.

Jackson, Peter, 1997. '*Kathoey*><gay><man: the historical emergence of gay male identity in Thailand.' In *Sites of Desire, Economies of Pleasure: Sexualities in Asia and the Pacific*, ed. Lenore Manderson and Margaret Jolly. Chicago and London: University of Chicago Press, 166–90.

-------- 2000. 'An explosion of Thai identities: global queering and re-imagining queer theory.' *Culture, Health & Sexuality* 2(4): 405–24.

-------- 2001. 'Interpreting "Sambia" masculine erotics: a question of sexuality or gender?' *The Asia Pacific Journal of Anthropology* 2(1): 109–13.

-------- 2009. 'Capitalism and global queering: national markets, parallels among sexual cultures, and multiple queer modernities.' *GLQ: A Journal of Lesbian and Gay Studies* 15(3): 357–95.

James, R.W. and I. Fraser (eds), 1992. *Legal Issues in a Developing Society*. Port Moresby: University of Papua New Guinea.

Jeffreys, Elena, 2010. 'Sex work, migration and trafficking identity matters: non-sex workers writing about sex work.' *Intersections: Gender and Sexuality in Asia and the Pacific* 23 (January). Online: http://intersections.anu.edu.au/issue23/jeffreys_review-essay.htm, accessed 11 March 2010.

Jenkins, Carol, 1994. *Situational Assessment of Commercial Sex Workers in Urban Papua New Guinea*. Report prepared for Papua New Guinea Institute of Medical Research, Goroka.

-------- 1996. 'The homosexual context of heterosexual practice in Papua New Guinea.' In *Bisexualities and AIDS*, ed. Peter Aggleton. London: Taylor and Francis, 191–206.

-------- 2000. *Female Sex Worker HIV Prevention Projects: Lessons Learned from Papua New Guinea, India and Bangladesh*. Geneva: UNAIDS.

-------- 2004. 'Male sexuality, diversity and culture: implications for HIV prevention and care.' Report prepared for UNAIDS, Geneva. Unpublished. Online: http://www.popline.org/node/264909, accessed 7 July 2014.

-------- 2006. 'Male sexuality and HIV: the case of male-to-male sex.' Paper presented at the Risks and Responsibilities: Male Sexual Health and HIV in Asia and the Pacific International Consultation Conference, New Delhi, 23–26 September.

-------- 2007. 'HIV/AIDS, culture, and sexuality in Papua New Guinea.' In *Cultures and Contexts Matter: Understanding and Preventing HIV in the Pacific*, Manila: Asian Development Bank, 5–69.

-------- 2010. 'Sex workers and police in Port Moresby (1994–1998): research and intervention.' In *Civic Insecurity: Law, Order and HIV in Papua New Guinea*, ed. Vicki Luker and Sinclair Dinnen. Canberra: ANU E Press, 153–64. Online: http://press.anu.edu.au?p=94091, accessed 8 April 2014.

Jenkins, Carol and Andrew Hunter, 2005. *Empowering Sex Workers: Does It Matter?* Report prepared for CARE Asia Regional Management Unit, Bangkok.

Jennett, Christine and Randal G. Stewart, 1987. *Three Worlds of Inequality: Race, Class and Gender*. South Melbourne, Vic: Macmillan.

Jinks, B., P. Biskup and H. Nelson, 1973. *Readings in New Guinea History*. Sydney: Angus and Robertson.

Johnston, Craig, 1985. 'Prostitution law reform in New South Wales: two shuffles forward, one stumble back.' In *Being a Prostitute: Prostitute Women and Prostitute Men*, ed. Roberta Perkins and Garry Bennett. Sydney, London, Boston: George Allen & Unwin, 261–73.

Johnstone, Joan Drikoré, 1993. 'The Gumini *Bisnis-Meri*: a study of the development of an innovative indigenous entrepreneurial activity in Port Moresby in the early 1970s.' Ph.D. thesis, Brisbane: University of Queensland.

Joint United Nations Programme on HIV/AIDS (UNAIDS), 1999. *Handbook for Legislators on HIV/AIDS, Law and Human Rights: Action to Combat HIV/AIDS in View of its Devastating Human, Economic and Social Impact*. UNAIDS/99.48E. Report prepared for Joint United Nations Programme on HIV/AIDS (UNAIDS), Geneva.

-------- 2008. *UNAIDS Terminology Guidelines (2008)*. Geneva: Joint United Nations programme on HIV/AIDS (UNAIDS).

-------- 2010. *Getting to Zero: 2011–2015 Strategy*. Geneva: Joint United Nations programme on HIV/AIDS (UNAIDS).

-------- 2011. *UNAIDS Terminology Guidelines (January 2011)*. Online: http://www.unaids.org/en/media/unaids/contentassets/documents/document/2011/jc1336_unaids_terminology_guide_en.pdf, accessed 8 June 2011.

Jolly, Margaret, 1996. 'Woman *ikat raet long human raet o no*?: Women's rights, human rights and domestic violence in Vanuatu.' *Feminist Review* 52 (Spring): 169–90.

-------- 2002. 'Introduction: birthing beyond the confinements of tradition and modernity?' In *Birthing in the Pacific: Beyond Tradition and Modernity?* Ed. Vicki Lukere and Margaret Jolly. Honololu: University of Hawai'i Press, 1–30.

-------- 2003. 'Epilogue.' *Oceania* 74(1/2): 134–47.

-------- 2010. 'Divided mothers: changing global inequalities of "nature" and "nurture."' In *The Globalization of Motherhood: Deconstructions and Reconstructions of Biology and Care*, ed. Wendy Chavkin and JaneMaree Maher. Abingdon, Oxon: Routledge, 154–79.

-------- 2012. 'Introduction—engendering violence in Papua New Guinea: persons, power and perilous transformations.' In *Engendering Violence in Papua New Guinea*, ed. Margaret Jolly, Christine Stewart with Carolyn Brewer, Canberra: ANU E Press, 1–46. Online: http://press.anu.edu.au?p=182671, accessed 31 March 2014.

Jolly, Margaret and Martha Macintyre, 1989. *Family and Gender in the Pacific: Domestic Contradictions and the Colonial Impact*. Cambridge and Melbourne: Cambridge University Press.

Jolly, Margaret and Lenore Manderson, 1997. 'Sites of desire and economies of pleasure in Asia and the Pacific.' In *Sites of Desire, Economies of Pleasure: Sexualities in Asia and the Pacific*, ed. Lenore Manderson and Margaret Jolly. Chicago: University of Chicago Press, 1–26.

Jolly, Margaret, Christine Stewart with Carolyn Brewer (eds), 2012. *Engendering Violence in Papua New Guinea*, Canberra: ANU E Press. Online: http://press.anu.edu.au?p=182671, accessed 31 March 2014.

Joseph, Sally, 2011. 'Working towards law reform for sex workers in PNG.' Paper presented at the Australasian HIV/AIDS Conference 2011. Canberra, 26–28 September.

Jowitt, Anita and Tess Newton Cain (eds), 2003. *Passage of Change: Law, Society and Governance in the Pacific*. Canberra: Pandanus Books.

Kapur, Ratna, 2000–2001. 'Postcolonial erotic disruptions: legal narratives of culture, sex, and nation in India.' *Columbia Journal of Gender and Law* 10: 333–84.

-------- 2002. 'The tragedy of victimization rhetoric: resurrecting the "native" subject in international/post-colonial feminist legal politics.' *Harvard Human Rights Journal* 15: 1–37.

Katyal, Sonia, 2002. 'Exporting identity.' *Yale Journal of Law and Feminism* 14(1): 98–176.

Kelly, Angela, et al., 2011. Askim na Save *(Ask and Understand): People who Sell and/or Exchange Sex in Port Moresby*. Sydney: Papua New Guinea Institute of Medical Research and the University of New South Wales.

Kidu, Carol, 2000. 'Reflections on change, ethnicity and conflict: family and ethnic violence in Papua New Guinea.' *Development Bulletin* 53 (November): 29–33.

-------- 2011. 'A national response to the HIV epidemic in Papua New Guinea.' *UN Chronicle* XLVIII(1) (May). Online: http://www.un.org:80/wcm/content/site/chronicle/home/archive/issues2011/hivaidsthefourthdecade/nationalresponsetohivpapuanewguinea, accessed 20 August 2011.

King, David, 1998. 'Elites, suburban commuters, and squatters: the emerging urban morphology of Papua New Guinea.' In *Modern Papua New Guinea*, ed. Laura Zimmer-Tamakoshi. Kirksville, MO: Thomas Jefferson University Press, 183–94.

King, Peter, Wendy Lee and Vincent Warakai (eds), 1985. *From Rhetoric to Reality? Papua New Guinea's Eight Point Plan and National Goals after a Decade*. Waigani, PNG: University of Papua New Guinea Press.

Kirby, Michael, 2000. 'Human rights—the way forward.' *Victoria University of Wellington Law Review* 36(4): 703–20.

Kituai, August Ibrum K., 1998. *My Gun, My Brother: The World of the Papua New Guinea Colonial Police, 1920–1960*. Honolulu: University of Hawai'i Press.

Knauft, Bruce M., 1993. *South Coast New Guinea Cultures: History, Comparison, Dialectic*. New York: Cambridge University Press.

-------- 1997. 'Gender identity, political economy and modernity in Melanesia and Amazonia.' *Journal of the Royal Anthropological Institute* 3(2): 233–59.

-------- 2003. 'What ever happened to ritualized homosexuality? Modern sexual subjects in Melanesia and elsewhere.' *Annual Review of Sex Research* 14, 137–59.

-------- 2007. 'Moral exchange and exchanging morals: alternative paths of cultural change in Papua New Guinea.' In *The Anthropology of Morality in Melanesia and Beyond*, ed. John Barker. Aldershot: Ashgate Publishing Ltd., 59–73.

-------- 2011. 'Men, modernity and Melanesia.' In *Echoes of the Tambaran: Masculinity, History and the Subject in the Work of Donald F. Tuzin*, ed. David Lipset and Paul Roscoe. Canberra: ANU E Press, 103–14. Online: http://press.anu.edu.au?p=146101, 10 April 2014.

Koczberski, G., G.N. Curry and J. Connell, 2001. 'Full circle or spiralling out of control? State violence and the control of urbanisation in Papua New Guinea.' *Urban Studies* 38(11): 2017–36.

Kowald, C., 1894. 'Appendix R: native habits and customs of the Mekeo District (Central Division).' In *Annual Report on British New Guinea 1892–1893*, Brisbane: Edmund Gregory, Government Printer.

Krishnaswamy, Sudhir, 2013. 'Naz Foundation: reading down the Supreme Court.' *Oxford Human Rights Law* 13 December. Online: http://ohrh.law.ox.ac.uk/?p=3733, accessed 31 December 2013.

Kulick, Don, 1992. *Language Shift and Cultural Reproduction: Socialization, Self, and Syncretism in a Papua New Guinean Village*. Cambridge and New York: Cambridge University Press.

Kyakas, Alome and Polly Wiessner, 1992. *From Inside the Women's House: Enga Women's Lives and Traditions*. Buranda, Qld: R. Brown.

Langmore, D., 1982. 'A neglected force: white women missionaries in Papua 1874–1914.' *Journal of Pacific History* 17(3): 138–57.

Langness, L.L., 1999. *Men and 'Woman' in New Guinea*. Novato, California: Chandler & Sharp, Publishers Inc.

Larmour, Peter (ed.), 1998. *Governance and Reform in the South Pacific*. Canberra: National Centre for Development Studies, The Australian National University.

Lattas, Andrew and Knut M. Rio, 2011. 'Securing modernity: towards an ethnography of power in contemporary Melanesia.' *Oceania* 81(1): 1–21.

Latukefu, Sione (ed.), 1989. *Papua New Guinea: A Century of Colonial Impact, 1884–1984*. Port Moresby: National Research Institute and University of Papua New Guinea.

Law Reform Commission of Papua New Guinea, 1975. *Report No. 1: Report on Summary Offences*. Waigani, PNG: Law Reform Commission of Papua New Guinea.

-------- 1975. *Report No. 2: Report on Abolition of Native Regulations*. Waigani, PNG: Law Reform Commission of Papua New Guinea.

-------- 1977. *Report No. 7: The Role of Customary Law in the Legal System*. Waigani, PNG: Law Reform Commission of Papua New Guinea.

-------- 1992. *Report No. 14: Final Report on Domestic Violence*. Boroko, PNG: Law Reform Commission of Papua New Guinea.

Lawrence, Peter, 1969. 'The state versus stateless societies in Papua and New Guinea.' In *Fashion of Law in New Guinea*, ed. B.J. Brown. Sydney, Melbourne, Brisbane: Butterworths, 15–37.

-------- 1970. 'Law and anthropology: the need for collaboration.' *Melanesian Law Journal* 1(1): 40–57.

Lepani, Katherine, 2007. '"In the process of knowing": making sense of HIV and AIDS in the Trobriand Islands of Papua New Guinea.' Ph.D. thesis, Canberra: The Australian National University.

-------- 2012. *Islands of Love, Islands of Risk: Culture and HIV in the Trobriands*. Nashville, TN: Vanderbilt University Press.

Lepowsky, Maria, 2001. 'The Queen of Sudest: white women and colonial cultures in British New Guinea and Papua.' In *In Colonial New Guinea: Anthropological Perspectives*, ed. Naomi McPherson. Pittsburgh: University of Pittsburgh Press, 125–50.

Levantis, Theodore, 2000. *Papua New Guinea: Employment, Wages and Economic Development*. Canberra: Asia Pacific Press.

Levine, Philippa, 2003. *Prostitution, Race, and Politics: Policing Venereal Disease in the British Empire*. New York: Routledge.

Lewis, D.C., 1996. *The Plantation Dream: Developing British New Guinea and Papua, 1884–1942*. Canberra: the Journal of Pacific History.

Lind, Andrew W., 1969. *Inter-Ethnic Marriage in New Guinea*. Port Moresby: New Guinea Research Unit.

Lindley, Jade and Laura Beacroft, 2011. *Vulnerabilities to Trafficking in Persons in the Pacific Islands*. Canberra: Australian Institute of Criminology. Online: http://www.aic.gov.au/documents/C/1/9/%7BC19D723B-44B8-4B02-9FA5-CB4470207AE7%7Dtandi428.pdf, accessed 4 December 2011.

Lindstrom, Lamont and Geoffrey M. White, 1994. *Culture, Kastom, Tradition: Developing Cultural Policy in Melanesia*. Suva: Institute of Pacific Studies.

Lipset, David, 2004. '"The trial": a parody of the law amid the mockery of men in post-colonial Papua New Guinea.' *Journal of the Royal Anthropological Institute* 10: 63–89.

Lipset, David and Paul Roscoe (eds), 2011. *Echoes of the Tambaran: Masculinity, History and the Subject in the Work of Donald F. Tuzin*. Canberra: ANU E Press. Online: http://press.anu.edu.au?p=146101, accessed 10 April 2014.

Llewellyn, Karl, 1931. 'Some realism about realism—responding to Dean Pound.' *Harvard Law Review* 44(8): 1222–64.

Loff, Bebe, Cheryl Overs and Paulo Longo, 2003. 'Can health programmes lead to mistreatment of sex workers?' *The Lancet* 361 (7 June): 1982–83.

Lohmann, Roger Ivar, 2007. 'Moral and missionary positionality: Diyos of Duranmin.' In *The Anthropology of Morality in Melanesia and Beyond*, ed. John Barker. Aldershot and Burlington: Ashgate, 131–47.

Lucas, John, 1972. 'Lae – a town in transition.' *Oceania* 42(2): 260–75.

Luhrmann, Tanya, 2004. 'Metakinesis: how God becomes intimate in contemporary US Christianity.' *American Anthropologist* 106(3): 518–28.

Luker, Vicki, 2003. 'Civil society, social capital and the churches: HIV/AIDS in Papua New Guinea.' Paper presented at the Governance and Civil Society Seminar, in Symposium Governance in Pacific States: Reassessing Roles and Remedies Conference, Suva: University of the South Pacific, 30 September–2 October.

Luker, Vicki and Sinclair Dinnen (eds), 2010. *Civic Insecurity: Law, Order and HIV in Papua New Guinea*. Canberra: ANU E Press, 141–52. Online: http://press.anu.edu.au?p=94091, accessed 8 April 2014.

Lukere, Vicki and Margaret Jolly (eds), 2002. *Birthing in the Pacific: Beyond Tradition and Modernity?* Honololu: University of Hawai'i Press.

Luluaki, John Y., 2003. 'Sexual crimes against and exploitation of children and the law in Papua New Guinea.' *International Journal of Law, Policy and the Family* 17(3): 275–307.

Lynch, C.J., 1968. 'Aspects of political and constitutional development and allied topics.' In *Fashion of Law in New Guinea: Being an Account of the Past, Present and Developing System of Laws in Papua and New Guinea*, ed. B.J. Brown. Sydney, Melbourne, Brisbane: Butterworths, 39–69.

-------- 1976. 'The adoption of an underlying law by the Constitution of Papua New Guinea.' *Melanesian Law Journal* 4(1): 37–66.

Macintyre, Martha, 1989. 'Better homes and gardens.' In *Family and Gender in the Pacific: Domestic Contradictions and the Colonial Impact*, ed. Margaret Jolly and Martha Macintyre. Cambridge and Melbourne: Cambridge University Press, 156–69.

-------- 1998. 'The persistence of inequality: women in Papua New Guinea since Independence.' In *Modern Papua New Guinea*, ed. Laura Zimmer-Tamakoshi. Kirksville, MO: Thomas Jefferson University Press, 211–30.

-------- 2000. '"Hear us, women of Papua New Guinea!" Melanesian women and human rights.' In *Human Rights and Gender Politics: Asia-Pacific Perspectives*, ed. Anne-Marie Hilsdon et al. London and New York: Routledge, 147–71.

-------- 2008. 'Police and thieves, gunmen and drunks: problems with men and problems with society in Papua New Guinea,' *The Australian Journal of Anthropology* 19(2): 179–93.

-------- 2011. 'Money changes everything: Papua New Guinean women in the modern economy.' In *Managing Modernity in the Western Pacific*, ed. Mary Patterson and Martha Macintyre. Brisbane: University of Queensland Press, 90–120.

Maibani-Michie, Geraldine and William Yeka, 2005. *Baseline Research for Poro Sapot Project: A Program for Prevention of HIV/AIDS among MSM in Port Moresby and FSW in Goroka and Port Moresby Papua New Guinea (PNG)*. Report prepared for Papua New Guinea Institute of Medical Research, Goroka, PNG.

Maibani-Michie, Geraldine et al., 2007. *Evaluation of the Poro Sapot Project: Baseline and End-of-Project (EOP) Studies: An HIV Prevention Program among MSM in Port Moresby and FSW in Goroka and Port Moresby*. Report prepared for Papua New Guinea Institute of Medical Research and Family Health International, Asia and Pacific Department, Goroka, PNG.

Malinowski, Bronislaw, 1948. *The Sexual Life of Savages in North-Western Melanesia: An Ethnographic Account of Courtship, Marriage, and Family Life among the Natives of the Trobriand Islands British New Guinea*, [3rd ed.]. London: Routledge & Kegan Paul.

Manderson, Lenore and Margaret Jolly (eds), 1997. *Sites of Desire, Economies of Pleasure: Sexualities in Asia and the Pacific*. Chicago: University of Chicago Press.

Marksbury, Richard A. (ed.), 1993. *The Business of Marriage: Transformations in Oceanic Matrimony*. ASAO Monograph No.14. Pittsburgh and London: University of Pittsburgh Press.

Martin, Keir, 2007. 'Your own *buai* you must buy: the ideology of possessive individualism in Papua New Guinea.' *Anthropological Forum* 17(3): 285–98.

Masenior, Nicole Franck and Chris Beyrer, 2007. 'The US anti-prostitution pledge: first amendment challenges and public health priorities.' *PLoS Medicine* 4(7). Online: http://www.humantrafficking.org/uploads/publications/Masenior_and_Beyrer.pdf, accessed 16 May 2011.

Mattes, J.R., 1969. 'The courts system.' In *Fashion of Law in New Guinea: Being an Account of the Past, Present and Developing System of Laws in Papua and New Guinea*, ed. B.J. Brown. Sydney, Melbourne, Brisbane: Butterworths, 71–82.

May, R.J. (ed.), 2009. *Policy Making and Implementation, Studies from Papua New Guinea*. Canberra: ANU E Press, 369–78. Online: http://press.anu.edu.au?p=78541m, accessed 31 March 2014.

May, Ronald James, A.J. Regan and Allison Ley (eds), 1997. *Political Decentralisation in a New State: the Experience of Provincial Government in Papua New Guinea*. Bathurst, NSW: Crawford House Publishing.

McCall, Leslie, 2005. 'The complexity of intersectionality.' *Signs* 30(3): 1771–800.

McClintock, Anne, 1993. 'Sex workers and sex work: introduction.' *Social Text* 11 (Winter): 1–10.

-------- 1995. *Imperial Leather: Race, Gender and Sexuality in the Colonial Conquest*. New York and London: Routledge.

McLaren, Margaret A., 2002. *Feminism, Foucault, and Embodied Subjectivity*. Albany, NY: State University of New York Press.

McMillan, Karen and Heather Worth, 2011. *Sex Workers and HIV Prevention in Fiji: after the Fiji Crimes Decree 2009*. Sydney: International HIV Research Group, UNSW.

McPherson, Naomi (ed.), 2001. *In Colonial New Guinea: Anthropological Perspectives*, Pittsburgh: University of Pittsburgh Press.

Meek, V. Lynn, 1982. *The University of Papua New Guinea: A Case Study in the Sociology of Higher Education*, St. Lucia and New York: University of Queensland Press.

Melbourne University Law Review Association Inc., 2010. *Australian Guide to Legal Citation 3rd Edition*. Melbourne: Melbourne University Law Review Association Inc.

Merry, Sally Engle, 1991. 'Law and colonialism.' *Law and Society Review* 25(4): 889–922.

-------- 2004. 'Law and identity in an American colony.' In *Law & Empire in the Pacific: Fiji and Hawai'i*, ed. Sally Engle Merry and Donald Brenneis. Santa Fe, NM: School of American Research Press, 123–52.

Merry, Sally Engle and Donald Brenneis (eds), 2004. *Law & Empire in the Pacific: Fiji and Hawai'i*. Santa Fe, NM: School of American Research Press.

Mill, John Stuart, 1992 [1859]. *On Liberty*. New York: Legal Classics Library.

Mills, Lennox A., 1943. 'Reed, Stephen Winsor: the making of modern New Guinea.' In *The Annals of the American Academy of Political and Social Science*. American Academy of Political and Social Science, 202.

Moore, Clive, 2001. *Sunshine and Rainbows: The Development of Gay and Lesbian Culture in Queensland*. St. Lucia, Qld: University of Queensland Press.

-------- 2005. 'Changes in Melanesian masculinities: an historical approach.' Paper presented at the Moving Masculinities: Crossing Regional and Historical Borders Conference. Canberra: The Australian National University, 29 November–2 December.

Moore, Dennis, Barry Richardson and Dianne Wuillemin, 1985. 'A comparison of rural and legal ranking of seriousness of crimes in Papua New Guinea.' *Melanesian Law Journal* 12: 149–58.

Moore, Henrietta L., 1999. *Anthropological Theory Today*. Cambridge: Polity Press.

Morris, H.F., 1974. 'A history of the adoption of codes of criminal law and procedure in British Colonial Africa, 1876–1935.' *Journal of African Law* 18(6): 6–23.

Mosko, Mark, 2010. 'Partible penitents: dividual personhood and Christian practice in Melanesia and the West.' *Journal of the Royal Anthropological Institute* 16(2): 215–40.

Murray, Sir Hubert, 1925. *Papua of Today: or an Australian Colony in the Making*. London: P.S. King & Son, Ltd.

Murray, Sir Hubert, 1912. *Papua or British New Guinea*. London: T. Fisher Unwin.

Murray, Stephen O., 1992. *Oceanic Homosexualities*. New York: Garland Publishing.

Namaliu, Rabbie, 1970. 'The good woman of Konedobu.' *Kovave* 1(2): 44–53.

Narokobi, Bernard, 1977. 'Adaptation of western law in Papua New Guinea.' *Melanesian Law Journal* 5(1): 52–69.

-------- 1980. *The Melanesian Way: Total Cosmic Vision of Life*. Boroko, PNG: Institute of Papua New Guinea Studies.

-------- 1982. 'History and movement in law reform in Papua New Guinea.' In *Law and Social Change in Papua New Guinea*, ed. David Weisbrot, Abdul Paliwala and Akilagpa Sawyerr. Sydney: Butterworths, 13–24.

-------- 1989. Lo Bilong Yumi Yet: *Law and Custom in Melanesia*. Suva: Institute of Pacific Studies of the University of the South Pacific and the Melanesian Institute for Pastoral and Socio-Economic Service.

-------- 1989. 'Law and custom in Melanesia.' *Pacific Perspectives* 14(1): 17–26.

Narrain, Arvind and Alok Gupta, 2011. 'Introduction.' In *Law Like Love: Queer Perspectives on Law*, ed. Arvind Narrain and Alok Gupta. Calcutta: Yoda Press, xi–lvi.

Narrain, Arvind and Alok Gupta (eds), 2011. *Law Like Love: Queer Perspectives on Law*, Calcutta: Yoda Press.

National AIDS Council of Papua New Guinea, n.d. *Papua New Guinea National Strategic Plan on HIV/AIDS 2004–2008*. Port Moresby: PNG National AIDS Council.

-------- 2001. *Review of Policy and Legislative Reform Relating to HIV/AIDS in Papua New Guinea*. Report prepared for National AIDS Council of Papua New Guinea, Port Moresby.

-------- 2004. *Statement of Facts on Police Raid at 3-Mile Guesthouse 12 March 2004*. Report prepared for National AIDS Council Secretariat, Port Moresby, PNG.

-------- 2010. *Papua New Guinea: National HIV and AIDS Strategy 2011–2015*. Port Moresby, PNG: National AIDS Council of Papua New Guinea.

National HIV/AIDS Support Project, 2006. *High Risk Settings Strategy Report: Moving Beyond Awareness*. Port Moresby: NHASP.

National Research Institute (Papua New Guinea), 2005. *Port Moresby Community Crime Survey, 2005: A Report Prepared for the Government of Papua New Guinea's Law and Justice Sector's National Coordinating Mechanism*. Boroko, PNG: National Research Institute.

National Sex and Reproduction Research Team and Carol Jenkins, 1994. *National Study of Sexual and Reproductive Knowledge and Behaviour in Papua New Guinea*. Goroka: PNG Institute of Medical Research (*National Study*).

Nelson, Hank, 1976. *Black, White and Gold: Gold Mining in Papua New Guinea, 1878–1930*. Canberra: Australian National University Press.

-------- 1982. Taim Bilong Masta: *The Australian Involvement with Papua New Guinea*, Sydney: Australian Broadcasting Commission.

-------- 2003. 'Dear Sir…: Evidence of civil society in the media of Papua New Guinea.' Paper presented at the USP/ANU/FDC Suva Symposium Conference, Suva, 30 September–2 October 2003.

Nilles, John, 1950/51. 'The Kuman of the Chimbu Region, Central Highlands, New Guinea.' *Oceania* 21(1): 25–65.

Norrie, Alan W., 1993. *Crime, Reason and History: A Critical Introduction to Criminal Law*. London: Weidenfeld and Nicolson.

O'Neill, Maggie, 1997. 'Prostitute women now.' In *Rethinking Prostitution: Purchasing Sex in the 1990s*, ed. Graham Scambler and Annette Scambler. London and New York: Routledge, 4–28.

Office of the United Nations High Commissioner for Human Rights (UNHCR) and Joint United Nations Programme on HIV/AIDS (UNAIDS), 1998. *HIV/AIDS and Human Rights: International Guidelines*, HR/PUB/98/1. Report prepared for United Nations, New York and Geneva: UNHCR and UNAIDS.

Ombudsman Commission of Papua New Guinea, 1981. *Final Report on the Kerevat National High School Enquiry*. Report prepared for National Parliament, Port Moresby.

-------- 2009. *Investigation Report into the Alleged Unlawful and Abuse of Human Rights by Police, Three Mile Guest House, Port Moresby, National Capital District*. Report prepared for National Parliament, Port Moresby.

Oram, Nigel, 1968. 'The Hula in Port Moresby.' *Oceania* 39(1): 1–35.

-------- 1976. *Colonial Town to Melanesian City: Port Moresby 1884–1974*. Canberra: Australian National University Press.

Osborne, P.G., 1964. *A Concise Law Dictionary* [5th ed.]. London, Sweet and Maxwell.

Ottley, Bruce L. and Jean G. Zorn, 1983. 'Criminal law in Papua New Guinea: code, custom and the courts in conflict.' *American Journal of Comparative Law* 31: 251–300.

Overs, Cheryl and Bebe Loff, 2013. 'Toward a legal framework that promotes and protects sex workers' health and human rights.' *Health and Human Rights* 15(1): 186–96.

Pacific Institute of Public Policy, 2011. *Youthquake: Will Melanesian Democracy be Sunk by Demography?* Pacific Institute of Public Policy. Online: http://www.pacificpolicy.org/, accessed 23 March 2011.

Pacific Parliamentary Assembly on Population and Development (PPAPD), 2004. *The Suva Declaration on HIV/AIDS by Pacific Parliamentarians*. Report of the 1st Conference for Pacific Parliamentarians on: The Role of Pacific Parliamentarians in the Fight against HIV/AIDS Conference, Suva, Fiji, 11–13 October (*Suva Declaration*).

Pacific Regional Rights Resource Team, 2005. *Pacific Human Rights Law Digest: Volume 1, PHRLD*. Suva: Pacific Regional Rights Resource Team.

Pacific Sexual Diversity Network, 2009. *Strategic Plan 2010–2013*. Online: http://afao.org.au/library_docs/international/PSDN_Strategic_Plan_2009.pdf, accessed 27 August 2011.

Paliwala, Abdul and David Weisbrot, 1982. 'Changing society through law: an introduction.' In *Law and Social Change in Papua New Guinea*, ed. David Weisbrot, Abdul Paliwala and Akilagpa Sawyerr. Sydney, Melbourne, Brisbane, Adelaide, Perth: Butterworths, 3–12.

Papua New Guinea, 1988. *National HIV/AIDS Medium Term Plan*. Port Moresby: Government of Papua New Guinea.

Parker, Richard and Peter Aggleton, 2003. 'HIV and AIDS-related stigma and discrimination: a conceptual framework and implications for action.' *Social Science & Medicine* 57: 13–24.

Patterson, Mary and Martha Macintyre, 2011. 'Introduction: capitalism, cosmology and globalisation in the Pacific.' In *Managing Modernity in the Western Pacific*, ed. Patterson and Macintyre. Brisbane: University of Queensland Press, 1–29.

Patterson, Mary and Martha Macintyre (eds), 2011. *Managing Modernity in the Western Pacific*. Brisbane: University of Queensland Press.

Patton, Cindy, 2002. *Globalising AIDS*. Minneapolis and London: University of Minnesota Press.

Perkins, Roberta, 1991. *Working Girls: Prostitutes, their Life and Social Control.* Canberra: Australian Institute of Criminology.

Perkins, Roberta and Garry Bennett, 1985. *Being a Prostitute: Prostitute Women and Prostitute Men.* Sydney: George Allen and Unwin.

Phetersen, Gail, 1993. 'The whore stigma: female dishonor and male unworthiness.' *Social Text* 37 (Winter): 39–64.

Phillips, Richard, 2002. 'Imperialism and the regulation of sexuality: colonial legislation on contagious diseases and ages of consent.' *Journal of Historical Geography* 28(3): 339–62.

-------- 2005. 'Heterogeneous imperialism and the regulation of sexuality in British West Africa.' *Journal of the History of Sexuality* 14(3): 291–362.

-------- 2006. *Sex, Politics and Empire: A Postcolonial Geography.* Manchester and New York: Manchester University Press.

PNG National HIV/AIDS Support Project (NHASP), 2002. *Workplace Policy Development Workshops Report.* Report prepared for PNG National HIV/AIDS Support Project, Port Moresby.

Pound, Roscoe, 1908. 'Common law and legislation.' *Harvard Law Review* 21(6): 383–407.

Ram, Kalpana, 1992. 'Modernist anthropology and the construction of Indian identity.' *Meanjin* 51(3): 589–614.

Reed, Adam, 1997. 'Contested images and common strategies: early colonial sexual politics in the Massim.' In *Sites of Desire, Economies of Pleasure: Sexualities in Asia and the Pacific*, ed. Lenore Manderson and Margaret Jolly. Chicago: University of Chicago Press, 48–71.

-------- 2003. *Papua New Guinea's Last Place: Experiences of Constraint in a Postcolonial Prison.* New York and Oxford: Berghahn Books.

Reed, Stephen Winsor, 1943. *The Making of Modern New Guinea with Special Reference to Culture Contact in the Mandated Territory*, Philadelphia: The American Philosophical Society.

Reid, Elizabeth, 2010. 'Putting values into practice in PNG: the Poro Sapot Project and aid effectiveness.' *Pacificurrents* 1.2 and 2.1. Online: http://intersections.anu.edu.au/pacificurrents/reid.htm, accessed 9 August 2010.

-------- 2010. 'Re-thinking human rights and the HIV epidemic: a reflection on power and goodness.' In *Civic Insecurity: Law, Order and HIV in Papua New Guinea*, ed. Vicki Luker and Sinclair Dinnen. Canberra: ANU E Press, 265–73. Online: http://press.anu.edu.au?p=94091, accessed 8 April 2014.

Reid, Patricia Mary, 2005. 'Whiteness as goodness: white women in PNG and Australia, 1960's to the present.' Ph.D. thesis, Brisbane: Griffith University.

Rew, Alan, 1974. *Social Images and Process in Urban New Guinea: A Study of Port Moresby*. St. Paul: West Publishing Co.

Robbins, Joel, 1994. 'Equality as a value: ideology in Dumont, Melanesia and the West.' *Social Analysis* 36: 21–70.

-------- 2004. *Becoming Sinners: Christianity and Moral Torment in a Papua New Guinea Society*. Berkeley: University of California Press.

-------- 2004. 'The Globalization of Pentecostal and Charismatic Christianity.' *Annual Review of Anthropology* 33: 117–43.

-------- 2007. 'Afterword: possessive individualism and cultural change in the western Pacific.' *Anthropological Forum* 17(3): 299–308.

Roberts, Jan, 1996. *Voices from a Lost World: Australian Women and Children in Papua New Guinea before the Japanese Invasion*. Alexandria, NSW: Millennium Books.

Roberts, Stephen H., 1928. 'Racial and labour problems.' In *The Australian Mandate for New Guinea: Record of Round Table Discussion*, ed. F.W. Eggleston. Melbourne: Macmillan, 74–84.

Robin, Robert W., 1982. 'Revival movements in the Southern Highlands Province of Papua New Guinea.' *Oceania* 52(4): 320–43.

Robinson, Shirleene (ed.), 2008. *Homophobia: An Australian History*. Annandale, NSW: Federation Press.

Rosi, Pamela and Laura Zimmer-Tamakoshi, 1993. 'Love and marriage among the educated elite in Port Moresby.' In *The Business of Marriage: Transformations in Oceanic Matrimony*, ed. Richard A. Marksbury. ASAO Monograph No. 14. Pittsburgh and London: University of Pittsburgh Press, 175–204.

Roulston, R.P., 1975. *Introduction to Criminal Law in New South Wales*. Sydney: Butterworths.

Rowley, Charles, 1966. *The New Guinea Villager: The Impact of Colonial Rule on Primitive Society and Economy*. New York: Praeger.

Rynkiewich, Michael A. and Roland Seib (eds), 2000. *Politics in Papua New Guinea: Continuities, Changes and Challenges*. Goroka, PNG: Melanesian Institute.

Sack, Peter, 1974. 'The range of traditional Tolai remedies.' In *Contention and Dispute: Aspects of Law and Social Control in Melanesia*, ed. A.L. Epstein. Canberra: Australian National University Press, 67–92.

-------- 1989. 'Law, custom and good government: the Derham Report in its historical context.' In *Papua New Guinea: A Century of Colonial Impact, 1884–1984*, ed. Sione Latukefu. Port Moresby: National Research Institute and University of Papua New Guinea, 377–97.

------- 1997. 'Colonial government, 'justice' and 'the rule of law': the case of German New Guinea.' In *European Impact and Pacific Influence: British and German Colonial Policy in the Pacific Islands and the Indigenous Response*, ed. Hermann J. Hiery and John M. MacKenzie. London: Tauris Publishers, 189–213.

-------- 2001. *Phantom History, the Rule of Law and the Colonial State: The Case of German New Guinea*. Canberra: Division of Pacific and Asian History, The Australian National University.

Sai, Anastasia, 2007. '*Tamot*: masculinities in transition in Papua New Guinea.' Ph.D. thesis, Melbourne: Victoria University.

Sandy, Larissa, 2006. '"My blood, sweat and tears": female sex workers in Cambodia—victims, vectors or agents?' Ph.D. thesis, Canberra: The Australian National University.

-------- 2007. 'Just choices: representations of choice and coercion in sex work in Cambodia.' *The Australian Journal of Anthropology* 18(2): 194–206.

Satish, Mrinal, 2013. 'Comment: breaking down the SC judgement on Section 377.' *IBN Live*. Online: http://ibnlive.in.com/news/comment-breaking-down-the-sc-judgement-on-section-377/439348-3.html, accessed 10 July 2014.

Sawer, Geoffrey, 1968. 'Introduction.' In *Fashion of Law in New Guinea: Being an Account of the Past, Present and Developing System of Laws in Papua and New Guinea*, ed. B.J. Brown. Sydney, Melbourne, Brisbane: Butterworths, 9–13.

Scambler, Graham and Annette Scambler (eds), 1997. *Rethinking Prostitution: Purchasing Sex in the 1990s*. London and New York: Routledge.

Scarlet Alliance, n.d. *State by State Laws in Australia*. Online: http://www.scarletalliance.org.au/laws/, accessed 8 July 2010.

-------- n.d. *Terminology*. Online: http://www.scarletalliance.org.au/issues/terminology/, accessed 20 March 2011.

-------- n.d. *Objectives*. Online: http://www.scarletalliance.org.au/object/, accessed 31 August 2011.

Scheper-Hughes, Nancy, 1994. 'An essay: AIDS and the social body.' *Social Science & Medicine* 39(7): 991–1003.

-------- 1996. 'Small wars and invisible genocides.' *Social Science & Medicine* 43(5): 889–900.

Scheper-Hughes, Nancy and Margaret M. Lock, 1987. 'The mindful body: a prolegomenon to future work in medical anthropology.' *Medical Anthropology Quarterly* 1(1): 6–41.

Schneebaum, Tobias, 1988. *Where the Spirits Dwell: An Odyssey in the New Guinea Jungle*. New York: Grove Press.

Schoeffel Meleisea, Penelope, 2008. *Gender and HIV in the Pacific Islands Region: A Review of Evidence, Policies and Strategies with Recommendations (Final Draft)*. Report prepared for UNDP Pacific Centre, Suva.

Secretariat of the Pacific Community (SPC), 2005. *The Pacific Regional Strategy on HIV/AIDS 2004–2008*. Noumea, New Caledonia: Secretariat of the Pacific Community.

Self, Helen J., 2003. *Prostitution, Women and Misuse of the Law: The Fallen Daughters of Eve*. London and Portland OR: Frank Cass Publishers.

Sepoe, Orovu V., 2000. *Changing Gender Relations in Papua New Guinea: The Role of Women's Organisations*. New Delhi: UBS Publishers' Distributors Ltd.

Shrivastava, Prachi, 2013. '7 creative (legal) reasons the Supreme Court found not to strike down section #377.' *Legally India*, 11 December. Online: http://www.legallyindia.com/201312114184/Constitutional-law/7-reasons-the-supreme-court-didnt-strike-down-377, accessed 14 December 2013.

-------- 2013. 'Column inches slamming SC's ruling overwhelm but 2009 academic argues how #377 is constitutional.' *Legally India*. Online: http://www.legallyindia.com/201312124187/Constitutional-law/section-377-judgment-reactions, accessed 14 December 2013.

Skorupski, John, 2005. 'Mill, John Stuart,' in *The Oxford Companion to Philosophy [2nd ed.]*, online: http://www.oxfordreference.com/view/10.1093/acref/9780199264797.001.0001/acref-9780199264797-e-1604?rskey=NAp1Zf&result=3, accessed 16 April 2014.

Spark, Ceridwen, 2010. 'Changing lives: understanding the barriers that confront educated women in Papua New Guinea.' *Australian Feminist Studies* 25(63): 17–30.

-------- 2011. 'Educated women in PNG: who are they today?' Paper presented at the Symposium PNG Today—and Tomorrow? Melbourne: Deakin University, 27 May.

Stephen, Sir James Fitzjames, 1883. *A History of the Criminal Law of England Vol. 2*. London: Macmillan.

-------- 1883. *A History of the Criminal Law of England Vol. 3*. London: Macmillan.

Stewart, Christine, 1993. *Law, Ethics and HIV/AIDS: Existing Law of Papua New Guinea*. Report prepared for Law Reform Commission of Papua New Guinea and Papua New Guinea Department of Health. Boroko, PNG: Law Reform Commission of Papua New Guinea and Papua New Guinea Department of Health.

-------- 1993. 'Existing law on HIV/AIDS in Papua New Guinea.' In *Law, Ethics and HIV: Proceedings of the UNDP Intercountry Consultation, Cebu, Philippines 3–6 May, 1993*, ed. Robert A Glick. New Delhi: United Nations Development Programme, 133–50.

-------- 2010. 'Enabling environments: the role of the law.' In *Civic Insecurity: Law, Order and HIV in Papua New Guinea*, ed. Vicki Luker and Sinclair Dinnen. Canberra: ANU E Press, 275–85. Online: http://press.anu.edu.au?p=94091, accessed 8 April 2014.

-------- 2010. 'The tale of an activist.' *HIV Australia* 8(2). Online: http://www.afao.org.au/library/hiv-australia/volume-8/hiv-and-png/gay-and-HIV-positive-in-PNG#.U74PZ19--5s, accessed 10 July 2014.

-------- 2010. 'The courts, the churches, the witches and their killers.' Paper presented at the Law and Culture: Meaningful Legal Pluralism in the Pacific and Beyond Conference. Port Vila, Vanuatu, 30 August–1 September 2010.

-------- 2012. '"Crime to be a woman?" Engendering violence against female sex workers in Port Moresby, Papua New Guinea.' In *Engendering Violence in Papua New Guinea*, ed. Margaret Jolly, Christine Stewart with Carolyn Brewer. Canberra: ANU E Press. Online: http://press.anu.edu.au?p=182671, accessed 31 March 2014.

Stewart, Christine and Pascoe Kase, 1993. 'Law, custom and the AIDS epidemic in Papua New Guinea.' In *Law, Ethics and HIV: Proceedings of the UNDP Intercountry Consulatation, Cebu, Philippines 3-6 May, 1993*, ed. Robert A. Glick. New Delhi: United Nations Development Programme, 63–76.

Stivens, Maila, 2000. 'Gender politics and the reimagining of human rights in the Asia-Pacific.' In *Human Rights and Gender Politics: Asia-Pacific Perspectives*, ed. Anne-Marie Hilsdon et al. London and New York: Routledge, 1–36.

Stoler, Ann Laura, 1995. *Race and the Education of Desire: Foucault's History of Sexuality and the Colonial Order of Things*. Durham and London: Duke University Press.

-------- 2003. *Carnal Knowledge and Imperial Power: Race and the Intimate in Colonial Rule*. Berkeley: University of California Press.

Strathern, Marilyn, 1975. *Report on Questionnaire Relating to Sexual Offences as Defined in the Criminal Code*. Report prepared for New Guinea Research Unit, Boroko, PNG.

-------- 1976. 'Crime and correction: the place of prisons in Papua New Guinea.' *Melanesian Law Journal* 4(1): 67–93.

-------- 1988. *The Gender of the Gift: Problems with Women and Problems with Society in Melanesia*. Berkeley: University of California Press.

Stuart, Ian, 1970. *Port Moresby Yesterday and Today*. Sydney: Pacific Publications.

Sullivan, Barbara Ann, 1997. *The Politics of Sex: Prostitution and Pornography in Australia since 1945*. New York: Cambridge University Press.

Sykes, Karen, 2007. 'Interrogating individuals: the theory of possessive individualism in the western Pacific.' *Anthropological Forum* 17(3): 213–24.

Tamata, Laitia, 2000. 'Application of Human Rights Conventions in the Pacific Islands Courts.' *Journal of South Pacific Law* 4. Online: http://www.paclii.org/journals/fJSPL/vol04/12.shtml, accessed 30 April 2010.

Taureka, R., 1973. 'Venereal disease and the law.' Paper presented at the Law and Development in Melanesia Waigani Seminar Conference, Waigani, PNG, April.

Todd, J.A., 1934/35. 'Native offences and European law in South-West New Britain.' *Oceania* 5: 437–60.

Treichler, Paula A., 1999. *How to have Theory in an Epidemic: Cultural Chronicles of AIDS*. Durham: Duke University Press.

Tryon, Darrell T. and Jean-Michel Charpentier, 2004. *Pacific Pidgins and Creoles: Origins, Growth and Development*. Berlin and New York: Mouton de Gruyter.

Tunick, Mark, 2002. 'Ethics, morality, and law.' In *The Oxford Companion to American Law*, ed. Kermit L. Hall. New York: Oxford University Press. *Oxford Reference Online*. Online: http://www.oxfordreference.com/views/ENTRY.html?subview=Main&entry=t122.e0313, accessed 21 April 2007.

UNDP Pacific Centre and UNAIDS, 2009. *Enabling Effective Responses to HIV in Pacific Island Countries: Options for Human Rights-Based Legislative Reform*. Suva, Fiji: UNDP Pacific Centre.

United Nations Human Rights Council, International Commission of Jurists and International Service for Human Rights, 2007. *The Yogyakarta Principles: Principles on the Application of International Human Rights Law in Relation to Sexual Orientation and Gender Identity*. Online: http://www.yogyakartaprinciples.org/principles_en.htm, accessed 11 April 2014 (*Yogyakarta Principles*).

United Nations, 2002–2006. *Millennium Development Goals Beyond 2015*. Online: http://www.unmillenniumproject.org/goals/, accessed 15 April 2014.

Viljoen, Frans, 2009. 'International Human Rights law: a short history.' *UN Chronicle* L(4) December. Online: http://www.un.org:80/wcm/content/site/chronicle/home/archive/Issues2009/internationalhumanrightslawashorthistory, accessed 6 August 2011.

Voeten, Erik, 2013. 'The recriminalization of homosexuality in India and the potential for broader backlash.' *Washington Post*, 11 December. Online: http://www.washingtonpost.com/blogs/monkey-cage/wp/2013/12/11/the-recriminalization-of-homosexuality-in-india-and-the-potential-for-broader-backlash/, accessed 16 December 2013.

Waldby, Catherine, Susan Kippax and June Crawford, 1993. '*Cordon Sanitaire*: "clean" and "unclean" women in the AIDS discourse of young heterosexual men.' In *AIDS: Facing the Second Decade*, ed. Peter Aggleton, Peter Davies and Graham Hart. London: Falmer Press, 29–39.

Walkowitz, Judith R., 1982. *Prostitution and Victorian Society: Women, Class, and the State*. Cambridge and New York: Cambridge University Press.

Wallace, Harvey and Cliff Roberson, 2001. *Principles of Criminal Law* [2nd ed.]. Boston: Allyn and Bacon.

Wardlow, Holly, 2001. '"Prostitution," "sexwork," and "passenger women": when sexualities don't correspond to stereotypes.' Paper presented at the 3rd IASSCS Conference, Melbourne, 1–3 October.

-------- 2002. 'Passenger-women: changing gender relations in the Tari Basin.' *Papua New Guinea Medical Journal* 45(1/2): 142–46.

-------- 2002. 'Headless ghosts and roving women: specters of modernity in Papua New Guinea.' *American Ethnologist* 29(1): 5–32.

-------- 2004. 'Anger, economy and female agency: problematizing "prostitution" and "sex work" among the Huli of Papua New Guinea.' *Signs* 29(4): 1017–39.

-------- 2006. *Wayward Women: Sexuality and Agency in a New Guinea Society.* Berkeley and Los Angeles, CA: University of California Press.

-------- 2008. '"You have to understand: some of us are glad AIDS has arrived": Christianity and condoms among the Huli, Papua New Guinea.' In *Making Sense of AIDS: Culture, Sexuality, and Power in Melanesia*, ed. Leslie Butt and Richard Eves. Honolulu: University of Hawai'i Press, 187–205.

-------- 2009. 'Whip him in the head with a stick!' In *The Secret: Love, Marriage, and HIV*, ed. Jennifer S. Hirsch et al. Nashville, TN: Vanderbilt University Press, 136–67.

Weeks, Jeffrey. 1977. *Coming Out: Homosexual Politics in Britain, from the Nineteenth Century to the Present.* London Melbourne New York: Quartet Books.

-------- 1989. *Sex, Politics, and Society: The Regulation of Sexuality since 1800.* London and New York: Longman.

Weir, Christine, 2008. '"White man's burden," "white man's privilege": Christian humanism and racial determinism in Oceania, 1890–1930.' in *Foreign Bodies: Oceania and the Science of Race 1750-1940*, ed. Bronwen Douglas and Chris Ballard. Canberra: ANU E Press, 283–303. Online: http://press.anu.edu.au?p=53561, accessed 31 March 2014.

Weisbrot, David, 1979. 'Judges and politicians.' *Legal Service Bulletin* 4(6): 240–45.

-------- 1980. 'Judges and politicians Pt II: the Wilson affair.' *Legal Service Bulletin* 5(5): 214–17.

-------- 1982. 'Integration of laws in Papua New Guinea: custom and the criminal law in conflict.' In *Law and Social Change in Papua New Guinea*, ed. David Weisbrot, Abdul Paliwala and Akilagpa Sawyerr. Sydney, Melbourne, Brisbane, Adelaide, Perth: Butterworths, 59–103.

-------- 1988. 'Papua New Guinea's indigenous jurisprudence and the legacy of colonialism.' *University of Hawai'i, Law Review* 10(1): 1–45.

Weisbrot, David, Abdul Paliwala and Akilagpa Sawyerr (eds), 1982. *Law and Social Change in Papua New Guinea*. Sydney, Melbourne, Brisbane, Adelaide, Perth: Butterworths.

Wetherell, David, 1996. *Charles Abel and the Kwato Mission of Papua New Guinea 1891–1975*. Carlton, Vic: Melbourne University Press.

Whiting, Amanda and Carolyn Evans (eds), 2006. *Mixed Blessings: Laws, Religions, and Women's Rights in the Asia-Pacific Region*. Leiden: Martinus Nijhoff Publishers.

Willett, Graham, 2000. *Living Out Loud: A History of Gay and Lesbian Activism in Australia*, St. Leonards, NSW: Allen & Unwin.

-------- 2008. 'From "vice" to homosexuality: policing perversion in the 1950s.' In *Homophobia: An Australian History*, ed. Shirleene Robinson. Annandale, NSW: Federation Press, 113–27.

Williams, Francis Edgar, 1969 [1936]. *Papuans of the Trans-Fly*. Oxford: Clarendon Press.

Willis, Ian, 1974. *Lae: Village and City*. Melbourne: Melbourne University Press.

Wojcicki, Allan M., 1987. 'Monocultural administration in a multicultural environment: the Australians in Papua New Guinea.' In *Colony to Coloniser: Studies in Australian Administrative History*, ed. J.J. Eddy and J.R. Nethercote. Sydney: Hale and Iremonger, 207–24.

-------- 1997. 'Colonial law as metropolitan defence: the curious case of Australia in New Guinea.' In *European Impact and Pacific Influence: British and German Colonial Policy in the Pacific Islands and the Indigenous Response*, ed. Hermann J. Hiery and John M. MacKenzie. London: Tauris Academic Studies, 214–30.

Wojcicki, Janet Maia, 2002. '"She drank his money": survival sex and the problem of violence in taverns in Gauteng Province, South Africa.' *Medical Anthropology Quarterly* 16(3): 267–93.

-------- 2002. 'Commercial sexwork or *ukuphanda*? Sex-for-money exchange in Soweto and Hammanskraal area, South Africa.' *Culture, Medicine and Psychiatry* 26: 339–70.

Wolfers, Edward P., 1975. *Race Relations and Colonial Rule in Papua New Guinea*. Sydney: Australia and New Zealand Book Company.

World AIDS Campaign, 2010. *Sex Work and the Law: The Case for Decriminalization*. Capetown, Amsterdam: World AIDS Campaign.

World Health Organization and UNAIDS, 2007. *Guidance of Provider-Initiated HIV Testing and Counselling in Health Facilities*. Geneva: World Health Organization.

Worsley, Peter, 1970. *The Trumpet Shall Sound: A Study of 'Cargo' Cults in Melanesia* [2nd ed.]. London: Paladin.

Wuillemin, Dianne, Barry Richardson and Dennis Moore, 1986. 'Ranking of crime seriousness in Papua New Guinea.' *Journal of Cross-Cultural Psychology* 17(1): 29–44.

Young, L.K., 1971. *Outline of Law in Papua and New Guinea*. Sydney, Melbourne, Brisbane: Law Book Company Limited.

Young, Michael, 1989. 'Suffer the children: Wesleyans in the D'Entrecasteaux.' In *Family and Gender in the Pacific: Domestic Contradictions and the Colonial Impact*, ed. Margaret Jolly and Martha Macintyre. Cambridge: Cambridge University Press, 108–34.

Yuval-Davis, Nira, 2006. 'Intersectionality and feminist politics.' *European Journal of Women's Studies* 13: 193–209.

Zimmer-Tamakoshi, Laura, 1990. 'Sexual exploitation and male dominance in Papua New Guinea.' In *Human Sexuality in Melanesian Cultures*, ed. Joel F. Ingebritson. Goroka, PNG: Melanesian Institute, 250–67.

-------- 1993. 'Nationalism and sexuality in Papua New Guinea.' *Pacific Studies* 16(4): 61–97.

Zimmer-Tamakoshi, Laura (ed.), 1988. *Modern Papua New Guinea*. Kirksville, MO: Thomas Jefferson University Press.

Zimmerman, Lorraine, 1973. 'Migration and urbanization among the Buang of Papua New Guinea.' Ph.D. thesis, Detroit, MI: Wayne State University.

Zocca, Franco, 2007. *Melanesia and its Churches: Past and Present*. Goroka, PNG: Melanesian Institute.

Zorn, Jean G., 1990. 'Customary law in the Papua New Guinea village courts.' *Contemporary Pacific* 2(2): 39–66.

-------- 1992. 'Common law jurisprudence and customary law.' In *Legal Issues in a Developing Society*, ed. R.W. James and I. Fraser. Port Moresby: University of Papua New Guinea, 103–27.

-------- 1994–1995. 'Women, custom and state law in Papua New Guinea.' *Third World Legal Studies* 13(7): 169–205. Online: http://scholar.valpo.edu/twls/vol13/iss1/7, accessed 11 April 2014.

-------- 2003. 'Custom then and now: the changing Melanesian family.' In *Passage of Change: Law, Society and Governance in the Pacific*, ed. Anita Jowitt and Tess Newton Cain. Canberra: Pandanus Books, 95–124.

-------- 2006. 'Women and witchcraft: positivist, prelapsarian, and post-modern judicial interpretations in PNG.' In *Mixed Blessings: Laws, Religions, and Women's Rights in the Asia-Pacific Region*, ed. Amanda Whiting and Carolyn Evans. Leiden: Martinus Nijhoff Publishers, 61–99.

-------- 2010. 'In memory of Bernard Narokobi.' *Pacificurrents* 1.2 and 2.1. Online: intersections.anu.edu.au/pacificurrents/zorn_memorial.htm, accessed June 2010.

-------- 2010. 'The paradoxes of sexism: proving rape in the Papua New Guinea courts.' *LAWASIA Journal* 2010: 17–58.

-------- 2012. 'Engendering violence in the Papua New Guinea courts: sentencing in rape trials.' In *Engendering Violence in Papua New Guinea*, ed. Margaret Jolly, Christine Stewart with Carolyn Brewer. Canberra: ANU E Press. Online: http://press.anu.edu.au?p=182671, accessed 31 March 2014.

Zorn, Jean and Peter Bayne (eds), 1975. *Lo Bilong Ol Manmeri: Crime, Compensation and Village Courts*. Port Moresby: University of Papua New Guinea.

Zorn, Jean G. and Jennifer Corrin Care, 2002. 'Everything old is new again: the underlying law act of Papua New Guinea.' *LAWASIA Journal* 2002: 61–97.

Cases

Papua New Guinea cases

Acting Public Solicitor v Uname Aumane, Aluma Boku, Luku Wapulae and Piope Kone [1980] PNGLR 510

Anna Wemay and Others v Kepas Tumdual [1978] PNGLR 173 (*Anna Wemay's Case*)

In the Matter of an Application under Section 57 of the Constitution; Application by Individual and Community Rights Advocacy Forum Inc (ICRAF); In re Miriam Willingal [1997] PNGLR 119 (*Willingal's Case*)

Monika Jon and Others v Dominik Kuman and Others (Unreported) N253, 8 August 1980 (*Monika Jon's Case*)

Public Prosecutor v Nahau Rooney (No.1) [1979] PNGLR 403

Public Prosecutor v Nahau Rooney (No.2) [1979] PNGLR 448

R v Bates (Unreported) SC255, 9 October 1962

R v C.E.C. Leech and Peter Yaku PNG National Archives Accession 454 Box 14619 Crown Prosecution File 5-9354 (*Leech Trial*)

R v Clemence Mandoma-Kausigor and Piki Piliu PNG National Archives Accession No. 454 Box 8139 Crown Prosecution File 5-8019 (*Kausigor's Trial*)

R v Clemence Mandoma-Kausigor; R v Piki Piliu (Unreported) FC3, 7 November 1969 (*Kausigor's Case*)

R v Hugh William Sitai PNG National Archives Accession 454 Box 14625 Crown Prosecution File 5-9468

R v Kauba-Paruwo [1963] PNGLR 18

R v John Bomai [1964] PNGLR 278

R. v John Passum, PNG National Archives Accession No.454 Box No.9621 File No.8596 1972

R v M.K. [1973] PNGLR 204 (*Mama Kamzo's Appeal*)

R v Mama Kamzo (Unreported) SC 671, 17 Febr 1972 (*Mama Kamzo's Trial*)

R v Siune Wel PNG National Archives Accession 454 Box 14625 Crown Prosecution File 5-9471 (*Siune Wel Case*)

R v Womeni-Nanagawo [1963] PNGLR 72

R v Yawi Huaimbore PNG National Archives Accession 454 Box 14625 Crown Prosecution File 5-9474

Re Wagi Non and Section 42(5) of the Constitution [1991] PNGLR 84

Samana v Waki (Unreported) N449 Amet J, 23 January 1984

SCR No 5 of 1982; Re Disputed Returns for the Kairuku-Hiri Open Electorate [1982] PNGLR 379

Secretary for Law v Kabua Dewake [1975] PNGLR 100

Smedley v the State [1980] PNGLR 379

State v Aubafo Feama & Ors [1978] PNGLR 301

State v John Puwa Bui (Unreported) N944, 14 December 1990

State v Johnny Mala, (Unreported, Unnumbered) National Court; CR 96 of 1997; 25–26th February 1997 (*JohnnyMala's Case*)

State v Kule [1991] PNGLR 404

State v Luku Wapulae (Unreported) N233, 4 June 1980

State v Pos [1991] PNGLR 208

Other jurisdictions

Bankstown City Council v Le 2003 WL 23103843; [2003] NSWLEC 362; [2005] ALMD 2742 (NSW, Australia)

Bowers v Hardwick 478 U.S. 186 (1986) (USA)

Croome v Tasmania (1997) 191 CLR 119 (Australia Clth.)

Heydon's Case (1584) 3 Co Rep 7a, 7b; 76 ER 637, 638 (England) (*Heydon's Case*)

Lawrence v Texas 539 U.S. 558, 578, 123 S.Ct. 2472, 156 L.Ed.2d 508 (2003) (USA)

McCoskar v The State [2005] FJHC 500 (Fiji)

Nadan v The State [2005] FJHC 1 (Fiji)

National Coalition for Gay and Lesbian Equality and Another v Minister of Justice and Others (CCT11/98) [1998] ZACC 15, §136 (South Africa)

Naz Foundation (India) Trust v Government of ACT of Delhi and Others WP(C) No.7445/2001, date of decision 2 July 2009, (India) (*Naz Case*)

Salgueiro da Silva Mouta v Portugal [2001] 1 F.C.R. 653 (European Court of Human Rights)

Suresh Kumar Koushal and another v Naz Foundation and Others, Civil Appeal No.10972 of 2013, 11 December 2013, (India) (*Naz Appeal*)

Legislation

Papua New Guinea

Constitution of the Independent State of Papua New Guinea

Criminal Code Act 1974

Criminal Code (Sexual Offences and Crimes Against Children) Act 2002

Customs Recognition Act 1963

Deserted Wives and Children Act 1951

HIV/AIDS Management and Prevention Act 2003

Human Rights Ordinance 1972

Informal Sector Act 2004

Interpretation Act 1975

Interpretation (Interim Provisions) Act 1975

Law Reform Commission Act 1975

Laws Repeal and Adopting Ordinance 1921–1939 (New Guinea)

Marriage Act 1963

National AIDS Council Act 1997

Native Administration Regulation (T.N.G.) (Chapter 315)

Native Customs (Recognition) Ordinance 1963

Native Regulation Act 1908–1967 (Papua)

Native Regulation 1888/1922 (Papua)

Native Women's Protection Ordinance 1951–1962 (Papua)

Police Act 1998

Police Offences Ordinance (New Guinea) 1925–1974

Police Offences Ordinance (Papua) 1912–1974

Prisons Ordinance (Papua) (repealed)

Public Health Act 1973

Public Order Ordinance 1971

Statute Law Revision (Amalgamation of Laws) Ordinance 1973

Summary Offences Act 1977

Underlying Law Act 2000

Vagrancy Ordinance (Papua) 1912–1964

Venereal Diseases Ordinance 1920–1947 (New Guinea)

Venereal Diseases Ordinance (Amalgamated) 1973 (Papua New Guinea)

Village Courts Act 1974

White Women's Protection Ordinance 1929 (Papua)

Other jurisdictions

Constitution of India 1949 (Ind)

Constitution of the Republic of South Africa Act No. 108 of 1996 (Saf)

Human Rights (Sexual Conduct) Act 1994 (Cth)

New Guinea Act 1929–1935 (Cth)

Papua Act 1905–1940 (Cth)

Papua and New Guinea Act 1949 (Cth)

Papua New Guinea Act 1971 (Cth) 1. The short title of this Act, which was in effect the 'constitution' of the two Territories until Independence, was changed by Section 1 of No.123 of 1971.

Papua New Guinea Act (No. 2) 1974 (Cth)

International treaties, agreements, documents

Convention for the Protection of Human Rights and Fundamental Freedoms (Europe) (ETS No. 5), 213 U.N.T.S. 222, entered into force 3 September 1953.

Convention on the Elimination of All Forms of Discrimination against Women, GA res 34/180, 34 UN GAOR Supp (No. 46) at 193, UN Doc A/34/46, entered into force 3 September 1981 (CEDAW).

Convention on the Rights of the Child, GA res 44/25, annex, 44 UN GAOR Supp (No 49) at 167, UN Doc A/44/49 (1989), entered into force 2 September 1990 (CRC).

International Covenant on Economic, Social and Cultural Rights, GA res 2200A (XXI), 21 UN GAOR Supp (No. 16) at 49, UN Doc A/6316 (1966), 993 UNTS 3, entered into force 3 January 1976 (ICESCR).

International Covenant on Civil and Political Rights, GA res 2200A (XXI), 21 UN GAOR Supp (No. 16) at 52, UN Doc A/6316 (1966), 999 UNTS 171, entered into force 23 March 1976 (ICCPR).

United Nations General Assembly Special Session on HIV/AIDS (UNGASS) *Declaration of Commitment on HIV/AIDS*, 27 June 2001 A/RES/S-26/2.

Universal Declaration of Human Rights, GA res 217A (III), UN Doc A/810 (1948) (UDHR).

Official documents

Commonwealth of Australia

1922. *Report to the League of Nations on the administration of the Territory of New Guinea 1914–1921*

1923. *Report to the League of Nations on the administration of the Territory of New Guinea 1922*

1924. *Report to the League of Nations on the administration of the Territory of New Guinea 1922–23*

1938. *Annual Report of the Territory of Papua 1937*

1960. *Parliamentary Debates*, House of Representatives, 23 August 1960

Great Britain

1894. *Annual Report on British New Guinea 1892–1893*

Queensland

1889. *British New Guinea: Report for the Year 1888*

Territory of Papua and New Guinea

1963. *Legislative Council Debates* VI:7

Territory of Papua New Guinea

1974. *Final Report of the Constitutional Planning Committee: Part I*

United Kingdom

1957. *Report of the Committee on Homosexual Offences and Prostitution.* London: HMSO, Cmnd. 247 (*Wolfenden Report*)

United Nations Trusteeship Council

1962. *Report of the 1962 United Nations Visiting Mission to the Trust Territory of New Guinea* (*Foot Report*)

Unpublished material

Papua New Guinea National Archives, Port Moresby

Crown Prosecution Files

Gwakarum Trials. Accession 454 Box 14648 Crown Prosecution Files Nos.9956, 9958

John Passum. PNG National Archives Accession No.454 Box No.9621 File No.8596

Mama Kamzo. Accession 454 Box 14612 Crown Prosecution File 5-9218

Prostitution. Accession No. 64 Box 1316 Crown Prosecution File N1-6-7

Siune Wel Cases. Accession 454 Box 14625 Crown Prosecution File 5-9468; Crown Prosecution File 5-9471; Crown Prosecution File 5-9474

Papua New Guinea Supreme Court Archives, Port Moresby

Prentice J Notebooks 1972. Box 2038 SCRA

Newspapers and periodicals

Papua New Guinea

(Papua New Guinea) Post-Courier (Port Moresby)

Rabaul Gazette

National of Papua New Guinea (Port Moresby)

Other

Fiji Times (Suva, Fiji)

Pacific Islands Monthly (Suva, Fiji)

Sydney Morning Herald

Other resources

Audiovisual

Hasluck, Paul, PMB Photo 6_12 'District Officer holding court.' From Sir Paul HASLUCK, *New Guinea Administration Series of Photographic Slides*, 1956, Nos.00121-00188, Pacific Manuscripts Bureau, The Australian National University.

Tau, Moses, 1999. 'Aito Paka Paka.' *Moses Says Aloha*. DVD Port Moresby: CHM Supersound.

Vinit, Thomas, 2004. 'HIV/AIDS Control—The PNG Way: World AIDS Day 2004.' Oilsearch Ltd. Powerpoint presentation.

Digital resources

ABC Radio Australia Pacific Beat. Online: http://www.abc.net.au/ra/pacbeat/.

ActNow! Online: http://www.actnowpng.org/blog.

Australia Network News, ABC Asia Pacific New Centre. Online: http://australianetworknews.com/.

Namorong Report. Online: http://medicmangi.blogspot.com/ (now redirected as http://namorong.blogspot.com/).

Oceanic Anthropology Discussion Group. Online: asaonet@listserv.uic.edu.

Oxford Reference Online. Oxford University Press, via The Australian National University. Online: http://www.oxfordreference.com.

Pacific Islands Legal Information Institute. University of the South Pacific School of Law. Online: www.paclii.org.

Papua New Guinea Department of Education. Online: http://www.education.gov.pg/.

pngInLaw, NiuMedia Pacific. Online: www.niumedia.com/pnginlaw.

Poro Sapot Database 2006–7 (outreach worker report forms).

SEX-WORK eForum 2004. Online: sex-work@eforums.healthdev.org.

United Nations Educational, Scientific and Cultural Organization (UNESCO), 'The official source of literary data,' *UNESCO Institute of Statistics*. Online: http://www.uis.unesco.org/Pages/default.aspx, accessed 11 April 2014.

University of Minnesota Human Rights Library. Online: http://www.umn.edu/humanrts.

www.ingramcontent.com/pod-product-compliance
Lightning Source LLC
Chambersburg PA
CBHW040934240426
43670CB00033B/2974